CHINESE AMERICANS AND

IN THE SERIES, ***Asian American History and Culture,***

EDITED BY

SUCHENG CHAN, DAVID PALUMBO-LIU,
MICHAEL OMI, K. SCOTT WONG, AND LINDA TRINH VÕ

Lisa Yun, *The Coolie Speaks: Chinese Indentured Laborers and African Slaves in Cuba*

Estella Habal, *San Francisco's International Hotel: Mobilizing the Filipino American Community in the Anti-Eviction Movement*

Thomas P. Kim, *The Racial Logic of Politics: Asian Americans and Party Competition*

Sucheng Chan, ed., *The Vietnamese American 1.5 Generation: Stories of War, Revolution, Flight, and New Beginnings*

Antonio T. Tiongson Jr., Edgardo V. Gutierrez, and Ricardo V. Gutierrez, eds., *Positively No Filipinos Allowed: Building Communities and Discourse*

Sucheng Chan, ed., *Chinese American Transnationalism: The Flow of People, Resources, and Ideas between China and America during the Exclusion Era*

Keith Lawrence and Floyd Cheung, eds., *Recovered Legacies: Authority and Identity in Early Asian American Literature*

Rajini Srikanth, *The World Next Door: South Asian American Literature and the Idea of America*

Linda Trinh Võ, *Mobilizing an Asian American Community*

Franklin S. Odo, *No Sword to Bury: Japanese Americans in Hawai'i during World War II*

Josephine Lee, Imogene L. Lim, and Yuko Matsukawa, eds., *Re/collecting Early Asian America: Essays in Cultural History*

Linda Trinh Võ and Rick Bonus, eds., *Contemporary Asian American Communities: Intersections and Divergences*

Sunaina Marr Maira, *Desis in the House: Indian American Youth Culture in New York City*

Teresa Williams-León and Cynthia Nakashima, eds., *The Sum of Our Parts: Mixed-Heritage Asian Americans*

Tung Pok Chin with Winifred C. Chin, *Paper Son: One Man's Story*

Amy Ling, ed., *Yellow Light: The Flowering of Asian American Arts*

Rick Bonus, *Locating Filipino Americans: Ethnicity and the Cultural Politics of Space*

Chinese Americans *and the* Politics of Race and Culture

EDITED BY

Sucheng Chan and Madeline Y. Hsu

TEMPLE UNIVERSITY PRESS
Philadelphia

Sucheng Chan is Professor Emerita of Asian American Studies and Global Studies at the University of California, Santa Barbara.

Madeline Y. Hsu is Director of the Center for Asian American Studies and Associate Professor of History at the University of Texas at Austin.

TEMPLE UNIVERSITY PRESS
1601 North Broad Street
Philadelphia PA 19122
www.temple.edu/tempress

Published 2008
Printed in the United States of America

Frontispiece photograph of Him Mark Lai by Frank Jang, 2006. Used with permission.

♾ The paper used in this publication meets the requirements of the American National Standard for Information Sciences—Permanence of Paper for Printed Library Materials, ANSI Z39.48–1992

Library of Congress Cataloging-in-Publication Data

Chinese Americans and the politics of race and culture / edited by
Sucheng Chan and Madeline Y. Hsu.
p. cm.—(Asian American history and culture)
Includes index.
ISBN-13: 978-1-59213-752-7 (cloth : alk. paper)
ISBN-13: 978-1-59213-753-4 (paper : alk. paper)
ISBN-10: 1-59213-752-0 (cloth : alk. paper)
ISBN-10: 1-59213-753-9 (paper : alk. paper)
1. Chinese Americans—History. 2. Chinese Americans—Social conditions. 3. Chinese Americans—Politics and government. 4. Chinese Americans—Ethnic identity. 5. Politics and culture—United States. 6. Racism—Political aspects—United States. 7. United States—Ethnic relations. 8. United States—Race relations. 9. Pluralism (Social sciences)—United States.
I. Chan, Sucheng. II. Hsu, Madeline Yuan-yin.
E184.C5C4795 2008
305.895'1073—dc22

200703829

2 4 6 8 9 7 5 3 1

In honor of

HIM MARK LAI

with utmost gratitude and respect for showing us better ways to write Chinese American history

which appeared in 1990, marked the academic coming of age of diaspora as a phenomenon worth studying and analyzing.

Many Chinese Americans are attracted by the idea of diaspora because it allows them to see themselves as part of a vast global network of social, cultural, economic, and political connections. Instead of being members of a racial/ethnic/cultural minority in the United States or any of the countries in which the Chinese now live and work, the existence of a Chinese diaspora allows all people of Chinese ancestry to think of themselves as members of the world's largest ethnic/national group. Chinese governments, from the days of the Chinese empire to the present, have always referred to these scattered compatriots as "overseas Chinese"—people whom China can still claim, control, and count on for support regardless of their citizenship in other nations. There lies the rub. Can Chinese in the diaspora be trusted in times of crisis in the countries in which they have settled? Or would they act as fifth columns should hostilities break out between their ancestral land and the nation(s) in which they happen to live? In the days when China was prostrate under the heels of Western imperialism during the nineteenth and early twentieth centuries, Western nations worried mainly about the huge numbers of Chinese and their allegedly insidious cultural and social differences; today, with China's resurgence as a world power, it is not just numbers and culture but also China's growing military strength, economic vitality, and technological advances that cause anxieties, especially to people living in the world's "only remaining superpower." How long will it take before China becomes a second superpower able to challenge U.S. hegemony on many fronts?

But diaspora is also problematic in an academic sense: It assumes the existence of an essentialized peoplehood precisely at a time when essentialism is being severely criticized. Members of a diaspora are said to identify with one another because they are part of a singular people with a shared history, culture, ethos, and language. Such an assumption ignores the influence of localities on their residents. That is, although members of a diaspora may live, go to school, work, marry, bear and rear children, die, and engage in all the minutiae of everyday life in other lands, the existence of a diasporic mentality implies that somehow these multiple facets of existence have less emotive power than the hallowed sense of common peoplehood. Instead of simply assuming the strength of such ties, scholars need to investigate, on the ground, how these bonds are sustained or broken and the factors that determine their strength and endurance or lack thereof.

Even more popular than diaspora is the idea of transnationalism. Although the two terms are often used interchangeably, they are not the same. Transnationalism implies multiplicity rather than singularity. As Nina Glick Schiller, Linda Basch, and Cristina Szanton Blanc, who first formalized the meaning of transnationalism, argued in *Towards a Transnational Perspective on Migration: Race, Class, Ethnicity Reconsidered* (1992), *Nations Unbound: Transnational Projects, Postcolonial Predicaments, and Deterritorialized Nation-States* (1994), and other writings, transnational migrants maintain simultaneous relationships with people and institutions in several nation-states. They may or may not yearn to "return" to a "homeland." Instead, they revel in their in-betweenness, their hybridity, their flexible citizenship. They are free to shuttle, like astronauts, around the globe. Although technological advances make such mobility—both physical and mental—possible, this kind of freedom is not available to everyone. The main beneficiaries of transnationalism are well educated and, in many instances, rich individuals who can work and invest wherever the best opportunities may be found. But there is another kind of transmigrants: contract workers and people without legal travel documents who are driven by poverty to risk their lives in order to earn a living outside their countries of origin so that they can send remittances home to feed families left behind. Among the latter groups, necessity, rather than liberty, is the driving force. Individuals of Chinese ancestry can be found among both well-to-do and poverty-stricken transmigrants not only at present but also historically. The paradox inherent in transnationalism is that its celebratory stance camouflages underlying realities of immense exploitation, severe suffering, and gross violations of human rights. Among elitist intellectuals, only a few call attention to the dark underside of transnationalism. However, as heirs and beneficiaries of the Asian American Movement (a small but identifiable part of the social movements of the 1960s and 1970s that fought for racial equality and social justice), should not Chinese American scholars be more cognizant of how ideologically loaded the term transnationalism really is?

Globalization, the third concept in the triad, was originally called "restructuring"—a reference to the transformation of "late" capitalism. Some time in the late 1960s and early 1970s, industrial production, instead of being confined to the so-called developed and industrialized nations of Europe and North America, as well as Japan, began to move to localities with plentiful low-paid labor. In place of the "Fordist" model of vertically integrated capitalist production, manufacturing became increasingly dispersed: Goods are no longer made and assembled in any single country. Jobs in what used to be called the "First World" (now more commonly referred to as "the North") are increasingly outsourced to the "Third World" (now often called "the South") or are relegated to immigrant labor, particularly that of women, in the more prosperous nations. Initially largely an economic phenomenon with an underlying ethos of consumerism, globalization today is also manifested in all forms of cultural production. Among scholars of Chinese America, globalization seems to be a less compelling concept than diaspora or transnationalism. Still, the word peppers many writings in contemporary Chinese American history. Like those who sing the praises of transnationalism, advocates of globalization claim that its universalizing tendency is a sign of human progress while blithely ignoring all the inequities it imposes on a worldwide scale. The tentacles of capitalism now reach into countless "global villages" to squeeze out the maximum profits from the backbreaking and eyesight-destroying labor of powerless workers living in countries with little protective legislation and no publicly funded socioeconomic safety nets. Thus, globalization likewise requires more critical analysis.

It is against the backdrop of these larger developments, both in academia and in the world at large, that the essays in this volume can be read. Each author explores a specific way, in a particular time and place, in which "culture" gained a political or economic force. We adopt the term "politics of culture" that Lisa Lowe and David Lloyd defined in their 1997 coedited work, *The Politics of Culture in the Shadow of Capital*. As they put it, " 'culture' obtains a 'political' force when a cultural formation comes into contradiction with economic or political logics that try to refunction it for exploitation or domination. Rather than adopting the understanding of culture as one sphere in a set of differentiated spheres and practices, we discuss 'culture' as a terrain on which politics, culture, and the economic form an inseparable dynamic." The chapters in this book, arranged in roughly chronological order, investigate the manner in which Chinese Americans have engaged in the politics of race and culture by deploying their "culture"—their representations and self-representations—to their own advantage, seizing the high ground from their historic detractors who used "Chinese culture" against them and placed them into an inferior and racialized slot in the host society. In this manner, Chinese Americans became players—limited though their influence might have been—in the American political arena, via the venue of culture, even before members of the immigrant generation were allowed to acquire naturalized American citizenship and to vote.

In the long introduction, Sucheng Chan tracks the changing trends in the writing of Chinese American history—a form of cultural production—from the mid-nineteenth century to the present. After briefly identifying the salient features in five periods of Chinese American historiography, Chan asks what difference the Asian American Movement has made in how community and academic historians have perceived and represented Chinese Americans. She argues that variations in the conceptual frameworks used and the choice of topics in historical and sociological studies reflected key developments in the larger society while scholarship itself helped transform Chinese American consciousness.

In Chapter 1, Mae Ngai reevaluates the significance of the case *Tape v. Hurley*, which upheld the rights of Chinese American children to a public school education, albeit in segregated schools. The issue of educational access underscored the contradictions in the status of Chinese Americans during the exclusion era (1882–1943): While acknowledging the rights of Chinese American children to a publicly funded education, it also highlighted the failure of the Chinese exclusion laws to prevent Chinese settlement. Ngai argues that the Tape family confronted the limits on their Americanization imposed by segregation by becoming brokers for the Chinese American community, a development that signaled the early formation of a Chinese American middle class. The experience of the Tape family reveals both the possibility and, ultimately, the impossibility of assimilation.

In Chapter 2, Josephine Fowler chronicles the activism of left-wing and Communist Chinese immigrants and their status within the U.S. Communist movement from the spring of 1927 to the beginning of 1933. In the early years, these individuals devoted a great deal of attention to events in China and expressed a strong desire to return there to participate directly in the ongoing Chinese revolution. By the early 1930s, however, their orientation began to change: They, as well as the Communist Party of the United States of America, felt compelled to address their isolation from the people living in Chinatowns—the very communities in which they tried to do political work. Drawing on newly declassified documents in the archives of the Comintern in Moscow, Fowler situates the history of Chinese immigrant activists within the context of global processes, thereby challenging the belief that Chinese immigrants were passive and were not interested in labor organizing or political activism.

Karen Leong and Judy Tzu-Chun Wu analyze, in chapter 3, how China's war against Japanese aggression in the 1930s and 1940s transformed the status of China and Chinese Americans in the imagination of mainstream Americans. Previously deemed racially inferior and perpetually alien, Chinese Americans increasingly were perceived as worthy allies and potential citizens of the American nation. Chinese Americans and European Americans worked together to construct a more sympathetic portrait of China and the Chinese people through the staging of pageantry, such as the Rice Bowl Parades, designed to solicit humanitarian aid for China and to stimulate tourism in American Chinatowns. Leong and Wu show how Chinese American women, who portrayed suffering mothers and starving children in war-torn China, played a central role in "selling" China as a country "worthy" of American patronage. Such spectacles worked by catering to American fantasies about "Oriental" beauties as gendered and racialized "Others."

Chapter 4 presents three examples of how the situation of Chinese Americans improved during World War II, allowing them to become "the good Asian in the good war." Scott Wong looks at the mainstream American as well as the Chinese American press, both of which valorized the Chinese; the visit of Mayling Soong (Madame Chiang Kai-shek), who spoke before both houses of Congress and charmed the American public as she toured the United States; and the passage of legislation to repeal the entire series of Chinese exclusion laws. Chinese Americans willingly participated in the construction and dissemination of these positive images, laying a foundation for a "model minority" stereotype much earlier than has been assumed by many scholars.

In Chapter 5, Madeline Hsu traces the shift from the racialization to the ethnicization of Chinese Americans during the cold war era. In this period, a number of Chinese American restaurateurs exemplified the American ideologies of capitalism and racial integration by successfully domesticating Chinese culture in the form of "authentic" cuisine for mainstream consumption. Hsu focuses on two famous restaurants and the strategic positionality of their owners as case studies to explore how ethnicity can function as a marketable and desirable asset rather than as a liability to be erased or overcome in post–World War II America.

Andrea Louie, in Chapter 6, examines transnationality among American-born Chinese who participate in the "In Search of Roots" program jointly sponsored by the Chinese Culture Center in San Francisco and the government of the People's Republic of China. This year-long program employs history lessons, archival research, genealogy projects, and a visit to ancestral villages in China to shape the identity-formation process of its participants. Analyzing the autobiographies written by the participants, Louie argues that the transnationality of American-born Chinese is mediated by contemporary political, economic, and social circumstances in both China and the United States. However, their country of birth and upbringing exerts a greater influence in shaping their cultural and ethnic affiliations.

In Chapter 7, Xiaojian Zhao studies one of the most energetic regional groups of contemporary Chinese immigrants, the *Changle ren* (Changle people) from the Fuzhou district in Fujian Province, China. A recent census taken by the Fuzhou government indicates that there are about 200,000 Changle ren in the United States, 170,000 of whom live and work in New York City. As a result of sensational media coverage of efforts to smuggle Chinese (a vast majority of them from Changle) into the United States, Changle ren have endured being negatively stereotyped as illegal immigrants. Within a relatively short period of time, however, they have demonstrated their entrepreneurship: Their presence in New York has revitalized that city's ethnic economy. Zhao concludes that this subcommunity provides a good example of how a new group of immigrants can negotiate power with earlier-established groups that had dominated the immigrant community for decades before the newcomers' arrival.

Taken together, these studies reveal how the writings of historians of Chinese America resonate with current academic trends in which cultural history, told within a transnational or diasporic framework, has (more or less) displaced social history. From the 1960s to the 1980s, many social historians relied on nonnarrative sources to reconstruct the lives of workers, peasants, women, and peoples of color who left few records of their existence, thoughts, and feelings. Such a methodology, full of statistical tables, produced new insights about hitherto neglected groups but often lacked human interest that can be teased out only from the life stories of individuals. Cultural history, in contrast, may contain a less extensive evidentiary base but offers a more heart-warming read. It is thus easy to understand why cultural history has gained great popularity so rapidly. In Chinese American historiography, cultural history is opening up possibilities that allow readers to view the lives of Chinese Americans in more complex, intricate, and intriguing ways.

A Note on Transliteration and Chinese Names

The transliteration of personal names in this book is inconsistent because the authors are reproducing the versions found in published writings. In those instances where the Chinese characters are not known, changing the published (English) spellings to a standardized transliteration system may in fact misrepresent the names. The pinyin transliteration system is used whenever the authors themselves are transliterating proper nouns from Chinese-language documents.

In the Chinese naming sequence, the family name (what Americans call "last name" and the British designate as "surname") precedes an individual's given name (what Americans call "first name" and "middle name" or "middle initial"). However, most Chinese living in the United States and other Western countries invert their names in order to conform to American and European usage. When the writings of such scholars residing in the Western world are listed in a bibliography or in an index in English-language publications, a comma follows the family (last) name.

In the Republic of China ("Taiwan") and in mainland China before it became the People's Republic of China ("Communist China") in 1949, a hyphen is used between the two words that form a person's given name—for example, Tsai Shih-shan. The first letter in the second word in a given name is not capitalized. When Tsai's Chinese-language publications are cited, his name in a bibliography or index is given as Tsai Shih-shan, with no comma after Tsai. However, because Tsai now lives and works in the United States, his name in English-language publications is inverted and given as Shih-shan Tsai. When citing such works in a bibliography or an index, a comma is used after Tsai:

Tsai, Shih-shan. The names of Chinese from Taiwan or pre-1949 China are almost always transliterated according to the Wade-Giles system.

A different convention prevails in the People's Republic of China: no hyphen is used between the first and second words in a person's given name—for example, Guan Shuyi. Scholars in the United States have adopted this naming practice: When Guan's works are listed in a bibliography or index, regardless of whether the work is in English or Chinese, the Chinese naming sequence is used, with no comma after Guan. Thus, the correct form is Guan Shuyi, and not Guan, Shuyi or Shuyi, Guan. Names of Chinese from the People's Republic of China are transliterated according to the pinyin system as they are pronounced in putonghua, the official spoken language in the People's Republic of China. (This spoken form used to be called Mandarin; many Chinese around the world still call it by the latter name.)

To make matters even more complicated, during the nineteenth and early twentieth centuries, Chinese immigrants in the United States did not hyphenate the first and second words in their given names or join them together. The first letter in each part of the name was capitalized—for example, Wong Kim Ark. Wong is the family name and Kim Ark (the two words together) is the given name. In bibliographies and indexes, the name should be Wong Kim Ark (and not Wong, Kim Ark, or Wong, Kim A., or Ark, Wong Kim, or Ark, Wong K.) Moreover, these names were not transliterated systematically and were often based on what U.S. consular officials abroad and immigration officials in ports of entry in the United States thought they heard and wrote down. Most of the pioneers were from Guangdong province, so the pronunciation of their names reflected the various dialects spoken in that province and not "standard" Mandarin.

Acknowledgments

We thank the anonymous reviewers for their positive and thoughtful evaluations that did not require us to make any changes in the manuscript. We are grateful to the following individuals and institutions for permission to reproduce the images in this book: Susan Snyder of the Bancroft Library at the University of California, Berkeley, for the image on the front cover of the paperback edition of this book; Frank Jang for the images on the dedication page and in the Introduction; Jack Kim, the Bancroft Library, and the Library of Congress for the images in Chapter 1; the Library of Congress for the images in Chapter 2; Martha Smalley, Joan Duffy, and Liam Haggerty of the Yale Divinity School Library for the image in Chapter 3; Judy Yung for the image in Chapter 4; Connie Young Yu for the image in Chapter 5; Andrea Louie for the image in Chapter 6; and Xiaojian Zhao for the image in Chapter 7. We very much appreciate the guidance of Janet Francendese and Charles Ault of Temple University Press, and Debbie Masi and Susan Baker of Westchester Book Services as the manuscript wound its way through the review and production process. We are also grateful to Julie Palmer-Hoffman, who copy-edited the manuscript, and Judith Daniels, who prepared the index with intelligence and care.

Josephine Fowler, the author of Chapter 2, died of breast cancer in 2006. According to her sister, she made "Herculean efforts" in the weeks before she passed away to complete the revision of her chapter, as well as to take care of the final details for her book, *Japanese and Chinese Immigrant Activists: Organizing in American and International Communist Movements, 1919–1933*, published posthumously in 2007 by Rutgers University Press. Her work, based on meticulous research in archives holding documents in four languages in several countries, is her legacy—a gift to colleagues interested in the history of international Communism in general and in Chinese American and Japanese American left-wing activists in particular.

We dedicate this book lovingly and respectfully to Him Mark Lai, the "dean" or "father" of Chinese American historiography, whose pathbreaking scholarship made our studies possible. Although we seek to emulate his prodigious labor of love, our work can never equal his monumental and enduring achievements.

Chinese Americans and the Politics of Race and Culture

Introduction

Chinese American Historiography: What Difference Has the Asian American Movement Made?

Sucheng Chan

From time to time, historians of Asian America have taken stock of the existing writings in the field. Roger Daniels, Shirley Hune, Sucheng Chan, L. Ling-chi Wang, and Gary Y. Okihiro have provided analytical overviews, whereas Shih-shan Henry Tsai, Sucheta Mazumdar, Charles J. McClain Jr., Gordon H. Chang, Chris Friday, Gail M. Nomura, Patricia N. Limerick, John Kuo Wei Tchen, Sylvia Junko Yanagisako, and Madeline Y. Hsu have discussed specific aspects of Asian American historiography. Daniels criticized historians of U.S. immigration for ignoring the migration from Asia;[1] Hune likewise faulted scholars for marginalizing Asian immigrants;[2] Chan argued that the nineteenth- and early twentieth-century history of Asian immigration should be seen within the twin contexts of Western imperialism and the uneven development of capitalism in the United States;[3] Wang pointed out that even the authors who were sympathetic to Asian immigrants had their own biases;[4] and Okihiro proposed alternative periodizations, assessed key historical debates, and presented what he considered to be the most important emerging themes.[5]

In the more specialized essays, Tsai alerted colleagues to the existence and utility of Chinese-language sources as well as histories penned by Marxist scholars in China;[6] Mazumdar called for a woman-centered perspective on Asian American history;[7] McClain refuted the belief that nineteenth-century Chinese immigrants were contract laborers imported by the Chinese Six Companies or its component associations;[8] Chang asked whose history scholars are talking about when writing Asian American history;[9] Friday lamented the absence of studies of Asian American workers in the historiography of U.S. labor;[10]

Nomura wanted to know why European American scholars place the burden of proof on Asian Americans to show that their lives have historical significance;[11] Limerick proposed that treating Asian American history as an integral part of the complex history of the American West will enrich both areas of academic inquiry;[12] Tchen queried how Asian American historiography might be different if we paid more attention to regions other than the Pacific Coast;[13] Yanagisako argued that nation, ethnicity, kinship, gender, and class should all be taken into account when investigating how an Asian American historical consciousness has been and is being constructed;[14] and Hsu urged scholars to recognize that the "homosociality" (warm relationships among men, be they nonsexual or sexual) in the largely "bachelor communities" in America's Chinatowns was, and is, a normative, and not a deviant form of social life. We need to move, she declared, beyond the false dichotomy between "bachelor" and family-centered societies.[15]

The scope of this introduction is narrower than the essays cited above. Instead of looking at the history of all Asian ethnic groups, I examine only selected books about Chinese Americans to illustrate how history writing and sociopolitical activism were inextricably intertwined and mutually constitutive during the years when the civil rights movement and the black power movement and their offshoots energized peoples of color, including Asian Americans, in the United States. A revisionist historiography helped create an alternative, often oppositional historical consciousness. I discuss the earliest works in some detail because they set the terms of the public policy and academic debates that have continued to the present day. My analysis of post-movement works, however, is very brief as they are readily available and have been widely reviewed in academic journals and because Asian Americanists know them well.

In two historiographical essays published in 1996, I identified the salient features in four periods of Asian American historiography: (1) the 1850s to the early 1920s, when partisan writings dominated the literature; (2) the mid-1920s to the early 1960s, when social scientists produced most of the studies; (3) the late 1960s to the early 1980s, when Asian American and European American scholars attempted to debunk anti-Chinese notions; and (4) the mid-1980s to the mid-1990s, when university-based Asian American historians came of age, professionally speaking. In an article published in 2007, I discussed a fifth period that emerged in the late 1990s when social history gave way to cultural history and when transnationalism, diaspora, and globalization became the key tropes in the literature.[16]

In the present study, I examine only one turning point that occurred when the Asian American Movement was most vibrant. I discuss three genres of pre-movement works—partisan tracts, sociological studies, and Chinatown "guides" or exposés—but owing to space limitations, I regretfully must leave out autobiographies, creative writings (except for a few nineteenth-century works), transcripts of state legislative and congressional hearings, books on Asian Americans containing sections on Chinese Americans (with several exceptions), and journal and newspaper articles. Despite its selectivity, this survey reveals that even though the militancy expressed by many participants of the Asian American Movement has long since dissipated, its legacy still resonates in multiple ways in both the community and the academy.

Partisan Writings

Journalists, missionaries, diplomats, labor leaders, publicists, and politicians started writing about Chinese immigrants almost as soon as they landed in the United States. Although some Chinese had appeared on the East Coast long before Chinese migrated in significant numbers to California and elsewhere in the American and Canadian West in search of gold and other means of sustenance, their presence along the Atlantic seaboard elicited curiosity more than hostility. In contrast, the large numbers who set foot along the Pacific Coast encountered opposition and discrimination early on. Partisan rhetoric tinged all the writings about the Chinese as Chinese immigration became a vociferously debated public policy issue, first in California and then in the nation.

Beginning in the early 1850s, short newspaper accounts, longer periodical articles, and pamphlets eventually burgeoned into a voluminous literature. Although the publications were numerous, they contained only a limited number of oft-repeated themes. Books published from the 1870s onward articulated these motifs in the greatest detail. Those written by missionaries William Speer, Otis Gibson, and Ira M. Condit, all of whom had served in China, and by diplomat George F. Seward, a former American minister (ambassador) in the U.S. legation (embassy) in China, exemplify the pro-Chinese arguments, whereas books by M. B. Starr, Willard B. Farwell, Pierton W. Dooner, Robert Woltor, and James A. Whitney reveal the anti-Chinese mindset. The authors in both camps based their arguments on their assessments of Chinese civilization and perceived the immigrants as representative bearers of that culture.

The bulk of Speer's hefty 681-page book is about the Chinese in China, but in six of his chapters he addressed the issues raised by Chinese immigration into the United States. He pointed out, in chapter 16, that the word *coolie* came from India, a caste society, but that castes never existed in China and that the Chinese in California were not "coolies" but "freemen." In chapter 17, he noted that although it was true that Chinese workers, in China as well as in the United States, received low wages, it was not their cheap labor but, rather, their industriousness, frugality, intelligence, and employability in a wide range of occupations that made them attractive to employers. Chapter 19 is devoted to a discussion of the Chinese Six Companies and the useful functions that organization performed.

However, Speer believed that when the Chinese became "secure in the possession of the ordinary rights of humanity, it is desirable that these companies should be discouraged." In chapter 20, he observed that "the saddest feature of the terrible trials of the Chinese [was] that so many of them were inflicted in the name of the law" and reproached Congress for allowing such a situation to exist. While admitting that the Chinese were indeed heathens, in chapter 21 he discussed the syncretic intricacies of Chinese religion, thereby (perhaps unwittingly) legitimizing the beliefs and rituals associated with that religion. In chapter 22, he declared that American civilization was "divinely designed to be a School of the Nations." For that reason, the Chinese who came to the United States could learn "our sciences," "the incalculable importance" of democratic politics, and Christianity. He hoped that they would help spread the glories of American civilization not only among their fellow trans-Pacific migrants but also in their villages and districts of origin.[17]

Unlike Speer's work, with its emphasis on China, all except the first chapter in Otis Gibson's study discuss various aspects of Chinese life in the United States, including the journey to America; San Francisco's Chinatown; the work the Chinese found in California; Chinese immigrant women; the impact of Christian missionary work on both the men and women; the antagonism against the Chinese; whether the Chinese Six Companies imported "slaves"; and the financial, moral, and political "facts and considerations bearing upon the Chinese Problem." Highlighting the remarkable economic growth of California, Gibson pointed out that the Chinese had "performed a considerable part of the unskilled labor in all these industries," which "could not have been developed" without them. He also asked, if Chinese labor were indeed as harmful to white working people as detractors of the Chinese claimed, "how is it that right here in California, where the Chinamen are the most numerous, the general condition of the white working-class is far better than in any other city of the United States, indeed of the world?" As for the charge that the Chinese presence was "demoralizing and ruining our boys," he observed, "in every instance they have taken their first lessons in the path of ruin in the whiskey shops and drinking saloons of our Christian civilization." Gibson saw only two valid objections to Chinese immigration: their slow rate of assimilation and their "overpowering numbers . . . coming from all parts of China." Still, to "prohibit the Chinese from entering this country requires . . . a marked departure from the broad principles upon which our Government is established, and which have been our boast and glory for a hundred years. Is the cause sufficient to require such a sacrifice?"[18] To him, the answer was no.

Ira M. Condit began his study with the premise that "one needs to see him [i.e., the Chinese] at home to fully appreciate him. . . . For capability, for reliability, for most of the sterling qualities which make for strength of character, the Chinese easily excel." He identified several prominent Chinese converts to Christianity in a chapter entitled "Acts of the Apostles in Chinese," drawing a parallel between the evangelical work the converts did among fellow Chinese, both in the United States and in China, with the proselytization carried out by Christ's original disciples. He argued that the "Chinaman" who came to the United States should be treated well because "he will never make America his permanent home. This is the very reason why we should give him the Gospel to take home with him. . . . To this nation is now being given one of the most wonderful opportunities that has ever been offered for helping forward the kingdom of God on earth."[19]

George F. Seward's work is a compendium of selected excerpts from the 1876 hearings before the U.S. Congressional Joint Special Committee to Investigate Chinese Immigration. As an advocate of the Chinese, however, he chose more segments that portrayed them in a positive light than in a negative one. Like Speer, he insisted that Chinese labor was free and that it did not displace but, rather, supplemented white labor; that Chinese vices were less dangerous than those of whites; and that "American race intolerance" impeded Chinese assimilation.[20] The issue of why the Chinese failed to assimilate would be debated over and over again in subsequent years.

Among the anti-Chinese authors, M. B. Starr, a "grand lecturer" for the People's Protective Alliance—an amalgamation of the Workingmen's Alliance of Sacramento, the Anti-Chinese League of San Francisco, and the Industrial Reformers that joined forces in 1873[21]—who traveled up and down the Pacific Coast giving anti-Chinese talks, began his book with a chapter entitled "Is the Coolie Trade Right When Viewed from a Scriptural Standpoint?" This was an apparent rebuttal to the writings of the pro-Chinese missionaries. He then listed all the evils brought about by Chinese immigration (including the corruption of public morals, finances, and paganism, as well as the reintroduction of slavery) and proposed such remedies as denouncing those who profited from the coolie trade, forming vigilante committees, "banishing . . . everything that is contaminating and impure," and preventing "the introduction of a leperous hord [*sic*] of serfs." He intoned, "This lovely land and glorious liberty of ours to enjoy, and then to transmit—to whom? to the heathen, to serfs, to a landed aristocracy, or to our posterity?"[22] It is clear that while targeting the Chinese, he also took aim at capitalists and landowners who benefited from Chinese labor.

Willard B. Farwell directed his ire at Chinese immigrants and the Christian missionaries who defended their presence. "Their religious zeal," he claimed, "blinds their ability to entertain a thought beyond making a Christian convert out of an idolator." Worse, the missionaries "either ignorantly or otherwise falsified facts, and suppressed or distorted the truth." Accusing them of "bigoted fanaticism," he particularly resented the fact that they pontificated about Chinese immigration as something "ordained by God." If people accepted that, he said, "then the opposition to it . . . is an unpardonable sin . . . then are we, indeed, in danger of eternal damnation."[23]

The rabidity of anti-Chinese sentiments is also highlighted in two works of fiction published in the 1880s. Pierton W. Dooner fanned fears of a race war by combining fact and fantasy, characterizing the "coolie invasion" as a "poison that is slowly corroding the vital principles of our national life." Citing China's "traditions of universal domination" and its penchant to absorb other lands, he painted a horrifying futuristic picture of how the Chinese would conquer the United States unless their immigration was stopped.[24] Robert Woltor offered another fear-mongering account of a potential Chinese invasion and conquest that he predicted would occur by 1899 in a tale that combined nativism, racism, and fin de siècle anxieties.[25]

James A. Whitney, a lawyer, while crediting Chinese civilization "from which have been drawn many of the discoveries without which the civilization of our western world would have been incomplete if not impossible," and acknowledging the deleterious effects of Western imperialism on China, nevertheless insisted on the urgent need to "stay the eastward migration of the Yellow race" by abrogating all treaties, particularly the Burlingame Treaty, between China and the United States. He claimed that China had no right to object to U.S. actions because China, too, had long excluded foreigners. The United States would simply be imitating China's example "in eliminating an objectionable element from a population characterized by the necessities, and imbued with the ideas, of an entirely different civilization."[26]

Unlike the authors of works that were either pro- or anti-Chinese, Charles R. Shepherd, director of Chinese Missions on the Pacific Coast for the American Baptist Home Mission Society, provided a dialectical view of the Chinese. In 1923, he published a book that spun out at length all the negative stereotypes of "Ah Sin," a name he borrowed from Bret Harte, detailing the vices of the "unregenerate Chinese," including gambling, smoking opium, killing, and prostituting women: "They have waxed fat, prosperous and powerful; and in addition to their own native wiles and cunning, have adopted many of the ideas and vices of the lower strata of American society. They constitute to-day the greatest single menace to peace, prosperity and social progress in every Chinese community in the United States."[27] Fifteen years later, he offered a counterpoint by documenting what the Chinese could be like if they were schooled properly. He told the story of the Chung Mei Home for Chinese Boys that he had established, highlighting how a Christian education and character-building manual labor turned the boys into worthy American citizens. Eddie Hing Tong, the first Chung Mei alumnus to graduate from the University of California, Berkeley, went to China to provide "Christian leadership among boys." Shepherd hoped that most of the other boys would follow Tong's footsteps and devote their lives to "Christian service."[28] The message conveyed by the two books taken together was that, yes, the Chinese indeed had vices, but "Christian living" could rescue and civilize them.

Long before the Asian American Movement raised the political consciousness of Chinese Americans, Chinese in the United States actively confronted the malevolent and benevolent but patronizing images that these defining works projected about them. Chinese diplomats in the United States, as well as resident Chinese merchants and others who were fluent in English, defended their compatriots in English-language publications. K. Scott Wong summarized their strategies as follows:

> They denied the anti-Chinese charges and paraded the virtues of Chinese history and culture; they sought equal treatment with other groups in America on the basis of class similarities; they defended the presence of the Chinese in America by comparing them favorably with others or by denigrating other immigrants and minority groups, often in Sinocentric terms; and they turned American democratic ideals back on their accusers, demanding that they live up to their own professed standards.[29]

Not only were America's democratic ideals in question; so was its Christian faith. As J. S. Tow, secretary of the Chinese Consulate General in New York, asked succinctly in 1923, was the prejudice against "the Mongolian race" a "Christian idea?"[30] One other form of self-defense that scholars who rely solely on English-language sources have failed to notice was the effects of exclusion on China itself. On the basis of a close reading of Chinese diplomatic correspondence, Shih-shan Henry Tsai concluded that anger over exclusion helped fuel modern Chinese nationalism.[31]

The themes in both these pro-Chinese and anti-Chinese writings continue to crop up in twenty-first-century writings, films, television, and radio. Today, China's booming export trade and increasing military prowess are causing anxieties among Americans to such an extent that the old anti-Chinese bogies are being reincarnated in public discourse.[32]

Social Science Studies

The partisan writings had a profound impact on research studies that appeared in their wake. Mary Coolidge, a sociologist who produced the first scholarly work on Chinese immigration, devoted her entire book to refuting the anti-Chinese arguments and offering her own explanations for why the anti-Chinese movement arose in California. Her reasons include the state's boom-and-bust economy, the nearly equal strength of the two major political parties, and the presence of a significant number of Southern slave owners who brought their slaves and racial prejudices with them when they came to

California during the gold rush. Her work adopted some of the strategies that the Chinese community spokespersons had used: comparing the Chinese favorably to certain groups of European immigrants, particularly the Irish, and faulting working-class European Americans for the violent outbreaks against the hapless Chinese, in the process revealing her own upper-class bias, just as the well-educated, urbane, English-speaking Chinese elite had done. She also reiterated several points made by Speer some four decades earlier: China, unlike India, had no caste system; Chinese immigrant workers were free men—hardworking, patient, careful, well-behaved, and adaptable, doing work that people of other national origins disdained.[33]

In the 1920s, social scientists associated with the Survey of Race Relations project directed by sociologist Robert E. Park published several volumes based on the data they had collected.[34] Although these studies by Roderick D. McKenzie, Eliot Grinnell Mears, and William C. Smith included the Chinese, they paid greater attention to the Japanese, whose presence in the United States was by then a larger public concern, and to the American-born second generation. Chinese exclusion having been in effect for more than four decades, the key issue was no longer Chinese immigration per se, but rather how the panoply of restrictive laws affected the legal status and economic opportunities of "resident Orientals." McKenzie's book is especially notable for placing the U.S. Chinese exclusion movement within the comparative context of similar efforts to exclude Chinese in "white" countries around the Pacific Rim, particularly Australia and Canada. He identified three major "problems" related to the exclusion laws and their enforcement: the creation of an incentive to enter the country illegally, a rise in the wages earned by immigrant Chinese workers as a result of their increasing scarcity in the labor market, and discrepancies in the interpretation and enforcement of the laws. The sociologists were also keenly interested in members of the second generation—U.S. citizens by birth—and their assimilation, or lack thereof. More important than the shift in topical emphasis, however, was the change in tone in these studies. Couched in the language and theories of sociology, the authors did not defend or attack Chinese immigration. Instead, they presented what they considered to be factual accounts and analyses in a manner approved by an ascendant positivist social science. The focus on assimilation, however, was not new: The partisan authors had already identified it as a problem half a century earlier.

Elmer Clarence Sandmeyer was the first professional historian to write about the Chinese. He revised his dissertation, completed in 1932, into a book published in 1939. Sandmeyer's analysis was less impassioned and more heavily footnoted than the preceding works. Concluding that the anti-Chinese movement was fueled by both a fear of economic competition and racial antipathy, he picked up and reprised most of the themes that had been broadcast by earlier anti-Chinese propagandists.[35]

Only a few books about Chinese Americans were published from the 1940s to the early 1960s, the output being dwarfed by writings about Japanese Americans. Milton R. Konvitz discussed the legal status of aliens in general and "Americans of Asiatic ancestry" in particular, bringing the earlier studies by Mears and McKenzie up to date. (Notice that the proper noun Konvitz used was "Americans," and not "Orientals" or "Chinese"—signaling an important perceptual shift.) He examined the country's right to exclude and expel aliens and the latter's right to become naturalized citizens, to remain citizens, to own land, work, use the natural resources of the land, go to school, and marry white Americans. Because the book appeared in 1946, after World War II had ended, its last chapter is about the court cases related to the wartime incarceration of Japanese Americans.[36]

Fred W. Riggs chronicled the activities of a pro-China lobby that he called a "catalytic group" and the actions of the Roosevelt administration and the U.S. State Department to push Congress to repeal all the Chinese exclusion laws, which it did in December 1943. Congress also granted the Chinese a token immigration quota of 105 persons a year and the right of naturalization. The repeal was meant to allay the long-felt grievances of China, an ally of the United States during World War II, over the injustice of Chinese exclusion. Riggs saw the repeal as a "preparatory step" that would eventually lead to a fundamental reformulation of the country's immigration laws after World War II. Among other changes, new legislation enacted in 1946 granted small quotas and the right of naturalization to immigrants from India and the Philippines. He also noted the congressional debates taking place when his book appeared in 1950—debates that led to the passage of the McCarran-Walter Act in 1952, which allotted immigration quotas and gave the right of naturalization to Japanese and Koreans. By examining the strategies and tactics of all the parties, both for repeal and against it, involved in the repeal campaign, Riggs, a political scientist, hoped to shed light on how pressure groups functioned in general and how the repeal campaign illustrated the manner in which the executive and legislative branches jockeyed for power.[37]

Four books published in the early and mid-1960s are noteworthy for different reasons. The first book published (in Hong Kong) by a Chinese American scholar, sociologist Rose Hum Lee, came out in 1960. While paying tribute to her mentors in the sociology department at the University of Chicago, Lee's framework was considerably broader than Robert E. Park's formulation. Instead of confining her study solely to the question of assimilation, she discussed the history of U.S.–China relations; pointed out that American Chinatowns were part of a worldwide Chinese diaspora; used a Weberian ideal-type approach to analyze Chinese culture; explored community organizations and immigrant families, all of which showed the impacts of Chinese exclusion; and evaluated the economic lives of Chinese Americans, their religious practices, and what she called "social disorganization" and "personal disorganization." Social disorganization referred to the "slot racket" (the "paper son" route to entering the United States), the dilemmas faced by students and intellectuals from China who could not return there after a Communist government came to power in 1949, overcrowded and dilapidated housing, and health problems. Personal disorganization included the deprivations experienced by old men without descendants in America to care for them, mental health problems, gangs and juvenile delinquency, and the plight of neglected children. In the last section of the book, Lee looked at the images that Chinese and Americans had of one another and the changing nature of majority–minority relations.[38] Whether or not scholars today agree with her take on these issues (some have denigrated her work because of her support for assimilation), it cannot be denied that she offered the broadest and most thorough analysis of Chinese communities in America up to that point. In fact, few books published in later years have matched the scope of hers.

The University of Washington Press published the next book by a writer of Chinese ancestry in 1962. The author, S. W. Kung, was a scholar and a former official in China, who specialized in international trade and economics. Whereas Rose Hum Lee had devoted one chapter to the Chinese diaspora, Kung throughout his book compared the experiences of the Chinese in the United States with those of Chinese in Canada, Southeast Asia, and Latin America, dissecting the reasons for the similarities and differences he noted and exploring the influence of U.S. exclusionary legislation on restrictive laws enacted in other countries that also singled out the Chinese. In addition, Kung offered detailed discussions of various displaced-persons and refugee acts that had some bearing on the Chinese. Discussion also focused on what kinds of Chinese were deported, who received "relief through private legislation" (i.e., laws passed to benefit particular individuals), illegal entrants, and the second generation. The book ends with a recitation of Chinese American contributions and achievements in an effort to counteract centuries of negative portrayals.[39]

In 1964, Harvard University Press published the work of Gunther Barth, a student of famed immigration historian Oscar Handlin. Barth's book, considered authoritative by scholars with no specialized knowledge of Chinese American history, has been widely quoted. He resurrected anti-Chinese stereotypes—"cheap labor," "sojourner," and "unassimilable"—and blamed the Chinese refusal to assimilate for white Americans' antagonism toward and discrimination against them. "The sojourners," he wrote, "were obstacles in the road to the realization of the California dream." In the eyes of many European Americans, he asserted, "California formed the pinnacle in the structure which reached from ocean to ocean and harbored the best form of human society." He further claimed that the

> credit-ticket system, by which the passage money was advanced to laborers in Chinese ports and repaid out of their earnings in California, became partly a disguised slave trade, managed chiefly by Chinese crimps and compradors who lured artisans, peasants, and laborers into barracoons and sold them to ticket agents. At Chinese ports and at San Francisco they were kept in confinement, watched, and terrorized by agents of Chinese societies who acted in the creditors' interest.[40]

Barth's book has angered many scholars and not only those of Chinese ancestry. Linda Shin, a European American historian of China, for example, noted that Barth's sources are "laden with notions of white racial supremacy."[41]

Ping Chiu's 1967 study of Chinese labor in California stands in stark contrast to Barth's sweeping moral judgments. A research monograph rather than a broad survey, Chiu's study relied on the statistical methods used by economic historians to analyze, with care and specificity, Chinese engagements in mining, railroad building, agriculture, and light industries that manufactured woolen products, textiles, clothing, shoes, cigars, soap, candles, watches, brushes, brooms, bricks, glue, and gun powder in California. He incisively discussed how the Civil War affected the state's economy when it disrupted the flow of East Coast–manufactured goods to California, thus allowing nascent industries in the still-young state to thrive. However, after the war ended, when cheaper, mass-produced goods from factories in New England and the mid-Atlantic states again flooded the California market, the industries in the state that survived were either those owned and run by Chinese entrepreneurs employing their countrymen or those owned by whites who hired Chinese labor. Chiu also provided a nuanced analysis of the myriad reasons that European American employers, in the post–Civil War years and during the depression of the 1870s, gave for preferring Chinese over white labor. To understand fully his arguments, however, one must know some economic theory—a topic that is beyond the scope of this chapter to discuss.[42]

Chinatown "Guides" and Exposés

During the same period that the above academic studies were published, there also appeared more widely read popular writings about Chinatowns. Books in this genre clearly reveal the process of Orientalization. Instead of attacking or defending Chinese immigration as the partisan writers had done, the authors of these journalistic accounts accepted the Chinese presence in the United States as a given and took advantage of the public's appetite for exotica to titillate their readers with highly colored descriptions of various aspects of Chinatown life.

The earliest lengthy discussion of Chinatown is found in Benjamin E. Lloyd's 1876 book about San Francisco, in which he devoted ten of the seventy-four chapters to the Chinese quarters. Lloyd touched upon all the topics that would reappear in later works. He began, in chapter 30, with a description of "the subjects of the Celestial Kingdom" and moved on to portray the Chinese population in San Francisco, the nature of their "town," their business habits, the sights and sounds of Chinatown at night, how a Chinese newspaper was typeset and produced, the religion of the Chinese, the Chinese Six Companies, and the work that missionaries were doing in Chinatown. He declared, "In San Francisco, it is but a step from the monuments and living evidence of the highest type of American civilization, and of Christianity, to the unhallowed precincts of a heathen race." According to him, the Chinese could take over the area that became Chinatown because "any building adjacent to one occupied by Chinese is rendered undesirable to white folks."

Yet, Lloyd's descriptions are not purely lurid, exoticized, or derogatory. In fact, he offered commonsensical explanations for why certain Chinese practices existed. He noted that the "Chinese are proverbially industrious and enterprising" and that "a Chinaman [will] cease to perform any work he has agreed to do, unless he receives his pay promptly at the appointed time." This statement contradicted not only the allegations of those who considered Chinese "coolies" to be slaves, but also his own assertion later in the book that the "slavery that exists in California . . . is the system of 'contract labor' practiced by both Americans and Chinese." Slaves receive no pay for their work, whereas contract laborers do earn wages. So one must assume that Lloyd used the words "slave" or "slavery" either as a metaphor or simply out of habit—a reflection of the zeitgeist in the latter half of the nineteenth century. He explained that the Chinese lived frugally because they were supporting "aged relatives at home, to whom they feel it is their most sacred duty to give their earnings. So great is their devotion to them that they deny themselves every luxury, and many times curtail the expenses for the actual necessaries [*sic*] of life." Furthermore, the "Chinese are very punctual in paying taxes, licenses, and all just public demands." (Note the word "just," which suggests that the Chinese might refuse to pay those taxes and fees that they considered unjust.)

In Lloyd's opinion, "gambling seems to be the besetting sin of the Chinese," whereas young girls who became prostitutes were "driven to this repulsive pursuit by the rigor of extreme poverty." As for Chinese religion, "because they as a nation have advanced in many things that tend to a high civilization, though almost opposite to our own, they may naturally think that *they are right* [emphasis in original], and we are wrong—that we are the heathens and barbarians." He thought that missionaries had not made much headway in converting the Chinese to Christianity because when the Chinese "see so many persons who disregard all religious teachings, they very naturally conclude that our religion is only a secondary matter at best." In addition, instead of lambasting the Chinese Six Companies as a "tribunal," as many writers and orators had done before and after him, he believed that the organization existed because the Chinese "fully understand the benefits of co-operation."

Despite his reasonable tone in the first nine chapters, Lloyd apparently could not resist ending the section of his book devoted to the Chinese with a graphic portrayal that undercut everything positive he had said earlier. This portrait is a good example of American Orientalism at work:

> Rival factions of the Chinese, sometimes come into hostile contact, and a bloody encounter ensues. . . . At such times the savage nature of the 'Heathen Chinee' is uppermost, and when wrought up to an ecstasy of wrath by the spirit of revenge, a devilish smile overspreads the face, and there is a sparkling in the eye, like unto the lurid flashes emitted from the fires of hell, that transforms John Chinaman's celestial countenance into the visage of a demon.[43]

In short, under the countenance of plodding, hardworking Chinese, there resided demons. Orientalism is both invidious and insidious because it uses non-European groups as foils for inscribing the superiority of European or American civilization and society: Anything non-Western is inferior and uncivilized.

Twenty-two years later, Louis J. Beck claimed that his book also painted an "impartial portraiture" of the Chinatown in New York City. However, like Lloyd, Beck could not help but let slip certain statements that contributed to the Orientalization of the Chinese as enticingly different beings, a people whose beliefs and behavior were totally incongruent with the American way of life. To Beck, it was not Chinese laborers but Chinese women, regardless of whether they were prostitutes or wives, who were "slaves" kept in bondage and seclusion by "their lords," or, worse, sold to the highest bidders.[44]

In 1899, Mary E. Bamford published a children's story about a Chinese boy named Ti who lived in a fishing village along the shores of San Francisco Bay. A charming and whimsical tale accompanied by numerous line drawings, she used Ti's adventures and misadventures as a vehicle to offer her readers glimpses of Chinese life in America. Most significant is the book's ending that depicts Ti's conversion to Christianity. Ti exclaims, "Teacher, great many little Chinese boys and girls in all Cal'forn'a! They don't know 'bout Jesus! Nobody teach them! Oh, teacher, it makes me feel bad! . . . Teacher, someday when I grow big, I go everywhere! I go tell all little Chinese girls and boys 'bout Jesus!" In response, the teacher resolves, "They ought to be reached. They ought to be taught. . . . Dear Lord, send forth more laborers into this, thine harvest!"[45] The missionary passion to grasp all opportunities to "save" or, as Bamford put it, "harvest" Chinese souls thus cropped up in works of fiction as well.

Thirty years would pass before the next batch of Chinatown guides appeared in print. In his 1930 book, journalist Bruce Grant claimed that the "inside story" of the tong wars had been related to him by Eng Ying Gong, also known as Eddie Gong, a leader of the Hip Sing Tong, who was listed on the title page as a coauthor. The story is told in the first-person singular in Gong's voice—obviously a narrative device to persuade readers that the story was authentic. The first battle between rival tongs occurred in 1875 over possession of a pretty prostitute; the wars would continue for another fifty years until the fighting tongs declared a truce mediated with the help of the Chinese Consolidated Benevolent Association (the so-called Chinese Six Companies).

The book contains spell-binding, racy details about the origins of the major tongs, including the Kwong Dock, Hip Sing, On Leong, Suey Sing, Suey On, Ong Yick, and Bing Kung tongs; the most colorful tong members (dubbed *hatchetmen*) and leaders, some of whom had Anglicized names like Little Pete and Big Queue Wai; the most famous battles; the weapons of choice and the ritualized protocols the fighters followed; and the tongs' extortion schemes. One little-known aspect of tong history is that tong membership was open not only to Chinese but also to Japanese and Filipino immigrants and European Americans. This ecumenical approach enabled each tong "to recruit a formidable fighting group." In the last chapter, Eddie Gong ponders the question "Will the tong survive?" His answer is a resounding yes because "a11 Chinese have a gift for organizing" and "the tong stands forth as the strongest organization to promote the welfare of the Chinese in America"—a view of the tongs that differed from that expounded by European American authors. Two kinds of Orientalizing touches in the book are easily discernible: The book uses dozens and dozens of sing-song Chinese names and weird-sounding terms and gives the chapter numbers both in Chinese characters that run horizontally from right to left and in English.[46]

Of the two books published on the topic in 1936, the author of one remains unknown. The author's name is given as Leong Gor Yun—a pseudonym meaning *two persons* (as pronounced in the Cantonese dialect). Some scholars believe the author was a man, others a woman; some think the author was Chinese, others non-Chinese. Regardless of who the author really was, the book claimed to turn Chinatown "inside out." It opens with a chapter entitled "Fu Manchu Exterior," which describes street scenes of shops bulging with disgust-eliciting merchandise: "The herb stores are perhaps the most oriental of all. Their windows are an anatomical nightmare with bears' galls, deer horns, sea horses, rhinoceros hide and dried creatures of land and sea, all for medicinal use." Chapter 23, the penultimate chapter, is entitled "Fu Manchu Interior" and delves into gambling, drug use (not just of opium but also of morphine, heroin, and cocaine, primarily by "Tong gunmen"), and various kinds of prostitution. Even though the author doubted "if there are more than 100 Chinese prostitutes in San Francisco, and still fewer in New York," he or she nevertheless felt compelled to discuss the brothels staffed by non-Chinese women, including a "particularly popular house in uptown New York . . . run by a white madam for the Oriental trade. . . . She always has over ten girls (so there is no traffic jam), between the ages of sixteen and twenty-four, who are white American, negro, Spanish, and Mexican." The author also takes note of the houses controlled by Chinese pimps employing white women and of white women who worked as "street pullers . . . [who] cruise around day and night . . . [going] to the laundries early in the morning or about noon-time, when the laundrymen are not busy." Leong Gor Yun observed wryly that "the laundrymen liked 'delivered goods,' " given their long hours of strenuous labor.

However, the book does contain some useful information not found in other contemporaneous writings. Long before historian Renqiu Yu introduced us to the history of the Chinese Hand Laundry Alliance and its challenge to the traditionalistic establishment in New York's Chinatown,[47] Leong Gor Yun had described this conflict in considerable detail (chapter 5) in a straightforward manner. The author also discussed a new kind of Chinese entering the country in the 1920s and 1930s—students from China pursuing higher education at American universities. Another topic he or she covered is the immigrants' involvement in China's republican revolution—not only the events of 1911 and 1912 that overthrew the Qing dynasty, but also Dr. Sun Yat-sen's subsequent battle against Yuan Shikai, who had declared himself emperor of a new dynasty in China.[48]

Charles C. Dobie, who first became acquainted with the Chinese when his parents employed Chinese domestic servants, wrote the second guide book published in 1936. Before launching into tales of Chinatown, he sketched the history of the Chinese in California in the first five chapters. In the final ten chapters, he painted vivid portraits of the Chinese Six Companies; the "highbinders" (another popular moniker for the hatchetmen) and the blackmail and assassinations these men perpetrated; prostitutes; "slaves—domestic and otherwise"; his own childhood memories; "the penchant of Chinamen for herding together like rabbits in a warren"; the comic efforts of officials in San Francisco to punish the Chinese; opium dens; street scenes; and Chinese festivals, theater, and religion. In short, even though he criticized other works that "chopped up a mess of exoticisms, stirred vigorously, added hot water and served a concoction as little fundamentally Chinese as a dish of chop-suey," while admitting that "it is hard to determine which was the more impressive to the fiction monger—the squalidness or the color," he himself nonetheless covered the same topics as the authors he chastised. He recognized that "it was [Chinatown's] sinister aspects, its delinquent phases which allured" and that the more terrifying the scene or description was, the more it thrilled its audience. Thus, Dobie fell into the same trap of catering to the public's yen for

Orientalized portrayals of a section of the city that he thought he had known well since his youth.[49]

A shift in emphasis can be seen in the books published in the first half of the 1940s, when public perceptions of the Chinese—in China as well as in the United States—underwent a fundamental change. Two books by Carl Glick, a native of Iowa, appeared in 1941 and 1943. Glick came to know the Chinese while working as the athletic director of a boy's club in New York's Chinatown. However, his earliest memories of the Chinese dated back to his boyhood when he visited San Francisco's Chinatown before the 1906 earthquake. In his 1941 book about his personal encounters with the Chinese, he confessed, "the very mention of a hatchetman frightened me. And I thought of Chinatown as a place one should never go to unless accompanied by the police. I have since met one or two so-called 'hatchetmen,' and have found them quite charming persons." Hatchetmen charming? Moreover, "they are today . . . neither terrifying or sinister. One I know is something of a poet. . . . He buys his clothes on Fifth Avenue and his ties at Macy's." Apparently, men formerly considered fearsome gangsters had evolved into urbane, well-dressed Chinese gentlemen no different from other New York gentlemen.

Glick pointed out that there were in fact two Chinatowns: "one seen from the outside by the tourists and sightseers, the other unseen, the Chinatown that exists behind close [*sic*] doors and shuttered windows." On the surface, Chinatown "is a place of strange odors, of exotic foods piled high in shop windows, of joss sticks, of cheap souvenirs, of softly murmuring Orientals standing about in groups seemingly doing nothing at all, of waiters from restaurants carrying trays of food on their heads up winding flights of stairways, of fantastic sights and sounds." But in the "real Chinatown . . . you might find an anxious mother bending over the cot of her sick child; you might find a grandfather instructing his children in good manners. You would find, I know, the sane and sensible home life of a hard-working people—the same sort of well-ordered, well-balanced home life that lies behind the close [*sic*] doors of any Middle Western family."[50] Sane and sensible. Well-ordered and well-balanced. At last, Chinese Americans are seen as normal human beings!

Thus, the model minority image came into being long before the 1960s—the decade conventionally accepted as the birth of the "positive" stereotype. However, the intended impact of the 1940s image differed from the 1960s version because the politics of the two periods were not the same. In the 1940s, praising the Chinese was a way to ensure that they would fervently support the war effort. In the 1960s, the not-so-hidden message was that those minorities who worked hard, did not protest, and played by the rules would in time be fully accepted in American society, unlike African Americans whose militant actions allegedly disrupted societal peace as they demanded equal rights for themselves.

By 1943, when Glick's second book came out, thousands of Chinese Americans had joined the U.S. armed forces, so Glick's story revolved around a Chinese American in his thirties, one Private Kung, who declined deferment, responded to "the invitation of the President" to serve his country (yes, the United States was "his" country), and was inducted into the U.S. Army. As the jacket copy advertised, the book also "answers, in highly entertaining form, a demand for more intimate and accurate information about our Eastern allies in a world rapidly becoming China-minded."[51]

A short pictorial account by Elizabeth Colman, published in 1946, underscored Glick's point. "The war greatly changed the situation," she wrote. "Thousands of Chinese-Americans and Chinese residents enlisted in the armed forces. Thousands were absorbed by defense industries. . . . The present phase of reconversion and the years to come will put to a serious test the sincerity of the will professed by the greater part of this nation to apply democracy at home. . . . Will we stick to our ideals and practice them, or will we let down those on whose help we relied when we desperately needed all able hands?"[52] Even in the twenty-first century, there is still no unequivocal answer to this question.

Despite this shift to more positive depictions, Orientalism had by no means disappeared. No book illustrates its persistence more clearly than Alexander McLeod's 1948 work. McLeod began in a seemingly benign way by stating that "since the San Francisco fire in 1906 a great change has come over the Chinese in California. In San Francisco the merchant, realizing the fire had removed much of the filth incidental to the Chinese quarter, turned his face against re-establishment of the sinister and crime-breeding conditions of early days, so today the Chinese are a credit to the Pacific coast and to themselves." Yet, his book is peppered with words and phrases that reveal his true perceptions of the Chinese. Taking a random sample, one finds the following: "mystery," "intrigue," "plots," "counterplots," "picturesque," "smuggling," "black mail," "strange," "mysterious," and "horde" on page 17; "arcane," "tribal," and "quaint" on page 18; "human tide" on page 19; "hordes of locusts" on page 23; "milling multitudes of destitute China," "novelty," and "amusing spectacle" on page 25; "grotesque" and "queer" on page 31; and "unperturbable" on page 32.

The topics McLeod covered are also familiar: Chinese gold miners, the coolie trade, what work the Chinese found, Chinese-language newspapers, opium dens, gambling joints, "the great Chinese slave market," the Chinese Six Companies, the tongs and their hatchetmen, Chinese religion, and Chinese theater. In the conclusion, he proclaims, "Old Chinatown is gone! San Francisco's quaint, mysterious, gorgeous, hideous old Chinatown has become a thing of history and tradition." Why, then, resurrect the stereotypes of yore? Because, he says, "when the lights are dimmed at midnight, and the stars shine down brightly on Chinatown, it is then that the ghosts walk, ghosts of a spine-tingling mystic past of Old Chinatown."[53] One might ask what ghosts is he talking about? The ghosts of intrepid Chinese pioneers who struggled to earn a living while facing immense hostility, or the piquant phantasmagoric images created by Orientalist writers exploiting Chinese "difference" to sell tabloids masquerading as serious books?

Richard Dillon, director of San Francisco's Sutro Library, rehashed the same tired themes in his 1962 book about hatchetmen, which the publisher announced was based on in-depth research.[54] What difference does research make when the sources used are impregnated with age-old bizarre assumptions that impugn the dignity of the subjects the author was writing about? The longevity of Orientalism is further apparent in journalist Gwen Kinkead's 1992 work, in which she bragged about her ability to penetrate the walls of Chinatown, "a closed society." She focused on how Chinese in New York City earn their living and on gambling, drug trafficking, people smuggling, polygamy, Chinese cuisine, and the failure of post-1960s immigrants to assimilate. To Asian Americanists, perhaps the only chapter in this book that is of some value is an eleven-page discussion of the activities, in the United States, of several exiled leaders of the student protestors who were killed or incarcerated during the revolt at Tiananmen in Beijing, China, in June 1989.[55]

So pervasive has been the urge to mark the Chinese as a feared alien "Other" that Chinese American authors themselves have not hesitated to exploit that image to promote tourism and to profit by the American public's fascination with spine-tingling exotica. In his 1948 Chinatown guide book, Garding Lui took his readers on a walking tour of the new Chinatown in Los Angeles, pointing out all the attractions that might interest visitors and claiming that "China City has shaken Hollywood" as "one out of every fourteen Chinese men and women in Los Angeles have worked in moving picture studios."[56] There are no hard statistics with which to evaluate the veracity of this claim, but if it is true, cinema must have by then become the most popular medium for circulating images that satisfy the desires of Europeans and Americans for the exotic. Why shouldn't shrewd Chinese American entrepreneurs also cash in on the marketability of such depictions?

In 1962, Calvin Lee, a restaurateur, lawyer, administrator at Columbia University, and author of Chinese cookbooks, warned his readers not to "expect me to create for you the mysterious and sinister atmosphere of Chinatown which Hollywood has portrayed, because it never existed."[57] Still, by calling Chinese ethnic communities "a country within a country" and titling his book *Chinatown, U.S.A.*—thereby robbing those communities of the specificities of time and place—he unwittingly helped propagate the incongruity, rather than the normalcy, of Chinese Americans. Finally, C. Y. Lee, author of *Flower Drum Song,* which Richard Rodgers and Oscar Hammerstein turned into a popular musical, saw fit to retell yet again in 1974 the story of the tong wars.[58]

This, then, was the existing literature confronting Chinese American and European American community-based as well as university-based historians in the late 1960s when they set out to rewrite Chinese American history. The fruits of their labor, in the form of books, articles, museum displays, films, and other expressive arts, will long endure in products that preserve some of the more significant legacies of the social movements of that era.

The Movement as a Turning Point

What has been called the Asian American Movement did not begin with a particular event or set of events that retrospectively became iconic. Rather, the term refers to a series of separate efforts undertaken by various groups of Asian Americans of diverse ideological tendencies and social affiliations in different parts of the country. What linked them was their desire to throw off the yoke of the Orientalist past and the adverse consequences it had imposed on their ancestors and themselves. In short, they were impelled not only by the desire to demolish materialist forms of gross injustice but also by the politics of representation. They aimed to raze the offensive images as they refashioned identities based on the "true" history of Asians in America. ("True" was a popular word in the days before postmodernism taught us that there is no single "truth.") In the most detailed study of the movement to date, William Wei concluded that it was "essentially a middle-class reform movement for racial equality, social justice, and political empowerment."[59] Wei's pronouncement has angered many old-time activists who claimed that the movement was not what Wei has depicted. Steve Louie, for example, characterized the movement as a "mass movement" that "stood for struggle to achieve self-determination in all aspects of our lives, to end all forms of oppression, and to end imperialist aggression. It was a radical movement that had many currents—including revolutionary ones—and not everyone in the movement agreed on means and ends."[60]

I characterize the movement as a multiclass, multiethnic, and multisited conglomeration that combined efforts to improve the lives of workers and poor people, to raise the political consciousness of all its participants, to transform detrimental stereotypes, and to assault the institutions entrenched in American society that had oppressed and continue to exploit various groups of people on the basis of race, ethnic origins, class, sex, sexual orientation, and handicap. Because the military conflicts in Vietnam, Laos, and Cambodia were the number one topic of public concern in the late 1960s and early 1970s, some Asian American activists, including me, also protested American involvement in these proxy wars that occurred during the cold war. The activists supported, at least rhetorically, national liberation movements in Third World countries or regions in Asia, Africa, Latin America, the Caribbean, and the Pacific that had been colonized by European powers and the United States. In short, like other social movements of that period, the Asian American Movement encompassed both materialist and symbolic concerns.

For Chinese Americans, rewriting the history of their people in the United States was, and is, an integral part of the struggles to disprove or correct the distorted, sensationalist, and racist representations that have been imposed on them. However, these anti-Chinese images are so deeply ingrained in the American popular as well as scholarly imaginations that they continue to lie dormant, lurking just beneath the surface, and can instantaneously reappear when forces in the larger society create conditions conducive to their resurrection. They remain, despite the efforts of community-based and university-based historians to eradicate them. For that reason, even though many younger scholars who do research in Chinese American Studies today have had no direct experience in the movement, they are nonetheless heirs to this tradition of struggle and self-empowerment.

Community-Based Historians

Chinese American community activists, as well as European American local history buffs, began to excavate and recover fragments of Chinese American history in the 1960s. Some of the larger Chinese ethnic communities in the United States established organizations to preserve those aspects of their heritage they deemed worthy of retention, to publicize their role in building the United States, to introduce more accurate or balanced versions of their history to the general public, and to claim their rightful place in American society. One of the oldest such organizations is the Chinese Historical Society of America, founded in 1963 in San Francisco by journalist Thomas W. Chinn, H. K. Wong, a businessman, restaurateur, and public servant, and other like-minded individuals. The society publishes a newsletter and a journal, *Chinese America: History and Perspectives*; sets up traveling exhibits of photographs and texts; hosts seminars; organizes conferences; and cosponsors a program to help young Chinese Americans do genealogical research and make contact with family members in the historic emigrant districts in Guangdong Province.[61]

Although there are many community historians, three stand out: Him Mark Lai, an engineer; Philip P. Choy, an architect; and Chinn, founder of several notable Chinese American periodicals in addition to the Chinese Historical Society of America. Following the publication of their collaborative works in 1969 and 1971, each has gone on to publish other books.[62] Him Mark Lai, in particular, has produced a seemingly endless stream of essays and books, presenting in-depth research based on Chinese-language sources that he searched for, found, gathered, archived, read, mulled over, and interpreted.[63] At age eighty-two, he remains marvelously productive. Nothing exemplifies the

Philip P. Choy (left), an architect, and Him Mark Lai (right), an engineer, are pioneer Chinese American community-based historians who coauthored the first two textbooks in Chinese American history. *(Photograph by Frank Jang, 2006. Used with permission.)*

community-based movement to recover Chinese American history better than Lai's Herculean efforts, and no one has melded community imperatives and academic concerns more seamlessly than he has done.

Born in San Francisco, educated in public and Chinese-language schools, and a graduate of the University of California at Berkeley, Lai spent much of his working years as an engineer at the Bechtel Corporation, but history is his true love. Beginning in 1967, he wrote a series of newspaper articles for the bilingual weekly *East/West: The Chinese American Journal*, founded by Gordon Lew and edited by Maurice Chuck, that became the kernel of the two textbooks he coauthored. These books were "bibles" that first-generation Asian Americanists relied on when beginning our teaching careers. As Madeline Hsu has observed, the fact that Lai never held a tenured position at a university has given him the freedom—a liberty that university-based scholars worried about tenure reviews, promotions, and academic prestige do not enjoy—to write whatever he wanted.[64] As a result of his decades-long labor of love, we finally know, from a Chinese American–centric perspective, the internal histories of many organizations based on common kinship, locality, and political ideology, as well as the *mentalité* (in the sense introduced by the French Annales school of historians) of various individuals and groups.

The fact that Lai's first article in a scholarly journal appeared in the *Bulletin of Concerned Asian Scholars* (*BCAS*) is historically significant.[65] *BCAS* was started by radical, anti–Vietnam War graduate students, young professors, and a few older ones to serve as a venue for presenting research and analyses that critiqued the conceptual frameworks and empirical evidence used in much of the work published by scholars specializing in Asian (area) Studies. The publication of Lai's article—a study of Chinese American leftist organizations—in the left-leaning *BCAS* emblematizes the convergence of several strands in the sociopolitical upheavals then occurring in many parts of the world. National liberation struggles and decolonization in the Third World, the anti–Vietnam War movement, the women's movement, the gay and lesbian movement, the student movement, and the counterculture movement were global phenomena, whereas the integrationist civil rights movement and the separatist black power, brown power, red power, and yellow power movements were specific to the United States. The work done by Chinese American community activists, therefore, dovetailed with parallel efforts being made by individuals and organizations in the larger society and, indeed, around the world.

The Chinese American community in the San Francisco Bay Area was by no means the only one to embark on projects of historical recovery and reconstruction in order to educate Chinese American themselves as well as the general public about the travails and triumphs of Chinese pioneers in America. In Seattle, Honolulu, Washington, DC, Los Angeles, New York, and some smaller cities, similar organizations sprang up to pursue the same ends. What they had in common was the recognition that a revisionist historiography can be a powerful tool to bring about fundamental social change to improve the status of Chinese Americans.

The Wing Luke Asian Museum in Seattle, now an affiliate of the Smithsonian Institution in Washington, DC, was founded in 1965 and is named after one of the first Chinese American officials elected to public office in the continental

United States. (Wing Luke served on the Seattle City Council from 1962 to 1965, but his political career was cut short when he died in a plane crash.) This organization is the only pan-Asian American museum in the United States with programs for twenty-six different Asian and Pacific Islander ethnic groups whose members reside in the state of Washington. The museum aims to bring about social change through interethnic and intergenerational dialogue by means of exhibits, seminars, research, and the restoration of significant sites with the help of grassroots participation.[66] In the early 1980s, it worked together with the Chinese Historical Society of the Pacific Northwest to publish a journal.[67]

The Hawaii Chinese History Center in Honolulu is the brainchild of Tin-Yuke Char. Born and raised in Hawaii, Char, like Him Mark Lai, learned Chinese during his childhood. At the Wah Mun School in Honolulu, he mastered Chinese well enough to attend and graduate with a B.A. in history from Yenching University in Beijing in 1928—the first Hawaiian Chinese to receive a degree from a university in China. His life is a prime example of the transnational existence of many Chinese Americans. After college, he taught at a middle school in China and wrote articles about China as a news correspondent for the *Honolulu Star-Bulletin* while simultaneously publishing articles about the Chinese in Hawaii in the *Chinese Political and Social Science Review*. Upon his return to Hawaii, he obtained an M.A. from the University of Hawaii and taught Chinese on that campus. From 1936 to 1939, he was back in China working as the registrar and director of admissions at Lingnan University in Guangzhou (Canton). Returning to Hawaii as war clouds gathered in East Asia, he became an insurance agent but kept up his interest in history. A meeting with Him Mark Lai in 1970 led to the establishment and incorporation of the Hawaii Chinese History Center the following year. The center has published many works by Char—most of them written after he retired from the insurance business—and by other community historians in the fiftieth state. Donations from the community supported the research that resulted in these publications.[68]

The Organization of Chinese Americans, founded in 1973, has its headquarters in Washington, DC, and branches in more than twenty cities. While monitoring trends in immigration laws, education, and the economy that may adversely affect the well-being of Chinese Americans, it encourages Chinese Americans to participate actively in civic and national life, to hone leadership skills, to fight against inequality in all its forms, and to enhance the images of Chinese in the United States. It publishes a newsletter and sponsored the publication of a handsome book with arresting photographs by Diane Mei Lin Mark and Ginger Chih that has been reprinted numerous times.[69]

In Los Angeles, the Chinese Historical Society of Southern California, founded in 1975 to disseminate knowledge about the Chinese in that region, likewise is concerned with changing the negative images of Chinese Americans that people in the larger society may still harbor. It supports research and collects documents, photographs, and artifacts. In the 1990s, members of the society worked diligently to purchase and restore a memorial shrine—a significant monument in the history of Chinese in the Los Angeles area—built in 1888 on the grounds of the Evergreen Cemetery. The society publishes a newsletter and the *Gum Saan Journal* and has sponsored the compilation of a book of oral history, an anthology of conference papers, and a family history.[70]

The Museum of Chinese in the Americas began life as the Chinatown History Project in 1980. Founded by John Kuo Wei Tchen, Charlie Lai, and other New York City–based artists, public intellectuals, and students, it was renamed the Chinatown History Museum in 1991. It changed its name again in 1995 in order to reflect its new diasporic perspective. Its goals are to find, preserve, curate, and disseminate historical information about Chinese throughout North, Central, and South America. While Charlie Lai serves as its executive director, Jack Tchen runs the Asian/Pacific American Studies Program and Institute at New York University. The close collaboration between the museum and the academic program demonstrates that universities and community organizations can work fruitfully together to conduct research and organize public forums in order to reach as many kinds of audiences as possible.

Other community-based scholars, some working alone, have published works that illuminate the lives of Chinese in specific localities. Gloria Hom wrote about the Chinese in Santa Clara County, California.[71] Doug Chin and Art Chin chronicled the history of the Chinese in Seattle.[72] Lavern Mau Dickson compiled a pictorial history of the Chinese in San Francisco.[73] Ruthanne Lum McCunn, who specializes in what she calls "biographical novels" and personal histories, published a number of books on notable Chinese Americans.[74] Jack Chen, a scholar from the People's Republic of China who settled in the United States in 1977, wrote a comprehensive history of Chinese Americans.[75] Eve Armentrout Ma and Jeong Huei Ma told the story of the Oakland Chinese community.[76] Victor Low published the only book-length study to date of Chinese struggles to ensure that their children would receive an education.[77] Peter C. Y. Leung preserved the story of the Chinese in Locke, the only rural Chinatown still in existence in the United States.[78] Connie Young Yu edited an anthology of oral histories of Chinese living in the vicinity of Stanford University.[79] H. K. Wong collected and published oral histories of the Chinese in San Luis Obispo, Bakersfield, Sonoma, Napa, and other small cities or towns.[80] Sylvia Sun Minnick corralled the resources of the San Joaquin County Historical Museum, the Haggin Museum in Stockton, the Stockton Public Library, and other county agencies to help her produce a detailed history of the Chinese in San Joaquin County, California.[81] Louise Leung Larson, the daughter of Tom Leung, a famous Chinese doctor of herbal medicine who practiced in

Los Angeles, and herself the first Chinese American woman to work as a reporter for a major American newspaper, recounted the interesting history of her family.[82] Lisa See narrated the life stories of her interracial relatives in their part-Chinese American and part-European American families.[83] Lani Ah Tye Farkas recorded the story of her multigenerational family whose members set down roots in remote La Porte, Plumas County, in the northern part of the Sierra Nevada Mountains, one of California's former gold mining regions.[84] Veteran journalist William Wong created another pictorial history, this one of Oakland.[85] All these works have enriched Chinese American historiography by adding texture, variegations, breadth, and depth to it.

While Chinese Americans were busy setting up historical societies and museums, non-Chinese local historical societies and museums also began to show an interest in the Chinese pioneers in their areas. The works of these two groups of community-based historians, however, differ in one important respect: Chinese Americans see their efforts as an integral part of their struggles to reclaim their history and broadcast their culture in order to enhance their current political and social well-being, whereas non-Chinese history buffs dug and continue to dig up buried aspects of their own regions' histories because the stories of the Chinese who had lived and worked there fascinated them; they did not and do not, however, seek to use such knowledge for political ends.

The non-Chinese local history buffs came from many different backgrounds. Sister M. Alfreda Elsensohn, a Catholic nun, edited an anthology of articles about the Chinese in Idaho.[86] The Oakland Museum published a bilingual catalogue to accompany its traveling exhibit on Chinese Americans.[87] Corinne K. Hoexter, a professional writer, used the life story of Ng Poon Chew—journalist, Christian minister, and popular speaker—as a vehicle for illustrating larger patterns in Chinese American history.[88] Lorraine B. Hildebrand, a librarian, wrote a book about the Chinese in Washington State as a part of the public programs commemorating the bicentennial of the American Revolution.[89] The Institute of Texan Cultures at the University of Texas at San Antonio put out two slim books on the Chinese in Texas.[90] Historians Jeffrey Barlow and Christine Richardson became interested in the Chinese in Oregon when they helped restore the Kam Wah Chung Building, in which Ing Hay, a Chinese doctor of herbal medicine, had his practice in a town named John Day in eastern Oregon.[91] Stan Steiner, author of many books about peoples of color in the United States, claimed that the Chinese had discovered and built America, and indeed "became America."[92] Milton Meltzer, a historian and biographer, penned a book about Chinese Americans for young readers.[93] Clark W. Brott, an archaeologist, excavated, studied, and wrote about the old Chinatown in Weaverville in northern California.[94] Historian Jonathan Goldstein traced Georgia's connections to China and the history of Chinese immigrants in his state.[95] Journalist Loren W. Fessler edited material that the China Institute in America had compiled for an overview of Chinese Americans.[96] Jeff Gillenkirk, a journalist, and James Motlow, a photographer, produced a pictorial history of Locke, the last remaining rural Chinatown in the United States.[97] David M. Brownstone and Irene M. Franck, publishers and writers, contributed the volume on Chinese Americans to the America's Ethnic Heritage series.[98] Florence Lister and Robert Lister, two archaeologists, catalogued and wrote about Chinese American artifacts dug up during an urban renewal project in Tucson, Arizona.[99] Journalist Arthur Bonner indefatigably searched for and found over three thousand newspaper and magazine articles about and pictures of the Chinese in New York and presented some of them in a book dedicated to the memory of Wong Chin Foo, one of the earliest Chinese immigrants to demand civil rights for his compatriots.[100]

The most ambitious project of this nature came into being in Riverside, California. A multiethnic "Save Riverside's Chinatown" campaign launched in 1984 with support from the Chinese-American Heritage and Progress Committee of the Inland Empire, the Chinese Historical Society of Southern California, the San Bernardino County Museum Associates, the Hemet Area Museum Association, the Riverside Municipal Museum Board, the Cultural Heritage Board of Riverside, and the Riverside County Historical Commission invited the Great Basin Foundation of San Diego to coordinate a large-scale archaeological and historical project to excavate, piece together, and present, in a film and two thick volumes of texts, drawings, and photographs, many facets of Chinese immigrant life in Riverside.[101]

Both groups of community-based historians, Chinese and non-Chinese, have emphasized the contributions that the Chinese have made to the United States. They have corrected misunderstandings, filled in gaps in what is known about Chinese Americans, and written new versions of Chinese American history in order to foster societal change. None, however, can be said to be "radical" in the sense of seeking to overturn the existing status quo. The latter task was what some Chinese American university-based scholars took upon themselves.

Leftist University-Based Scholarship

University-based scholars can be divided into three groups: Chinese American leftists who decry the racism, class oppression, sexism, and imperialism of "Amerika" (a spelling popular among militants in the 1960s and 1970s); Chinese American scholars who try, like their community-based counterparts, to publicize the tribulations that Chinese Americans have endured and the contributions they have made and are still making in order to assert their rights as citizens and residents in a multiethnic America; and European American scholars sympathetic to the hardships that peoples of color have experienced in the United States.

The worldview of the leftists, many but not all of whom were or still are Marxists, can be reconstructed from the countless flyers, pamphlets, and other writings they produced in the late 1960s and 1970s. An easier way to grasp what their vision entailed is to look at two anthologies published by the Asian American Studies Center at the University of California, Los Angeles, and in a book edited by sociologists Lucie Cheng of UCLA and Edna Bonacich of the University of California at Riverside. These works played a crucial role in inscribing "Asian America/n/s" as political concepts that underpinned a pan-Asian American identity. *Roots*, the first Asian American Studies anthology published in 1971, singled out identity, history, and community as the field's central tropes. Among the stereotypes that contributors to the volume debunked were "sojourner" and "successful model minority." They proposed "internal colonialism," "Third World peoples," "history of struggles," "resistance," "self-determination," and "yellow power" as alternative conceptual frameworks. They also pondered how close a relationship Asian Americanists should foster with scholars specializing in Asian (area) Studies. Finally, as Marxist-oriented writers, they pointed out that there were or are exploiters not only in white society but within Asian American communities as well.[102]

Five years later, the second anthology, *Counterpoint*, rolled off the press. The articles in it are considerably more analytical and academic than those in *Roots*, reflecting a (perhaps reluctant) recognition of the fact that if Asian American Studies wished to remain alive, it must institutionalize itself on university campuses. The chapters in part I present concepts, critiques, and perspectives. The contemporary issues discussed in part II include education; the mass media; land, labor, and capital; and recent immigration—that is, topics less embedded in personal and collective consciousness than the articles in *Roots* had been. *Counterpoint* also has a large section on literature, a reflection of the fact that various Asian American expressive arts were springing to life in the wake of the Asian American Movement. It is in these creative writings and art works that quests for existential meaning increasingly reside.[103] In retrospect, *Counterpoint* can be seen as a transitional work—one that moved from the intense yearnings of Asian American youth for identities of their own making to a more formal analysis of how Asian American Studies can challenge, modify, and transform the traditional disciplines.

A neo-Marxist framework organizes the chapters in *Labor Immigration under Capitalism*, a collective work by faculty and graduate students at UCLA and Edna Bonacich of the University of California at Riverside. The chapters written by Bonacich and Lucie Cheng are the most theoretical in the book and lay out in great detail how Asian labor migration was part of the worldwide expansion of capitalism. However, there is an unresolved disjuncture between the empirical evidence presented in the case-study chapters and Bonacich's and Cheng's overarching theoretical constructs.[104] Despite this problem, the book is a pioneering work that announced the theoretical coming of age of Asian American Studies.

Peter Kwong, a political scientist, is another scholar who has consistently adhered to the tenets of Marxism. In two books about New York's Chinatown, he focused on its workers and the political and labor struggles they engaged in. He delineated the class structure of Chinese ethnic communities and analyzed the residents' relationships to political developments in China, on the one hand, and to the American labor movement, on the other. Kwong's third book investigated the Chinese currently being smuggled into the United States—what he called the contemporary version of the "pig trade"—and how ethnic ties in this instance are used to smother the class consciousness of these recent immigrants. He faulted American organized labor and the lackadaisical enforcement of U.S. laws meant to protect workers for their failure to ameliorate the plight of these superexploited individuals once they land in the United States.[105]

Other books that delve into Chinese American labor history but are not explicitly Marxist include works by Sucheng Chan, Paul C. P. Siu, Renqui Yu, and Chris Friday. I studied the critical roles that Chinese immigrants played in the development of California agriculture in a wide variety of capacities. As a political scientist who retooled myself into a historian, I used the methodologies of agricultural and economic history, cultural geography, historical sociology, and social history to make sense of the massive amount of data I collected from the manuscript schedules of the U.S. census of population and from old documents archived in county recorders' offices. In the conclusion, I sketched the differences between the class structure of urban and rural Chinese enclaves in California and between these enclaves and Chinese ethnic communities in Southeast Asia.[106]

Sociologist Paul C. P. Siu's landmark work on Chinese laundrymen in Chicago relied on a key anthropological method—participant observation—to describe and analyze the lives of his subjects. Siu carried out the research in the 1930s but did not submit the write-up as a Ph.D. dissertation until 1953. Three decades later, historian John Kuo Wei Tchen, recognizing the richness and complexity of Siu's study—a work that compellingly portrays the daily lives of the laundrymen—deftly edited it for publication.[107]

Historian Renqiu Yu's well-researched treatise on the Chinese Hand Laundry Alliance of New York and its efforts to break the virtual stranglehold that the traditionalistic organizations had on the ethnic economy is another study attentive to the ideological and political cleavages within Chinese immigrant communities. He described how the traditionalistic leaders within these ethnic enclaves deployed ethnicity to trump class consciousness. Using Chinese-language sources, Yu showed how various segments of Chinese American communities perceived and acted on their self-interests.[108] Siu's and Yu's studies, taken together, provide the fullest understanding available of a particular group of Chinese workers, whose class status was indeterminate because they usually owned and managed the shops in which they carried out back-breaking labor. That is to say, laundrymen were simultaneously owners of small businesses (and were thus members of the petit bourgeoisie) and proletarian laborers.

Another historian, Chris Friday, incisively analyzed the historical interactions among Chinese, Japanese, and Filipino immigrants, as well as European American women, who worked in salmon canneries along the Pacific Coast. He chronicled how an "aristocracy of labor" emerged among Asian cannery workers in a manner similar to what had developed in the American labor movement, in which a selected group of union members and their leaders carved out a privileged position for themselves. In time, Filipino workers became the most militant of all and most sympathetic to unionization because members of the "aristocracy" (most of whom were older Chinese) were blocking their upward mobility within the cannery work force.[109] These four labor histories by Chan, Siu, Yu, and Friday not only elucidate the workplace conditions encountered by various kinds of workers, but they also reflect the influence of the "working class culture" school of thought introduced by such labor historians as Herbert Gutman and immigration historians like John Bonard.

Chinese American-Centered Studies

In contrast to the Marxist-oriented authors, most Chinese American and European American scholars who have been rewriting Chinese American history since the 1970s do not try to incite revolution, be it intellectual or sociopolitical. Rather, they attempt to produce balanced, layered, and nuanced accounts of the historical and contemporary lived experiences of Chinese Americans. Their work can be divided into several categories: general surveys, both historical and contemporary; new studies on some old topics, particularly the controversies over pre–World War II Chinese immigration and the anti-Chinese movement; local and regional studies; women's and family histories; and cultural histories that employ concepts that did not yet exist in earlier years when the task of historical reclamation began. Even though they pick up old subject matter, they break new ground and shed light on hitherto unexamined aspects of those topics.

General Surveys

The first academic Chinese American histories published in the late 1960s and 1970s were general surveys of what was then popularly called "the Chinese American experience." Betty Lee Sung, a former librarian and a writer for the Voice of America who later became a prolific sociologist, began *Mountain of Gold*, published in 1967, with the sentence "I was an angry young woman!"

Incensed by the "grossly distorted" caricatures of the Chinese in America, she set out to rectify a situation she characterized as "a fixation about the Chinese that demands the sensational, the lurid, the peculiarities, and the mysteries." To counteract this legacy, she told the stories of many individuals and discussed a large variety of Chinese American contributions to U.S. society. "This book is not a refutation or whitewash," she stated, "nor is it a public relations scheme. I have tried to present the facts, and the facts speak for themselves."[110] That same penchant for facts led her to publish many additional books: One presents a statistical profile of the Chinese in the United States based on the 1970 census of population, a second analyzes Chinese American manpower and employment conditions and needs, a third looks at Chinatown gangs, a fourth discusses transplanted Chinese children, a fifth examines Chinese immigrant children in New York City, and a sixth investigates Chinese American intermarriage.[111]

Anthropologist Francis L.K. Hsu,[112] sociologist Stanford Lyman,[113] William L. Tung, a professor of international law and East Asian Studies,[114] political scientist Pao-min Chang,[115] historian Shih-shan Henry Tsai,[116] historian-cum-anthropologist Franklin Ng,[117] historian Benson Tong,[118] and political scientist Peter Kwong and historian Dušanka Miščević (the last two as coauthors)[119] have all also penned general surveys. All except two of these books (those by Chang and Kwong and Miščević) were manuscripts solicited for inclusion in various book series. Hsu's work belongs in the "Minorities in American Life" series, Lyman's is a part of the "Ethnic Groups in Comparative Perspective" series, Tung's is in the "Ethnic Chronology" series, Tsai's is in the "Minorities in America" series, and the books by Ng and Tong are both contributions to "The New Americans" series. This fact demonstrates that from the late 1960s until the present, publishers were and still are riding the waves created by the ethnic and racial consciousness movements. They wanted and still want to include works on various immigrant and domestic minority groups in response to changing perceptions of the nature of American society—from a European American–dominated one to a multiethnic (but by no means equal) one. As shrewd entrepreneurs with their eyes on the bottom line, publishers, particularly commercial ones, recognize that ethnic histories at all reading levels, including books for young people, by authors such as Claire Jones in the "In America" series and Franklin Ng in the "Discrimination" series,[120] sell. Finding authors from the ethnic groups in question to write such books allows publishers to parade the cultural and intellectual "authenticity" of their products. Another contribution to overviews of the Chinese in America is a volume of collected essays edited by literary scholar Susie Lan Cassel, in which the contributors examine both old and new subjects.[121] Although all these books served useful functions, the study by Kwong and Miščević is the most incisive and up-to-date. It is the only general survey that analyzes Chinese American participation in the Asian American Movement and in identity politics; the fundamental demographic, social, economic, and political changes that came about as a result of post-1965 Chinese immigration; and the inescapable interweaving of transnational developments that link China and the United States.

Chinese Immigration and the Anti-Chinese Movement

In research monographs meant for academic, rather than general, audiences, scholars have not yet finished analyzing pre-1965 Chinese immigration and the anti-Chinese movement—two themes that are repeatedly reincarnated in one form or another, given the fact that they were what I call "defining traumatic events" in the history of Chinese America. Stuart Creighton Miller argued against Mary Robert Coolidge's California thesis by demonstrating that negative perceptions of the Chinese were formed long before sizable numbers of Chinese set foot on American soil.[122] Alexander Saxton showed how the "Chinese question" was imbricated in the development of the American labor movement, in which unions formed by journeymen in the skilled crafts kept out unskilled laborers but pacified them with attacks against Chinese workers. Combining labor history and cultural history, Saxton also examined the ideological and psychological factors in the anti-Chinese movement.[123] Cheng-Tsu Wu edited a collection of documents with commentaries on various manifestations of anti-Chinese prejudice for the "Ethnic Prejudice in America" series.[124] Delber L. McKee exposed the increasingly draconian measures that immigration officials used to implement the Chinese exclusion laws and counterpoised Chinese exclusion and the U.S. Open Door Policy in East Asia, dissecting the tensions between the two policies and the dilemmas faced by U.S. policymakers because of this divergence.[125] Shih-shan Henry Tsai, in the first Chinese-centric book-length study based on Chinese-language sources, chronicled how Chinese diplomats stationed in the United States dealt with and protested Chinese exclusion. He also linked the immigration imbroglio to the 1898 Reform Movement and the 1911 Revolution in China.[126] Thus, years before transnationalism became an intellectually chic concept, Miller, McKee, and Tsai (all historians) had already published studies couched in transnational terms.

Despite its importance, the exclusion era did not receive serious scholarly treatment until 1991 when I edited a collection of essays on how the Chinese exclusion laws affected Chinese American communities and how the Chinese fought in American courts against their ever-more-restrictive implementation.[127] Lucy E. Salyer, a legal historian, analyzed how the Chinese exclusion laws helped shape U.S. immigration law and tracked changes in the successive stages of the sixty-one-year history of Chinese exclusion. In documenting the rise of the American administrative–bureaucratic state, she concluded that the "immigration law resulting from this struggle [between the judicial and executive branches] stood at odds with one of the most esteemed Anglo-American principles—the rule of law."[128] Historian Erika Lee expanded Salyer's analysis by demonstrating that Chinese exclusion not only affected the evolution of U.S. immigration law, but also changed the very nature of the U.S. nation-state itself. Chinese exclusion, she argued convincingly, transformed America from a proverbial nation of immigrants to a gatekeeping nation. Through a careful reading of thousands of documents, Lee brought the memory of dozens of immigrants back to life while delineating the race, class, gender, and nativity/citizenship dimensions of Chinese immigration, both legal and illegal, during the exclusion era.[129]

Attorney and sociologist Estelle T. Lau documented yet other aspects of the history of the exclusion era. She argued that "the Chinese community and the immigration service were shaped *in relation to* [emphasis added] each other through acts of resistance that were, on the one hand, 'opportunistic and individualistic,' but 'neither random nor idiosyncratic.'" To highlight "the reciprocal relations between the power of the state and the power of civil society" (she considered Chinese communities as integral parts of U.S. civil society), she examined everyday practices—especially the discretionary power available to immigration officials—at the points of entry. By placing greater emphasis on discourse analysis than did either Salyer or Lee, Lau teased out patterns in how power was exercised, as well as the unintended consequences of those practices on Chinese "paper families," the disquieting level of mistrust among community members due to their fear of exposure and deportation, the consequent isolation of the Chinese from mainstream society, and the evolution of a subculture of vigilance and vindictiveness within the immigration bureaucracy.[130]

In the 1990s and early 2000s, scholars also began to take new looks at the anti-Chinese movement and Chinese resistance to it. Resistance is a theme that reverberates in many postmovement studies, and attention to its existence is what makes them different from the premovement ones. Charles J. McClain Jr., a historian and a lawyer, offered the most detailed and probing analysis of how the Chinese used the American judicial system to garner some civil rights for themselves and documented the great success of the Chinese litigants and their lawyers. Even more important, a number of the Chinese cases set precedents for certain constitutional principles that have endured to this day.[131]

In a different vein, historian Andrew Gyory published a thoroughly revisionist book in 1998 in which he tried to restore the honor of the U.S. labor movement that Alexander Saxton and political scientist Gwendolyn Mink had excoriated as racist.[132] He argued that European American workers were not against Chinese immigration per se; rather, what they objected to was imported contract labor. The blame for Chinese exclusion, he concluded, should be placed at the foot of politicians, particularly those running for national office, who expediently used anti-Chinese rhetoric and legislative action to garner votes.[133] Another study of the anti-Chinese movement by historian Najia

Aarem-Heriot also downplayed the role of European American labor. Instead, she placed the anti-Chinese campaign within the broader framework of U.S. race relations, comparing the exploitation and disenfranchisement of African Americans, especially after Reconstruction, with the racial discrimination against Chinese Americans.[134]

The concept that has transformed the study of Chinese immigration most profoundly in recent years is transnationalism. Madeline Hsu is the first historian to document empirically the transnational ties between Chinese migrants in the United States and their villages and districts of origin. Imaginatively using a variety of never-before-tapped Chinese-language sources, she showed how separated members of transnational families struggled to keep their ties intact during the exclusion era and how magazines published in Taishan district and circulated in Chinese diasporic communities around the world kept the migrants overseas informed of events in their homeland.[135] Historian Adam McKeown took transnationalism to its logical end: In a comparative study of Chinese migration to Chicago, Hawaii, and Peru, he argued forcefully that scholars should stop writing nation-based narratives that focus on either China or the countries where Chinese migrants have settled. Instead, he insisted that they pay paramount attention to the networks that migrants have created that linked and continue to link them not only to their homeland but also to migrants who had or have gone to other lands.[136] The latest addition to these studies of transnationalism is the third volume in the Chinese exclusion-era trilogy that I edited, in which the contributors discussed the flow of people, economic resources, technology, and political and cultural ideas between China and the United States, in the process illustrating the multifaceted nature of transnational ties.[137]

Though the advent of the transnational framework seems to bear little relationship to the Asian American Movement, the easy adoption of that conceptual turn by Asian Americanists, in fact, was made possible by the movement. From the beginning, many scholars who studied Asian America were quite aware of the enduring ties between Asian immigrants and their homelands, but some deliberately downplayed those bonds because it was more urgent to debunk the "sojourner" or "perpetual foreigner" myths so that Asian Americans could claim their rightful place in American society. Between the late 1960s, when Asian American Studies was established, and the 1990s, when transnationalism took academia by storm, significant changes had occurred in U.S. society. As a consequence of the revolts by peoples of color, women, gays and lesbians, and other groups whose members felt victimized, it has become less acceptable to express racism, sexism, homophobia, and other forms of hostility openly. These protest movements forced many institutions in American society to allow, however grudgingly, changes that made them more inclusive and diverse. Thus, even though various aspects of globalization, especially the instantaneous transmission of electronic media, made transnational linkages very visible, it was the sociopolitical gains achieved in the 1960s and 1970s that made it possible for Asian American scholars to highlight and embrace the transnational dimensions in the lives of Asian Americans because they now worry a lot less than they did in the past about the sociopolitical implications of proclaiming multiple identities and loyalties.

At the dawn of the twenty-first century, authors also turned their attention away from historical Chinese immigration to the contemporary influx of immigrants, both legal and illegal, of Chinese ancestry from many areas of the world. Ko-lin Chin analyzed how Chinese are being smuggled into the United States clandestinely. Unlike Peter Kwong, who saw the smuggled-in migrants primarily as superexploited workers, Chin focused on the minutiae related to the transnational smuggling schemes—the air, sea, and land routes that the "snake heads," who mastermind and control every step of the process, use; the "safe houses" that restrict, in the name of protection, the options open to the smuggled-in people after their arrival; and the inconsistencies in U.S. policies that hamper the country's ability to stem the flow.[138]

Two geographers, Laurence J. C. Ma and Carolyn Cartier, edited a book of collected essays that discussed the Chinese diaspora in terms of space, place, mobility, and identity. In a truly global manner, the contributors examined Chinese transnational migrants in Malaysia, Singapore, Thailand, Vietnam, various countries in Latin America, the United States (with a separate chapter on Hawaii), Canada, Germany, Australia, and New Zealand.[139] Wanning Sun, a specialist in media studies, looked at how television, films, videos, and the internet are fueling the desire of Chinese in many parts of China to leave home for supposedly greener pastures overseas. She discussed how the stay-at-home population fantasizes about life in richer countries while those abroad remember the homeland in selective ways. Both processes are helping to engender a new Chinese transnational imagination.[140] In a multidisciplinary book coedited by Peter H. Koehn and Xiao-huang Yin, the contributors examined other dimensions of transnationality. They described the many ways in which Chinese Americans are influencing U.S.–China relations through transnational interactions. Students, scientists and other professionals, businesspeople, creative writers and artists, journalists, and philanthropists have all been involved in mediating the relationships between the People's Republic of China and the United States since the two countries reestablished diplomatic ties.[141]

Local and Regional Histories

Local and regional histories continue to be produced. What is new is that their authors no longer try to arouse curiosity and excite their readers in order to sell books. Not surprisingly, given the long history of the Chinese in California, the largest number of post–Asian American Movement academic histories focus on various localities in the Golden State; the second most-studied locality is New York City. Other regions or cities with a significant number of Chinese residents are now also covered in the scholarly literature.

Victor and Brett de Bary Nee, a sociologist and a literary scholar, respectively, published in 1972 the first collection of oral histories told by Chinese residents in San Francisco—a multitude of voices talking not only about the narrators' own lives but also about the goings-on in their community. Because it is a heartwarming book with a great deal of human interest, it remains popular as a text for classroom use.[142] Psychologist Chalsa Loo and her collaborators also based their book on field research that investigated many aspects of the quality of life in San Francisco's Chinatown in the 1980s. They explored residential mobility, the conflicts between urban renewal and historical preservation, overcrowding and its effects, the residents' difficulties in learning English, their physical and mental health, and the changing status of women. Although they highlighted certain squalid aspects of that urban enclave, their goal was quite different from that of earlier writers who fixated on the peculiarities of Chinatown. What Loo and her coauthors did was to call public attention to the lack of adequate social services in that neighborhood and the hardships that such a lacuna created. That is to say, instead of blaming the victims, they hoped that their research findings would enable community activists to pressure local authorities to provide better social services to an underserved population.[143]

Anthropologist Bernard Wong and Ethnic Studies scholar Timothy Fong each contributed to studies on contemporary Asian immigrants. Wong discussed how post-1965 immigrants—from Hong Kong, Taiwan, China, and other locations around the world—rapidly spilled out of the boundaries of the old Chinatown into suburban areas in San Francisco often dubbed the "new Chinatown," in the process transforming the increasingly heterogeneous Chinese communities in the San Francisco Bay area in fundamental ways. He looked at the new immigrants' reliance on family connections to enhance their competitiveness as they established hundreds of businesses, many of which have transnational linkages to Chinese entrepreneurs in the diaspora. He further pointed out that the new professionals think globally as they strategize to maximize the economic well-being and social standing of their families.[144]

Fong, a former journalist and now a professor of Ethnic Studies with a keen eye for details, used both participant observation and documentary research to draw a multifaceted portrait of Monterey Park, California, located eight miles east of downtown Los Angeles, a community he dubbed the "first suburban Chinatown." What happened in Monterey Park is a template that many suburban areas of the larger cities in the United States soon reproduced.

Fong's most valuable insight is his observation that allegiances based on class, date of immigration, and nativity can override ethnic loyalty in a multiethnic city like Monterey Park where coethnics can and do line up on opposite sides of various local issues.[145]

Exciting as recent developments have been, scholars interested in Chinese America have not forgotten history, as studies by Yong Chen, Nayan Shah, and Sandy Lydon demonstrate. Transnationalism framed historian Yong Chen's cultural and social history of the Chinese community in San Francisco. Using Chinese-language sources, he depicted the *mentalités*, both individual and collective, of its residents from 1850 to 1943. Although he touched on some of the same subjects as those found in the old partisan writings, he portrayed the activities in a different light. Like Erika Lee, who highlighted the changes in Chinese immigration patterns over time, Chen tracked how the community evolved historically, with each phase distinguished by characteristics specific to its time and place. Despite the persistence of trans-Pacific ties, Chen called attention to the "Americanness" of Chinese San Francisco, unlike some authors who insist on seeing only its "Chineseness."[146]

Nayan Shah, another historian, published a complex portrait of the Chinese in San Francisco that elucidated the intersection of race and disease. He analyzed how public health officials have played a crucial role in marking Chinese immigrants as sickly "Others" whose very bodies threatened the well-being of European Americans. This is an old theme that has been expressed repeatedly since the mid-nineteenth century. A fear of contamination, perversity, and what Shah called "queer domesticity" (referring to the "bachelor" communities in which most Chinese male immigrants lived until after World War II) added fuel to the anti-Chinese movement. Such allegedly contagious and hence dangerous characteristics, the detractors of the Chinese believed, could be erased only through "respectable domesticity"—that is, by the establishment of heterosexual families on American soil.[147] More so than other historical studies, Shah's work reflects the influence of the Birmingham school of cultural studies on the writing of Asian American history.

There are also studies that examine Chinese communities in California outside of San Francisco. In 1974, anthropologist Melford Weiss published a study of Sacramento that hinged on the theoretical concerns of his discipline in the 1960s and 1970s. Using a diachronic approach, he examined the historical precedents (in China) the immigrants brought as their cultural baggage, their adaptation in America, the social organization of their communities, and their assimilation or lack thereof. To readers today, his study sounds dated because he saw these processes in static and reified ways. However, he did note that a new group of Chinese Americans had emerged as a result of the Asian American Movement. In addition to "traditionists" and "modernists," there were now also "activists" who not only expressed "disenchantment, disappointment, and often disgust with the policies of the American bureaucracy" but also rejected "the values of their forebears."[148]

Historian Sandy Lydon's book recovered an almost lost segment of Chinese American history. He told the story of immigrants who found livelihood in the small communities around Monterey Bay—Monterey, Watsonville, Santa Cruz, Salinas, and Castroville—and in even more remote locations in the Pajaro and Salinas valleys. There, the Chinese—farmers, farm workers, fishermen and fisherwomen, railroad builders and maintenance workers, and common laborers—lived in ways that differed from those of their urban compatriots. Lydon recognized that most of the sources he used were full of "racial slurs and exaggerations." Still, by reading against the grain, he treated the evidence he found as "rare documents of the Chinese presence"—an approach that enabled him to move the story of these Chinese pioneers to a more central and visible location in the regional history of the area he studied.[149]

The Chinese in New York City, which contains the nation's largest Chinese-ancestry community today, have also received scholarly attention. In addition to the three books by Peter Kwong discussed earlier, six significant studies have been published. Chia-ling Kuo analyzed how voluntary associations providing social services helped to change the power structure in New York's Chinatown in the 1970s. Although the book does not contain information about the Asian American Movement, the new associations that Kuo analyzed were both a cause and a result of that movement.[150] Xinyang Wang combined statistical analyses with a reading of Chinese-language newspapers to retrieve a part of the history of the Chinese in New York City. Unlike in San Francisco's Chinatown during the late nineteenth and early twentieth centuries, where the residential pattern became increasingly segregated, many Chinese in New York, particularly laundrymen and restaurant owners and workers, were able to live in largely white neighborhoods until the 1950s "even while housing discrimination and harassment against them were rampant." They did so for economic reasons: They wanted to be close to their potential customers. Wang concluded that "making a living . . . was sometimes even more crucial . . . than fighting and avoiding discrimination."[151]

Anthropologists Bernard Wong and Hsiang-shui Chen and sociologists Min Zhou and Jan Lin have provided additional insights into New York's Chinatown. Their emphasis, like Wang's, is on survival. Using biographical sketches, Wong disclosed what kinds of people live in Chinatown and how they make a living. In addition to discussing the traditionalistic community organizations, he briefly described the new associations that had sprung up and the youth who had formed and joined gangs; in so doing, he demonstrated that Chinese Americans today are heterogeneous and no longer fit into easily discernible molds.[152] Chen's study dealt with new immigrants from Taiwan and how they differ from the pre-1965 immigrants from Guangdong Province. He documented how their presence amid many other ethnic groups has complicated race and ethnic relations in Flushing, in the borough of Queens, New York (a New York counterpart to Monterey Park). The area in which the Chinese have congregated cannot be called a Chinatown; instead, it is a multiethnic community within which the Chinese are stratified by class, educational attainment, Chinese dialect, and English proficiency. He concluded that there has been considerable mobility between classes—both downward, when immigrants are unable to find jobs commensurate with their education and training, and upward, when they save up to launch their own small businesses.[153]

In contrast to the dire picture that Asian American Movement activists painted of Chinese American ghettos with countless unmet needs, sociologist Min Zhou's portrayal of New York's Chinese community is optimistic. She emphasized the many opportunities open to its residents, who can work their way up from their entry-level jobs as laborers, busboys, shop assistants, and garment workers by learning entrepreneurial skills from their employers, who may, in time, help some faithful employees to start their own businesses. Zhou also revealed that the ethnic enclave is not an isolated entity but is connected in various ways to the larger society. In short, ethnic resources are important, and Chinatown offers an alternative route to immigrant incorporation by helping immigrants to adapt to life in the United States.[154] Instead of focusing on immigrant incorporation within the context of the U.S. nation-state, sociologist Jan Lin located New York's Chinatown within a global network of postindustrial world cities in an age marked by flexible and dispersed capitalist production. More sensitive to the importance of the symbolic realm in human existence than sociologists who have not been influenced by cultural studies, Lin mapped out the role of tourism, voyeurism, and cinema in defining the fluid, multisited experiences of today's Chinese transnational migrants. His book demonstrates how the global and local intersect and are mutually constitutive—an idea promulgated by scholars in global studies.[155]

Haitian American anthropologist Michel S. Laguerre, in a comparative study of Chinatown, Japantown, and Manilatown in San Francisco, further refined globalization theory as it is applied to Asian Americans to explicate the relationship between transnationalism and globalization. He called these communities "global ethnopoles" and argued that they are the products of transnational processes that occur within the "logic" or "modalities" of globalization. As "nodes in a network of sites linking the ethnopole to the homeland and its residents and to other diasporic sites as well," they are "sustained by the four sectors of the *diasporic economy*—namely, the *enclave economy*, characterized by those who own businesses in the enclave; the *ethnic economy*, which includes those who have businesses outside the enclave; the *transethnic* or *transurban* economy, which results from the interface with the *mainstream economy*, and the *transnational economy*, which comprises those transactions with an overseas headquarters or subsidiary in another country." The boundaries of ethnopoles are simultaneously constricted and expansive. On the one hand, the geographic spaces that ethnopoles occupy have been limited historically by segregation and housing discrimination; by what Laguerre calls the minoritization, stigmatization, racialization, marginalization, and exoticization of space; by quarantines and bodily regulations; and by exclusion. On the other hand, cities in which ethnopoles exist can never fully contain them because of their residents' ties to localities beyond the confines of the cities and nations in which they exist.[156]

Unlike the historical ethnic enclaves (or, less euphemistically, ghettos) that evolved into the present-day ethnopoles that Laguerre examined, communities in the so-called Silicon Valley of California with large Asian American populations are new configurations. These towns and cities have grown as the computer industry has flourished. Chinese Americans and Indian Americans make up a large proportion of the computer hardware and software engineers, as well as the venture-capital entrepreneurs who start new companies. These busy people commute regularly between California and Taiwan or China or, in the case of Indian Americans, between California and Bangalore or other cities in India with burgeoning high-technology industries. In a study of Taiwanese immigrants in Silicon Valley, landscape architect Shenglin Chang analyzed how these highly-educated, globe-trotting, and wired-to-the-Internet professionals often own residences in two or more countries, each of which they consider "home." What is most interesting is that they not only bring Chinese cultural practices to America, but also export the California suburban landscape with its single family houses, clipped lawns, lush semi-tropical vegetation, swimming pools, and barbeque pits to new industrial-cum-residential parks in Taiwan built according to the California high-technology "campus" and suburban templates.[157]

In another study of Silicon Valley, Bernard Wong interviewed and observed immigrants from China, Taiwan, and Hong Kong, as well as American-born professionals of Chinese descent, and chronicled how they build social networks that facilitate entrepreneurship within a global economy. Wong emphasized that there are both benefits and costs to leading transnational lives, that the paths such transmigrants traverse are not linear and unidirectional, and their identities are not based on cultural allegiance alone but are, instead, the products of pragmatic business calculations and practices. As they search for ways to maximize profit and to ensure the safety and comfort of their families, they weigh the relative economic vitality of different countries and the taxation and foreign-investment policies in the pertinent nation-states.[158]

Lest we think of globalization and transnationalism as phenomena that emerged only in the late twentieth century, historian John Kuo Wei Tchen reminded us that global circuits did not arise only in recent years. Rather, they have existed for centuries, linking different areas of the world and disparate cultures together in myriad ways. He used the stories of Chinese who resided and worked in New York City before there was a Chinatown there to elucidate a larger point: Chinese ideas, goods, and people have long played a role in forming an American national identity. (Literary scholars David Palumbo-Liu and Colleen Lye have made the same point.) Tchen traced how Europeans' and Americans' perceptions of and attitudes toward China changed from an initial admiration for and fascination with the glories of Chinese civilization to a demonization of an allegedly inalterably alien people whose culture could never be reconciled with an ascendant, progressive, and exceptionalist American civilization.[159]

None of the studies of Chinese communities elsewhere in the United States matches the theoretically sophisticated approaches of Jan Lin, Michel Laguerre, Jack Tchen, Shenglin Chang, and Bernard Wong, but they do fill important gaps in our knowledge. Sociologist Clarence E. Glick revised and updated his Ph.D. dissertation after he retired from the faculty at the University of Hawaii decades after he had done the original research to produce the fullest history we have of the Chinese in Hawaii.[160] Sociologists James Loewen and Robert Seto Quan and anthropologist Lucie Cohen studied the Chinese in the South, where they functioned as a middleman minority sandwiched between the white majority and the black minority.[161] Sociologist Rose Hum Lee, journalist Craig Storti, archaeologist Priscilla Wegars, historian Liping Zhu, and historian Marie Rose Wong wrote about Chinese communities in the American West. Historian Arif Dirlik compiled an anthology of journal articles about the Chinese in the same region that displays the broad range of their experiences.[162] The geographic scope of Chinese American Studies continues to broaden: Three recent studies examined Chinese communities in Philadelphia, Atlanta, and St. Louis—cities that have not historically housed large numbers of residents of Chinese ancestry.[163]

The History of Women and Families

Until Judy Yung began to publish the results of her research on Chinese American women, women's history was a gaping void in Chinese American historiography. Yung's first book, published in 1986, used a lot of photographs and a short text to tell their stories—tales that contain hitherto unknown aspects of these women's historical experiences.[164] This initial publication was followed, in 1995, by a social history of Chinese American women in San Francisco during the first half of the twentieth century and, in 1999, an anthology of documents that she had relied on as the evidentiary basis of her 1995 book.[165] These three books follow the same triumphalist approach that has characterized other recent works in Chinese American history. That is, because they recount hardships overcome with fortitude and determination, readers cannot help but be inspired by such accounts.

Peggy Pascoe, another feminist historian, looked at the experiences of young Chinese women who were "rescued" from brothels and oppressive living environments by Protestant women missionaries. She used their stories to analyze a larger phenomenon—the rise and decline of the "moral authority" that European American women possessed in the late nineteenth and early twentieth centuries. Many found a calling in Christian service, so their experiences, like those of male missionaries who worked in China and in American Chinatowns, illuminate another part of the problematic nexus between Christianity and Chinese immigration.[166]

Benson Tong, another feminist historian, also told a triumphalist tale—this one about prostitutes who survived brutal conditions and tried in various ways to escape their bondage and to better their lot. Tong gathered evidence from many sources—manuscript censuses, newspaper articles, government documents, records of missionary organizations, and a few creative writings and autobiographical snippets—to make his case.[167] Historian George Peffer was likewise interested in prostitutes but for a different reason. To him, prostitutes served as a foil for his main concern—"respectable" Chinese women who came as members of families. He analyzed the Page Law, which excluded women whom immigration officials suspected were being brought to America to staff brothels. He also investigated staff in the U.S. consulate in Hong Kong and port authorities in San Francisco who were charged with implementing the Page Law, and examined the corruption of these officials as well as the relative effectiveness of the barriers they erected to keep out Chinese women.[168]

Historian Huping Ling penned a general history of Chinese American women by combining life stories and a sampling of immigration records, interviews, information from miscellaneous collections of papers, and articles in Chinese-language newspapers. Her book, which covers the period from the 1840s to the 1990s, includes discussions of prostitutes, merchants' wives and daughters, female students, professionals, and even laborers and farmers. In my opinion, however, some of her generalizations may be too sweeping, given the sparse sources on some subgroups of women.[169]

Two books are concerned with Chinese American women workers in contemporary U.S. society. Sociologist Stacey Yap studied women who became community workers and the multiple means they used to promote the well-being of those whom they sought to help. These women were very much a part of the Asian American Movement, and Yap framed their stories within the internal colonialism model popular during the heyday of that movement. The goal of these women, as that of their "brothers" (the terms "sisters" and "brothers" were widely used among movement activists), was to transform U.S. society through massive structural changes.[170] Historian Xiaolan Bao produced a detailed study of women workers in the garment industry in New York City. What intrigued her was the fact that some twenty thousand garment workers, a majority of them women, went on strike in 1982. She conducted over a hundred interviews to understand how they developed such "progressive" (another oft-used movement concept) consciousness. She elucidated how class and ethnicity worked at cross-purposes within the Chinese immigrant community and how race undercut the proletarian solidarity that is supposed to exist between European American union organizers and Chinese American workers.[171]

Chinese American families are the central concern in three recent books. Historian Xiaojian Zhao combined accounts in Chinese-language newspapers, newsletters, and magazines; oral histories; official U.S. immigration records; and federal statutes and court cases to reconstruct—or rather, to construct for the first time—the history of family formation and trans-Pacific reunification during World War II and the postwar period before 1965. She discovered that many of the women who entered as "war brides" were not brides at all but were, in fact, wives who had been separated from their husbands for decades. Zhao's book is the first full-fledged study we have of those crucial years when significant changes were occurring in Chinese American communities.[172]

In another study of intra-family dynamics, anthropologist Maria Chee explained how transnational families function among Chinese migrants from Taiwan—an understudied group in Chinese American Studies. She discussed how women see migration, thus highlighting the fact that migration is a gendered process that affects men and women differently. She further explored power relations between men and women; how women workers juxtapose their responsibilities as workers, wives, and mothers; and the impacts of globalization on marriages that must be sustained despite geographical separation and the existence of dual households located thousands of miles apart.[173]

Separated families are nothing new: Chinese migrants in the United States and elsewhere have had hundreds of years of experience in maintaining such geographically split families. Reading closely family letters preserved by one transnational family, historian Haiming Liu illustrated how such a family could remain intact despite momentous upheavals in China and major changes in America over the course of more than a century. Chinese migration, he observed, was "a socially embedded, group-oriented, and family-supported movement."[174] In addition, chapter 5 of Estelle Lau's study discussed above (under the subheading *Chinese Immigration and the Anti-Chinese Movement*) contains the complex stories of how several real-cum-fictive immigrant families were created as their members strategically dealt with the exclusion laws and the changing procedures and practices used to enforce them over time.

Even in studies of families, not much attention has been paid to children. Aside from two of Betty Lee Sung's books mentioned above, the only book-length study of Chinese American children was written by Vivian S. Louie, a professor of education. She examined the central importance of education in immigrant families: Parents see education as a reliable channel for upward mobility and thus sacrifice a great deal to ensure that their children will succeed academically. The pressure to do well in school, however, places enormous stress on the students who are burdened with guilt should they fail to live up to their parents' (often unreasonable) expectations. However, Louie discovered that despite such pressures, many Chinese American college students ultimately break free and find their own paths to fulfillment.[175]

Cultural History

Aside from women's and family history, another segment of Chinese American history has flourished since the rise of the Asian American Movement. Although the partisan writers of the nineteenth century and the Orientalizing and self-Orientalizing authors of Chinatown studies relished, in a voyeuristic way, certain aspects of Chinese culture, cultural history was an underresearched topic until the 1990s. However, judging from the books published in recent years and the rapid ascendance of cultural history, which has virtually displaced social history (the latter was considered to be methodologically innovative from the 1960s to the 1980s because many of its practitioners used nonnarrative sources to recreate the experiences of long neglected groups), it is highly likely that this subfield in Chinese American historiography will boom and bloom in the foreseeable future. I use the term "cultural history" broadly and loosely to refer not only to studies of the various expressive arts and artists but also to works concerned with identities, representations and self-representations, ideologies, beliefs, discourses, and religious rituals.

Books about how Chinese Americans have been portrayed in novels, short stories, poetry, films, plays, paintings, illustrations, photographs, and posters began appearing in the early 1980s. William F. Wu analyzed images of Chinese Americans in American popular fiction published between 1850 and 1940 and found that they were invariably depicted as a yellow peril eager to invade America.[176] Feminist film studies scholar Gina Marchetti's exploration of films with Chinese characters revealed that these were filled with fantasies of seduction, rape, captivity, rescue, and tragic love. She showed how such films exploited race, sex, and violence to succeed at the box office.[177] James S. Moy, a professor of theater history and theory, looked at Chinese characters in plays, cartoons, exhibits in museums, films, photographs, circuses, and pornography. He proposed that Orientalist drama and other media gained popularity by fetishizing stereotypical notions of Chinese Americans that were intentionally constructed to appeal to mainstream audiences.[178] Another theater studies scholar, Josephine Lee, analyzed how Asian American playwrights stage identities that may affect how individuals of Asian ancestry perform facets of their race and ethnicity offstage as well as on. Such an approach goes against traditional assumptions that insist that plays, like other works of art, should be evaluated according to "universal," "objective," or "neutral" aesthetic standards—that is, drama for drama's sake. At the same time, Lee warned about the danger of assuming that what is presented on stage mirrors "reality." Rather, meanings emerge from the complex interactions of performers and spectators. More than any other cultural scholar, Lee explicitly recognized the connection between the Asian American Movement and the establishment of local theaters as hospitable venues where works by Asian American artists can be performed.[179]

Historian Robert G. Lee examined the key tropes in depictions of "Orientals" in popular culture. They include the "heathen Chinee" as a pollutant in a Christian nation, the "coolie" as a threat to the livelihood of white workers, the "third sex" as a form of deviancy in a family-based society, "inner dikes and barred zones" (the latter refers to regions of the world whose inhabitants were prohibited from immigrating into the United States) as the sources of the "yellow peril," the "model minority" and its relationship to the cold war, and "gooks" as enemies in racialized wars.[180] Krystyn R. Moon, another cultural historian, studied how the Chinese have been represented in music, vaudeville, and other kinds of performance from the 1850s to the 1920s. European American actors, made up in "yellow face," more often than not played caricatured Chinese characters in these productions that Moon called "white fantasies of the way Chinese bodies should look and sound based on a dichotomous relationship that differentiates 'us' from 'them.'" Moon's most intriguing discovery, however, is that African American musicians and actors also used "Chinese stereotypes as a way of underscoring the Americanness of black people and the inherent foreignness of Chinese immigrants."[181]

Art historian Anthony W. Lee probed the works of artists and photographers for whom "no collection of photographs about San Francisco or the developing West could quite do without an image of Chinatown. . . . The experience of Chinatown as a 'place' of the imagination seems best characterized as part alluring, part repulsive. . . . Chinatown is best described as a district for indulgence, not a space where the Chinese live and work."[182] The simultaneity of allure and repulsiveness likewise informs the work of historian Mary Ting Yi Lui, who used the 1909 murder of a European American Sunday school teacher in New York City, for which crime her Chinese lover was alleged to be responsible, as a lens through which to decipher the dangerous and transgressive social and sexual relations between Chinese and non-Chinese. Although scholars in Asian American Studies have long known that opposition to Chinese female prostitution was an important element in the anti-Chinese movement, Lui's book is the first to analyze the complicated ways in which race, gender, and sexuality were intertwined.[183]

In contrast to the works that reveal how non-Chinese perceive Chinese Americans, Ronald Riddle's study of Cantonese opera attempted to tell the story from the perspective of the Chinese actors and musicians.[184] A book about the fifty-seven-year career of world-renowned cinematographer James Wong Howe, born in Guangdong Province in 1899 and named Wong Tung Jim, explicated how he used light and shadow to convey powerful emotions with consummate artistry.[185] Three books about Chinese American actress Anna May Wong, born in Los Angeles in 1905 and named Wong Liu Tsong, offer glimpses of what she had to overcome to succeed in her chosen profession. Although she had starred in more than fifty films and had international admirers, she was passed over for the lead female role in the film based on Pearl S. Buck's *The Good Earth*—a role that went to a European American actress.[186]

Studies of religion have also found their way into Chinese American cultural history. Religion, of course, is an important component of all cultures as it deals with the deepest yearnings and fears of human beings and is the wellspring of faith and commitment. The missionaries who worked among the Chinese, were they still alive, would be delighted with the burgeoning number of Chinese American Christians. This increase in number is reflected in the literature: Karl Fung told the story of the Chinese Community Church in San Diego; Lawrence Palinkas examined the discursive practices of two Chinese Mandarin-speaking churches in the same city; Kenneth J. Guest studied the relationship between religion and survival among Chinese in New York's Chinatown; Fenggang Yang, through participant observation in an evangelical congregation in Washington, DC, explored how its members develop adhesive (a concept first introduced by Korean American sociologists Won Moo Hurh and Kwang Chung Kim) identities that fuse their Christian faith and traditional Chinese values; and Russell Jeung delved into how panethnic Asian American churches institutionalize themselves.[187] Although Christianity is making headway among Chinese Americans, Sue Fawn Chung and Priscilla Wegars reminded us that old rituals performed at funerals in the past continue to offer solace when death occurs.[188]

Identity remains a central concern in Chinese American historiography. Focusing on the period from the 1930s to the 1990s, Ethnic Studies scholar Gloria Chun authored a book on how Chinese American identity and culture were and still are constantly reinvented.[189] The contributors to a volume of essays that K. Scott Wong and I coedited proposed that identity is not monolithically associated with one's "culture" but is, rather, a self-image and sense of belonging that is continuously being constructed and reconstructed. Although this book deals with the Chinese exclusion era, its conclusions are applicable to other periods as well.[190] Historian Henry Yu looked specifically at the first cohort of Chinese American sociologists trained at the University of Chicago and argued that their identity as panethnic "Orientals" was a precursor to the Asian American identity that emerged in the 1960s. Although from today's perspective, these scholars' embrace of the "middleman minority" concept as something that aptly described their own plight may make them seem like Uncle Toms, they accepted the moniker because being "marginal men" or "marginal women" (the latter term, however was never used in that masculinist period) was an improvement over being perpetual foreigners.[191] Elionne L. W. Belden traced how Chinese Americans in contemporary Houston claim a Chinese identity and argued that identity is not something one inherits but is, rather, an attribute consciously absorbed.[192]

Going back to an earlier period, historian Shehong Chen dissected the complexities of trans-Pacific interactions and the evolution of Chinese American identities. Closely reading articles in Chinese-language newspapers, she teased out different political perspectives held by the immigrants who identified with three strands of Chinese political thought in the late 1910s and the 1920s. She demonstrated that the immigrants in the United States did not unquestioningly accept all the political ideas and cultural practices flowing out of China but formed their own opinions independently.[193] Karen J. Leong, a feminist historian, analyzed the biographies of the three women—Pearl S. Buck, Anna May Wong, and Mayling Soong (Madam Chiang Kai-shek)—whom she considered most crucial in transforming the American public's images of China during the 1930s and 1940s. As Leong saw it, Anna May Wong's life and career illuminate the conflicts between art and race, between representation and self-representation.[194] Historian K. Scott Wong produced the first book-length study of how Chinese Americans fared during World War II—an event that transformed their standing in the United States and their self-images and brought about changes in the public perceptions of them. For the first time, the larger society saw them as "good" Asians who helped fight the "good war."[195] In her study of the life of Dr. Margaret Chung, the first Chinese American female medical doctor, historian Judy Wu revealed how deftly Chung experimented with a variety of lifestyles as she became a celebrity during World War II.[196]

Anthropologist Andrea Louie studied an ongoing program, "In Search of Roots," to see how young Chinese Americans are negotiating identities that reflect their transnational family histories by discovering and affirming ties across the Pacific.[197] In a multiple-award-winning book that contains a chapter on the Chinese, historian Mae Ngai traced how the figure of the illegal alien has been constructed in legal as well as public discourse as yet another form of racial difference.[198] These books in cultural history, in addition to illuminating the complex nature of Chinese American identities, explicitly reveal the gendered and class-based process of image and self-image formation. In contrast to the earlier (mostly) externally imposed Orientalist depictions, recent works illustrate how Chinese Americans, as agents in the making of their own history, have played and continue to play important creative roles in struggles to gain control over the public representations of themselves.

Conclusion

This literature review demonstrates how closely Chinese American history and historiography are related. The subjects that authors choose to write about, the tone of the literature produced, and the uses to which knowledge is put all underpin the idea that there are no eternal "objective" truths. Although the same facets of Chinese immigrant life have been discussed since the 1850s, the manner in which authors have approached their subjects differs from one individual to the next and from one historical period to the next. There being no singular "correct" way to write Chinese American history, we are at liberty to use history as a tool to help reinvent ways of looking at ourselves, our communities, and our world. Thus, whether or not we choose to think of ourselves as activists or reformers, we, as beneficiaries of the Asian American Movement, can and must play a vital role in efforts to regain the dignity and self-respect that racism and other forms of oppression had denied us in the past.

NOTES

1. In "Westerners from the East: Oriental Immigrants Reappraised," *Pacific Historical Review* 35, no. 4 (1966): 373–83, Roger Daniels noted that more has been written about the "excluders" than the "excluded" because his fellow historians had "very little understanding of the excluded, insisting or implying that Asians were somehow outside the canon of immigration history" (375). He expanded this theme and updated his review of the literature in "American Historians and East Asian Immigrants," *Pacific Historical Review* 43, no. 4 (1974): 449–72; and "North American Scholarship and Asian Immigrants, 1974–1979," *Immigration History Newsletter* 11, no. 1 (1979): 8–11. In *Asian America: Chinese and Japanese in the United States since 1850* (Seattle: University of Washington Press, 1988), he repeatedly demonstrated that Asian immigrants were more similar to European immigrants than they were different. Thus, he insisted, they should be treated as a part of American immigration history and society.

2. Shirley Hune echoed Daniels's observations in *Pacific Migration to the United States: Trends and Themes in Historical and Sociological Literature* (Washington, DC: Research Institute on Immigration and Ethnic Studies, Smithsonian Institution, 1977), when she complained that scholars who call immigrants from Asia and the Pacific "sojourners" are marginalizing them in U.S. immigration history. She further observed that it is wrong to assume that every aspect of the lives of Chinese immigrants has been determined by their ancestral cultural norms. In her later work, Hune focused on the historiography of Asian/Pacific Islander women: *Teaching Asian American Women's History* (Washington, DC: American Historical Association, 1997); "Asian American and Pacific Islander Women as Historical Subjects: A Bibliographic Essay," in *Asian/Pacific Islander Women: A Historical Anthology*, eds. Shirley Hune and Gail M. Nomura (New York: New York University Press, 2003), 385–400.

3. In a 1978 review essay, "Commentary: Contextual Frameworks for Reading *Counterpoint*," *Amerasia Journal* 5, no. 1 (1978): 115–29, I proposed two frameworks to help move the writing of Asian American history away from its U.S.-centric biases. I argued that, first, historians must examine the multifaceted impacts of European and American imperialism on international migrations, particularly the movement of Asian workers to other continents; and second, it is important to recognize that the development of U.S. capitalism has been uneven in various regions of the country and that until the early twentieth century the American South and West, as well as emerging urban racial/ethnic ghettos, were de facto "colonies" of the industrializing East Coast and Midwest. As such, the social and economic conditions in the American South and West were amenable to the use of nonwhite coerced or semicoerced labor: enslaved African Americans in the South, peonized Mexican Americans in the Southwest, and exploited Asian Americans along the Pacific Coast. In a 1990 essay, "European and Asian Immigration into the United States in Comparative Perspective, 1820s to 1920s," in *Immigration Reconsidered: History, Sociology, and Politics*, ed. Virginia Yans-McLaughlin (New York: Oxford University Press, 1990), 37–75, I combined my earlier call for placing Asian immigration history within an international context with a criticism of the sojourner concept. My concerns were more U.S.-centric in "We Too Built America," *Halcyon: A Journal of the Humanities* 17 (1995): 49–63, in which I contended that "historians who wish to integrate Asian immigrants and Asian Americans into American history must . . . redefine the country's regions, reconceptualize the notion of the frontier, and highlight the analytical salience of race, ethnicity, class, and gender in American history" (52). My goal in two 1996 historiographical essays, "The Writing of Asian American History," *Magazine of History* 10, no. 4 (1996): 8–17, and "Asian American Historiography," *Pacific Historical Review* 65, no. 3 (1996): 363–99, was to introduce the existing literature to scholars who were not specialists in the field, and not to critique earlier studies.

4. In "Asian American Studies," *American Quarterly* 33, no. 3 (1981): 339–54, L. Ling-chi Wang asserted that even pro-Asian writers, whom he called "apologists," harbored "personal biases. . . . Coolidge and Lasker . . . articulated the liberal but class-biased perspective of their times; ironically, their vigorous defense of the system that severely exploited Chinese and Filipino labor put them on the same side as their opponents on the question of race. Their concern over the adverse impact of exclusionary laws on American access to, and dominance in, Asia likewise illustrated the intricate ties between domestic racial policy and international relations" (342). He called for community-based research and writing to counteract the deficiencies of university-based scholarship.

5. Gary Y. Okihiro began his forays into Asian American historiography with "Oral History and the Writing of Ethnic History: A Reconnaissance into Method and Theory," *Oral History Review* 9 (1981): 27–46; "The Idea of Community and a 'Particular Type of History,'" in *Reflections on Shattered Windows: Promises and Prospects for Asian American Studies*, ed. Gary Okihiro et al. (Pullman: Washington State University Press, 1988), 175–83; "Fallow Field: The Rural Dimension of Asian American Studies," in *Frontiers of Asian American Studies: Writing, Research, and Commentary*, ed. Gail M. Nomura et al. (Pullman: Washington State University Press, 1989), 6–13; and "African and Asian American Studies: A Comparative Analysis and Commentary," in *Asian Americans: Comparative and Global Perspectives*, ed. Shirley Hune et al. (Pullman: Washington State University Press, 1991), 17–28. In *Teaching Asian American History* (Washington, DC: American Historical Association, 1997) and *The Columbia Guide to Asian American History* (New York: Columbia University Press, 2001), two major historiographic works, he was concerned with "definitions and delimitations of the field of study, its purposes and objects, its literature, the methods and theories that inform it, and the interpretations and narratives that constitute it" (xv).

He divided authors into anti-Asianists, liberals, and Asian Americanists and explained that the "center of reference for this book is the United States" despite the fact that "Asians came to the Americas by way of . . . currents of [global] commerce and conquest beginning in the mid-sixteenth century" and "their classification as Asians was a European invention" (xiv).

6. Shih-shan Henry Tsai was the first university-based scholar to stress that Chinese Communist historiography and Chinese-language sources can open up new vistas in historical studies of Chinese immigrants. He argued that the writings of historians in China, despite their Marxist lenses, can nevertheless be useful: "Chinese Immigration through Communist Chinese Eyes: An Introduction to the Historiography," *Pacific Historical Review* 43, no. 3 (1974): 395–408, and "Historical Sources on Chinese Immigration to America: An Evaluation," *Committee on East Asian Libraries Newsletter* 50 (July 1976): 38–44.

7. Sucheta Mazumdar, like Shirley Hune, has repeatedly affirmed the critical importance of including women in Asian American history. In "General Introduction: A Woman-Centered Perspective on Asian American History," in *Making Waves: An Anthology of Writings by and about Asian American Women*, ed. Asian Women United of California (Boston: Beacon Press, 1989), 1–22, she discussed the "lines along which women have shaped, and been shaped by, the history of Asian America"(1). In "Beyond Bound Feet: Relocating Asian American Women," *Magazine of History* 10, no. 4 (1996): 23–27, she averred, "insisting on writing the history of only those who continued to live within the territorial boundaries of the U.S. tells only half the story. . . . A global perspective which links the men and women on both sides of the Pacific allows us to reclaim histories of those women who never managed to cross the seas"(24-25). In "What Happened to the Women? Chinese and Indian Male Migration to the United States in Global Perspective," in *Asian/Pacific Islander Women: A Historical Anthology*, eds. Shirley Hune and Gail M. Nomura (New York: New York University Press, 2003), 58–74, she explored how the emigration of men "produced a new division of labor within the family/household unit in Asia, recasting women's roles in both family and society"(58) and restructuring gender relations. In particular, she criticized the "argument that the restrictive laws account for the paucity of Chinese women in the United States" and argued that "it was unlikely that the married women would have migrated even if the laws had allowed, because the economic system was built around male migration and female domestic labor"(58 and 60).

8. In a rebuttal to Patricia Cloud and David W. Galenson, "Chinese Immigration and Contract Labor in the Late Nineteenth Century," *Explorations in Economic History* 24, no. 1 (1987): 22–42, Charles J. McClain argued that assertions that the Chinese Six Companies imported Chinese contract laborers were based on sparse, controversial evidence, some of it mere hearsay. In "Chinese Immigration: A Comment on Cloud and Galenson," *Explorations in Economic History* 27, no. 3 (1990): 363–78, he concluded that "there is no convincing evidence in the record of the legislative hearings of 1876 that the Chinese district associations ever imported bound Chinese laborers into the United States during the 19th century or controlled their movement or employment while there. . . . Our knowledge of the immigration rests entirely upon the statements of contemporary outside (mainly Caucasian) observers . . . and in attempts by contemporary scholars to extrapolate this evidence" (376-77).

9. In a review of three books by Roger Daniels, Ronald Takaki, and Sucheng Chan, Gordon Chang pondered larger issues in "Asian Americans and the Writing of Their History," *Radical History Review* 53 (1992): 105–14. He asked, "Who are 'Asian Americans' after all? Are there historic/cultural/psychological ties that bind people from Asia into an identifiable entity? Or are they simply different national immigrant groups who happen to be from the same region of the world?" (107).

10. Chris Friday criticized labor historians for ignoring workers of color in "Asian American Labor and Historical Interpretation," *Labor History* 35, no. 4 (1994): 524–46. To bridge the gap between labor history and Asian American history, in his own book, *Organizing Asian American Labor: The Pacific Coast Canned-Salmon Industry, 1870-1942* (Philadelphia: Temple University Press, 1994), he examined the intricate interplay of ethnic solidarity, class divisions within ethnic communities, discriminatory laws, and employers' divide-and-conquer tactics that promoted antagonism between white and Asian American workers and blunted the latter's militancy. He paid special attention to the concept of a two-tiered segmented labor market and evaluated its applicability in Asian American labor history.

11. Gail M. Nomura, in "Significant Lives: Asia and Asian Americans in the History of the U.S. West," *Western Historical Quarterly* 25, no. 1 (1994): 69–88, claimed a place for Asian Americans in the history of the American West by asking, "Why is significance *ascribed* to European American settlers, while people of color must *achieve* it? . . . Since I assume no static, exclusive, dominant center in U.S. western history, my discussion is not, and cannot be, a study of margins"(69-70). Instead, she questioned "the borders that define this region" (70) and tried to fathom why European Americans "refuse to acknowledge Asian elements in defining the 'core' of America" (72).

12. Like Nomura, Patricia Limerick queried how the historiography of the American West would be different if peoples of color were included in it. In "Common Cause? Asian American History and Western American History," in *Privileging Positions: The Site of Asian American Studies*, ed. Gary Y. Okihiro et al. (Pullman: Washington State University Press, 1995), 83–99, she noted that "as a society resting on such a recent and unstable foundation of conquest, the American West was and is a place of constantly contested legitimacy . . . a place where white Americans felt precarious . . . [and] took on a multi-front campaign for supremacy, simultaneously working to subordinate Indians, Hispanics, Asians, and African Americans"(91). She reminded her readers that "Asian Americans were founding participants in Western American society; their actions transformed, and indeed, are now transforming, many parts of the Western natural, urban, and social landscapes" (98).

13. John Kuo Wei Tchen, in "Conjuring Ghosts in a Journey East," in *Privileging Positions: The Site of Asian American Studies*, ed. Gary Y. Okihiro et al. (Pullman: Washington State University Press, 1995), 101–22, declared, "I believe Asian/Pacific American individuals and scholars ultimately have to go eastward because the Atlantic Northeast has historically been the hub of power from which this nation developed socio-economically and culturally"(105). Moreover, "the nineteenth-century Hawaiian and Pacific coast settlements, and the earlier migrations of Chinese and Filipinos to the Americas with Spanish colonizations, were in fact extensions of the Atlantic-centered world of European and Euro-American empire-building and nationalisms"(109).

14. Sylvia Junko Yanagisako, in "Transforming Orientalism: Gender, Nationality, and Class in Asian American Studies," in *Naturalizing Power: Essays in Feminist Cultural Analysis*, eds. Sylvia Yanagisako and Carol Delaney (New York: Routledge, 1995), 275–98, viewed the teaching of Asian American history on university campuses as a cultural practice imbued with ideologies of nation, gender, ethnicity, kinship, and social class that seeks to meld disparate groups of Asian immigrants and their progeny into an entity with a common historical memory. This "celebratory narrative of endurance and survival," however, is "selectively constructed"(279) and privileges the largely male working-class pioneer generation and drowns out other aspects of Asian American history.

15. In "Unwrapping Orientalist Constraints: Restoring Homosocial Normativity to Chinese American History," *Amerasia Journal* 29, no. 2 (2003): 230–53, Madeline Hsu bemoaned how Orientalism "has restricted our thinking about Asian Americans," especially

our understanding of "the bachelor era of Chinese American history on its own terms" (231). She pointed out that in traditional China, "participation in homosexual relationships . . . did not preclude heterosexual relationships" (245). Rather, what mattered was the power differential between the "penetrator" and the "penetratee," and not the partners' sexual orientation. She urged readers to see "the dynamics and satisfactions of masculine lives experienced in fraternity with other men, not as aberrations from heterosexual, family-oriented ideals but as . . . a set of norms and values with equal resonance in Chinese culture and society" (249).

16. Chan, "The Writing of Asian American History"; Chan, "Asian American Historiography"; and Chan, "The Changing Contours of Asian American Historiography," *Rethinking History* 11, no. 1 (2007): 125–47.

17. William Speer, *The Oldest and the Newest Empire: China and the United States* (Cincinnati, OH: National Publishing Co., 1870).

18. Otis Gibson, *The Chinese in America* (Cincinnati, OH: Hitchcock and Walden, 1877; repr., New York: Arno Press, 1978). The quotes are from 348, 352, 356–57, and 373.

19. Ira M. Condit, *The Chinaman as We See Him and Fifty Years of Work for Him* (Chicago: Fleming H. Revell, 1900; repr., New York: Arno Press, 1978). The quotes are from 7 and 54.

20. George F. Seward, *Chinese Immigration: Its Social and Economical Aspects* (New York: Charles Scribner's Sons, 1881). The excerpts compiled by Seward are from U.S. Congress, Joint Special Committee to Investigate Chinese Immigration, *Report*, 44th Cong., 2d. sess. (Washington, DC: Government Printing Office, 1877). Two other compilations of excerpts from the testimonies given by pro-Chinese individuals are *Memorial, Six Chinese Companies, An Address to the Senate and House of Representatives of the United States: Testimony of California's Leading Citizens* (1877; repr., San Francisco: R and E Research Associates, 1970); and *Memorial, The Other Side of the Chinese Question: To the People of the United States and the Honorable the Senate and House of Representatives: Testimony of California's Leading Citizens* (1886; repr., San Francisco: R and E Research Associates, 1971).

21. Najia Aarim-Heriot, *Chinese Immigrants, African Americans, and Racial Anxiety in the United States, 1848–82* (Urbana: University of Illinois Press, 2003), 164–66.

22. M. B. Starr, *The Coming Struggle: What the People on the Pacific Coast Think of the Coolie Invasion* (San Francisco: Bacon and Co., 1873). The quote is from 113.

23. Willard B. Farwell, *The Chinese at Home and Abroad* (San Francisco: A. L. Bancroft, 1885). The quotes are from 60–61 and 66.

24. Pierton W. Dooner, *Last Days of the Republic* (San Francisco: Alta California Publishing House, 1880).

25. Robert Woltor, *A Short and Truthful History of the Taking of Oregon and California by the Chinese in the Year A.D. 1899* (San Francisco: A. L. Bancroft, 1882).

26. James A. Whitney, *The Chinese and the Chinese Question*, 2nd ed. (New York: Tibbals Book Co., 1888). The quotes are from 24, 196, and 143.

27. Charles R. Shepherd, *The Ways of Ah Sin: A Composite Narrative of Things as They Are* (New York: Fleming H. Revell, 1923).

28. Charles R. Shepherd, *The Story of Chung Mei* (Philadelphia: Judson Press, 1938).

29. K. Scott Wong, "Cultural Defenders and Brokers: Chinese Responses to the Anti-Chinese Movement," in *Claiming America: Constructing Chinese American Identities during the Exclusion Era*, ed. K. Scott Wong and Sucheng Chan (Philadelphia: Temple University Press, 1998), 3–63. The quote is from 4.

30. J. S. Tow, *The Real Chinese in America* (New York: Academy Press, 1923). The quote is from 149.

31. Shih-shan Henry Tsai, *China and the Overseas Chinese in the United States, 1868–1911* (Fayetteville: University of Arkansas Press, 1983).

32. Okihiro, *Columbia Guide*, 201–3, discusses some contemporary anti-Asian works.

33. Mary Roberts Coolidge, *Chinese Immigration* (New York: Henry Holt, 1909).

34. Eliot Grinnel Mears, *Resident Orientals on the American Pacific Coast: Their Legal and Economic Status* (New York: Institute of Pacific Relations, 1927; rev. ed., Chicago: University of Chicago Press, 1928); William C. Smith, *The Second Generation Oriental in America* (Honolulu: Institute of Pacific Relations, 1927); Roderick D. McKenzie, *Oriental Exclusion: The Effect of American Immigration Laws, Regulations, and Judicial Decisions upon the Chinese and Japanese on the American Pacific Coast* (Chicago: University of Chicago Press, 1928); and William C. Smith, *Americans in Process: A Study of Our Citizens of Oriental Ancestry* (Ann Arbor, MI: Edwards Brothers, 1937).

35. Elmer Clarence Sandmeyer, *The Anti-Chinese Movement in California* (Urbana: University of Illinois Press, 1939).

36. Milton R. Konvitz, *The Alien and the Asiatic in American Law* (Ithaca, NY: Cornell University Press, 1946).

37. Fred W. Riggs, *Pressure on Congress: A Study of the Repeal of Chinese Exclusion* (New York: King's Crown Press, Columbia University, 1950).

38. Rose Hum Lee, *The Chinese in the U.S.A.* (Hong Kong: Hong Kong University Press, 1960).

39. S. W. Kung, *Chinese in American Life: Some Aspects of Their History, Status, Problems, and Contributions* (Seattle: University of Washington Press, 1962).

40. Gunther Barth, *Bitter Strength: A History of the Chinese in the United States, 1850–1870* (Cambridge, MA: Harvard University Press, 1964). The quotes are from 2, 34, and 67.

41. Linda P. Shin, untitled review essay on three books: Gunther Barth, *Bitter Strength*; Betty Lee Sung, *The Story of the Chinese in America*; and Stanford Lyman, *Chinese Americans*; in *Counterpoint: Perspectives on Asian America*, ed. Emma Gee et al. (Los Angeles: University of California, Los Angeles, Asian American Studies Center, 1976), 36–40.

42. Ping Chiu, *Chinese Labor in California, 1850–1880: An Economic Study* (Madison: State Historical Society of Wisconsin, 1967).

43. Benjamin E. Lloyd, *Lights and Shades in San Francisco* (San Francisco: A. L. Bancroft, 1876). The quotes are from 236–37, 244, 259, 245, 253, 255–56, 272, 276, and 292.

44. Louis J. Beck, *New York's Chinatown: An Historical Presentation of the People and Places* (New York: Bohemia Publishing, 1898).

45. Mary E. Bamford, *Ti: A Story of San Francisco's Chinatown* (Chicago: David C. Cook, 1899). The quote is from 93.

46. Eng Ying Gong and Bruce Grant, *Tong War! The First Complete History of the Tongs in America; Details of the Tong Wars and Their Causes; Lives of Famous Hatchetmen and Gunmen; and Inside Information as to the Workings of the Tongs, Their Aims and Achievements* (New York: Nicholas L. Brown, 1930). The quotes are from 48, 280, and 287.

47. Renqiu Yu, *To Save China, to Save Ourselves: The Chinese Hand Laundry Alliance of New York* (Philadelphia: Temple University Press, 1992).

48. Leong Gor Yun, *Chinatown Inside Out* (New York: Barrows Mussey, 1936). The quotes are from 23 and 224–25.

49. Charles Caldwell Dobie, *San Francisco's Chinatown* (New York: D. Appleton-Century, 1936). The quotes are from 2–3, 233, and 245.

50. Carl Glick, *Shake Hands with the Dragon* (New York: McGraw-Hill, 1941). The quotes are from 8–9, 81, and 84.

51. Carl Glick, *Three Times I Bow* (New York: McGraw-Hill, 1943).

52. Elizabeth Colman, *Chinatown, U.S.A.* (New York: John Day, 1946). The quote is from 15.

53. Alexander McLeod, *Pigtails and Gold Dust* (Caldwell, ID: Caxton Printers, 1948). The quotes are from 8 and 320.

54. Richard H. Dillon, *The Hatchet Men: San Francisco's Chinatown in the Days of the Tong Wars, 1880–1906* (New York: Ballantine Books, 1962).

55. Gwen Kinkead, *Chinatown: A Portrait of a Closed Society* (New York: HarperCollins, 1992).

56. Garding Lui, *Inside Los Angeles Chinatown* (n.p.: 1948).

57. Calvin Lee, *Chinatown, U.S.A.: A History and Guide* (Garden City, NY: Doubleday, 1965). The quote is from xii.

58. C. Y. Lee, *Days of the Tong Wars: California, 1847–1896* (New York: Ballantine Books, 1974).

59. William Wei, *The Asian American Movement* (Philadelphia: Temple University Press, 1993), 1.

60. Steve Louie, review of William Wei, *The Asian American Movement*, in *Amerasia Journal* 19, no. 3 (1993): 155–59; and Steve Louie and Glenn K. Omatsu, eds., *Asian Americans: The Movement and the Moment* (Los Angeles: University of California, Asian American Studies Center Press, 2001).

61. The Chinese Historical Society of America has published three volumes of conference papers, *The Life, Influence and the Role of the Chinese in the United States, 1776–1960: Proceedings/Papers of the National Conference Held at the University of San Francisco, July 10–12, 1975* (San Francisco: Chinese Historical Society of America, 1976); Genny Lim, ed., *The Chinese American Experience: Papers from the Second National Conference on Chinese American Studies (1980)* (San Francisco: Chinese Historical Society of America and the Chinese Culture Center, 1984); and *The Repeal and Its Legacy: Proceedings of the Conference on the 50th Anniversary of the Repeal of the Exclusion Acts* (San Francisco: Chinese Historical Society of America, 1994).

62. Thomas W. Chinn, H. Mark Lai, and Philip P. Choy, eds., *A History of the Chinese in California: A Syllabus* (San Francisco: Chinese Historical Society of America, 1969); H. Mark Lai and Philip P. Choy, *Outlines: History of the Chinese in America* (San Francisco: the authors, 1972); Him Mark Lai, Yuk Ow, and Philip P. Choy, *A History of the Sam Yup Benevolent Association of San Francisco* (San Francisco: Sam Yup Association, 1975); Him Mark Lai, Genny Lim, and Judy Yung, *Island: Poetry and History of Chinese Immigrants on Angel Island, 1910–1940* (San Francisco: Hoc Doi, a project of the Chinese Culture Foundation, 1980; repr., Seattle: University of Washington Press, 1986); Him Mark Lai, Joe Huang, and Don Wong, *The Chinese of America, 1785–1980* (San Francisco: Chinese Culture Foundation, 1980); Thomas W. Chinn, *Bridging the Pacific: San Francisco Chinatown and Its People* (San Francisco: Chinese Historical Society of America, 1989); Philip P. Choy, Lorraine Dong, and Marlon K. Hom, *The Coming Man: 19th Century American Perceptions of the Chinese* (Hong Kong: Joint Publishing Co., 1994); and Anne Bloomfield, Benjamin Anaian, and Philip P. Choy, *History of Chinese Camp: Cultural Resources Inventory, Tuolumne County, California* (Sonora, CA: Tuolumne County Historic Preservation Review Commission, 1994). Two of Lai's bibliographies have benefited countless colleagues as they researched Chinese American history: Him Mark Lai and Karl Lo, *Chinese Newspapers Published in North America, 1854–1975* (Washington, DC: Association of Research Libraries, Center for Chinese Research Materials, 1977); and Him Mark Lai, *A History Reclaimed: An Annotated Bibliography of Chinese Language Materials on the Chinese of*

America, eds. Russell Leong and Jean Pang Yip (Los Angeles: University of California, Los Angeles, Asian American Studies Center, 1986).

63. Him Mark Lai, *Cong Huaqiao dao Huaren: Ershi shiji Meiguo Huaren shehui fazhan shi* [From overseas Chinese to Chinese Americans: a history of the development of Chinese American society during the twentieth century] (Hong Kong: Joint Publishing Co., 1992); Lai, *Becoming Chinese American: A History of Communities and Institutions* (Walnut Creek, CA: AltaMira Press, 2004); and Lai, *Transnational Politics and the Press in Chinese American History: Collected Essays of Him Mark Lai* (Urbana: University of Illinois Press, 2008). The last two volumes are collections of some of Lai's articles, most of which first appeared in the journal of the Chinese Historical Society of America, *Chinese America: History and Perspectives*. His newspaper articles up to 1995 are listed in an untitled *Festschrift* pamphlet prepared by his colleagues and admirers in honor of his seventieth birthday. I thank Madeline Y. Hsu for sharing a copy of this pamphlet with me.

64. Madeline Y. Hsu, "Foreword: The Life and Times of Him Mark Lai," in Lai, *Becoming Chinese American*, xvii.

65. Him Mark Lai, "A Historical Survey of Organizations of the Left among the Chinese in America," *Bulletin of Concerned Asian Scholars* 4, no. 3 (1972): 10–20. Lai subsequently published three revised and updated versions of this study.

66. Among the Wing Luke Asian Museum's publications is a collection of oral histories and photographs edited by Ron Chew, the museum's executive director: *Reflections of Seattle's Chinese Americans: The First 100 Years* (Seattle: University of Washington Press and the Wing Luke Asian Museum, 1994).

67. Douglas W. Lee, ed., *Annals of the Chinese Historical Society of the Pacific Northwest*, 1983 and 1984.

68. The Hawaii Chinese History Center has published many books, sometimes in conjunction with the University of Hawaii Press (formerly named the University Press of Hawaii). It has also served as the distributor of books published by other community organizations. Its main publications include Tin-Yuke Char, comp. and ed., *The Sandalwood Mountains: Readings and Stories of the Early Chinese in Hawaii* (Honolulu: University Press of Hawaii, 1975); Tin-Yuke Char, *The Bamboo Path: Life and Writings of a Chinese in Hawaii* (Honolulu: Hawaii Chinese History Center, 1977); Tin-Yuke Char and Wai Jane Char, *Chinese Historical Sites and Pioneer Families of Kauai* (Honolulu: Hawaii Chinese History Center, 1980); Tin-Yuke Char and Wai Jane Char, *Chinese Historical Sites and Families of the Island of Hawaii* (Honolulu: University of Hawaii Press for the Hawaii Chinese History Center, 1983); Wai Jane Char and Tin-Yuke Char, *Chinese Historical Sites and Pioneer Families of Rural Oahu* (Honolulu: Hawaii Chinese History Center, distributed by the University of Hawaii Press, 1988); James H. Chun, *The Early Chinese in Punaluu* (Honolulu: Yin Sit Sha, distributed by the Hawaii Chinese History Center, 1983); Violet L. Lai, assisted by Kum Pui Lai, *He Was a Ram: Wong Aloiau of Hawaii* (Honolulu: University of Hawaii Press for the Hawaii Chinese History Center and the Wong Aloiau Association, 1985); and Edward Seu Chen Mau, *The Mau Lineage* (Honolulu: Hawaii Chinese History Center, 1989). Diane Mei Lin Mark, *Seasons of Light: The History of Chinese Christian Churches in Hawaii* (Honolulu: Chinese Christian Association of Hawaii, 1989), is another book published by a community organization in Hawaii. Freelance writer Bob Dye produced *Merchant Prince of the Sandalwood Mountains: Afong and the Chinese in Hawaii* (Honolulu: University of Hawaii Press, 1997).

69. The Organization of Chinese Americans sponsored the research and publication of Diane Mei Lin Mark and Ginger Chih, *A Place Called Chinese America* (Dubuque, IA: Kendall/Hunt, 1982; 2nd ed., 1985; 3rd ed., 1993).

70. Publications sponsored by the Chinese Historical Society of Southern California include *Gum Saan Journal*; a collection of women's oral histories, *Linking Our Lives: Chinese American Women of Los Angeles* (Los Angeles: Chinese Historical Society of Southern California and the University of California, Los Angeles, Asian American Studies Center, 1984); Louise Leung Larson, *Sweet Bamboo: A Saga of a Chinese American Family* (Los Angeles: Chinese Historical Society of Southern California, 1989; repr., Berkeley and Los Angeles: University of California Press, 2001); and Chinese Historical Society of Southern California, ed., *Origins and Destinations: 41 Essays on Chinese America* (Los Angeles: Chinese Historical Society of Southern California and University of California, Los Angeles, Asian American Studies Center, 1994).

71. Gloria Sun Hom, ed., *Chinese Argonauts: An Anthology of the Chinese Contributions to the Historical Development of Santa Clara County* (Los Altos, CA: Foothill Community College, 1971).

72. Doug Chin and Art Chin, *Uphill: The Settlement and Diffusion of the Chinese in Seattle* (Seattle: Shorey Book Store, 1973).

73. Laverne Mau Dicker, *The Chinese in San Francisco: A Pictorial History* (New York: Dover Publications, 1979).

74. See the following works by Ruthanne Lum McCunn: *An Illustrated History of the Chinese in America* (San Francisco: Design Enterprises, 1979); *Thousand Pieces of Gold: A Biographical Novel* (San Francisco: Design Enterprises, 1981); *Sole Survivor* (San Francisco: Design Enterprises, 1985); and *Chinese American Portraits: Personal Histories, 1828–1988* (San Francisco: Chronicle Books, 1988).

75. Jack Chen, *The Chinese of America: From the Beginning to the Present* (San Francisco: Harper & Row, 1980).

76. Eve Armentrout Ma and Jeong Huei Ma, *The Chinese of Oakland: Unsung Builders* (Oakland, CA: Chinese Historical Research Committee, 1982).

77. Victor Low, *The Unimpressible Race: A Century of Educational Struggle by the Chinese in San Francisco* (San Francisco: East/West Publishing Co., 1982).

78. Peter C. Y. Leung, *One Day, One Dollar: Locke, California, and the Chinese Farming Experience in the Sacramento Delta* (El Cerrito, CA: Chinese/Chinese American History Project, 1984).

79. Connie Young Yu, *Profiles in Excellence: Peninsula Chinese Americans* (Palo Alto, CA: Stanford Area Chinese Club, 1986).

80. H. K. Wong, *Gum Sahn Yun: Gold Mountain Men* (n.p.: the author, 1987).

81. Sylvia Sun Minnick, *Sam Fow: The San Joaquin Chinese Legacy* (Fresno, CA: Panorama West Books, 1988).

82. Larson, *Sweet Bamboo.*

83. Lisa See, *On Gold Mountain: The One-Hundred-Year Odyssey of a Chinese-American Family* (New York: St. Martin's Press, 1995).

84. Lani Ah Tye Farkas, *Bury My Bones in America: The Saga of a Chinese Family in California, 1852–1996* (Nevada City, CA: Carl Mautz, 1998).

85. William Wong, *Oakland's Chinatown* (Charleston, SC: Arcadia, 2004).

86. M. Alfreda Elsensohn, *Idaho Chinese Lore* (Cottonwood: Idaho Corporation of Benedictine Sisters, 1971).

87. Oakland Museum, *Three Generations of Chinese—East and West* (Oakland, CA: Oakland Museum, 1973).

88. Corinne K. Hoexter, *From Canton to California: The Epic of Chinese Immigration* (New York: Four Winds Books, 1976).

89. Lorraine Barker Hildebrand, *Straw Hats, Sandals, and Steel: The Chinese in Washington State* (Tacoma: Washington State American Revolution Bicentennial Commission, 1977).

90. Institute of Texan Cultures, *The Chinese Texans* (San Antonio: University of Texas at San Antonio, Institute of Texan Cultures, 1978); and Marian L. Martinello and William T. Field Jr., *Who Are the Chinese Texans?* (San Antonio: University of Texas at San Antonio, Institute of Texan Cultures, 1979).

91. Jeffrey Barlow and Christine Richardson, *China Doctor of John Day* (Portland, OR: Binford and Mort, 1979).

92. Stan Steiner, *Fusang: The Chinese Who Built America* (New York: Harper & Row, 1979).

93. Milton Meltzer, *The Chinese Americans* (New York: Thomas Y. Crowell, 1980).

94. Clark W. Brott, *Moon Lee One: Life in Old Chinatown, Weaverville, California* (San Diego: Great Basin Foundation, 1982).

95. Jonathan Goldstein, ed., special issue, "Georgia's East Asian Connection, 1733–1983," *West Georgia College Studies in Social Sciences* 22 (June 1983).

96. Loren W. Fessler, ed., China Institute in America, comp., *Chinese in America: Stereotyped Past, Changing Present* (New York: Vantage Press, 1983).

97. Jeffrey Gillenkirk and James Motlow, *Bitter Melon: Stories from the Last Rural Chinatown in America* (Seattle: University of Washington Press, 1987).

98. David M. Brownstone and Irene M. Franck, *The Chinese-American Heritage* (New York: Facts on File, 1988).

99. Florence C. Lister and Robert H. Lister, *The Chinese of Early Tucson: Historical Archaeology from the Tucson Urban Renewal Project* (Tucson: University of Arizona Press, 1989).

100. Arthur Bonner, *Alas! What Brought Thee Hither? The Chinese in New York, 1800–1950* (Madison and Teaneck, NJ: Fairleigh Dickinson University Press, 1997).

101. Great Basin Foundation, *Wong Ho Leun: An American Chinatown*, vol. 1, History; vol. 2, Archaeology (San Diego: Great Basin Foundation, 1987).

102. Amy Tachiki, Eddie Wong, Franklin Odo, and Buck Wong, eds., *Roots: An Asian American Reader* (Los Angeles: University of California, Los Angeles, Asian American Studies Center, 1971).

103. Emma Gee, Bruce Iwasaki, Mike Murase, Megumi Dick Osumi, Jesse Quinsaat, and June Okida Kuramoto, eds., *Counterpoint: Perspectives on Asian America* (Los Angeles: University of California, Los Angeles, Asian American Studies Center, 1976).

104. Lucie Cheng and Edna Bonacich, eds., *Labor Immigration under Capitalism: Asian Workers in the United States before World War II* (Berkeley and Los Angeles: University of California Press, 1984).

105. See the following works by Peter Kwong: *Chinatown, New York: Labor and Politics, 1930–1950* (New York: Monthly Review Press, 1979); *The New Chinatown* (New York: Hill and Wang, 1987); and *Forbidden Workers: Illegal Chinese Immigrants and American Labor* (New York: New Press, 1997).

106. Sucheng Chan, *This Bittersweet Soil: The Chinese in California Agriculture, 1860–1910* (Berkeley and Los Angeles: University of California Press, 1986).

107. Paul C. P. Siu, with an introduction by John Kuo Wei Tchen, ed., *The Chinese Laundryman: A Study in Social Isolation* (New York: New York University Press, 1987).

108. Renqiu Yu, *To Save China, to Save Ourselves: The Chinese Hand Laundry Alliance of New York* (Philadelphia: Temple University Press, 1992).

109. Chris Friday, *Organizing Asian American Labor: The Pacific Coast Canned-Salmon Industry, 1870–1942* (Philadelphia: Temple University Press, 1994).

110. Betty Lee Sung, *Mountain of Gold: The Chinese in America* (New York: Macmillan, 1967). A paperback edition was published under a different title: *The Story of the*

Chinese in America (New York: Collier Books, 1967; repr., 1972, 1975). The quotes are from 1 and 8.

111. See the following works by Betty Lee Sung: *Statistical Profile of the Chinese in the United States: 1970 Census* (Washington, DC: U.S. Department of Labor, Manpower Administration, 1975; repr., New York: Arno Press, 1978); *A Survey of Chinese-American Manpower and Employment* (New York: Praeger, 1976); *Gangs in New York's Chinatown* (Washington, DC: Department of Health, Education, and Welfare, Office of Child Development, 1977); *Transplanted Chinese Children* (Washington, DC: Department of Health, Education, and Welfare, Administration for Children, Youth, and Families, 1979); *The Adjustment Experience of Chinese Immigrant Children in New York City* (New York: Center for Migration Studies, 1987); and *Chinese American Intermarriage* (New York: Center for Migration Studies, 1990).

112. Francis L. K. Hsu, *The Challenge of the American Dream: The Chinese in the United States* (Belmont, CA: Wadsworth, 1971).

113. Stanford M. Lyman, *Chinese Americans* (New York: Random House, 1975). See also the following works by Lyman: *The Asian in the West* (Reno and Las Vegas: University of Nevada, Desert Research Institute, Western Studies Center, 1971); *The Asian in North America* (Santa Barbara, CA: ABC-Clio, 1977); and *Chinatown and Little Tokyo: Power, Conflict, and Community among Chinese and Japanese Immigrants to America* (Millwood, NY: Associated Faculty Press, 1986).

114. William L. Tung, *The Chinese in America, 1820–1973: A Chronology and Fact Book* (Dobbs Ferry, NY: Oceana, 1974).

115. Pao-min Chang, *Continuity and Change: A Profile of Chinese Americans* (New York: Vantage Press, 1983).

116. Shih-shan Henry Tsai, *The Chinese Experience in America* (Bloomington: Indiana University Press, 1986).

117. Franklin Ng, *The Taiwanese Americans* (Westport, CT: Greenwood Press, 1998).

118. Benson Tong, *The Chinese Americans* (Westport, CT: Greenwood Press, 2000).

119. Peter Kwong and Dušanka Miščević, *Chinese America: The Untold Story of America's Oldest New Community* (New York: New Press, 2005).

120. Claire Jones, *The Chinese in America* (Minneapolis: Lerner, 1972); and Franklin Ng, *Chinese American Struggle for Equality* (Vero Beach, FL: Rourke Corp., 1992).

121. Susie Lan Cassel, ed., *The Chinese in America: A History from Gold Mountain to the New Millennium* (Walnut Creek, CA: AltaMira Press, 2002).

122. Stuart Creighton Miller, *The Unwelcome Immigrant: The American Image of the Chinese, 1785–1882* (Berkeley and Los Angeles: University of California Press, 1969).

123. Alexander Saxton, *The Indispensable Enemy: Labor and the Anti-Chinese Movement in California* (Berkeley and Los Angeles: University of California Press, 1971).

124. Cheng-Tsu Wu, ed., *"Chink!" A Documentary History of Anti-Chinese Prejudice in America* (New York: World Publishing, 1972).

125. Delber L. McKee, *Chinese Exclusion and the Open Door Policy, 1900–1906: Clashes over China Policy in the Roosevelt Era* (Detroit: Wayne State University Press, 1977).

126. Shih-shan Henry Tsai, *China and the Overseas Chinese in the United States, 1868–1911* (Fayetteville: University of Arkansas Press, 1983).

127. Sucheng Chan, ed., *Entry Denied: Exclusion and the Chinese Community in America, 1882–1943* (Philadelphia: Temple University Press, 1991).

128. Lucy E. Salyer, *Laws Harsh as Tigers: Chinese Immigrants and the Shaping of Modern Immigration Law* (Chapel Hill: University of North Carolina Press, 1995), 248.

129. Erika Lee, *At America's Gates: Chinese Immigration during the Exclusion Era, 1882–1943* (Chapel Hill: University of North Carolina Press, 2003).

130. Estelle T. Lau, *Paper Families: Identity, Immigration Administration, and Chinese Exclusion* (Durham, NC: Duke University Press, 2006). The quotes are from 2–3.

131. Charles J. McClain Jr., *In Search of Equality: The Chinese Struggle against Discrimination in Nineteenth-Century America* (Berkeley and Los Angeles: University of California Press, 1994).

132. Gwendolyn Mink, *Old Labor and New Immigrants in American Political Development: Union, Party, and State, 1875–1920* (Ithaca, NY: Cornell University Press, 1986).

133. Andrew Gyory, *Closing the Gate: Race, Politics, and the Chinese Exclusion Act* (Chapel Hill: University of North Carolina Press, 1998).

134. Najia Aarim-Heriot, *Chinese Immigrants, African Americans, and Racial Anxiety in the United States, 1848–82* (Urbana: University of Illinois Press, 2003).

135. Madeline Y. Hsu, *Dreaming of Gold, Dreaming of Home: Transnationalism and Migration between the United States and South China, 1882–1943* (Stanford, CA: Stanford University Press, 2000).

136. Adam McKeown, *Chinese Migrant Networks and Cultural Change: Peru, Chicago, Hawaii, 1900–1936* (Chicago: University of Chicago Press, 2001).

137. Sucheng Chan, ed., *Chinese American Transnationalism: The Flow of People, Resources, and Ideas between China and America during the Exclusion Era* (Philadelphia: Temple University Press, 2005).

138. Kwong, *Forbidden Workers*; Ko-lin Chin, *Smuggled Chinese: Clandestine Immigration to the United States* (Philadelphia: Temple University Press, 1999).

139. Laurence J. Ma and Carolyn Cartier, eds., *The Chinese Diaspora: Space, Place, Mobility, and Identity* (Lanham, MD: Rowman and Littlefield, 2003).

140. Wanning Sun, *Leaving China: Media, Migration, and Transnational Imagination* (Lanham, MD: Rowman and Littlefield, 2002).

141. Peter H. Koehn and Xiao-huang Yin, eds., *The Expanding Roles of Chinese Americans in U.S.-China Relations: Transnational Networks and Trans-Pacific Interactions* (Armonk, NY: M.E. Sharpe, 2002).

142. Victor G. and Brett de Bary Nee, *Longtime Californ': A Documentary Study of an American Chinatown* (New York: Pantheon Books, 1972).

143. Chalsa M. Loo, *Chinatown: Most Time, Hard Time* (New York: Praeger, 1991; repr. paperback ed. with a new title, *Chinese America: Mental Health and Quality of Life in the Inner City*, Thousand Oaks, CA: Sage, 1998).

144. Bernard P. Wong, *Ethnicity and Entrepreneurship: The New Chinese Immigrants in the San Francisco Bay Area* (Boston: Allyn and Bacon, 1998).

145. Timothy P. Fong, *The First Suburban Chinatown: The Remaking of Monterey Park, California* (Philadelphia: Temple University Press, 1994).

146. Yong Chen, *Chinese San Francisco: A Trans-Pacific Community* (Stanford, CA: Stanford University Press, 2000).

147. Nayan Shah, *Contagious Divides: Epidemics and Race in San Francisco's Chinatown* (Berkeley and Los Angeles: University of California Press, 2001).

148. Melford Weiss, *Valley City: A Chinese Community in America* (Cambridge, MA: Schenkman, 1974), 233.

149. Sandy Lydon, *Chinese Gold: The Chinese in the Monterey Bay Region* (Capitola, CA: Capitola Book, 1985).

150. Chia-ling Kuo, *Social and Political Change in New York's Chinatown: The Role of Voluntary Associations* (New York: Praeger, 1977).

151. Xinyang Wang, *Surviving the City: The Chinese Immigrant Experience in New York City, 1890–1970* (Lanham, MD: Rowman and Littlefield, 2001), 129.

152. Bernard P. Wong, *Chinatown: Economic Adaptation and Ethnic Identity of the Chinese* (New York: Holt, Rinehart and Winston, 1982).

153. Hsiang-shui Chen, *Chinatown No More: Taiwan Immigrants in Contemporary New York* (Ithaca, NY: Cornell University Press, 1992).

154. Min Zhou, *Chinatown: The Socioeconomic Potential of an Urban Enclave* (Philadelphia: Temple University Press, 1992).

155. Jan Lin, *Reconstructing Chinatown: Ethnic Enclave, Global Change* (Minneapolis: University of Minnesota Press, 1998).

156. Michel S. Laguerre, *The Global Ethnopolis: Chinatown, Japantown, and Manilatown in American Society* (New York: St. Martin's Press, 2000). The quotes are from 12 and 20.

157. Shenglin Chang, *The Global Silicon Valley Home: Lives and Landscapes within Taiwanese American Trans-Pacific Culture* (Stanford, CA: Stanford University Press, 2006).

158. Bernard P. Wong, *The Chinese in Silicon Valley: Globalization, Social Networks, and Ethnic Identity* (Lanham, MD: Rowman and Littlefield, 2006).

159. John Kuo Wei Tchen, *New York before Chinatown: Orientalism and the Shaping of American Culture, 1776–1882* (Baltimore: Johns Hopkins University Press, 1999).

160. Clarence E. Glick, *Sojourners and Settlers: Chinese Migrants in Hawaii* (Honolulu: Hawaii Chinese History Center and the University of Hawaii Press, 1980).

161. James W. Loewen, *The Mississippi Chinese: Between Black and White* (Cambridge, MA: Harvard University Press, 1971; 2nd ed., Prospect Heights, IL: Waveland Press, 1988); Robert Seto Quan, *Lotus among the Magnolias: The Mississippi Chinese* (Jackson: University Press of Mississippi, 1982); and Lucy M. Cohen, *Chinese in the Post-Civil War South: A People without a History* (Baton Rouge: Louisiana State University Press, 1984).

162. Rose Hum Lee, *The Growth and Decline of Chinese Communities in the Rocky Mountain Region* (New York: Arno Press, 1978); Craig Storti, *Incident at Bitter Creek: The Story of the Rock Springs Chinese Massacre* (Ames: Iowa State University Press, 1991); Priscilla Wegars, ed., *Hidden Heritage: Historical Archaeology of the Overseas Chinese* (Amityville, NY: Baywood, 1993); Liping Zhu, *A Chinaman's Chance: The Chinese of the Rocky Mountain Mining Frontier* (Niwot: University Press of Colorado, 1997); Marie Rose Wong, *Sweet Cakes, Long Journey: The Chinatowns of Portland, Oregon* (Seattle: University of Washington Press, 2004); and Arif Dirlik, ed., *Chinese on the American Frontier* (Lanham, MD: Rowman and Littlefield, 2001).

163. Jae-Hyup Lee, *Dynamics of Ethnic Identity: Three Asian American Communities in Philadelphia* (New York: Garland, 1998); Jianli Zhao, *Strangers in the City: The Atlanta Chinese, Their Community, and Stories of Their Lives* (New York: Routledge, 2002); and Huping Ling, *Chinese St. Louis: From Enclave to Cultural Community* (Philadelphia: Temple University Press, 2004).

164. Judy Yung, *Chinese Women of America: A Pictorial History* (San Francisco: Chinese Culture Foundation, 1986).

165. Judy Yung, *Unbound Feet: A Social History of Chinese Women in San Francisco* (Berkeley and Los Angeles: University of California Press, 1995); and Yung, *Unbound Voices: A Documentary History of Chinese Women in San Francisco* (Berkeley and Los Angeles: University of California Press, 1999).

166. Peggy Pascoe, *Relations of Rescue: The Search for Female Moral Authority in the American West, 1874–1939* (New York: Oxford University Press, 1990).

167. Benson Tong, *Unsubmissive Women: Chinese Prostitutes in Nineteenth-Century San Francisco* (Norman: University of Oklahoma Press, 1994).

168. George Anthony Peffer, *If They Don't Bring Their Women Here: Chinese Female Migration before Exclusion* (Urbana: University of Illinois Press, 1999).

169. Huping Ling, *Surviving on the Gold Mountain: A History of Chinese American Women and Their Lives* (Albany: State University of New York Press, 1998).

170. Stacey G. H. Yap, *Gather Your Strength, Sisters: The Emerging Role of Chinese Women Community Workers* (New York: AMS Press, 1989).

171. Xiaolan Bao, *Holding up More Than Half the Sky: Chinese Women Garment Workers in New York City, 1948–92* (Urbana: University of Illinois Press, 2001).

172. Xiaojian Zhao, *Remaking Chinese America: Immigration, Family, and Community, 1940–1965* (New Brunswick, NJ: Rutgers University Press, 2002).

173. Maria W. L. Chee, *Taiwanese American Transnational Families: Women and Kin Networks* (New York: Routledge, 2005).

174. Haiming Liu, *The Transnational History of a Chinese Family: Immigrant Letters, Family Business, and Reverse Migration* (New Brunswick, NJ: Rutgers University Press, 2005), 3.

175. Vivian S. Louie, *Compelled to Excel: Immigration, Education, and Opportunity among Chinese Americans* (Stanford, CA: Stanford University Press, 2004).

176. William F. Wu, *The Yellow Peril: Chinese Americans in American Fiction, 1859–1940* (Hamden, CT: Archon Books, 1982).

177. Gina Marchetti, *Romance and the "Yellow Peril": Race, Sex, and Discursive Strategies in Hollywood Fiction* (Berkeley and Los Angeles: University of California Press, 1993).

178. James S. Moy, *Marginal Sights: Staging the Chinese in America* (Iowa City: University of Iowa Press, 1993).

179. Josephine Lee, *Performing Asian America: Race and Ethnicity on the Contemporary Stage* (Philadelphia: Temple University Press, 1997).

180. Robert G. Lee, *Orientals: Asian Americans in Popular Culture* (Philadelphia: Temple University Press, 1999).

181. Krystyn R. Moon, *Yellow Face: Creating the Chinese in American Popular Music and Performance, 1850–1920s* (New Brunswick, NJ: Rutgers University Press, 2005). The quotes are from 166–67.

182. Anthony W. Lee, *Picturing Chinatown: Art and Orientalism in San Francisco* (Berkeley and Los Angeles: University of California Press, 2001), 19.

183. Mary Ting Li Lui, *The Chinatown Trunk Mystery: Murder, Miscegenation, and Other Dangerous Encounters in Turn-of-the-Century New York City* (Princeton, NJ: Princeton University Press, 2005).

184. Ronald Riddle, *Flying Dragons, Flowing Streams: Music in the Life of San Francisco's Chinese* (Westport, CT: Greenwood Press, 1983).

185. Todd Rainsberger, *James Wong Howe: Cinematographer* (San Diego: A. S. Barnes, 1981).

186. Anthony B. Chan, *Perpetually Cool: The Many Lives of Anna May Wong (1905–1961)* (Lanham, MD: Scarecrow Press, 2003); Philip Leibfried and Chei Mi Lane, *Anna May Wong: A Complete Guide to Her Films, Stage, Radio, and Television Work* (Jefferson, NC: McFarland, 2004); and Graham R. G. Hodges, *Anna May Wong: From Laundryman's Daughter to Hollywood Legend* (New York: Palgrave, 2004).

187. Karl Fung, *The Dragon Pilgrims: A Historical Study of a Chinese-American Church* (San Diego: Providence Press, 1989); Lawrence A. Palinkas, *Rhetoric and Religious Experience: The Discourse of Immigrant Chinese Churches* (Fairfax, VA: George Mason University Press, 1989); Kenneth J. Guest, *God in Chinatown: Religion and Survival in New York's Evolving Immigrant Community* (New York: New York University Press, 2003); Fenggang Yang, *Chinese Christians in America: Conversion, Assimilation, and Adhesive Identities* (University Park: Pennsylvania State University Press, 1999); and Russell Jeung,

Faithful Generation: Race and New Asian American Churches (New Brunswick, NJ: Rutgers University Press, 2005).

188. Sue Fawn Chung and Priscilla Wegars, eds., *Chinese American Death Rituals: Respecting the Ancestors* (Walnut Creek, CA: AltaMira Press, 2005).

189. Gloria Heyung Chun, *Of Orphans and Warriors: Inventing Chinese American Culture and Identity* (New Brunswick, NJ: Rutgers University Press, 2000).

190. K. Scott Wong and Sucheng Chan, eds., *Claiming America: Constructing Chinese American Identities during the Exclusion Era* (Philadelphia: Temple University Press, 1998).

191. Henry Yu, *Thinking Orientals: Migration, Contact, and Exoticism in Modern America* (New York: Oxford University Press, 2001).

192. Elionne L. W. Belden, *Claiming Chinese Identity* (New York: Garland, 1997).

193. Shehong Chen, *Being Chinese, Becoming Chinese American* (Urbana: University of Illinois Press, 2002).

194. Karen J. Leong, *The China Mystique: Pearl S. Buck, Anna May Wong, Mayling Soong, and the Transformation of American Orientalism* (Berkeley and Los Angeles: University of California Press, 2005).

195. K. Scott Wong, *Americans First: Chinese Americans and the Second World War* (Cambridge, MA: Harvard University Press, 2005).

196. Judy Tzu-chun Wu, *Dr. Mom Chung of the Fair-Haired Bastards: The Life of a Wartime Celebrity* (Berkeley and Los Angeles: University of California Press, 2005).

197. Andrea Louie, *Chineseness across Borders: Renegotiating Chinese Identities in China and the United States* (Durham, NC: Duke University Press, 2004).

198. Mae M. Ngai, *Impossible Subjects: Illegal Aliens and the Making of Modern America* (Princeton, NJ: Princeton University Press, 2004).

1

History as Law and Life: *Tape v. Hurley* and the Origins of the Chinese American Middle Class

Mae M. Ngai

Perhaps the most significant development in contemporary immigration studies has been the so-called transnational turn. In the field of Chinese American studies, the concept is not entirely new, as China-oriented politics have long been prominent in overseas Chinese communities and as such have been the central problematic in political historiography, manifest in titles like "To Bring Forth a New China, to Build a Better America" and *To Save China, to Save Ourselves*. Recent scholarship has both built on previous work and drawn from newer theoretical interventions in migration studies, while also continuing the practice of alliteratively transnational titling. For example, Madeline Hsu's *Dreaming of Gold, Dreaming of Home* renders with deep insight the social world of Chinese migrant families, a world that existed simultaneously in villages in southern China and in American Chinatowns.[1]

Transnational research focuses on the immigrants, on the first generation. In a sense, the synchronic nature of the project elides the question of generational change over time. Scholars are beginning to consider the impact of transnational migrant culture on the American-born generation. Gloria Chun and Haiming Liu have written about second-generation Chinese Americans who, facing employment discrimination in the United States, sought career opportunities in China during the 1930s.[2] But in general, our understanding of longer-term processes of incorporation and settlement in the host country continues to be shaped by canonical assumptions in sociology and history about the assimilation of the American-born generations: that is, that immigrant incorporation follows a generational path of Americanization and socioeconomic mobility. These remain powerful influences on our thinking, for even when traveled slowly and against obstacles of racial discrimination, there remains an assumption of that path as normative. In this chapter, I try to rethink these assumptions. I do not mean to argue from the outset for a transnational second generation,[3] but I do want to suggest that exclusion and inclusion were not necessarily successive phases of immigrant incorporation. Rather, these processes were intimately entwined, especially in the formation of the Chinese American middle class.

I illustrate this process by examining the 1885 civil rights case, *Tape v. Hurley*.[4] In that case, the California Supreme Court ruled that Chinese children could not be excluded from public schools. I consider the place of the decision in the longer-term trajectories of Chinese American civil rights and of the Tape family itself. Methodologically, I propose to combine legal and social history—that is, to use both "law" and "life." I examine the experience of individual social actors alongside broader socio-legal trends in the stream of historical time, to try to get at social processes and meanings that are not otherwise easily revealed.

Much of what we know about *Tape v. Hurley* and the Tape family is based on a handful of documents. These comprise the court's ruling; the affidavit submitted to the court by Joseph Tape; and a letter written to the San Francisco school board by Joseph Tape's wife, Mary, which was printed in the *Daily Alta*, after the court handed down its ruling. Only a few scholars have researched the case and these studies have been based mainly on newspaper accounts of the controversy and have approached the case through the context of education policy.[5] Chinese American historians have also taken an interest in Mary Tape, who by all accounts was an extraordinary woman, being a painter, photographer, and amateur telegraphist. In 1892, the *Morning Call* ran a feature about her artistic endeavors.[6] Beyond these few documents and articles, however, we know little, if anything, about the Tape family's history, whether before or after *Tape v. Hurley*.

To meet this empirical challenge, I have researched a broader range of historical documents spanning a longer period of time, including census records, maps, directories, newspapers, photographs, immigration case files and administrative records, transcripts of government hearings, and the like. My research suggests that *Tape v. Hurley* marked a turning point both in the status of the Chinese in California and in the lives of members of the Tape family. I argue that these two trajectories converged in a process of class formation. The Tape family was an exemplar of a "brokering class" that emerged in the nineteenth and early twentieth centuries as the legal status of the Chinese was being worked out in the federal courts. The brokers were go-betweens that facilitated transactions between mainstream American institutions and the Chinese community. They included immigration and transportation agents, labor contractors, language interpreters, and other kinds of ethnic entrepreneurs. They were a relatively small group—for only a few Chinese had the language and cultural skills to work for American offices—but their work was indispensable for the immigration and settlement of the Chinese. I argue that the brokers were central, constitutive figures of the first generation of the Chinese American middle class.

Tape v. Hurley and the Peculiarity of Chinese American Civil Rights Jurisprudence

In *Tape v. Hurley,* the California Supreme Court ruled in 1885 that public schools in California could not exclude Chinese children on account of race. The holding in the case, a straightforward reading of the statute, is unremarkable, which is perhaps why the case has not received the same attention as the landmark constitutional cases decided by the U.S. Supreme Court in the same decade, notably the Chinese exclusion cases (*Chae Chan Ping* and *Fong Yue Ting*) and *Yick Wo v. Hopkins.*[7]

In 2004, *Tape v. Hurley* received a boost of publicity as many programs commemorating the fiftieth anniversary of *Brown v. Board of Education* included it as part of an effort to broaden the public's understanding of civil rights and education by looking at Asian American and Latino experiences. For example, the Smithsonian's Museum of American History included *Tape v. Hurley* in its exhibit on *Brown*; and the Chinese Historical Society of America in San Francisco sponsored a program on the two decisions. In the context of these commemorations, *Tape* was typically described as a kind of forerunner to *Brown.* In fact, Tape is both temporally and substantively more proximate to *Plessy v. Ferguson,* in which the Supreme Court justified the "separate but equal" doctrine, than it is to *Brown.* For when the court ruled that Chinese could not be excluded from public schools, San Francisco immediately established a segregated Chinese school. *Tape v. Hurley*, then, was a kind of Pyrrhic victory.[8]

But *Tape* is also not exactly like *Plessy.* In the latter case, the Court established for African Americans a second-class citizenship but excluded the Chinese in America from citizenship. The distinction was clear to Supreme Court Justice John Marshall Harlan. In his famous "color-blind" dissent in *Plessy,* Justice Harlan compared the Negro citizen with the Chinese foreigner. Whereas the former had shed his blood for the nation and deserved the full rights of citizenship, Harlan argued, the Chinese were "*a race so different from our own* that we do not permit those belonging to it to become citizens of the United States. Persons belonging to it are, with few exceptions, absolutely excluded from our country."[9]

The problem of Chinese segregation thus must be understood in the context of a complex negotiation of the status of the Chinese that was being worked out in the federal courts in the late nineteenth century, a status that came under competing pressures of exclusion and inclusion. Put another way, the Chinese Exclusion Act of 1882 aimed to stop Chinese immigration and denied the Chinese the right of naturalization, but—Justice Harlan's dissent notwithstanding—the exclusion law could not altogether eliminate the presence of the Chinese in the United States. These included laborers already lawfully domiciled, merchants and others exempt from the exclusion laws, and those born on U.S. soil. What rights, if any, these Chinese possessed remained a contested issue throughout the late nineteenth century.

California's first laws on common-branch schooling provided for segregated schools for "Negroes, Indians, and Mongolians," but the Chinese found even segregated schools hard to come by.[10] The first school for the Chinese in San Francisco, started in 1853, was not a public school but was funded by Chinese merchant leaders and white Christian missionaries. English classes for some twenty Chinese boys and men were held in a small room on Sacramento Street. Contemporaries understood the link between language acquisition and assimilation. An observer wrote that the students, fifteen to forty years of age, reportedly made "rapid progress" and showed "eagerness to become acquainted with our language, manners and customs. We venture to assert that if the Chinese can be induced to settle permanently among us, that in time our country will be greatly benefited by their accession."[11]

For the missionaries, English-language instruction was, of course, linked to the goal of conversion and to the missionaries' hopes of recruiting native (Chinese) Christians for missionary work in China. The Presbyterian minister William Speer, who spent four years in China before opening the first Chinese mission in San Francisco in 1853, wrote, "I have considered it an important branch of my missionary work to impart a knowledge of the English language, literature and science . . . and such things as would best illustrate our later advancement and tend to disabuse their minds of idolatrous fears and superstitions."[12]

Indeed, in the late nineteenth century, teaching English was the central conversion strategy used by those missionaries working among the Chinese in America. According to the Reverend Ira Condit, the Chinese were "extremely suspicious" of Christians and "had no desire to learn the religion of those who had treated them so unjustly and cruelly. . . . [But] as the Chinese were anxious to learn English, the plan of Chinese Sunday Schools was adopted." Guy Maine, who directed the Episcopal Church's "Chinese guild" in New York, similarly described English-language instruction as a "practical method" of uplift "by first making intelligent men then Christians." The Congregationalists bluntly advocated "baiting the Gospel hook with the English alphabet."[13]

The rate of conversion was, in fact, rather low. Speer reportedly baptized only one Chinese convert during a half-dozen years in San Francisco. According to a survey by the Chinese Sabbath School Association in 1892, there were more than 7,300 Chinese in thirty-six states "reached regularly or occasionally with Christian instruction," of whom only 734, or 10 percent, had been baptized as Christians.[14]

Nearly all the Protestant mission–sponsored schools and classes were for adults and were held during evenings and on Sunday. Only in San Francisco, where there was a relatively larger and more settled community, did the missionaries operate day schools for children. Speer, who was dedicated both to religious conversion and to opposing race discrimination against the Chinese community, directly appealed to the school board to provide instruction for the Chinese, arguing that "as taxpayers, they have a civil right to school privileges."[15]

With Speer's prodding, the San Francisco school board in 1857 unanimously agreed that "Asiatics, and particularly the Chinese youths, should have every opportunity to acquire a knowledge of the English language." School board member Goddard said that the board's aim should be to "Americanize the Chinamen," who paid more taxes and were better behaved than the "low class of American citizens." But the board voted not to admit Chinese to the evening school, on grounds that their presence would excite white students.[16]

Instead, the school system provided limited resources for a separate Chinese school. Beginning in 1859, the board paid for a teacher for a single class for Chinese pupils, which was held in the "gloomy basement" of Speer's Presbyterian mission in Chinatown. Bible reading was the principal form of instruction. The superintendent of schools, James Denman, was pessimistic about the project. "The prejudices of caste and religious idolatry are so indelibly stamped upon their character and existence," he said, that teaching them was "almost hopeless."[17]

Yet the teacher, Mr. Lanctot, soon proudly reported that the "little Celestials were very apt at learning. The younger ones knew nothing whatever of the English language on entering, but they picked it up with marvelous facility. Writing they learned with even greater ease than Yankees." Denman's successor, George Tait, acknowledged in 1864 the school's "good results," which he considered all the more remarkable in light of the fact that "missionaries [in China] after a life-long devotion to the spiritual regeneration of this unprogressive and unimpressible race, show little fruit of their exhaustive labor."[18]

The reason for the school's success was no mystery; as the missionaries understood, the Chinese in America were motivated to learn English so that they could get along in the new society. The Chinese pupils included some children but mostly comprised teenagers and young adults, the sons of merchants, who were sent to acquire the knowledge they needed to "transact business with [white Americans] and . . . to act as clerks and interpreters for their countrymen."[19] Observers noted that these older students attended school only long enough to acquire a working knowledge of English—as Speer conceded, "only a few necessary words and sentences, to assist in mining, traveling, bartering, marketing, and procuring various kinds of employment." Some school board members believed that the Chinese pupils' motives were opportunistic, even though the city also sponsored an evening school for adult European immigrants to meet a similar demand.[20]

Other critics opposed the "long prayers and reading [of] the Bible" in the Chinese Primary School and argued, "so long as the school was supported by the public moneys, it was wrong to allow it to be construed as a religious school." Nevertheless, the arrangement was the least expensive for the school board—that is, next to having no school at all. Over the years, the board frequently closed the school, citing low attendance or lack of funds, only to reopen weeks or months later, under pressure from the community. At times, the board authorized only evening classes, which catered to adult learners.[21]

The sporadic nature of public schooling was consistent with the indeterminate general status of the Chinese in the pre-exclusion years. Before the 1870s, the Chinese lived and worked in a dispersed pattern in San Francisco: They were employed in a variety of occupations and manufacturing, and many workers lived not in the Chinese quarter but near their places of employment. For example, a community of Chinese fisherman lived near the bay at the mouth of Mission Creek, which is how the area became known as China Basin. Others lived near the Tubbs Ropewalk and several woolen factories near Potrero Point.[22] This is not to say that the Chinese were just another group of settlers. There was always racism against the Chinese, but it was not yet ubiquitous or codified. Many white San Franciscans found the Chinese a curious but a benign, even necessary, presence, for the manufacturing and commercial class depended on Chinese labor and on Chinese connections for trade to China. Chinese labor, of course, was highly regarded as cheap and plentiful in an otherwise tight labor market. Chinese merchants not only imported and exported goods for the resident Chinese community but were also engaged in large-scale Sino-American commerce, exporting "immense quantities" of quicksilver, flour, wheat, and barley to Hong Kong and Chinese ports. White elites praised Chinese merchants as excellent businessmen and considered them honorable, intelligent, and prompt in their dealings, more "high-minded, correct, and truthful" than any other nationality in San Francisco.[23]

But racial animosity toward the Chinese grew in the 1870s. The opening of the transcontinental railroad brought to San Francisco growing numbers of Euro-American migrants from the East Coast; Chinese laborers, who had formerly been employed in the construction of the railroad; and a national market, which introduced new pressures on local manufacturing and wages. The economic recessions of the 1870s exacerbated the growing sense of competition between Chinese and Euro-American laborers. By the late 1870s, there was a full flowering of anti-Chinese racism in San Francisco. That racism fueled mob violence, the expulsion of Chinese workers from many manufacturing jobs, and a hardening of residential segregation.[24]

The anti-Chinese movement, which vociferously agitated for exclusion, just as adamantly opposed granting rights to resident Chinese. After all, its rallying cry was "the Chinese must go"—its aims were exclusion and expulsion, not segregation, which was the policy for African Americans and American Indians. Racist thinking blamed the Chinese for being unassimilable, yet that same thinking opposed education precisely because it threatened to incorporate, even assimilate and, hence, permanently establish the Chinese population. The exclusionists believed that the practice of keeping out new immigrants would be for naught if a permanent settlement were allowed to establish and accrete by natural increase. The *Call* summed up the danger of public schooling: "The [Chinese] race is striving to take root in the soil. They desire or profess to desire, to mingle their youth with ours, with a view, doubtless, to more thorough assimilation in the body politic."[25]

Public education was thus one of the first casualties of the anti-Chinese movement. In 1871, the San Francisco school board terminated support for the Chinatown school, upon the recommendation of James Denman, who had returned to the position of school superintendent. Denman found sanction in California's 1870 school law, which required districts to operate separate schools for "African and Indian children" but omitted any mention of the Chinese or "Mongolians." There is no record explaining the change in the law; it may well have reflected the growing animosity toward the Chinese in California. In any event, Denman concluded that San Francisco had "no obligation to continue support" for the schooling of the Chinese.[26]

The closing came at a time when there was a growing population of school-age Chinese children in California. By the 1870s and early 1880s, there were three thousand Chinese children in the state, two-thirds of whom lived in San Francisco. Education was no longer the concern only of young adults in mercantile and other businesses. Yet only a few hundred Chinese children attended the missionary schools each year.[27]

Throughout the 1870s, the school board ignored or dismissed numerous individual and collective petitions from the Chinese for admission to public schools. In 1878, the state legislature similarly disregarded a petition from 1,300 Chinese residents of San Francisco, Sacramento, and other towns, on behalf of three thousand Chinese children residing in California. "Chinese merchants and laborers," the petitioners averred, "being under the protection of your Constitution and laws, are entitled to the same rights and privileges accorded to foreigners generally." Excluding the Chinese from the benefit of public education when they paid over $40,000 a year in taxes to the state, the petitioners added, "we hold to be unjust."[28]

Then, in October 1884, Joseph and Mary Tape tried to enroll their eight-year-old daughter, Mamie, in Spring Valley primary school on Union Street in San Francisco. The principal, Miss Jennie Hurley, refused to admit Mamie because the school board had explicitly instructed all school principals to deny entry to children of Chinese descent, under pain of dismissal. Jennie Hurley, like Mamie Tape, was the daughter of an immigrant. Miss Hurley's father was a carpenter who migrated from Ireland first to New Brunswick, Canada, and then to California in the 1850s. In 1884, Jennie Hurley was forty years old; she had not married but had made her career in the public schools, rising from teacher to principal, which was unusual for a woman in those days. Her professional attainment no doubt required political as well as administrative skills. This meant that she would have gotten along with school superintendent Andrew Jackson Moulder.[29]

Moulder was a die-hard racist who had long vowed to "resist, to defeat, and to prohibit" the admission of "Africans, Chinese, and Diggers [American Indians] into our white schools." He, too, was a migrant—he had come to California from the slave-holding South. A wealthy lawyer, he was active in state politics; in his capacity as state superintendent of schools in the 1850s and 1860s and then as superintendent in San Francisco, he successfully lobbied for laws that not only segregated the public schools but also imposed sanctions against local school districts and officials that violated the law.[30]

After Jennie Hurley barred Mamie from Spring Valley School, Joseph Tape went to the Chinese consul's office in San Francisco and asked for assistance. The vice-consul, Frederick A. Bee—a white attorney who represented the Chinese Six Companies in the 1870s—lodged a protest with the school board and retained a lawyer to sue on Mamie's behalf. The lawyer, William Gibson, was son of the Reverend Otis Gibson, the Methodist missionary who was a prominent defender of the Chinese in California.[31] Both Bee and William Gibson argued that the exclusion of Mamie Tape violated both state law and the Fourteenth Amendment, "especially so in this case as the child is native-born."[32]

Notwithstanding Moulder's considerable influence in state politics, California had amended its state education law in 1880 to provide public schooling for all children in the state. The law specified that "schools must be open for the admission of all children" and that only "children of filthy or vicious habits, or children suffering contagious or infectious diseases" could be excluded.[33] Coming in the period following the Civil War, the reform was aimed chiefly at eliminating California's "colored schools." It resulted from many years of lobbying on the part of the state's small but persistent black population, as well as from a move by elites, who considered the funding of the colored schools a tax burden during economically difficult times.[34]

Moulder did not believe that the 1880 law applied to the Chinese. He had an ally in the state superintendent of public instruction, William Welcher, who agreed that the law was "meant to apply only to the African race." Excluding the Chinese from the schools, Welcher emphasized, was consistent with the California constitution's declaration that the Chinese were "dangerous to the well-being of the state."[35]

The school board concurred. If the Chinese were admitted to public schools, it asked, "will assimilation begin and race mixture follow?" It proclaimed: "Guard well the doors of the public schools that they do not enter. For however stern it might sound, it is but the enforcement of the law of self-preservation . . . by which we hope presently to prove that we justly and practically defend ourselves from this invasion of Mongolian barbarism."[36]

However, confronted with the plain wording of the statute, the court ruled against the school board's exclusion of Mamie Tape. The judge was not unsympathetic to the board's concerns. According to the Sacramento *Union*, Judge Maguire stated that "if evil resulted followed this decision it was not the fault of the judiciary. The Legislature possessed the power to provide separate schools for distinct races." The board appealed to the state supreme court but, in the meantime, rushed to Sacramento and secured a law authorizing the creation of separate schools for "Mongolian" children. The state supreme court upheld the lower court's ruling in favor of Mamie Tape. The San Francisco school board immediately announced that it would open a separate Chinese primary school in Chinatown.[37]

Tape v. Hurley signaled an important shift in the status of the Chinese, for it had in effect recognized their presence and elevated them to the status of African Americans and American Indians. This may seem a dubious promotion, but it was an important concession that distinguished between exclusion as a policy goal and presence as a social fact. Indeed, *Tape v. Hurley* was decided during the same time that the status of the Chinese was being adjudicated in the federal courts. These Chinese cases followed two tracks. On one track, a series of immigration and deportation cases upheld Chinese exclusion and pronounced the doctrine of Congress's plenary, or absolute, power over matters of immigration.[38] However, along a second track, the courts ruled that the equal protection clause of the Fourteenth Amendment applied to resident Chinese and that the citizenship clause applied to Chinese born on U.S. soil. Thus were two policies, exclusion and inclusion, born and entwined, creating a fundamental tension in the status of Chinese in America.

Today, we take the universality of principles like equal protection and birthright citizenship as self-evident meanings of the Fourteenth Amendment. But in the late nineteenth century, this was not certain. After the Civil War, when Congress amended the naturalization law to include in its scope "persons of African nativity and descent," in addition to "white persons," it chose its words deliberately in order to exclude the Chinese from the privilege of naturalization. Once Chinese exclusion was enacted, it became commonly argued that, in the words of Supreme Court Justice Harlan, "imposing" citizenship on

Chinese born "accidentally" on U.S. soil "contradicted the will of Congress to exclude" the Chinese.[39]

The federal justices who decided the Chinese cases made no effort to hide their racial animus toward the Chinese. The civil rights cases might be best understood in terms of Derrick Bell's theory of interest convergence. In other words, the courts were willing to concede certain rights to the Chinese because it suited other agendas. In *Wong Kim Ark*, for example, the Supreme Court narrowly upheld birthright citizenship of Chinese Americans because to deny them would have jeopardized the "citizenship of thousands of persons of English, Scotch, Irish, German or other European parentage, who have always been considered and treated as citizens."[40]

Just as important, federal judges found in the Chinese civil rights cases occasion to extend the application of the Fourteenth Amendment to economic rights. Before *Yick Wo*, the Supreme Court had limited the Fourteenth Amendment to protecting the civil rights of the former slaves, which was also an effort to limit the scope of federal powers after the Civil War.[41] *Yick Wo*, which concerned the city's regulation of laundries, widened the scope of the equal protection clause to include the right of individuals to pursue "ordinary trades" free from state interference. To achieve this aim, *Yick Wo* applied the equal protection clause to all "persons," not just citizens. The move was underscored with the Court's ruling—announced on the same day as *Yick Wo*—in the *Santa Clara* case, which recognized the right of corporations to equal protection.[42] *Yick Wo*, then, was an important moment in the development of laissez faire economic policy, a bridge on the road to *Lochner*.[43]

The Chinese immigration and civil rights cases established the basic doctrine that continues to apply to all immigrants in the United States—in matters of admission aliens are not protected by the Constitution, and in matters of expulsion they have only very limited procedural rights. However, when aliens are territorially present, they have rights of equal protection and of substantive due process. The two principles exist in constant tension, each qualifying the meaning of the other.[44] But whereas in the case of European immigrants, the presumption of assimilation and eventual citizenship has generally tended to privilege their inclusion, the Chinese were until the mid-twentieth century defined principally in terms of their exclusion.[45]

The Tape Family: Roads Taken and Not Taken

Let us turn now to the plaintiffs in *Tape v. Hurley* and to the public statements made by Joseph and Mary Tape. These documents purposefully project an image of the Tapes as a highly assimilated family. Joseph Tape's affidavit to the court explained that he and his wife had been married in a Christian church and in conformity with state law; that he had been engaged continuously for the last ten years in the business of draying and expressing; and that his family had lived continuously in the same place of residence for the past seven years. In other words, he was a stable, working, and moral family man, not a sojourner or a "coolie." Moreover, he wrote, "Fifteen years ago I discarded my queue, and have never since worn one. My wife and I are now, and for fifteen years past, have been clothed in the American costume. The said Mamie Tape is now and always has been dressed in the American costume, in the manner common and usual for a child of her years."[46]

A family photograph taken during the school dispute supported the image of assimilation. The family presents itself in Western-styled clothing; the parents' garments in particular are typical of contemporary Victorian fashion, although it is impossible to know whether these were their own clothes or costumes provided by the studio. Perhaps more telling as to the purpose of the photograph is Mamie, who is positioned strategically at the center. Instead of the neutral gaze favored in family portraiture, her look is proud, almost defiant. She holds her brother's hand, giving unity to the family's image while also possibly steadying her nerves.

In these words and images, the Tapes presented themselves as a heteronormative bourgeois family, far removed from the stereotype of sojourning coolies and prostitutes. In fact, this was a typical strategy used by all ethnoracial groups in civil rights cases, in which plaintiffs create a social distance between themselves and the unassimilated lower classes. Aimed at minimizing racial bias by minimizing racial difference—as if to say, "see, we are just like white people"—the legal strategy was akin to the racial "uplift" ideology that was widespread among African American and other nonwhite minorities in the late nineteenth and early twentieth centuries.[47]

Mary Tape's letter to the school board again reinforced the image of the Tapes as a bourgeois family. That letter was written as an angry protest when, after Mamie Tape won her case at trial, the school board announced that it would create a segregated school for the Chinese. Mrs. Tape wrote: "Dear sirs: Will you please to tell me! Is it a disgrace to be Born a Chinese? Didn't God make us all!!! . . . Do you call that a Christian act to compell my little children to go so far to a school that is made in purpose for them." She continued:

> My children don't dress like the other Chinese. They look just as phunny amongst them as the Chinese dress in Chinese look amongst you Caucasians. . . . Her playmates is all Caucasians ever since she could toddle around. If she is good enough to play with them! Then is she not good enough to be in the same room and studie with them? You had better come and see for yourselves. See if the Tape's is not same as other Caucasians, except in features. It seems no matter how a Chinese may live and dress so long as you know they Chinese. Then they are hated as one. There is not any right or justice for them.

The Tape family, ca. 1885. From the left, Joseph, Emily, Mamie, Frank, and Mary. *(From the Mary Tape collection. Courtesy of Jack Kim.)*

Finally, Mary Tape swore: "Mamie Tape will never attend any of the Chinese schools of your making! Never!!! I will let the world see Sir What justice there is When it is govern by the Race prejudice men!"[48]

Joseph Tape's affidavit was most likely written by his lawyer, following conventional practice, but the emotion and grammatical imperfection of Mary Tape's letter indicates that she wrote it herself. There is more expressive latitude in a letter than in an affidavit, and perhaps gender difference also allowed the female or mother's voice to register more affect (although the anger in Mrs. Tape's letter exceeds the normative middle-class female voice). It is unclear whether Mrs. Tape intended her letter just for the school board or for the general public, but her outrage evinced an understanding that segregation was a badge of race inferiority.[49]

These documents make the Tapes appear proud and heroic as they refuse to submit to discriminatory policies and practices. Indeed, the image of resistance to racial oppression is favored in academic and lay narratives about *Tape v. Hurley*, and undoubtedly it has much appeal.[50] Yet their resistance seems to be grounded in their claim that they are the "same as other Caucasians." That is, they make a claim to whiteness, not that they, as Chinese, should be treated the same as whites. The Tapes seem to be ambivalent about, if not outright rejecting, an identity as Chinese, "except in features."

A number of questions arise. What accounts for the Tapes' apparent assimilation and their view that they are the "same as Caucasians"? What explains their agency? Moreover, if we read *Tape v. Hurley* not as an unalloyed civil rights victory but as part of a trend that established both segregation and exclusion, we will also want to know how that trend influenced the Tape family. To answer these questions, we need to step back from these documents and view them not as products of an isolated moment but in the broader context of the family's development over time.

The Tapes had come to the United States in the 1860s, before exclusion, when things were still fluid for Chinese immigrants. They came separately, each at a young age and without parents, and they each lived among white people. He was fourteen when he arrived; his Chinese name was Zhao Qia, or Chew Dip in Cantonese. He worked for a Scots dairy farmer on Van Ness, first as a servant boy and then driving the milk wagon, laying the basis for his future career as a teamster and expressman.[51] She was only eleven when she came; although the circumstances of her arrival are indeterminate, we know that she was raised in the home of the Ladies Protection and Relief Society, a residence for abandoned children. She was the only Chinese child at the home. She did not have a Chinese name that she ever acknowledged but was called Mary McGladery after the assistant matron in the home who raised her. Miss McGladery taught the girl to read and write English, to play the piano, and to draw.[52]

At the time, nearly all Chinese in San Francisco were first-generation immigrants. The few merchant families with American-born children lived in the Chinese quarter and were not acculturated to American ways. We might think of Chew Dip and Mary McGladery as proto-Chinese Americans. They had adopted American manners and customs, but they were not "assimilated" because they were not actually integrated into the mainstream of society. They were liminal subjects, the only Chinese in their respective worlds and marked by a double difference—different from the white people around them, different from other Chinese.

After they married in 1875, they took the name Tape, most likely because "Joe Tape" sounded a little like "Chew Dip," and built a little house with a stable in the back on Green Street in a neighborhood called the Cow Hollow (now Pacific Heights). At the time, there were few people living in the area and almost no other Chinese—just a few domestic servants living in the homes of whites and, a bit further out near the Presidio, a few Chinese who held vegetable plots and a peach orchard.[53]

Chew Dip was not able to build a business in general drayage, probably because by the mid-1870s there was already too much prejudice against the Chinese. But he did find a niche working for Chinese merchants, hauling their imported goods up from the docks to Chinatown, and then expressing baggage for the Chinese immigrants arriving on Pacific Mail steamships. The young couple may have chosen to live in the Cow Hollow because Mary was not comfortable in Chinatown; unlike her husband, who was from Taishan, she did not speak Cantonese and did not have Chinese friends. Mary's inability to speak Cantonese also meant that she and Joseph spoke English, not Chinese, to each other.[54]

Mary Tape's domestic and social activities suggest a woman who was highly acculturated to conventional middle-class, Euro-American social norms. She birthed her children at home, attended by a Euro-American doctor. Unlike most Chinese merchants' wives in America, who were confined to the home, Mary participated in civil society. She exhibited her paintings at the Mechanics Institute's juried art shows, and as she became interested in photography, she joined the California Camera Club, an amateur society. By the 1890s, she had established a small reputation in San Francisco as a maker of lantern slides.[55]

Still, the Tapes sustained contacts with other Chinese, mainly through Joseph's business dealings. The vegetable men from the Presidio routinely left *bok choy* and *gailan* (Chinese cabbage and broccoli) on the Tapes' doorstep, as they passed through the Cow Hollow on their way to the Chinese quarter. Joseph also hired a Chinese nanny (*ah-ma*) to take care of his wife when she was ill.[56] Although details are sparse, the Tape household appears to have been a culturally hybrid space, where English was the dominant (but not only) language spoken, Chinese food was consumed, and company was mixed. Although highly acculturated to American ways, the Tapes were apparently more bicultural than asserted in Mary Tape's letter, that they were "same as Caucasians, except in features."

The Tapes could not have been unaffected by the anti-Chinese movement that gripped San Francisco politics in the late 1870s and 1880s. They could not have been unaware of this climate when they tried to enroll Mamie in Spring Valley school, but perhaps they harbored the hope that the girl, who spoke English and who could already read and write, would not be treated like ordinary Chinese.[57] Years later Mamie Tape recalled that her father was "determined to have us educated and [fought] like heck" to get her admitted to school.[58] The elder Tapes' commitment reflected their desire for assimilation. They were both literate in English, if not formally schooled, and they knew that their children had to be educated in order to participate in and be accepted by white society. Moreover, Mary's unusual upbringing by the English matron McGladery ensured that the Tapes' commitment applied to their daughters and not just to their son.

The creation of the segregated Chinese Primary School, however, suggested that assimilation, which had been a tenuous proposition at best, was now impossible. Indeed, notwithstanding their mother's vow that her children would "never!!!" attend the Chinese school, Mamie and her younger brother Frank were the first students to arrive when the Chinese Primary School opened, just five days after Mrs. Tape wrote her letter. For the Tapes, the decision to go to the Chinese school represented their determination to educate their children, but it also must have meant that they realized that the path to full acceptance by white society was closed. It is this recognition of their inability to assimilate that accounts for the deep anger in Mary Tape's letter.

According to a news story in the *Evening Bulletin*, a certain irony pervaded the first day of school. The Tape children were "dressed neatly in clothes like those worn of American children," but having never been to school before, they were "restless," unaccustomed to schoolroom discipline. The other four children who came to school, ten- and twelve-year-old boys wearing "queues and distinctive style of [Chinese] clothing," had all been to mission schools. The reporter observed that they all could read and write English, were proficient in arithmetic, and complied with the teacher's method of instruction.[59]

For several years, the Tape children commuted to Chinatown, riding to school each morning in their father's horse-drawn wagon. But things on Green Street were changing. By 1890, the block had become completely built up with a row of vernacular housing, and the neighborhood was filled with Euro-Americans of the middling class. Frank fought with the Irish boys in the neighborhood.[60] The Tapes also worried that their children's marriage prospects would be dim unless they met other Chinese. Interracial unions were not uncommon in the Northeast, but in California both law and social custom precluded such marriages. Mamie Tape recalled, "The folks moved downtown [to Chinatown], because there was too much *fan-yun* (fanren, or "barbarians," i.e. white people) they thought, [so they wanted us] to get acquainted with some Chinese boys and girls." In 1891, the Tapes moved to Chinatown.[61]

By now the Chinese Primary School had some seventy students. There were just two girls, including Mamie. Mamie and Frank probably did look "phunny" next to the other children in Chinese attire and likely took some abuse for their acculturation and privilege (they brought roller skates to school). Mary Tape did her best to maintain a household organized around Euro-American norms, with Western-style furnishings and music lessons. But the Tape children were also becoming Sinicized. Most important, they learned to speak Cantonese. They had already learned some Chinese at home, from their mother's nanny, but now they needed it to survive the Chinatown school yard.[62]

At least on one occasion, the Tape children wore Chinese outfits to school. They appear, so clothed, in a group photograph of the Chinese Primary School's pupils, taken in 1890 by Isaiah Taber, one of San Francisco's leading photographers.[63]

Mamie is the only girl in the photograph. Frank is seated to her right, his forelock tucked under the edge of his cap. In contrast to the plain dress worn by the other children, Mamie and Frank are wearing stylish garments made of silk. Mamie's dress is that of the current fashion in Shanghai,[64] suggesting not only the family's wealth but ongoing social and cultural knowledge, if not contact with China, as well. Most likely, Mamie and Frank did not wear these clothes to school every day but donned them especially for the occasion. But still, one wonders, did they like wearing Chinese clothes because it made them more like their friends? Or did they do so under pressure from the teacher—or from their parents?

Taber carefully composed the sitting, positioning the better-dressed children in the front two rows and Mamie at their center. But the children in plainer dress dominate the photograph. Taber achieved this effect by placing a very tall boy at the center of the back row; his height and his simple dark-colored gown, accentuated by the two boys flanking him in white, command our attention. It seems that Taber wished the Euro-American viewer to see a group of pupils of the laboring class, even though most of them, regardless of their dress, were children of merchant families. Because the exclusion laws did not allow Chinese laborers to bring wives into the country, there were few families of the laboring class at the time.[65]

An 1890 photo of the pupils at the Chinese Primary School in San Francisco taken by the well-known photographer Isaiah Taber. Mamie is the only girl in the picture. Her brother Frank is to her right. *(Courtesy of the Bancroft Library and Library of Congress.)*

Taber was not unsympathetic to the Chinese, but he was clearly invested in presenting a homogenous image to his audience. A photograph that included children in Western-style dress would have disrupted the common understanding of Chinese difference. It would also have given lie to the claim that the Chinese were unassimilable—the fundamental rationale for exclusion and segregation. Indeed, Joseph and Mary had both refuted that racist logic during Mamie's lawsuit by stating that she was "always clothed in the American costume." Both Taber and the Tapes believed that one's manner of dress signaled one's identity. Yet, they also understood that one could manipulate the signal to project a desired image that the putative authenticity of the bearer could, in fact, be staged.[66]

Mamie and Frank went to the Chinese school through the eighth grade. By then, enrollment had grown and the school had run out of space. The board came up with a plan to move the Chinese school into the basement of Commercial High School, on Powell Street between Clay and Sacramento. The fact that the high school had been closed and condemned as unsafe did not seem to worry the board, which calculated that the new site would save $1,000 a year.

The Chinese Primary School was already run on a meager budget; by one account, the expense of the existing school was $2,800 a year, far less than the $8,000 it received from the state to educate Chinese students.[67]

But the plan faced heated opposition from white property owners on Powell Street, which was one block outside the territory that had come to be defined as the Chinese quarter. The up-and-coming residents of Powell Street now associated themselves with the elites on the adjacent Nob Hill. They deployed incendiary language to police the racial boundary, claiming that the Chinese had an offensive smell and warning that that the value of their property would drop by 25 percent if Chinese began "strutting" along Powell Street. School board members offered plans to require the Chinese students to enter and leave the school by way of a side alley or a back staircase, which the board proposed to build "up over the forty-five foot hill from Clay Street," but these failed to appease the Powell Street residents. The board found an alternate site for the school on Clay Street.[68]

Perhaps it was this ugly incident that prompted the Tapes to leave Chinatown. Or maybe it was just the accumulation of racist incidents, large and small, that continued to dog the Chinese of San Francisco. True, the elder Tapes maneuvered around the strictures of segregation—Joseph worked for the Pacific Mail Steamship Co., and Mary was known as "the Americanized Chinese lady" among the city's artists and photographers.[69] But it was another matter that their children were growing up in Chinatown. Here, they were being socialized under conditions of racial isolation and the stigma of segregation.

Mamie and Frank, who had completed primary school, might have continued their education in San Francisco; in 1905, the board began to admit Chinese students to the regular city high schools. But the two younger Tape children, Emily and Gertrude, were still in primary school in Chinatown. To continue there meant that they would continually suffer from insults, like the decision that even the back entrance to the basement of a condemned school building was too good for them because it was in a white neighborhood. So, in 1895 Joseph bought a house on Russell Street in Berkeley, in a newly subdivided area in the south part of town, just a block from the Southern Pacific's rail line on Shattuck, and the family moved across the bay.[70]

Emily and Gertrude went to school in Berkeley, which did not segregate its schools. Frank went to Berkeley Commercial High School, although it is unclear whether he graduated. Mamie did not continue in school, yet she was probably the most educated Chinese girl in San Francisco at the time. Although the Tape family lived in Chinatown for only about five years, their stay there was terribly important. Joseph Tape's business success, of course, depended on a Chinese clientele, and his office would always be in Chinatown. Living in Chinatown was, perhaps, even more important for the Tape children. Attending the public school there not only gave them formal schooling, but more important, it made them part of a social cohort of Chinese

Americans. The Tape girls would all marry Chinatown boys. In 1897, Mamie married Herman Lowe, who was born in Chinatown and educated in the Baptist mission school there, and the couple settled in Chinatown. In 1901, Emily Tape married Robert Leon Park, the son of a Chinatown teamster. In 1913, Gertrude, the youngest Tape child, married Herbert Chan, the son of a Chinatown merchant.[71]

The men who married into the Tape family were themselves second-generation Chinese Americans who also became interpreters and brokers. In 1905, Frank Tape, Herman Lowe, and Robert Park's brother Edward were among the first Chinese to get jobs as interpreters for the Immigration Bureau. Robert Park worked as the official Chinese interpreter for the San Francisco Hall of Justice (the city's criminal court). The most highly educated member of the extended Tape family, Park graduated from high school in San Francisco and attended the University of California. He was a founding member of the Native Sons of the Golden State, the forerunner of the Chinese American Citizens Alliance, as well as a president of the powerful Sam Yup (Sanyi) Association.[72]

Joseph Tape himself became quite wealthy from the baggage monopoly he held for the Pacific Mail and the Southern Pacific Railroad and from myriad other kinds of brokering work, all related to the business of immigration. He became the Chinese passenger agent for the Pacific Mail Steamship Company and the Southern Pacific Railroad as well as a bonds broker, who guaranteed the departure of Chinese arriving in San Francisco on transit tickets for Mexico and Cuba and of Chinese ship crewmen desiring shore leave while in port.[73] A journalist described Tape's office in Chinatown as a quintessential immigrant brokerage and clearinghouse, a "link between Orient and the Occident" that served as an "informal information bureau where [immigrants'] problems are solved and questions are answered."[74] Joseph Tape's work and connections also provided jobs for his relations; at various times, Frank Tape and Herbert Chan worked directly for Joseph or held jobs with the Pacific Mail and the Southern Pacific.[75]

Joseph and Mary Tape's effort to distance themselves and their children from other Chinese was not, in the end, a strategy that would lead the family to economic or social achievement. The better strategy, as they discovered, the strategy that turned their liminality to greatest advantage, would be to play the broker and the interpreter.

The Rise of the Brokering Class

The broker is an interstitial subject, who translates and facilitates transactions between two cultures. Guides, envoys, translators, notaries, negotiators, and labor contractors are common figures in histories of conquest, colonialism, and immigration. Some possess iconic status in nation-founding myths, like La Malinche, Cortés's translator–mistress, and Squanto, the Wampanoag at Plymouth. Every immigrant group in American history has had its brokers—the Italian *padrone*, the Irish ward boss, the Mexican *coyote*. Bilingual and bicultural, the brokers were able to navigate the institutions of the host society on behalf of its newcomers.[76]

The Chinese immigration brokers and language interpreters were arguably the first "hyphenated" Chinese Americans. Contemporaries commonly called people like the Tapes "Americanized Chinese" well before sociologists theorized and circulated the concept of "assimilation."[77] In contemporary journalistic accounts, "Americanized Chinese" were defined by conversion to Christianity, acquisition of the English language, and adoption of Western-style clothing and customs. Writing in the early 1960s, sociologist Milton Gordon would consider these to be evidence of acculturation, a step toward assimilation. But Gordon also considered language and "exterior" matters like dress to be superficial adaptations to the "cultural patterns" of the host society. He believed that the "adoption of core values and life goals" indexed more durable acculturation, although he did not specify those values and goals. Although Gordon believed that acculturation was a prerequisite for assimilation, he did not believe that the former inevitably led to the latter.[78]

According to Gordon's concept, it is difficult to say just how acculturated the Tapes were. The Tapes were associated with the Presbyterian Chinese mission, but there is no evidence that they were baptized or that they were devout. They seem to have been like many other Americanized Chinese, who learned from the mission schools and churches Western social mores and conventions but not a deep sense of religiosity.[79] The Tapes' entrepreneurialism might be considered an American "core value," but it was also quintessentially Chinese. In any event, we can say that during Chinese exclusion, acculturation, even if extensive, did not lead to structural assimilation.

The brokers' knowledge and practice of American ways held a special premium in the segregated and marginalized community of Chinese immigrants. Their position as middlemen gave them an unusual measure of power. The brokers found their markets in the legal and social world of Chinese immigration, and brokering became particularly lucrative under the regime of legal exclusion. Although many immigration brokers engaged in legitimate businesses—in Tape's case, in expressing, bonding, and ticketing—exclusion also created an underground economy that supported illegal immigration. Indeed, exclusion generated a robust market for selling fake certificates of identity and coaching books, for arranging surreptitious border crossings and jumping ship, and for bribing immigration inspectors. Chinese secret societies ("tongs") controlled much of the smuggling business, but they invariably involved persons in the employ of transportation companies and the government.

Corruption was not limited to the Chinese but involved Euro-Americans as well, including ship's officers, immigration officials, and attorneys.[80]

Joseph Tape was implicated several times in illegal smuggling schemes, although he was never arrested. Twice he was suspected of having a role in alleged plots to land stowaways and in "substitution" schemes, whereby Chinese seamen, employed on trans-Pacific steamships and bonded (by Tape) for shore leave while docked at San Francisco, remained in the United States while Chinese wishing to return to China took their places on the return voyage.[81]

If Joseph Tape eluded arrest, his son Frank was not as fortunate. The younger Tape's career as a Chinese interpreter for the Immigration Bureau was marked by notoriety and scandal. In the 1910s, Tape, who was assigned to the Seattle immigration office, came under suspicion for alleged extortion of Chinese immigrants seeking admission into the country. He was acquitted of criminal charges of conspiracy to smuggle aliens after a sensational trial that involved the murder of a witness in Seattle's Chinatown.[82] Tape lost his job with the bureau and returned to San Francisco, where he worked at his father's bonding business. Within a few years, he had reinvented himself as a respectable middle-class citizen, marrying a Chinese American socialite and becoming, in 1923, the first Chinese American to serve on a jury in San Francisco. The *Chronicle* lauded him as a "real American."[83]

Conclusion

As gatekeepers and facilitators, brokers and interpreters like the Tapes operated along apposite vectors of immigrant experience: inclusion and civil rights, on the one hand, and exclusion and illegal immigration, on the other. They protested and profited from the discrimination against their co-ethnics; they enabled and subverted the regime of exclusion. The brokers were both esteemed and mistrusted by Chinese immigrants and Euro-Americans alike, their loyalties doubted on all sides. The very structure of brokering, however, involved pleasing or serving two sides, so that loyalties were necessarily divided. The broker had to know how to navigate that divided terrain through negotiation, manipulation, and accommodation; ultimately, the broker's loyalty was to his own survival and advancement. The Tapes' involvement in illegal immigration was thus not necessarily inconsistent with their advocacy for civil rights; each trend derived from their interstitial location and from their pursuit of self-interest.

Among the Euro-American ethnic groups, the power of brokers diminished with the social mobility of the second generation. The Chinese exclusion laws, however, meant that the Chinese American brokers had greater power over a longer period of time. But it also meant that they occupied a more prolonged liminal status. They were prototypes of another sociological figure, the "marginal man," the racial or cultural hybrid, who lived with a foot in each culture but belonged fully to neither. Sociologists imagined the marginal man as a figure of alienation and conflict; but they also saw him as a pioneer at the vanguard of group assimilation.[84]

The Chinese American brokers, however, did not pave the way for immigrant assimilation or racial amalgamation. Indeed, their existence, their fortunes as well as their woes, derived from the persistence of exclusion and segregation. But the brokers were pioneers of another sort. The history of the Tape family is a story about how immigration and exclusion created a site for the accumulation of wealth and social status among the first Chinese Americans as well as a site for the production of a Chinese American ethnic identity, an identity that valorized acculturation, education, and material success. In this version of Chinese American history, exclusion and inclusion were not successive phases of immigrant incorporation but were dynamically entwined, the result of a legal status that combined exclusion from immigration and naturalization with limited inclusion for residents and birthright citizens, a status that was defined in part by *Tape v. Hurley*. In this story, we might discern, in the checkered careers of self-fashioning and entrepreneurial agency of families like the Tapes, some of the processes that shaped class formation and social organization in early Chinese America.

NOTES

This essay is drawn from my biography of the Tape family, forthcoming from Houghton Mifflin. I am grateful to Him Mark Lai, Judy Yung, and Jack Kim for assistance with sources. For critical comments I thank Madeline Hsu, Sucheng Chan, and participants of seminars at the Davis Center for Historical Studies, Princeton University, and at Stanford Law School, where earlier versions of the essay were presented.

1. Him Mark Lai, "To Bring Forth a New China, to Build a Better America: The Chinese Marxist Left in America to the 1960s," *Chinese America: History and Perspectives* 8 (1992): 3–82; Renqui Yu, *To Save China, to Save Ourselves: The Chinese Hand Laundry Association of New York* (Philadelphia: Temple University Press, 1992); Madeline Hsu, *Dreaming of Gold, Dreaming of Home: Transnationalism and Migration between the United States and South China, 1882–1943* (Stanford, CA: Stanford University Press, 2000); see also Adam McKeown, *Chinese Migrant Networks and Cultural Change: Peru, Chicago, Hawaii, 1900–1936* (Chicago: University of Chicago Press, 1999). On the transnational turn, see Shelley Fisher Fishkin, "Crossroads of Culture, the Transnational Turn in American Studies," *American Quarterly* 57, no. 1 (March 2005): 17–55; Mae M. Ngai, "Transnationalism and the Transformation of the Other," *American Quarterly* 57, no. 1 (March 2005): 56–65; and Alfred Hornung, "Transnational American Studies," *American Quarterly* 57, no. 1 (March 2005): 67–73.

2. Gloria Chun, *Of Orphans and Warriors: Inventing Chinese American Culture and Identity* (New Brunswick, NJ: Rutgers University Press, 2000); Haiming Liu, *The Transnational History of a Chinese American Family: Immigrant Letters, Family Business, and Reverse Migration* (New Brunswick, NJ: Rutgers University Press, 2005).

3. This would have to be addressed empirically. My research suggests a variable experience among the second generation. For a study of second-generation identity formation in the contemporary era of globalization, see Philip Kasinitz, John Mollenkopf, and Mary C. Waters, eds., *Becoming New Yorkers: Ethnographies of the New Second Generation* (New York: Russell Sage, 2004).

4. *Tape v. Hurley*, 66 Cal. 473 (1885).

5. Charles Wollenberg, *All Deliberate Speed: Segregation and Exclusion in California Schools, 1855–1975* (Berkeley and Los Angeles: University of California Press, 1976); Charles McClain, *In Search of Equality: The Chinese Struggle against Discrimination in Nineteenth-Century America* (Berkeley and Los Angeles: University of California Press, 1994), chapter 5; Victor Low, *The Unimpressible Race: A Century of Educational Struggle by the Chinese in San Francisco* (San Francisco: East/West Publishing, 1982). Low's work, which relies largely on a reading of the San Francisco *Evening Bulletin*, was an important starting point for my research.

6. "What a Chinese Girl Did: An Expert Photographer and Telegrapher," *Morning Call*, November 23, 1892. See also "Our Chinese Edison," *San Francisco Examiner*, August 4, 1889. Unless otherwise indicated, all newspapers cited in this chapter were published in San Francisco.

7. *Chae Chan Ping v. United States*, 130 U.S. 581 (1889); *United States v. Fong Yue Ting*, 149 U.S. 698 (1893); *Yick Wo. v. Hopkins*, 118 U.S. 356 (1886).

8. *Brown v. Board of Education*, 347 U.S. 483 (1954); *Plessy v. Ferguson*, 163 U.S. 537 (1896).

9. *Plessy v. Ferguson*, at 561 (emphasis added).

10. Low, *Unimpressible Race*, 17.

11. "School for the Chinese," *Daily Alta*, June 9, 1853.

12. Ira M. Condit, *The Chinaman as We See Him and Fifty Years of Work for Him* (Chicago: Revell, 1900), 91; Timothy Tseng, "Ministry at Arms' Length: Asian Americans in the Racial Ideology of Mainline Protestants, 1882–1952" (Ph.D. diss., Union Theological Seminary, 1994), 52; "Claims of the Chinese on Our Common Schools, Card from the Rev. Mr. Speer," *Evening Bulletin*, June 20, 1857.

13. Condit, *The Chinaman as We See Him*, 93, 102–3; Guy Maine, "Report of Chinese Guild," in *Yearbook of St. Bartholomew's Parish, New York* (New York: Archives of the Diocese of New York, Episcopal Church, 1914), 1909; Wesley S. Woo, "Protestant Work among the Chinese in the San Francisco Bay Area, 1850–1920" (Ph.D. diss., Graduate Theological Union, Berkeley, CA, 1983), 118.

14. "Statistics of the Chinese Churches, Missions, Schools, and Institutions in North America," compiled by Chinese Sabbath School Association (New York, 1892), New York Public Library. According to the survey, there were 271 Protestant schools and missions in the United States and Canada, mostly run by Baptist, Presbyterian, Congregational, Methodist, and Episcopal churches. On conversion figures, see also Condit, *The Chinaman as We See Him*, 115.

15. In San Francisco, the Baptist Mission, Methodist Chinese Church, and Women's Occidental Board of the Presbyterian Church each sponsored day schools. "Statistics of Chinese Churches," 2–3; "Claims of the Chinese on Our Common Schools."

16. Low, *Unimpressible Race*, 7.

17. Wollenberg, *All Deliberate Speed*, 32.

18. Low, *Unimpressible Race*, 23.

19. Ibid., 27.

20. "Claims of Chinese on Our Common Schools."

21. Low, *Unimpressible Race*, 16, 27.

22. Christopher Lee Yip, "San Francisco's Chinatown: An Architectural and Urban History" (Ph.D. diss., University of California, 1985), 96; *Memorial, Six Chinese Companies, An Address to the Senate and House of Representatives of the United States: Testimony of California's Leading Citizens* (San Francisco, December 8, 1877), 21, 25.

23. Testimony of Cornelius B. S. Gibbs, cited in Frederick A. Bee, *Memorial, The Other Side of the Chinese Question: To the People of the United States and the Honorable the Senate and House of Representatives, Testimony of Leading Citizens, Read and Judge* (San Francisco, 1886), 30, 38–39, 47–48.

24. Alexander Saxton, *The Indispensable Enemy: Labor and the Anti-Chinese Movement in California* (Berkeley and Los Angeles: University of California Press, 1971); Yong Chen, *Chinese San Francisco, 1850–1943: A Trans-Pacific Community* (Stanford, CA: Stanford University Press, 2000).

25. *Daily Morning Call*, March 7, 1878.

26. Wollenberg, *All Deliberate Speed*, 33. Wollenberg also points out that regardless of the change in state law, the Chinese were still entitled to public education according to the 1868 Burlingame Treaty with China. From another angle, permanent settlement—especially if it entailed birthright citizenship—undermined exclusion by creating a legal method of entry for those Chinese claiming U.S. citizenship. More than a decade before *Wong Kim Ark*, the San Francisco press fretted that a Ninth Circuit ruling recognizing the citizenship of Chinese born in the United States "still leave[s] open the door for admission on proof of 'citizenship,'" anticipating, of course, the paper-son strategy, by which immigrants gained admission by claiming they were sons of native-born Chinese, that would sustain Chinese immigration throughout the exclusion era. *U.S. v. Wong Kim Ark*, 149 U.S. 649 (1898); *In re Look Tin Sing*, 21 F. 905 (1884); "Citizenship and the Interpreter," *Evening Call*, November 10, 1884, 2. On paper sons, see Erika Lee, *At America's Gates: Chinese Immigration during the Exclusion Era, 1882–1943* (Chapel Hill: University of North Carolina Press, 2003); Mae Ngai, *Impossible Subjects: Illegal Aliens and the Making of Modern America* (Princeton, NJ: Princeton University Press, 2004), chapter 6.

27. Census of Chinese children in "San Francisco Items," *Sacramento Union* February 4, 1885; data on Chinese attending nonpublic schools in Low, *Unimpressible Race*, 54. Yong Chen's sampling of the U.S. census in San Francisco indicated a marked increase in the number of U.S.-born children after 1870. Chen, *Chinese San Francisco*, 56.

28. Petition, "To the Honorable the Senate and the Assembly of the State of California, Signed by 1300 Chinese, Including the Principal Chinese Merchants of San Francisco, Sacramento, etc." [1877], trans. by J. G. Kerr, Bancroft Library, University of California, Berkeley.

29. U.S. Census of Population, 1870, 1880.

30. Low, *Unimpressible Race*, 17.

31. Gibson, who ran the Methodist mission in Chinatown, testified before many official commissions on behalf of the Chinese during the 1870s and wrote the lengthy tract *The Chinese in America* (Cincinnati: Hitchcock and Walden, 1877). He was despised by nativists, who burned him twice in effigy and attacked his mission on Washington Street.

32. Frederick Bee quoted in *Evening Bulletin*, October 4, 1884.

33. General School Law of California, Sec. 1662 (1880).

34. Wollenberg, *All Deliberate Speed*, 25–27.

35. *Evening Bulletin*, January 15, 1885; Wollenberg, *All Deliberate Speed*, 40.

36. San Francisco Board of Supervisors, *Report of the Special Committee on the Condition of the Chinese Quarter and the Chinese in San Francisco* (San Francisco, 1885), 59–62.

37. *Sacramento Union*, January 10, 1885, 8. Assembly Bill 268 added the following to Section 1662: "and also to establish separate schools for children of Mongolian or Chinese descent. When such separate schools are established Chinese or Mongolian children must not be admitted into any other schools." The provision was repealed in 1947.

38. The doctrine of plenary power in immigration was set in the *Chinese Exclusion Case* and *Fong Yue Ting*.

39. *Wong Kim Ark,* at 731 (J. Harlan, dissenting).

40. *Wong Kim Ark,* at 694.

41. *Slaughterhouse cases*, 83 U.S. 36 (1873).

42. *County of Santa Clara v. Southern Pac. RR*, 18 F. 385 (C.C.D. Cal. 1883), affirmed 118 U.S. 394 (1886). Morton Horowitz has persuasively argued that the theory of corporate personality did not emerge until the turn of the century and was then read back onto *Santa Clara*; the "real significance" of the case, according to Horowitz, was that it expanded the scope of the Fourteenth Amendment. See Morton Horowitz, *The Transformation of American Law, 1870–1960* (New York: Oxford University Press, 1992), 69.

43. *Lochner v. New York*, 198 U.S. 45 (1905). Justice Stephen Field, who in 1872 first argued for economic rights in his dissent in the *Slaughterhouse* cases, sat on the federal Circuit Court of Appeals, Ninth Circuit, in the 1880s and used the Chinese cases to rewrite his *Slaughterhouse* dissent into Ninth Circuit law, which then culminated in the Supreme Court's *Yick Wo* decision in 1886. See Thomas Wuil Joo, "New 'Conspiracy Theory' of the Fourteenth Amendment: Nineteenth Century Chinese Civil Rights Cases and the Development of Substantive Due Process Jurisprudence," 29 USF L. Rev. 353 (Winter 1995).

44. Linda Bosniak, "Membership, Equality, and the Difference That Alienage Makes," 69 NYU L. Rev. 1947 (December 1994).

45. Congress repealed the Chinese exclusion laws in 1943, as a wartime political measure aimed at combating Japanese propaganda that the United States held racist policies against Asians. Chinese Repeal, Act of December 17, 1943 (57 Stat. 600).

46. *Tape v. Hurley*, 66 Cal. 473 (1885), Affidavit for Writ of Mandate, 3–4.

47. The National Association for the Advancement of Colored People (NAACP) and the Japanese American Citizens League (JACL) were always careful to choose for test cases plaintiffs who were assimilated and middle class. When deployed in legal cases, however, the claims of the plaintiffs can not be taken at face value. Affidavits and photographs are carefully scripted briefs, not untrue but often based on selective truths made for the purpose of argument. On racial uplift, see Kevin Gaines, *Uplifting the Race: Black Leadership, Politics, and Culture in the Twentieth Century* (Chapel Hill: University of North Carolina Press, 1996).

48. *Daily Alta*, April 16, 1885, 1.

49. Newspapers routinely published correspondence between individuals and the school board and board of supervisors, probably as an easy method of reporting on the business of these official bodies.

50. Mrs. Tape's letter is read in Asian American Studies courses and can be found on various Asian American civil rights Web sites. The letter began to circulate after it was reprinted in Judy Yung, ed., *Unbound Voices: A Documentary History of Chinese Women in San Francisco* (Berkeley and Los Angeles: University of California Press, 1999); more recently, the letter was featured in the Organization of American Historians' *Magazine of History* (Winter 2001).

51. In some documents, "Chew" is written as "Jeu." Joseph Tape's obituary states that he delivered milk for Matthew Sterling's dairy farm on Van Ness Avenue in San Francisco. Sterling is listed in the 1870 census with a fourteen-year-old Chinese male servant in his

household. "Joseph Tape, Local Pioneer Is Dead," *Daily Gazette* (Berkeley), March 11, 1934, 16; U.S. Census of Population, 1870.

52. "What a Chinese Girl Did." The assistant matron Mary McGladery, but not the child, is listed in the 1870 census.

53. The U.S. Census of Population, 1880, lists Joseph Tape's residence at 1771 Green Street. The Sanborn Fire Insurance Map for San Francisco (Vol. 2, 1893) shows only three houses on the 1700 block of Green Street. The Tapes' neighbors were Euro-Americans of the middling class, a carpenter and a printer's widow. The only other Chinese in the neighborhood were a few random domestic servants. Discussion of vegetable men in Him Mark Lai and Philip Choy, interview with Mamie Tape Lowe and Emily Lowe Lum, July 29, 1972, Portland, Oregon (copy in possession of author). I am grateful to Him Mark Lai for sharing this tape recording with me.

54. "What a Chinese Girl Did."

55. On home births, see Interview with Mrs. Herman Lowe, July 7, 1930, file 5017/562, Records of the Immigration and Naturalization Service, RG 85, National Archives—Pacific Alaska region (Seattle); on Mary Tape's artistic endeavors, see *Art Catalogue of the Twentieth Industrial Exposition of the Mechanics Institute of the City of San Francisco, 1885* (San Francisco: P. J. Thomas, 1886), 51–53, 104; "Our Chinese Edison"; Peter Palmquist, *Shadowcatchers: A Directory of Women in California Photography before 1901* (Acatia, CA:P.E. Palmquist, 1990), 215. On domestic isolation of Chinese merchants' wives in America, see Judy Yung, *Unbound Feet: A Social History of Chinese Women in San Francisco* (Berkeley and Los Angeles: University of California Press, 1995).

56. Lai and Choy, interview with Mamie Lowe and Emily Lum.

57. Florence Eveleth, the teenaged daughter of Mary Tape's friend and neighbor, Sarah Eveleth, taught Mamie and Frank reading and arithmetic. She later took credit for encouraging the Tapes to enroll Mamie in school and even for urging Joseph Tape to sue after Mamie was denied entry. This may have been the case, although Tape would not have needed a white person to tell him about his rights. Chinese businessmen were adept at using American courts, and the Chinese Six Companies and Chinese consul were already bringing test cases; Tape knew people in the consul's office, having served as an interpreter for them at times. Florence [Eveleth] Fontecilla, Statement made to E. C. Benson, inspector in charge, March 29, 1940, file 12016/8690, San Francisco district 12016 case files, Records of the Immigration and Naturalization Service, RG 85, National Archives and Records Administration—Pacific-Sierra Region (hereafter "INS-SF"). On Chinese merchants and the courts, see Todd Stevens, "Brokers between Worlds: Chinese Merchants and Legal Culture in the Pacific Northwest, 1852–1925" (Ph.D. diss., Princeton University, 2003). On test cases, see McClain, *In Search of Equality*.

58. Lai and Choy, interview with Mamie Lowe and Emily Lum.

59. *Evening Bulletin*, April 14, 1885, cited in Low, *Unimpressible Race*, 71–72.

60. Sanborn Fire Insurance Company map of San Francisco, 1893, vol. 2 (microfilm); Fontecilla statement to E. C. Benson. On Frank fighting with Irish boys, see oral history interview with Ruby Kim Tape by Jeffrey Chan, December 12, 1974, Combined Asian American Resources Oral History Project, Bancroft Library, University of California, Berkeley.

61. Lai and Choy, interview with Mamie Low and Emily Lum. California and most western states barred blacks, American Indians, and "Mongolians" from marrying whites. In northeastern states, which did not have antimiscegenation laws, Chinese men frequently married white women. A number of Chinese men who studied at Yale University as part of the Chinese Educational Mission, including its founder Yung Wing, married middle-class Euro-American women. See Thomas LaFargue, *China's First Hundred: Educational Missions*

in the U.S. (Pullman: Washington State University Press, 1987). In New York City, Chinese laborers commonly married Irish and native-born white and black women. See John Tchen, *New York before Chinatown: Orientalism and the Shaping of American Culture, 1776–1882* (Baltimore: Johns Hopkins University Press, 1999); Mary Lui, *The Chinatown Trunk Mystery: Murder, Miscegenation, and Other Dangerous Encounters in Turn-of-the-Century New York* (Princeton, NJ: Princeton University Press, 2005).

62. Lai and Choy, interview with Mamie Lowe and Emily Lum.

63. Photograph by Isaiah Taber, 1891, brk00001331_16a, Bancroft Library, University of California, Berkeley, available online in Chinese in California Collection, Library of Congress (http://memory.loc.gov/cgi-bin/query/D?cic:1:./temp/~ammem_UyqX:); on Taber, see also Anthony Lee, *Picturing Chinatown: Art and Orientalism in San Francisco* (Berkeley and Los Angeles: University of California Press, 2001).

64. See fashion plate #15 (1891, Shanghai) in Zhou Xibao, *Zhongguo gudai fushi shi* (Taipei: Nantian, 1989), 533. I thank Dorothy Ko for this reference.

65. Erika Lee, *At America's Gates*, 92–94.

66. The process could also work in reverse. Interestingly, not a few Chinese Christian preachers in the late nineteenth and early twentieth centuries presented themselves in Chinese dress, perhaps as a way to suggest to prospective converts that Christianity did not make one less Chinese. By the turn of the century, the Chinatown missions were also sponsoring Chinese-language schools. These practices underscored the missionaries' principal aim, which was not to Americanize but to prepare the Chinese for evangelical work in China. See Woo, "Protestant Work among the Chinese," 123. For contemporary photographs of Chinese Christians in both Western- and Chinese-style dress, see Louis Beck, *New York's Chinatown* (New York: Bohemia Publishing, 1898), 235, 267, 279; Condit, *The Chinaman as We See Him*, 121, 128–34, 159.

67. Low, *Unimpressible Race*, 79–80.

68. Ibid.

69. Palmquist, *Shadowcatchers*, 215.

70. Lai and Choy, interview with Mamie Lowe and Emily Lum; Wollenberg, *All Deliberate Speed*, 44. Joseph Tape purchased the house, a two-bedroom Victorian cottage, from the developer William Bissell, for about $1,000. Berkeley property assessment records, 1895, 1896, Bancroft Library, University of California, Berkeley. I thank Daniella Thompson for this reference.

71. U.S. Census of Population, 1910, 1920; Lai and Choy, interview with Mamie Lowe and Emily Lum; Statement of Robert Park, January 31, 1921, file 12016/1898, San Francisco District 12016 case files, INS-SF; Statement of Wong Fun [mother of Herbert Chan], November 15, 1920, file 24563/9–4, San Francisco District 12016 case files, INS-SF.

72. "Chinese Blood Goes into the Bureau," *Morning Call* April 4, 1905, 7; Statement of Robert Park, January 31, 1921, INS-SF; U.S. Census of Population, 1900, 1910; Lai and Choy, interview with Mamie Lowe and Emily Lum; *History of the Sam Yup Benevolent Association* (San Francisco: Sam Yup Benevolent Association, 2000), 214.

73. Tape's expressing business for passengers arriving on Pacific Mail ships and Southern Pacific trains is described in advertisements that appeared regularly in *Zhongxi Ribao* during the first two decades of the 1900s. In 1907, Tape was described as a "wealthy expressman . . . [who] is engaged by railroad and steamship companies to look after Chinese immigrants in transit through the U.S." See *Morning Call*, April 4, 1904. The U.S. Census of Population, 1910, lists Joseph Tape as a "transportation clerk" for the Southern Pacific Railroad. On Tape's bonding business, see Edward White to Commissioner General, exhibits A and C, May 10, 1922, file 12019/01, entry 9, Records of the Immigration and Naturalization

Service, RG 85, National Archives (Washington) (hereafter "INS"). A reporter described the Tapes' business as the "link between Orient and the Occident" in San Francisco's Chinatown. They "handle the bonding work among the Chinese for the Pacific Mail Steamship Company, the Southern Pacific, and the Toyo Kisen Kaisha Steamship Company, besides settling many business matters for the people of Chinatown. They maintain an informal information bureau where problems are solved and questions answered." "Former Policeman and U.S. Investigator Takes up New Post," clipping fragment, ca. 1923, copy in Frank Tape file, Him Mark Lai papers, Ethnic Studies Library, University of California, Berkeley.

74. "Former Policeman and U.S. Investigator Takes up New Post."

75. Before working for the Immigration Bureau, Frank Tape held a job as "transportation guide" for the Southern Pacific Railroad. U.S. Census of Population, 1900. Herbert Chan worked as a clerk for the Pacific Mail Steamship Company and as an assistant to Joseph Tape's bonding work. Letter from Herbert Chan to Railton, March 1, 1922, box 52aE, Records of the Pacific Mail Steamship Co., Huntington Library (San Marino, CA); Edward White to Commissioner General, May 10, 1922, INS.

76. Norma Alarcón, "Traddutora, Traditoria: A Paradigmatic Figure of Chicana Feminism," *Cultural Critique* 13 (Fall 1989): 57–87; Neal Salisbury, "Squanto: Last of the Patuxets," in *Struggle and Survival in Colonial America,* ed. David G. Sweet and Gary B. Nash (Berkeley and Los Angeles: University of California Press, 1981), 228–46; Gunther Peck, *Reinventing Free Labor: Padrones and Immigrant Workers in the North American West, 1890–1930* (New York: Cambridge University Press, 2000).

77. The most influential theory of immigrant assimilation was developed by Robert E. Park and the "Chicago school" of sociology in the interwar period. Park argued that a defining social process of modern society, especially urban society, was the "race relations cycle," in which immigrants and racial minorities experienced successive stages of contact, competition, accommodation, and eventual assimilation. Robert E. Park, *Race and Culture,* vol. 1, *Collected Works* (New York: Free Press, 1950), 149–50.

78. Here Gordon revised Park's view that assimilation was organic and inevitable; Gordon's pessimism derived in large part from the persistent socioeconomic subordination of urban blacks and Puerto Ricans, which vexed social scientists in the 1960s. Milton M. Gordon, *Assimilation and American Life: The Role of Race, Religion, and National Origin* (New York: Oxford University Press, 1964). For a recent appraisal of assimilation theory, see Richard Alba and Victor Nee, *Remaking the American Mainstream: Assimilation and Contemporary Immigration* (Cambridge, MA: Harvard University Press, 2002). Alba and Nee argue that assimilation does not mean only integration into the social and economic mainstream but can also include incorporation into subordinated or marginalized social structures.

79. I could not establish definitively that the Tapes belonged to the Presbyterian mission church, but the evidence suggests an association, if not membership. The elder Tapes were married in 1875 by the Reverend Augustus Loomis, head of the San Francisco mission. After Mamie Tape married Herman Lowe, the couple lived across the street from the women's rescue mission on Sacramento Street, and Mamie became a close friend of Tien Fook Wu (Wu Tianfu), the assistant to Donaldina Cameron, matron of the Presbyterian mission for Chinese women, although Mamie herself was not a churchgoer. Frank Tape and Robert Park are mentioned in mission publications. The Tapes were also probably associated with the Knox Presbyterian Church in Berkeley, which was built across the street from their home there in 1896. *Tape v. Hurley*, [Joseph Tape] Affidavit for Writ of Mandate; Lai and Choy, interview with Mamie Lowe and Emily Lum; author interview of Carolyn Lum, August 8, 2005, Portland, OR; Ira Condit, "Americanized Chinese," *Woman's Work* 17 (August 1902): 219.

80. On practices of illegal immigration and corruption in the Immigration Bureau, see Erika Lee, *At America's Gates*, 189–222.

81. Richard H. Taylor to Commissioner General, "Escape of Chinese Crewmen," July 2, 1909, file 52114/4A, INS; "Chinese Smuggled in by Mail Ships," July 24, 1908 [San Francisco *Examiner*], file 52114/4, INS; John B. Densmore, Report to Secretary of Labor Wilson, January 11, 1916, INS (microfilm, supplemental reel 4); Statement of Watchman David F. Graham, December 8, 1915, INS (microfilm, supplemental reel 4). See also Robert Barde, "The Scandalous Ship Mongolia," *Steamboat Bill* 250 (August 2004): 112–18.

82. Testimonies of Frank Tape, Henry White, Ralph Bonham, and Seid Gain Jr. (August 1914), in "Smuggling of Asiatics," *Industrial Relations: Final Report and Testimony* (Washington, DC: Government Printing Office, 1916), 6121–29, 6154–73. See also the following articles in the *Seattle Times*: "Tape Arrested on Smuggling Charge," April 16, 1914; "Chinese Shot as Sequel to Tape Inquiry," September 21, 1914; "Chinese Suspect Gives Himself Up," October 7, 1914; "Defendants Win in Tape Prosecution," December 11, 1914.

83. On dismissal of Frank Tape, see Ralph Bonham, Memorandum to Commissioner General, August 22, 1914, and Commissioner General, Memorandum for the Secretary, September 2, 1914, file 5300/910B, INS; on jury service, see "First Chinese Called on Jury Here Real American," *Chronicle,* March 20, 1923.

84. Robert E. Park, *Race and Culture*, 111–12, 354–56; Everett V. Stonequist, *The Marginal Man: A Study in Personality and Culture Conflict* (New York: Scribner's Sons, 1937).

2

The Activism of Left-Wing and Communist Chinese Immigrants, 1927–1933

Josephine Fowler

In the wake of Chiang Kai-shek's anti-Communist coup in China in April 1927, as the ongoing intraparty struggle within the Kuomintang (KMT, the Nationalist Party) became ever more fierce, the Workers Party of America (renamed in 1929 as the Communist Party of the United States of America—CPUSA) formally recognized its Chinese immigrant members by forming, in May, a Chinese National Fraction of the party. Two months later, when the KMT–Chinese Communist Party (CCP) United Front had ended but in name, there was a corresponding collapse of cooperative relations between KMT branches in the United States and the Workers Party of America. At the beginning of the following year, the Communist International (Comintern) and the Central Executive Committee (CEC) instructed the Chinese members in the United States "to dissolve all branches of the KMT that we controlled and to withdraw from the KMT." The Comintern also forced Chinese immigrant Communists to resign from their positions in *Kuo Min Yat Po*, the KMT party organ.[1]

For too long, left-wing and Communist Chinese immigrants have been absent from the landscape of the history of the American Communist movement and in Chinese American history. Asian Communism has been seen strictly as a phenomenon in the non-Western world. The first scholar to challenge this master narrative was Him Mark Lai, who began in the early 1970s to recover painstakingly the history of activism among left-wing Chinese in America. In his pathbreaking article, "To Bring Forth a New China, to Build a Better America: The Chinese Marxist Left in America to the 1960s," Lai offered both the first periodization and a detailed narrative of the Chinese Marxist Left.[2]

Building on Lai's work and drawing on materials in the newly opened Comintern archives in Moscow, I examine the experiences of Chinese immigrants who were active in the American and international Communist movements from the spring of 1927 through the latter part of 1933. Up to the early 1930s, activists devoted much attention to events in China and expressed a strong interest in returning to China at some not-too-distant future time to participate directly in the revolutionary movement there. By late 1933, the Central Committee (CC) of the Chinese National Fraction within the CPUSA had moved away from policies that had isolated Chinese party members from surrounding Chinese ethnic communities in the United States toward more broad-based cooperation with organizations that shared "similar ends in view" and that drew in "unorganized and undeveloped workers." At the center of these new efforts was the "mass" organization, the American Friends of the Chinese People, formed in the spring of 1933. Even as the activists began to embrace this new policy, they continued to put much energy into finding ways to support the Chinese revolution and sustain close ties with the CCP.[3]

At the same time, Chinese immigrant party members were forced to wage another struggle within the movement itself. In addition to their isolation, a small membership, the repeated loss of leading members who left for the USSR and China, a perpetual lack of funds, ongoing and bitter factional struggles among district and national party leaders, harassment by the KMT and by U.S. immigration authorities, and the ever present threat of arrest leading to deportation, issues of concern to Chinese communities within the United States were ignored by the American party leadership. To complicate matters further, these party leaders expected the Chinese immigrant activists to conform to policies that construed all members of the American party as individuals who were eligible for naturalized U.S. citizenship while simultaneously treating them as natives of China. Even among party leaders who worked closely with and demonstrated their commitment to sustaining the Chinese activists' efforts, the paramount interest was to support the revolutionary forces in China and to defend the Soviet Union. When it came to developing strategies and organizing at the local level, the activists were largely alone.

The membership of the American party during the 1920s was, in Nathan Glazer's words, "overwhelmingly composed of relatively recent immigrants." By 1925, the party included an English section and eighteen organized foreign-language federations. In that year, however, the party reorganized itself in a process commonly referred to as Bolshevization, which aimed to "Americanize" the party and to root it in the "American" working class. In short, the foreign-language federations were to be abolished, and the basic unit of the party was to become either the "shop nucleus" or the "street nucleus."[4] Members of the various foreign-language groups did not universally accept such a process without question as they struggled to reconcile ethnic self-identity with internationalism and to cope with pressures to "Americanize."[5]

At the top of the party was the national office. In descending order of authority came the district, the subdistrict, the section or local (consisting of street and shop units in a given area), and the shop unit or nucleus. Various departments, which were also organized at the national, district, section, and shop unit levels, supervised the daily work carried out by members of fractions who worked within nonparty "mass" organizations, such as fraternal and cultural associations and branches of the International Labor Defense (ILD) and the U.S. Section of the Anti-Imperialist League (also known as the All-America Anti-Imperialist League, American Section—AAAIL).[6] In general, fractions consisted of small groups of party members working within nonparty organizations, whereas foreign-language members "with a special interest in foreign-language work were organized into 'sections' or 'bureaus.'"[7] However, in the case of Chinese members, both non-Chinese and Chinese party members used interchangeably the terms *fraction*, *bureau* (or *buro*), and *section* to refer to the Chinese members' structures at the national and local levels.

The Apparatus for Chinese-Language Work in the Party

Organizational efforts advanced quickly during the second half of 1927. On April 13, 1927, the District Executive Committee (DEC) of District 13 (California, Arizona, and Nevada) resolved that a "Chinese fraction be formed"; around the beginning of May the "fraction was organized." In June, after forming a "provisional National Executive Committee of Left-wing Chinese Fraction," the Chinese National Fraction decided "to call [a] conference of left wing representatives." Among the issues to be addressed at this conference were "Support of Hankow, Support of Soviet Russia, [and] Cooperation with [the] Communist Party." In October, at the first national conference held in Chicago, participants wrote a constitution for the Chinese National Fraction in America. In November, some of them secretly established a National Bureau or Buro (also known as the Central Bureau or Buro) of the Chinese National Fraction "under the leadership of the Central Committee of the Communist Party of America," consisting of five members and situated in San Francisco. At the end of the year, approval was given to launch a weekly mimeographed Chinese-language "Chinese Communist paper," *Kungchang*.[8]

Shi Huang (aliases Tontien and Dongsheng),[9] the first secretary of the National Bureau of the Chinese National Fraction, had been the leader of a group of Qinghua University students in China who in the spring of 1923 had formed a group called Chaotao, the objective of which, according to Him Mark Lai, "was to effect national salvation through political action," taking inspiration from "the revolutionary spirit of Sun Yat-sen and V. I. Lenin." The following summer, Shi and group member Xu Yongying (Hsu Yung-ying, also known as Y. Y. Hsu) met with Chinese Communist Party founder Li Dachao and Sun Yat-sen. They imparted to the other group members that they had learned from the two senior revolutionaries that the group's "primary objective" was "to promote and support the revolutionary cause in China."[10] That fall, Shi and fellow Chaotao member Ji Chaoding (Chi Ch'ao-ting, also known as C. T. Chi) left for the United States. Once there, Shi entered Stanford University, while Chi traveled eastward and enrolled at the University of Chicago. By the following fall, in the wake of the May Thirtieth Massacre in Shanghai,[11] all the remaining Chaotao members except Luo Zongtang had come to the United States to study. They included Xu Yongying, Zhang Yucang (Chang You-jang), Mei Ru'ao, Hu Dunyuan, and Luo Jingyi, who stood out not only because she was the sole woman in the group but also because she was fluent in Cantonese, which would prove to be of great value to the activists in America. Under the direction of Shi, they gathered as a group in Berkeley, California, and "unanimously resolved that while seeking an education in this country they would actively work to further the goals of the Chinese Revolution"[12] and to "spreading the ideas of communism and revolution among the Chinese workers and students" in America.[13] When the group's first national conference was held, there were only "two and [a] half and not well-organized branches." The Chinese National Fraction had eighteen members, of whom ten classified themselves as "workers" and eight as students. Two other members had recently "1eft [the] U.S. for Europe."[14]

Given these small numbers, it is not surprising that other sources give far more subdued accounts of the work being carried out under the leadership of the Chinese National Fraction during the months following its formation. An unnamed "Chinese comrade," who delivered a "Chinese report" to a District 13 DEC meeting held in San Francisco in early May 1928,[15] first stated the aims of the fraction—namely, "to carry on work among the Chinese workers, do anti-Imperialist [*sic*] work and to train comrades to go back to China and carry on the work there." After noting that the Chinese National Fraction's National Bureau was located in San Francisco and citing party membership figures (a total of "about 24," with five in San Francisco, eight in New York, three in Chicago, three in Madison, and four in Philadelphia), he proceeded to detail the activities pursued over the past year. Marking what would become a trend over the years, it was not the members of the "CP group," but rather, members of the "CY Group" (also known as Young Workers League or Young Communist League—YCL), numbering "about 9 in S.F.," that had been most active. They had "organized a workers club with about 19 member [*sic*]," "publish[ed] a paper regularly," and "conduct[ed] many mass meetings." They were also "organizing a restaurant workers union" and were trying "to establish a workers school under the auspices of the students group," which was "under the control of the CY group." In the wake of the KMT-CCP split in China, the removal of "our editor," Xu, from the "KMT paper," and withdrawal of party members from the KMT, the main endeavor of the activists was to form, in January 1928, a "united front organization," Meizhou Yonghu Zhongguo Gong-Nong Geming Da Tongmeng (American Grand Alliance Supporting the Chinese Workers and Peasants Revolution—ACWP), with "the purpose of attacking and exposing the KMT."[16] Shortly after, the ACWP began issuing a mimeographed Chinese-language weekly newspaper, *Xianfeng Zhoukan* (The Vanguard), as its organ.[17] The ACWP also established other branches in cities with significant numbers of progressive Chinese and attempted to persuade Japanese party members to act in solidarity with the Chinese members in both national and immigrant arenas.[18]

Four months earlier, in a letter to AAAIL Secretary Manuel Gomez, Chinese activists in San Francisco had shed light on the prospects for "spreading the ideas of communism and revolution among the Chinese workers and students" in America. They summed up the dilemma as follows: "Nearly all the Chinese residents here are Cantonese. . . . Only two of the seven Chinese comrades here (Suarez [Chang Hen Tang or Benjamin Fee] and Tsetung [S. S. Lo]) are Cantonese, while the rest are not Cantonese and cannot speak the Cantonese dialect." Actually, one other "comrade," Luo Jingyi, in San Francisco at that time was not only a native speaker of Cantonese but also a talented orator and teacher who "moved everybody in the audience" when she delivered speeches to San Francisco's Chinese community about the Chinese people's "resistance against imperialism," and who, under Shi Huang's instruction, also gave lessons in Mandarin to the community.[19] For most of the other activists, "It is very difficult for us to work among a people with whom we cannot communicate in the same language. This language difference has greatly handicapped our work in the past." In addition, "all the Chinese Comrades here are students, not workers," which made it "difficult for the students to mix up with the workers and still the more difficult when the former are engaged in their studies."[20] Moreover, "The majority of the Chinese comrades here are 'outsiders,' and do not intend to stay in American [*sic*] for more than five years." The end result: "At present we can hardly get some chinese [*sic*] workers here into our fraction and even if we can, they are not qualified to take important responsibilities."[21]

The last two points were not strictly true because YCL member Benjamin Fee, the son of an American-born interpreter, had been working "at various jobs as a cook in San Francisco" since his arrival in the United States in 1923. Similarly, Xavier Dea (Xie Chuang—also known as Dea Chang, Dea Wood, or

Dea Woo) had been "a restaurant worker, a fruit gatherer, and did some other kinds of work" since he came to the United States in 1923, and he, too, had joined his father, a local fruit store merchant, in San Francisco.[22] These comments raise an important issue that the left-wing Chinese activists would later acknowledge at their second national conference in February 1929 when they looked self-critically at their efforts thus far. They wrote that one of "the principal causes of our defects" was "underestimation of the revolutionary potentialities of the masses, condemnation of masses, segregation from masses, and defetism [*sic*]."[23] Ironically, being active in local Chinese communities was more difficult than at the national and international levels.

A month earlier, Shi Huang had reported to Gomez that the first meeting of the Central or National Bureau of the Chinese National Fraction, held on November 20, 1927 in San Francisco, had grappled with two pressing and knotty matters, namely, "APPLICATION FOR MEMBERSHIP" and "THE QUESTION OF APPROACHING THE CHINESE AS COMMUNISTS." The crux of the second dilemma was that "The Central Bureau holds that unless some Chinese comrades are ready to approach the Chinese as communists and openly preach Communism, it will be very difficult to win over the Chinese workers and sympathizers to our side. But there is danger of being deported if the American Government discovers." In theory, the solution was straightforward: "find some Chinese comrades who have American citizenship, to do this work."[24] Implementing the solution, however, proved far more difficult. At the second national conference held more than a year later, "native place" was not noted in the membership lists or mentioned in the discussion. Rather, one had to go to the second to the last page of the report, in the section "TASKS OF THE CHINESE FRACTION," to find a reiteration of the earlier directive: "Recruit more working class elements and native born Chinese into the Party."[25]

In addressing the question of recruiting members, focus shifted from within the Chinese community to the relationship between the Chinese activists and the larger party leadership. The participants decided upon two "method[s] of procedure." According to the first scenario, the District Organizer (DO) should refer a Chinese applicant's "application card" to the "imperialist [*sic*] Committee of the National Office of the American Party and the Imperialist Committee will refer it to the Central Bureau of the Chinese National Fraction for approval." Alternatively, the "Chinese Branches may also introduce new members." However, in the event an applicant was considered "suspicious," not only should the first method "be resorted to" but also "approval of the National office of the American Party should be obtained."[26] A month later, the Anti-Imperialist Committee approved a motion that reaffirmed the authority of the Chinese National Bureau, declaring: "we approve the recommendations of the Chinese Bureau relative to the approach of new members and relative to the regulations for taking Chinese members in to the Party."[27]

Meanwhile, the party leadership had already arrived at a decision on the matter. About seven months earlier and in response to District 13 DO Emanuel Levin's question, secretary-general of the American party, Jay Lovestone, reaffirmed the authority of the party leadership: "All members must go through the National Office when they are received, so that we may check up with the connections we have here." Levin also raised the issue of disclosure. He understood that Chi was "in charge" of "admission of Chinese to the Party," and that Chi had informed Shi that their membership was "to be kept secret from the rest of the party." Although he considered this "a very wise move at this time," there seemed "to be a tendency here to treat this question by some of the other members just as we would other workers."[28] To this, Lovestone responded, "In almost all cases the connection should be confidential, not public. This does not mean they should not attend unit meetings, however. They should participate in unit meetings, but should exercise greater care than others."[29]

That there existed confusion if not open disagreement over the rules is evident. Lovestone's statement revealed the basic contradictions in the party's treatment of its Chinese members. On the one hand, like "other workers," all Chinese membership applications must "go through the National Office," but in evaluating these applications, the National Office would turn to "the connections we have here." It is highly likely that these contacts were valued for their access to information about each individual's relationship to the KMT branches in America and in China, as well as to the CCP. In simultaneously denying the special circumstances of the Chinese members and recommending that they remain ever sensitive to these circumstances, Lovestone was perpetuating the age-old misreading of the situation confronting the Chinese in America and placing the burden of exclusion on the shoulders of the Chinese activists themselves.

Left-wing Chinese immigrant activists, however, could never forget the realities of exclusion and discrimination. As they noted at their second national conference in February 1929, "our work among Chinese in America cannot fail to give due attention to the question of national minority," namely, the "vicious social prejudice fostered by American imperialists and the social, political, and economic discrimination and oppression against the Chinese."[30] Nor did they seek to sever their connections with China. In fact, among this first cohort of leading Chinese immigrant party members, there was a strong orientation toward events in China and a great deal of interest in returning to China in the near future to participate directly in the revolutionary movement there.

Until the end of 1927, left-wing activists devoted much energy to working within the KMT and, importantly, "under the name of the KMT"[31] even as they debated whether to continue the policy of cooperation under a united front. In a jointly written letter relayed by Shi in early December 1927, Chi and

Y. C. Chang reported on their interview with the former head of the political department of the Chinese revolutionary army, Comrade Teng Yen Ta. They had learned that the "majority of the Chinese communist party are not in favor of cooperating with the KMT as they did before." Although they had not been informed of the "attitude of the Communist International," Chi and Chang believed that "we should change our policy." More specifically, they "express[ed] the opinion that the policy of the Chinese national [*sic*] Fraction in America should be on the same line with the Chinese Party." They were "in favor of converting the KMT members directly into Communists." They "also stress[ed] the importance of organizing the left wingers of the KMT."[32] Shi reported that the next issue of the left-wing Chinese-language newspaper *Hu Tang Te Kau*, of which he was editor, would "be devoted to the discussion of cooperation between the KMT and the Communist Party," calling attention to the fact that this was "at present the most important question confronting every responsible member of the party."[33]

This question lay at the center of the raging battle then taking place at the highest levels of the Comintern over the disastrous failures of the united front policy. In late December, members of the party's Anti-Imperialist Committee, led by Director of the Anti-Imperialist Department Gomez,[34] began to debate such questions as how Chinese immigrant Communists should "prepare for a split in the KMT here" while at the same time "immediately organizing all possible forces in a left wing, welding together expelled branches and connecting them with left wing . . . [*sic*] in the KMT, etc." A motion was passed that explicitly linked the Chinese immigrant Communists directly to the revolutionary movement in China even at the cost of any support for the activists' commitments to U.S.-based activism. "The chief task of the Chinese Communists in America is to mobilize around themselves and their leadership the Chinese workers and peasants in an open organization, locally and later on nationally, for the purpose of giving organized support to the Chinese Revolution." In using the descriptor "Chinese workers and peasants" to refer to Chinese laborers in the United States, the national leaders once again showed their confusion over the difference between the Chinese in the United States and those in China as they dogmatically applied a China-based model in the U.S. context.[35]

Building Mass Organizations of "Asiatic Workers"

When it came to anti-imperialist initiatives and mass organizations, party leaders generally marginalized "Asiatic workers." There is no mention in the records of the AAAIL, which like the ACWP was formed some time in early 1928, or of the ACWP or the organization that succeeded it at the end of 1929, the All-America Alliance of Chinese Anti-Imperialists (AACAI—also known as the Chinese Anti-Imperialist Alliance of America).[36] Rather, one finds only scattered references to anti-imperialist organizations of Chinese in the United States and to "Orientals" as "individuals and representatives of organizations." Nor were members of ACWP invited to participate in the AAAIL's 1929 "national tour on the subject 'The Struggle against World Imperialism, The Frankfort [*sic*] Congress and Latin-America.'" Only more than halfway into the tour did the secretariat of District 13 decide that "speakers would include [Benjamin] Fee, [and a] Filipino (if possible)."[37] Such neglect existed despite the fact that a number of leading left-wing and Communist Chinese immigrant activists were appointed to the General Council of the U.S. Section of the AAAIL, which, like the ACWP and the Chinese Bureau, was headquartered in New York City.[38] Among party members were K. M. Chen, Li Daoxuan (Li Tao Hsuan, alias Toddy, referred to as "Chinese, student"), Zhang Bao (Mo Zhengdan or Me Guoshi, aliases Xuehan and James Mo, also referred to as "Chinese, student"), Y. Y. Cheng, and Chi. Among nonparty members were Tsiang Hsi-Tseng (referred to as "Chinese, intellectual"), and Hu Dunyuan (Thomas T. Y. Hu), a representative of the Chinese Students Alliance.[39]

For their part, in January 1929 Fee reported that the Chinese National Fraction had resolved to organize an "Oriental branch, of All America Anti-Imperialist League," toward which aim "the Chinese Fraction and Japanese comrades formed the Sino-Japanese Anti-Imperialist Federation." Although "this league is not yet functioning," the Chinese activists were nonetheless "prepared to draw up the work for all Oriental workers on the Pacific Coast for Anti- Imperialist work."[40]

Perhaps spurred to action by the efforts of the Chinese and Japanese activists, sometime in the first part of 1929 the national party leadership took the initiative: The Administrative Committee of the U.S. Section of AAAIL issued a "Call for a National Convention of the All-America Anti-Imperialist League (United States Section). To Be Held in New York City, April 20–21, 1929." Among other groups, the call was "addressed to all anti-imperialist organizations of Chinese, Japanese, Hindoos [*sic*] and others residing in the United States . . . as well as to all the branches of the United States Section of the All-America Anti-Imperialist League."[41] As it happened, given the convening of "special Negro, Latin-American and Far Eastern conferences,"[42] the New York conference was pushed to June 15 and broadened to include conferences in Chicago and San Francisco. The timing of the party's actions was connected to the Second World Congress of the League Against Imperialism and for National Independence scheduled for July. In "view of this, and under the instructions of the International Secretariat," AAAIL International Representative Louis Gibarti wrote the secretariat "to request the C.P. of the U.S.A. to give the utmost possible support to this important international work."[43]

In mid-May, the DEC of District 13 formed a committee to organize "a Pacific Coast Bureau of our Asiatic fractions, which shall work toward the

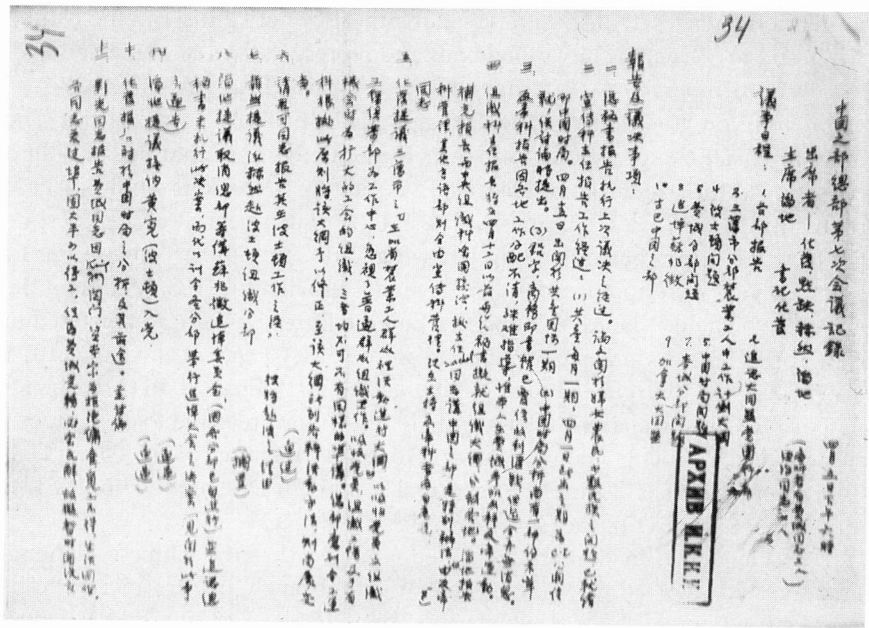
34

中國支部總部第七次會議記錄

АРХИВ ИККИ

building of mass organizations of Asiatic workers, with the aim of calling a conference to organize an Asiatic federation, mostly along anti-Imperialist [*sic*] lines." At a meeting a week later, the group learned that Gibarti had written that a regional Anti-Imperialist League Conference was to be held no later than June 2, 1929. Two days after that, the Committee on Oriental Work met to discuss this matter; and later that night, newly appointed District 13 DO Emil Gardos wrote to Gibarti informing him of the committee's criticisms—the problem of "slowness of the National Office in informing us about this Conference" and the more serious charge, "that no anti-imperialist work whatsoever was done in the past. All the comrades know of was the formation of some Party-committee last year, which did not work whatsoever." There was no reference to San Francisco-based Chinese activists' anti-imperialist efforts.[44]

Still, recognizing "the importance of this work," the committee "decided to go ahead" to convene the "Western Conference" on June 23. Plans included "the arranging of smaller conferences through the Seattle District and the Los Angeles Subdistrict," which would then "send delegates to the Frisco Conference," and the mobilizing of "a group of people to sign the call." Gardos elaborated,

> We are laying of course great emphasis to the drawing in of the Mexicans, Orientals, Negroes etc in this work. Among the signers of the Conference call we hope to have the editors of the Chinese left

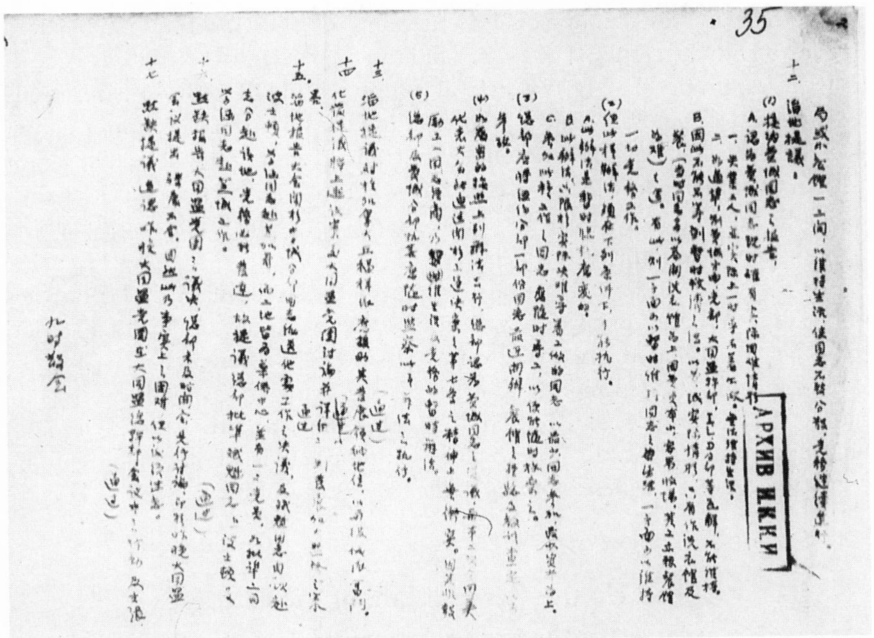
35

АРХИВ ИККИ

Minutes of the seventh meeting of the Chinese National Fraction's Central or National Bureau, Communist Party of the United States of America, April 5, 1929. The agenda is shown at the beginning (right side) of the first page of the two-page document, followed by a discussion of the items under numbered headings (the numbers are shown at the top of each page). Present at the meeting were Li (secretary), Xu (acting secretary), James Mo, and Xavier Dea. Note the stamps in Cyrillic letters—an indication that this copy had been transmitted to the Soviet Union. *(Courtesy of the Library of Congress.)*

> Kuo-min-tang paper, Pa blo [*sic*] Manlapit, who is in L.A.[,] the chairman of the CUCM (Mexican indep. Union in Los Angeles) and a few more representatives of oppressed peoples. . . . We will also try to secure prominent liberals, such as Upton Sinclair, Robert Whittaker, Austin Lewis, etc and active AFL trade-unionists, presidents of 1–2 local unions, together with our own comrades to sign the call, such as [Anita] Whitney, H[arrison] George, Japanese and Chinese comrade [*sic*], etc.

These were ambitious and surprising plans indeed—ambitious in regard to "the drawing in of the Mexicans, Orientals, Negroes";[45] surprising because of the aim to bring together such a broad constituency at a time when the party was for the most part openly hostile to cooperating with "liberals" and "AFL trade-unionists."[46] It was "the opinion of the DEC that there is a splendid field for anti-imperialist work in the Western Coast and we are going to do our best in that direction."[47]

When the Western Regional Conference of the AAAIL, U.S. Section, opened on Sunday, June 30, 1929, in San Francisco's California Hall, a remarkably diverse group of sixty-two delegates representing fifty-two organizations assembled. Delegate Ben Falcon, representing the Philippine Legion of Labor, pointed out what was most notable about this gathering, namely, that it was "the first Conference which he attended, where white workers speak against racial discrimination and where there is a unity between all colors and races in fighting capitalism, the common enemy."[48]

At the end of June, instructions were given for "Building AAAIL Branches in Localities Where None Exist." Specifically, the "backbone of the organization must be the affiliated organizations and nationality branches." The former should include "trade unions and other labor organizations, political organizations, liberal groups, anti-militarist societies, etc.," and the latter, "Chinese, Filipino, Latin American."[49] Meanwhile, Chinese activists redoubled their energies to organize Chinese workers in their own communities.

"Lead Up the General Life of the Chinese Masses in America"

In late 1927, left-wing Chinese activists began to pay greater attention to the struggles of workers in Chinese communities within the United States. The shift, as Lai points out, was especially important because "it marked the reorientation towards the labor movement of many in the Chinatown left who had outgrown their student careers." For instance, before former university student Xu Yongying (alias Huafa) left for the East Coast in late spring of 1928, party members Li Gan and Xu advised Xavier Dea and his classmates to reorganize Sanminzhuyi Yanjiushe (Society for the Study of the Three People's Principles) into the Gongyu Quluobu (Kung Yu Club—After Working Hours Club). Along with Dea, who became a leader in the club, the roughly dozen or so active members included other former San Francisco Chinese Students' Association activists as well as a number of workers from Chinatown. Then, in early 1928, in a further effort to reach out to Chinatown's workers, the club again transformed itself, this time into the Huaren Gongrenhui (Chinese Workers' Club).

In spite of the change in orientation, the group was unable to remove itself from intraparty politics. It split into a pro-KMT faction, Huaqiao Gonghui (Overseas Chinese Club), that focused on providing job placements, and a left-wing faction that reclaimed the name Kung Yu Club and continued to work with the American labor movement. However, once reformed, both the original Kung Yu Club in San Francisco and a branch that formed in Walnut Grove, California, which was also called the Kung Yu Club, sought to take part in and initiate labor organizing drives among Chinese workers in the area. The club in San Francisco tried to organize Chinatown restaurant workers. Apparently, Lai writes, "This attempt failed when the organizers made demands so out of line with Chinatown realities that few workers found them credible."[50]

The Chinese activists' labor organizing at the local level was by no means limited to actions taken by this single group. In his report to the District Convention in January 1929, Benjamin Fee enumerated the labor groups formed and other labor-oriented initiatives in which they had participated. Fee played a leading role not only at the local level in San Francisco's Chinatown but also at the district and national levels among the non-Chinese party leadership. He often represented the Chinese National Fraction and "Chinese workers" before or on party committees, in spite of the fact that he was a YCL rather than a CP member, because he was fluent in English and Chinese.[51]

One of the arenas in which the Chinese Fraction was active at the local level and in which Fee was a leader was youth work. Fee summarized the activities of the Young Workers League (YWL) Unit #7 (composed of the Chinese Students Alliance in U.S.A. and the Chinese Youth in S.F. [San Francisco]), calling attention to its success in "captur[ing] the Students Alliance."[52] Although Fee's report did not indicate a special interest in labor issues on the part of left-wing Chinese students and youth, the report by YWL representative Minnie Carson revealed that "in S.F. the comrades refused to do industrial work . . . and gave an excuse that the work is not important because we have no proletarian workers in that nucleus." In contrast, the young Chinese activists proved a striking and ironic exception to the rule: "The Chinatown nucleus is the only active nucleus in industrial work. They organized a club, laundry work and industrial work." Unlike the party as a whole, these activists had a more flexible understanding of what constituted "industrial" work within the immigrant economy.[53]

Nor was this the only instance in which Chinese youth stood out in terms of dedication to the movement. When it came to election work, Carson reported, "When the comrades were called upon to distribute leaflets, only the Chinese comrades reported for this work" despite the fact that at this time few Chinese were eligible to vote. Finally, they were among the most outspoken on issues of discrimination. For instance, following the recent formation of a "University fraction in Berkeley," the "segregation question of Berkeley was brought up." Members pointed out that the university "tried to keep the Orientals[,] Negroes[,] and Mexicans, students from the University campus and around the schools." Carson added, "Immediately all the Orientals called a mass meeting," which was attended by a League representative who "presented a policy which they were to follow."[54]

Less than a month later, at the second national conference the bureau issued a fuller statement, "Work among the Masses," articulating the larger set of beliefs that underlay the Chinese activists' efforts to organize Chinese workers in their local communities. As Communists who were dedicated to the class struggle, as well as the struggle against all forms of imperialism, with the ultimate goal of bringing about the "Proletarian World Revolution," they placed their activism at the local level within this larger framework: "To work among the masses is the basic task of the Fraction. Our line of work is to educate the Chinese workers in America in their class struggle, to arouse their class consciousness, to organize them into real working class organizations, to work within the already established workers' associations in order to win them over, and to bring them together with the workers of other nationalities in America to fight against American Imperialism." Impossibly ambitious as such a declaration appeared to be, it was immediately followed by a remarkably frank admission of failure: "But we must admit that not much satisfactory result has been brought about."[55]

The report cast a critical eye at what had been done thus far. The number of members had increased from eighteen in September 1927 to thirty-three in February 1929 in spite of the fact that nine had "Left U.S. for Europe [en route to Moscow] in August 1928." However, there were many weaknesses in the Chinese National Fraction's work:

> We have published a labor monthly called Kon Yu, Which [*sic*] is the first and the only labor Chinese publication in America. It was not very well editied [*sic*] and its circulation is still not very extensive. We have organised [*sic*] several labor associations such as the Kong [*sic*] Yu Club, in Walnut Grove, the Chinese Workers Association in California, the Kong [*sic*] Yu Club in San Francisco, the Chinese Workers' Alliance in New York, the Chinese section fo [*sic*] the International Labor Defense in Philadelphia, etc. Chiefly due to inexperience on our part, we have not been able to develop these organisation[s] [*sic*] into the desired shape. The present situation is that one has been disintegrated (N.Y.). One has fallen in the hands on the right wing (Calif.)[,] one is not well controlled[,] and two (San Francisco and Philadelphia) are without larger membership.[56]

The comrades also remained active "within the old organizations like the Seamen's Clubs in Phia. [*sic*] and N.Y. and the Unionist Guild in San Francisco," had "approached . . . women workers in San Francisco," and had "distributed leaflets among the Chinese workers telling them not to break the strike and to give full support" to the striking "Pullman Negro Porters." Furthermore, they had "carried on a campaign to aid the Chinese Trade Unions" and attempted "to make connection with the Chinese Seamen working on the foreign ships along the West Coast." Unfortunately, "due to strict vigilance of the ship owners and them [*sic*] immigration offecers [*sic*]," the latter effort had "not been yet successful." Given the relatively small number of activists in various cities, the record was dizzying in scope and level of activity. However, none of the above merited special praise, which was reserved for a single action that "must be recorded as a great step forward in our work among the Chinese masses"—the recent strike of Chinese laundrymen and women in which "our comrades there were able to some extent to direct the movement, and became connected with the strikers."[57]

The laudatory comments were well deserved as the action was indeed significant on a number of counts. First, the very fact that the strike had occurred among Chinese laundry workers, who were organized into the Sai Fook Tong (Chinese Laundry Workers Union), in which "about 15% are women workers," was noteworthy.[58] Second, the workers had won all their demands "except pay for time lost" as a result of their weeklong strike beginning at noon on Monday, January 28, 1929. These included the twin demands "All workers, men and women, to belong to the Union," and "No discrimination."[59] Throughout the process of organizing the walkout, the union followed democratic procedures.[60] Third, the action involved both the party's "Chinese Units, League and Party," and non-Chinese party organizers. Among the Chinese activists, "Billy" played the key role in his capacity as representative of the Kung Yu Club along with Dea as representative of the ACWP, the two serving with "Manus" on the Advisory Committee to the Strike Committee. Also active was Fee; among non-Chinese party activists "Manus" and "Ellen" were the lead organizers, with Emanuel Levin providing some assistance and guidance.[61] Fourth, the strike was significant in terms of the breadth of support it received. Notably, "the Japanese Workers Club (our own organization) issued leaflets in Japanese which were translated into Chinese also. [C]alling upon the Japanese workers to help the Chinese workers and not to act as scabs, urging them to place their solidarity before the Chinese strikers." In addition, the ILD offered to place "the services of the ILD at the disposal of the strikers, that they will take over the defense in case of any persecution." Within the Chinese community, support came from the Kung Yu Club, the Chinese Labor Alliance, ACWP, the Union Guild, some Chinese papers, and both YCL and party members. Given the broad level of support, it is surprising that news of the strike did not spread very far among the non-Chinese party rank and file. Because of this, DEC member Joe Modotti resolved, "As a member of the Buro, hereafter I will make a point of arranging frequent meetings with the Chinese comrades for the purpose of mutual help and work."[62] But the rank and file and party organizers were, in fact, never told about what was happening next door in the Chinese community.[63]

The strike was a landmark: It was the first time a Chinese organization was invited to attend a meeting of the San Francisco Labor Council thanks to strenuous efforts on "Billy's" part. Indeed, even the notoriously anti-Chinese *Seamen's Journal* published an article that said: "This incident is of historic significance—first, because never before had a duly accredited delegate of organized Chinese workers appeared on the floor of San Francisco Labor Council; second, because the strike illustrates forcibly the terrible contrast in the working conditions of white and yellow." Nonetheless, the journal saw no contradiction in broadcasting its harangue about the "threat" and "menace" of "Asiatics."[64]

Even with this recent victory so fresh in the minds of the assembled group, national conference participants in February acknowledged many weaknesses in their work. After detailing problems at the local level, the report summarized "the principal causes of our defects." Of the eight points, all but two centered on internal factors—problems of "language and dialect difficulties," with "Cantonese working class comrades . . . not all participat[ing] actively in Party work"; "condemnation of the masses, segregation from masses"; and "1ack of a clear analysis of the conditions of the Chinese community." The two external causes were "poor relation[s] with the Party[,] lack of guidence [*sic*] and assistance from the Party," and "tremendous financial difficulties." This was not the first time that the Chinese National Bureau had called attention to the last two problems,[65] which, from the perspective of the activists, were connected.

Nor had the Chinese party members avoided raising the twin subjects in their respective districts. The same report noted, "our Philadelphia comrades complained that they had contact with the D.O. only when the District wants money." And in January, Fee called to the notice of his district the "serious inattention of the Party." Of particular concern was the situation in Chicago where "the DO there did not know there was a Chinese Buro even." On the financial question, the report listed a string of instances in which the CEC had not come through with aid: "The casese [*sic*] of subsidiary to the publication of the Chinese 'Communist' in the end of 1927, of sending comrades abroad [to study in Moscow before going to China] in the Summer of 1928, of subsidiary of the 'Communist' and delegate to the National Conference of the Fraction this year are some examples."[66]

Although the leading members of the Chinese National Fraction for the most part framed the issue as a problem, what was equally apparent from their remarks was that the activists enjoyed an unusual degree of independence relative to the party leadership. For instance, in reviewing the "Organizatiional [*sic*] Problems of the Fraction," the February 1929 report noted: "With the exception of San Francisco the Chinese Units do not have organizational contact with the District. They work independently and are quided [*sic*] only [*sic*] by the National Buro." The report astutely pointed out that "lack of attention on the part of District was the cause of the independent character of the Chinese Unit in the Disricts [*sic*]." From the perspective of at least one party leader, such behavior should serve as a model for others. At the District Convention in January, Emanuel Levin singled out the Chinese and Filipino members for praise: "We must all understand Communist initiative better; the Chinese report and San Juan report gave an example of real initiative. The Chinese and Filipinos speak various dialects and cannot understand each other and have accomplished a great deal."[67]

It did not follow, however, that the party leadership welcomed such independence. In July 1929, the national leadership leveled severe criticism at the Chinese immigrant Communists for convening a national conference.[68] Five months after the gathering, then-secretary of the bureau Li Daoxuan relayed the new directives issued by P. Smith, secretary of the "recently established" CEC of the Language Department: "The Chinese Buro is an agent of the C.E.C. and does not represent the Chinese party members as a national group[.] It follows that the Chinese Party members can hold no national conference hereafter, neither can they creat [*sic*] the Buro . . . that all members of the Buro must reside in New York; that the Chinese Buro is now under the jurisdiction of the Department." According to Comrade Smith, "the Buro had to be reorganized."[69] Once again the party leadership was refusing to acknowledge the special position of Chinese immigrants within the American nation. As "aliens ineligible to citizenship," they were not at liberty to shed their identity as a "national group" and assimilate into the larger society. Nor could the group operate directly under the jurisdiction of the party's Language Department—no members of the Language Department knew Chinese and few Chinese activists knew English.

The activists themselves had already reorganized the bureau with its transfer from San Francisco to New York shortly after the national conference in February. It consisted of Li as secretary, Xu as acting secretary, He Zhifen (Chee Fun Ho, alias Hazen) and two others as central committee members (one possibly being H. T. Chang, as he was named "industrial organizer of the Buro," and the other being Xavier Dea), and Zhang Bao as an alternate.[70] In October the Language Department "appointed to the Buro: Li (student), Liu (worker), Lo (worker), Mo (worker) and Chi (student). Comrade Li was appointed secretary."[71] At the first meeting of the new Chinese National Bureau held on October 25, 1929, a number of decisions were made, including initiating the process of reevaluation that would culminate by the end of that year in ACWP's reorganization as AACAI. In addition, the Bureau "request[ed] the Party to help set up an indepent [*sic*] printing press in N.Y.," and it "decided that the Chinese 'COMMUNIST' [*Kungchang*] shall be still published twice a month."[72]

Finally, Li reported publication of a special pamphlet 'The Chinese in America and our Tasks.' Even as he reminded the group of "the organizational mistake and also factional opportunist formulations" for which Smith had reprimanded them, Li "emphasized the usefulness of the parts dealing with the

Chinese community." The aim in producing such a publication was "to draw critism [*sic*] and suggestions from Chinese comrades so that it will be a basis for a better and more correct program of action among the Chinese." This comment did not necessarily imply that either Li or the other members of the bureau were unwilling to follow specific party directives or the larger party line, although on at least one occasion they cautioned against accepting directives from the Comintern "simply as a matter of discipline." Rather, "the correct path" should be one that has been "verified by the experiences" of the American party and "especially of the Chinese branch."[73] Li was fully cognizant of the fact that the bureau must look not to the party leadership but to their fellow activists for recommendations regarding a "more correct program of action among the Chinese."[74]

About two months later, as part of the nationwide recruiting campaign, which aimed to move the party in the direction of "becoming the mass political Party of the working class of the United States," Li prepared a document, "Instruction of the Chinese Buro." Following party procedure, Li submitted "an excerpt from the instruction in Chinese" to the CC of the Language Department. The first two sections covered only "essential points" that were "also published in the Language [Department's] paper, the 'Communist.' " The third section, however, was not only "a direct translation from the Chinese version" but also "was omitted [from the Language Department's paper] due to the secret character of the work of the Chinese comrades."[75]

In the third section, before listing the "General Points of the Campaign," Li outlined the larger context. Four "conditions" must be emphasized: first, the current "radicalization of the American workers . . . [to] not exclude the Chinese"; second, the "rising of the new revolutionary wave in China," coupled with the "revolutionary influence" of "the heroic struggle of the American workers" over "the Chinese Workers"; third, the "Reorganization of the Chinese Fractions," which meant that the Chinese party members now "join the regular Party units . . . and understand more about the line, tactics, and work of the Party as a whole"; and fourth, the "Secret Character of the work of the Chinese Comrades." Of the four, the last condition was the one "which differentiates the method for the recruiting Drive [*sic*] of the Chinese Fractions to some extent from that of the Party." "In other words," Li explained, "we must successfully apply the general line of the Party to the specific conditions under which we work." In particular, "unlike the Party that can publicly appeal for membership, we can recruiting [*sic*] new members mostly from those we have organized in our fraternal organizations where the Chinese worke [*sic*] can be testified [*sic*] and trained before joining the Party." Thus, once again, Chinese immigrant Communists were articulating the delicate and contradictory nature of the position they occupied. Even as they acquiesced to party protocol and "join[ed] the regular units," they were compelled to point out that the "specific conditions under which we work" necessitated that the fourth condition override the third and that they be allowed to continue to work separately within their own immigrant communities.[76]

Isolation and the need for secrecy were not the only dilemmas that left-wing Chinese activists confronted at that time. In Philadelphia and New York, the far more pressing problems were unemployment, underemployment, and the resulting poverty. Li reported at the end of May 1929, "during the past two months comrades in Philadelphia and New York most of them lose jobs." Thus, it was "absolutely impossible for the Buro to tax the membership."[77] Similarly, "reports from comrades in Philadelphia" indicated that the activists there were "really in a difficult situation":

> The unemployed workers couldn't find jobs in a short time, thus their livings are not supported. . . . Therefore temporary relief measures have to be taken. In Philadelphia, only workers in laundry and restaurants could get support for their livings (currently workers are mostly in laundry, this is mainly due to the small capitals they have and also to the competition from the farmers). On the one hand, they can earn support for their livings; on the other hand, all the party's activities are still maintained.

In response to these reports, the Chinese National Fraction's National Bureau emphasized that relief measures were only "temporary and subject to change" and that "these methods are only applied to those who really have problems in finding new jobs. The fewer the participants and the shorter the time, the better." Moreover, recipients of this assistance were reminded that they "should keep looking for jobs so that the supply could be saved for others once they get jobs." On a more positive note, the bureau mentioned that "some comrades in New York recently opened a restaurant" and recommended that the National Bureau "should summarize the experiences and lessons," presumably so that they might serve as a possible model for those in Philadelphia.[78]

With the onset of the Great Depression, the situation became even more dire. Zhang Bao recalled that just as "a large number of people were unemployed," so the "Chinese people there faced the same situation." During 1931–32, the activists reported "instability in work," and in Boston there was "*fear for work*." By late August 1932, Zhang reported that the Chinese Bureau in New York was "in such bad financial condition that it can hardly buy stamps and envelops [*sic*]," not through any fault of their own but because "most of the Chinese comrades are unemployed." Although in the past, both during the second half of 1928 and more recently, individual members of the bureau had spent money "from their pockets" on office expenses and to "send comrades to Moscow," this was no longer an option. Even the most privileged members, namely, the students, could no longer keep the bureau afloat[79] because in late August 1929, when news of their "revolutionary activities" reached China, Qinghua University had cut off its financial support for Xu, Chi, and several other left-wing students. To make ends meet, Xu "sold newspapers on the street, polished shoes for pedestrians, and waited at tables in restaurants."[80]

Another problem that continued to haunt the activists wherever they were located was the combined threat posed by immigration authorities, the KMT right-wing, and local police, who could not only harass the foreign-born but also threaten them with deportation. For instance, in 1929, "the San Francisco police, perhaps egged on by the KMT right-wing, raided the headquarters of the San Francisco Chinese Students club [*sic*] and closed it for alleged communist activities."[81]

To sum up the situation at the end of the 1920s, it is clear that the Chinese immigrant Communists had achieved a remarkable consolidation of their apparatus, with the establishment of a national bureau and local branches in New York, San Francisco, Philadelphia, Boston, Chicago, and Madison, and regular publication in Chinese of not only *Kungchang*, *Xianfeng Zhoukan*, *Kung Yu* (*Gong Yu,* the Chinese edition of *The Worker*), and *Chinese Students Monthly,* but also "Marine Workers," "Restaurant Workers," "Laundry Workers" and "Agricultural Workers."[82] In addition, the National Bureau directed a number of mass organizations, including the AACAI; a Chinese Workers Club in San Francisco; Chinese branches of the ILD in Philadelphia, San Francisco, and New York; and a Chinese Section of the Food Workers Industrial Union in New York. It had fractions within the Chinese Seamen's Club in Philadelphia, the Chinese Unionist Guild, the Chinese Workers Alliance in Chicago, and the Chinese Students Alliance in the United States. Yet, the activists worked within a context in which successes were highly vulnerable to setbacks, if not dissolution of the organizations altogether.[83]

Taking "A Great Step Forward of the Communist Movement among Chinese Masses in America"

On April 3, 1930, the first issue of the AACAI's Chinese-language newspaper *Xianfeng Bao* [*Chinese Vanguard*] appeared. Such an event was no small feat. Just to be able to launch the publication, the bureau ran up $1,900 in expenses. In addition, a "monthly deficit of $200.00 for six months" was projected.[84] In its former incarnation as *Xianfeng Zhoukan*, the mimeographed paper had served as the organ of the ACWP. By contrast, this new "printed weekly" was to "carry strictly a party line, and develop wider connections preparing the ground for an official party organ. For the time being," however, it would be "a Party organ without a label."[85]

This description of the transformed newspaper suggested the subtle change in orientation then taking place among the leading Chinese immigrant Communists at the beginning of the 1930s. First, "overt activities in support of the Chinese revolution had ebbed among the Chinese in America. The Kuomintang right, in collaboration with the police and supported by the conservative merchants, gained control in the community."[86] However, as loyal Communists who adhered to and therefore viewed events through the lens of Third Period doctrine, this was a time of crisis and revolutionary possibility.[87] "Our Party must take advantages [*sic*] of the growing favorable situation to educate and organise [*sic*] the Chinese masses and lead them closer to the general life and struggle of the American working class." What is especially significant is not simply the issuing of this directive but the fact that the activists suggested a need to foreground local work over efforts to "rally them [the Chinese masses] to the support of the revolutionary struggles in China."[88]

At the same time, in a move that seemed to work at cross-purposes to the above directive, members of the CC expressed a strong desire to strengthen relations with the Chinese in China and to build close ties with the CCP. For instance, in discussing why such "a mass agitation organ is IMPERATIVE," they called attention to the "strong reactionary propaganda among the tremendous Chinese population, (about 15 Chinese dailies alone in America)," and made the following additional points: "Furthermore, the coming weekly is not only the revolutionary organ of one million Chinese in this continent, but is also the organ of the nearly eight million Chinese outside China. . . . It is needless to mention the importance of this Paper to the C.P. of China, because . . . we have set up a printing shop which will supply partially propaganda materials to the latter in time of need."[89]

The Chinese immigrant Communists obviously understood that their activism not only was bound up with the Communist movement in China but was also international in scale: They identified with and pledged commitment to speak on behalf of the millions of "Chinese outside China." The CC of the CPUSA made it clear that the bureau had in no way abandoned or even moderated its revolutionary beliefs and commitments. In deciding "to enlarge the 'Chinese Vanguard,'" the bureau had received "the approval of the Party, the Chinese Delegation at Moscow and also the Eastern Department of the Comintern." The CPUSA's secretary of the Language Department CC endorsed the Chinese Bureau's joint proposals "to organize a wide campaign in connection with the Soviet Congress in China, May 30th," and "to have greetings sent through the Chinese Vanguard weekly [*sic*] to China." The question of "enlist[ing] support to the Chinese revolution . . . concern[ed] not only the Chinese Bureau of our Party but the whole Party."[90]

There were, in fact, several contradictory forces at work. On the one hand, the bureau was beginning to grapple more seriously with the problem of "segregation from [the] masses" and was forced to work within an increasingly dangerous and inhospitable environment. On the other hand, according to Third Period doctrine, Communists were entering a period of sharpening contradictions, and "the increasing revolutionary activities of workers and peasants in Americas greatly influenced the Chinese masses here." As members of a national section of the Comintern, it was the duty of the Chinese immigrant Communists to act as the vanguard of such a revolutionary upsurge. Giving added weight to this duty, ideological, cultural, and personal connections tied the Chinese activists in America to Chinese revolutionaries in China, in Moscow, and elsewhere in the world, as well as to the leadership of the Eastern Department of the Comintern. The American party firmly supported the National Bureau's alignment with the Chinese revolutionary movement and its efforts to direct attention to anti-imperialist struggles overseas.[91]

During the first two years of the 1930s, the Chinese National Fraction and its branches in the United States both grew and stagnated. In June and July of 1930, there were 72 party members out of 285 members in "Org. controlled by the Party" but only 2 party members out of 105 members in "Org. influenced by the Party." In February 1929, there had been only 33 party members, which means that in sixteen months the nationwide membership had increased by 39 members. As small as such an increase might seem, it must be seen against the backdrop of the severe penalties incurred by party members whose identities local KMT leaders or immigration authorities discovered. Under these circumstances, perhaps as significant a measure as formal membership in the party was the material assistance given to activities organized by the National Bureau, its branches, and the mass organizations it directed. For example, the bureau received a "Collection among Chinese" totaling $1,000 as "INCOME" for launching *Xianfeng Bao*.[92]

Local branches of the bureau enjoyed some success in the party-led unemployed movement. In January 1931, under the leadership of Dea, the Kung Yu Club in San Francisco formed a San Francisco Chinese Unemployed Alliance as a branch of the larger party-led Unemployed Council in San Francisco. It mobilized "several hundred unemployed Chinese in Chinatown to march on the Chinese Six Companies [Chinese Consolidated Benevolent Association, CCBA] to demand immediate relief." "Later many of these participants also joined a massive demonstration of the unemployed in San Francisco's business district." As Lai comments, "this marked one of the earliest instances of American Chinese taking part in such an event outside Chinatown." This initiative was part of a broad effort to expand its base in the Chinese community. "Since 1930 . . . the Seamen group, the unemploed [*sic*] alliance, the needle trades group had been formed." Shortly after the above demonstration, the Kung Yu Club established the Huagong Zhongxin (Chinese Workers Club) to assist Chinese workers looking for work as well as to rally them in support of the Chinese revolution.[93]

Perhaps the most striking instance of success occurred in the maritime industry. In the wake of the bureau's decision to encourage "all comrades who were or are seamen" to join the Marine Workers Industrial Union, and "under the direction of the Union leadership to intensify the work among the Chinese seamen in the cities and on the ships," by May 1932, "the work [had] shown definite progress." Capitalizing on this progress, a "Chinese Bureau of the Union was created to be responsible to the Executive Committee of the Union to work among the Chinese seamen." Success was most evident in Philadelphia. "One of the most outstanding acheivements [*sic*] is the *penetration into the Chinese Seamens* [*sic*] *Club* (Lien Yee Shei, reactionary mass organisation [*sic*] under the control of Kuomintang) in Philadelphia. As the result of our work, practically all rank and file members of the Culb [*sic*] *joined the Marine Workers Industrial Union in Phila*. (Those who joined number about thirty five) and the old reactionary club was declared disolved [*sic*]."[94] It is noteworthy that what was considered progress had occurred among Chinese workers whose occupation was mobile and outside the territorial bounds of New York, Philadelphia, and San Francisco.

Furthermore, the bureau accomplished a great deal in its work among youth. For instance, in 1931 it was noted, "In San Francisco, the Chinese Buro is making progress in youth work and are now organizing sports clubs etc." Also, the bureau controlled the youth organization Mass Voice, whose membership included thirty-five YCL members. Although the bureau could boast about the formation of the Resonance Association, "an organization of Chinese youth for the struggle against imperialism" based in San Francisco, and the reappearance of *Resonance*, now a four-page printed monthly edited by Fee, circulation of the publication was "not wide and subscription is small." Plus, the association had only a membership of fifteen.[95] More fledgling were the efforts in women's work. The national conference in February 1929 declared, "The recruiting of women members into the Party and adequate attention of the Party on this work are quite urgent." Yet, two years later, the bureau was said to be moving in a positive direction only because it had "committees for women's work in district Bureaus for work among women workers." As for the press, success was moderate. Party papers issued included *Xianfeng Bao*, *Kung Yu*, and *The Mass Voice*, with a circulation in February 1931 of 1500, 500, and 500, respectively, and an overall "percentage growth in last year" of 15 percent.[96]

However, signs of stagnation were also evident. In 1930, "only the Anti-imperialist Alliance and the Resonance Association and the I.L.D. Chinese Branches numbered about 250." When it came to bureau publications, "In 1930 only the *Chinese Vanguard* was published with an actual circulation of about 500–600, as compared with the present [1933] of 900."[97] Finally, as an indication of the situation in the San Francisco branch in particular, at a meeting in January of the District 13 Language Bureau "with the Secretaries of the Language fractions," Dea, "reporting for the Chinese fraction," presented a fairly bleak picture of local activism. There were only "10 Party members" and an "ILD branch with 24 members, Party members included. [The] Alliance for Support of Chinese Revolution [was] not functioning. Chinese Labor League is going to issue two bulletins, one to the Food Workers and the other to the Needle Trade Workers. Anti-Imperialist League not functioning."[98] The bureau was obviously encountering difficulty in fulfilling its aims of "educat[ing] and organiz[ing] the Chinese masses" in America during the early 1930s.

As of February 1931, out of a nationwide total of thirty-three functioning fractions, only a "very small number" existed "in organizations controlled by our class enemies." As for organizations "controlled by us," growth was slow and uneven and was "mainly due to anti-Japanese sentiment and suffering from mass unemployment."[99]

Finally, harassment increased and resulted in arrests and deportations. In late 1930, Li, secretary of the bureau, was arrested and threatened with immediate deportation "for his political belief and activity." In spite of defense efforts by the bureau and, after some delay, by the ILD National Office in New York, as well as a "flood of protests," including one by American philosopher and educator John Dewey who knew Li as a "regular student at Columbia U.," Li was ordered deported to China. After further negotiations, immigration officials permitted him to be deported to the USSR.[100]

Around this same time on the other coast, Xavier Dea and Wei Minghua were subjected to similar treatment. Recalling the sequence of events that followed Dea's arrest, Zhang Bao related that Dea "surrendered to the immigration office on May 14th, 1931 upon the information of his activities by the Kuomintang and imperialist agents in S.F." Dea, he continued, "was in jail since then until he was granted voluntary departure, started for the Soviet Union from S.F. on May 6th, 1932." The process leading up to his departure was anything but easy. Dea suffered "indescribable turture [*sic*] and discrimation [*sic*]" on Angel Island. Wei was arrested on November 16, 1931, in Los Angeles at an ILD membership meeting "when anti-war leaflets were found on his car by members of the 'Red Squad.'" He, too, was granted permission to "depart voluntarily" to the Soviet Union, leaving on May 22, 1932.[101]

On the East Coast, sometime in August 1932, Zhang himself became the target of sustained harassment. He was forced to resign from his position as head of the bureau and seemingly disappeared. The bureau apparently did not know that in late August the party leadership helped Zhang escape to the Soviet Union, where he received permission to transfer his membership from the CPUSA to the Communist Party of the Soviet Union.[102] On September 1, the bureau learned most rudely that "the secret service agents [were] still looking for J. M. [James Mo]" when the agents appeared on "the 2nd floor of the Worker Center at a lecture conducted by the Anti Imperialist League" and "question[ed] a non-party comrade," whom they had "mistaken" for Zhang.[103]

Not surprisingly, the bureau was plunged into a crisis. Henry Hahn, newly appointed secretary of the bureau, explained:

> Since Comrade Mo's affair the work of the Buro had been carried on in an unorganized manner and now especially the situation becomes acute. There is no fund for postage and other material, and as Comrade Hahn is recalled from Philadelphia to take the place of Comrade Mo as secretary, he has since stayed at Mo's place[.] [*sic*] Due to Mo's departure the place is to be given up. The question rises as to a suitable place for the documents and for work, because the available places are open to outside workers.

Even as he reassured party leader Earl Browder that all this was "not to say that we ask the secretariat to look for a place or to solve this small difficalties [*sic*] for us," Hahn nonetheless closed his postscript with the following recommendation: "In view of the fact that white terror is intensified, we suggest that the secretariat instruct the A.I.L. to release the Chinese comrades from open." (The end of the sentence is cut off by the margin of the page, but presumably Hahn was referring to "open" meetings of the Anti-Imperialist League.) Although not mentioned by Hahn, we know from another source that Hahn's own situation may have been far less secure than his reassurances might lead one to believe. At an earlier meeting of the National Bureau where Hahn was approved as the new secretary of the bureau, a motion was adopted "to take up with the Secretariat about finding for Hahn some sort of paying position in sympathetic or other organizations so as to make Hahn's stay in New York possible . . . because of Hahn's health."[104]

In spite of the seeming thoroughness and candor of the many reports filed by the activists, one issue was not discussed—namely, the continuing separation between the members of the bureau and the so-called Chinese masses in communities in America. This issue came to the fore following the reorganization of the Chinese National Fraction's National Bureau in October 1929. In July 1931, in a letter addressed to Hahn, Chow En Len, who had recently "resigned from the post of secretary of the New York Branch," along with fellow activists Wong Hwin and Lee Chen harshly criticized the "situation of the Alliance of the Chinese Anti-Imperialists."[105] Largely written in the first person, and "in the tone and by the hand of Chow," the letter declared:

> Since the organization og [*sic*] the Alliance, there has not [been] any progress during the past several years. In N.Y.C., the number of members has not increased. Especially at the present time, the conditions are partially dead, and consititute [*sic*] a condition of backwardness. . . . Some comrades told me that the backwardness of the Alliance

> was due to the leading comrades in the top, who are not trying their utmost for thd [*sic*] work among the workers, who are not speaking for the workers. Some are just pretend [*sic*] to be revolutionary. Some have the nervous disease about female sex, to become outstanding in the name of the Party. Their attitude of an [*sic*] rotten egg has been now finally discovered by the workers in the fraction. Afterwards we dont [*sic*] have to believe in what they say.

While acknowledging poor revolutionary credentials—"my experiences and past records in the revolutionary movement are shallow and weak"—Chow nonetheless reminded Hahn that he had been a member of "the Alliance for about one year, and have been trained by the Party in the work I should do." In addition, he had "observed from several months."[106]

The letter writers exhorted: "Since they have done this [*sic*] rotten things and were discovered by us, we must put all our forces to sweep them completely. . . . Comrade Han [*sic*]: Wake up quickly! Prepare for the bright future that is to come! Forward with the class struggle to accomplish the tasks unfinished by our forerunners." In a postscript, they demanded the following:

> The Chinese Fraction under the monopoly of a few students is going from bad to worse. We cannot [*sic*] tolerate any longer. We decide to demand its complete reoganisation [*sic*] at the next Fraction meeting. *If our demand is not passed, then we may not appeal. We will organise [sic] another organisation [sic] as a counter organisation [sic] to oppose it.* . . . Without the abolishion [*sic*] of these several students, there can be no development in the work among the Chinese masses. This I have said long ago.[107]

Clearly, the letter revealed not only the inability of the Chinese immigrant Communists to continue pursuing older strategies but also the emergence of heightened criticism of the divide between them and ordinary working people in Chinese communities in America.

The National Bureau responded swiftly to the criticism, though its response was surprisingly mild and included no demands for punishment.[108] Rather, having arrived at the conclusion that "these several comrades were instigated by talks and conversations which brought about the misunderstanding and misconception about the Bureau," the bureau sent letters to "each of the three comrades," calling attention not so much to the substance of the criticism but rather to the tone and mode in which it had been delivered. As party members, they should "exercise real Bolshvic [*sic*] spirit." In addition, they must heed the following rule: "Inner Party disputes should not be broadcast to nonparty members and you should not attck [*sic*] our own auxiliary organisations [*sic*] among the non-Party masses." Instead, "You must send in your concrete criticisms and suggestions[.] You [*sic*] must follow the line of the party, base[d] on the organisational [*sic*] tightness of the Party, observe the iron discipline of the Party and send in your ruthless criticisms!"[109]

Perhaps the bureau's apparent leniency was due at least in part to the fact that the "three comrades" touched upon a matter that the bureau had already acknowledged as a problem—the predominance of "intellectuals" and "students" and their haughty "attitude" toward workers, the "Chinese masses in Chinatown."

The American Defense of the Chinese People

On January 18, 1933, a "meeting of a group of comrades to form the organization for support of the Chinese Revolution" was held at the Japanese Workers Club. Among those present were "J. Loeb, Trebst, Huafa[xu] and Hahn." Having met previously and received "proposals made by the Chinese Buro," the group chose a name for the organization, "Friends of the Chinese People"; determined the composition of the committee; and wrote an "Outline for Program." The main thrust of the program was to support the Chinese people's "resistence [*sic*] to Japanese invasion" and their "struggle for national liberation in all its phases," as well as American armed intervention and "all forms of political and economic American privileges in China." To carry out these aims, the organization was mandated "to cooperate with all organisations [*sic*] which have similar ends in view toward oppressed peoples." This last point was reflected in the choice of committee members, which included leading Chinese immigrant Communists Xu, Chi, and Hahn; non-Chinese party leaders in District 2, such as Anthony Bimba and Moissaye J. Olgin; and prominent nonparty figures, such as the intellectual Philip J. Jaffe (who was the third cousin of Chi's wife, Harriet Levine) and "John Dewey, Stokofsky, Elmer Rice, George Counts, Harry F. Ward, Scott Nearing, [and] Lewis Gannes." The group also resolved to approach "Trade Unions and Literary organizations."[110]

The Chinese activists, under Xu's initiative, began to grapple more seriously with the problem of "separation from the masses." Yao Xiaoping recounts that through Xu's efforts to make contact with Chinese workers in New York's Chinatown, he had "become aware of the overemphasis" by the Chinese Bureau and the AACAI on the political situation in China and on revolutionary movements elsewhere overseas, resulting in the "neglect of the real sufferings and problems in the daily lives" of these workers. In an article published in the February 15, 1933, issue of *Xianfeng Bao*, Xu offered a "candid self-criticism" of the group, calling attention to their contemptuous attitude and to "their overzealous concern for abstract concepts and theory." He asked, "if we overlook their problems, and if we cannot even understand the needs of the masses, how can we expect to attract the masses?"[111]

Several months later, another meeting was held that focused more broadly on a "Campaign for the Defence [*sic*] of the Chinese Revolution." It is not known who was present at this meeting, but based on Jaffe's recollection of a meeting "in a small Bronx apartment" in May 1933, it would seem likely that no one from the "outside" was there. According to Jaffe, whom Chi had invited, "there is probably no question that, except for me, everyone in the apartment that evening was a member of the American Communist Party."[112]

The new organization, Friends of the Chinese People, was to form one arm of a multipronged effort. The group would employ the following means: use of the "Chinese Press," in particular *Xianfeng Bao* and *The Unemployed*, which should be given "a name similar to 'Breadless Chinese,' and shall become the voice of the broadest masses of unemployed Chinese and bankrupt tradesmen and craftsmen," and "Tchuin Chin (Voice of the Masses) . . . as a trade union organ"; the dissemination of literature among "American workers and toilers"; the mobilization of workers in the war and transportation industries to stop the shipment of arms to Japan and China; and grassroots organizing efforts among Chinese in America to build "self-aid organisations [*sic*]" and to defend those "who are arrested for deportation, or who are being oppressed by American imperialism." Finally, the National Bureau CC should enforce the following code of conduct: "To impress all comrades with the necessity of maintaining illegal work among the Chinese comrades. The comrades who are in mass organisations [*sic*] in hostile organizations, or who return to China, must not appear as Communists, but must present themselves as anti-Japanese, anti-imperialist, etc." This last point was not simply a matter of individual behavior; rather, it concerned the issue that lay at the center of the change in orientation then being advocated by leading Chinese immigrant Communists in America.[113]

The crux of the matter was spelled out in the final comments. Referring to the publication of *China Today,* it was noted that critics had said that the paper held "too narrow an approach to the Chinese people." The paper allegedly promoted "news about Soviet China" to the neglect of "the anti-Japanese, anti-imperialist struggle." The proposed remedy zeroed in not only on the editorial policy of *China Today* but also on the organizational policies of the new broad-based campaign: "This should be reversed so that *the main emphasis must be placed on the anti-Japanese, anti-imperialist struggle,* to appeal to the broadest sections of the Chinese people. In a similar way, the League of Friends of the Chinese People must be broadened out so that it can draw in all elements who are against Japanese imperialist [*sic*] and against Chiang Kai-Shek, establishing a united front with elements who support General Tsai Ting Kai, who are anti-Japanese and anti-Chiang Kai-Shek."[114]

In fact, at the meeting of the Chinese Bureau CC on January 20, 1933, two days after the meeting at which the mass organization, Friends of the Chinese People, was first given a name and program, those present had already explicitly articulated the shift. Among the points "on [the] basis of which a program" was "to be drafted by Hahn" was the following directive: "Should make a turn in anti-Japanese imperialist work among the Chinese: liquidate the non-cooperation attitude of the past, penetrate into the masses by participating in the anti-Japanese collection drive, into aviation training corps, etc. . . . When we have not yet gain [*sic*] the confidence of the masses, there must not be any split with them, or any action taken which would lead to a split with the masses."[115]

At the same time, even as they abandoned the "non-cooperation attitude of the past," the activists must simultaneously "make clear to them [i.e., the Chinese masses] our independent even minority stand." Moreover, the official line of party and nonparty groups alike should reflect the change: "The party fractions, the Chinese Alliance, and the organizations under our influence and leadership must make known such attitude and stand, and by earnest and sincere explanation, persuasion, convince and lead the masses forward." One of the recommended ways that the Chinese Fraction would make known its independence and sincerity was to "begin with small struggle . . . to break through the old practice of 'non-offendism,' politeness, the fear of hurting the 'face' of the merchant-gentry or relatives."[116]

By early April, in response to the CPUSA CC's suggestion to name the new organization "Friends of Revolutionary China," "the initiative group of Comrades" decided, instead, to name it the "American Defense of the Chinese People." In a long letter, the group explained the thinking that underlay their decision. First, reacting to Japan's increased aggression against China, Eugene Chen, the foreign minister of the nationalist government, called Japan's behavior "a formidable indication of preparations for a war with the United States." So, the group considered the new name "more suitable." Second, unlike a "more revolutionary" name, such as "Friends of Revolutionary China," the chosen name would facilitate broad-based work: "With this name, we can work on the widest possible front. The unorganized and undeveloped workers can be drawn in, as well as the petty bourgeois liberals, and many other elements." In other words, the aim was not simply to "attract those who are already within the Red Orbit" but, rather, to "capitalize the large Anti-Japanese sentiment existing thruout [*sic*] the country." They declared, "Our new organization should be the leader in this endeavor." On a tactical level, "Mass protests held under the auspices of the AMERICAN DEFENSE of the CHINESE PEOPLE will be more effective, and receive much more recognition by the Capitalist Press and official Washington, than if the same protests were made by an organization with a revolutionary name."[117]

Sandwiched between the above points were two statements that seemed to contradict the rest of the analysis. The first was the following statement: "Our objectives, as expressed in our revolutionary program, and our directive forces will remain the same, irrespective of the name we adopt." The second was a declaration that sounded as if it were part directive, part warning: "Unorganized workers, Socialist Party members, Liberals and the petty bourgeoisie, must subscribe to our revolutionary program before joining the organization. This would be an essential condition for all prospective members, no matter which of the two names we may adopt." Although there was no further discussion of a potential conflict, the issue was hinted at in the statement entitled "Party Line in the Organization": "We adopted a broad name and program not mainly for the purpose to reach the petty bourgeois liberals, but to draw in unorganized and undeveloped workers."[118] At that very moment, however, Xu was also pressing members of the Chinese Fraction to address the neglect of Chinese workers' problems in America. That there might be evidence of conflict over the proposed change in orientation should come as no surprise. Less predictable is the impact of the changes on the attitude and policy with regard to the activists' work.

In the responses to a questionnaire during the second half of 1933, the Chinese activists noted, "The total membership of all organisations, now in round figure number [is] 3,180," an increase from "about 250" in 1930. However, "the chief characteristic then as now is the duprication [*sic*] in membership—one belongs to more than one organisation [*sic*], especialy [*sic*] party members." A brief commentary on the "foremost tasks in the mass organisations [*sic*]" raised a familiar problem as well as another less discussed problem: first, "The drive for new members drawing in new element as instrument for liquidation of the sectarian tendencies of the party members"; and second, the "urgent need" for an "intensive drive to liquidate illiteracy both in the Chinese and the English languages." It appears that there was growing acceptance of the necessity, though perhaps not agreement on the method, to begin to address the problem of how to bridge the divide between committed party members and working people in Chinese communities in order to mobilize the masses to support the bureau's "revolutionary program."[119]

There is some evidence that beginning in the early 1930s the activists began to experience some success in mobilizing a broad constituency that included ordinary Chinese working people; Japanese, Filipino, and American workers; and so-called liberal elements. The most promising fields were the "anti-Japanese invasion united front" and the related antiwar and antifascist struggles. For instance, the front page of the January 30, 1933, issue of the *Western Worker* ran the following headline: "1500 AT CHINESE CONSULATE PROTEST HUANG PING ARREST; ANTI-WAR MEETINGS ON COAST FIGHT MUNITION SHIPMENTS." The text revealed that "five hundred workers, including 150 Chinese and Filipinos marched through Chinatown today demanding the release of Huang Ping, member of the Executive Committee of the Anti Imperialist League, arrested in Peiping January 4 by the Kuomintang." Nor would this demonstration of solidarity remain an isolated event. Barely a month later, the *Western Worker* flashed another headline: "2500 AT JAPANESE, GERMAN CONSULATES OF S.F. PROTEST FASCIST TERROR AND WAR PREPARATIONS AGAINST THE SOVIET UNION." This time, a "parade in which Chinese, Japanese, Germany [*sic*], Filipino and American workers joined, went through Chinatown and other districts crowded with thousands of workers. Banners in were carried in various languages making a most impressive parade." And in early April, it was reported that a "delegation of one hundred, composed of American, Japanese and Chinese workers will call on Mayor Rossi . . . to protest the official welcoming of the Japanese ships and demand that the money to be so used be immediately turned over for unemployed relief."[120]

Conclusion

Even as Chinese immigrant Communists moved toward embracing a policy that advocated cooperation "with all organizations which have similar ends in view," they also sought ways to support the Chinese revolution and to sustain close ties with the Chinese Communist Party. For example, "at the beginning of the 1930s, the Chinese Bureau received letters from the CCP via Hong Kong, asking for money to be sent to certain people in Hong Kong to rescue comrades who were in jail. Each time, we sent a lot of American dollars."[121]

It should not be thought that support flowed in only one direction. Zhang remembered that the Chinese Bureau "often received magazines" from "comrades" in China. Also, at the January 20, 1933, meeting of the National Bureau CC, it was reported that "books bought from contributions to the Chinese Vanguard from comrades in S.U. [Soviet Union] be sent to the RESONANCE—to the amount of 100.00 R" [presumably, R referred to rubles]. At this same meeting, it was noted that the "request by comrades in S.U. to reprint coupon with China Soviet currency cannot be complied with, because expense is too great." A recommendation was made that the bureau "write comrade in charge with the work there to economies [*sic*], and use the 'Map' coupons."[122]

The Chinese National Fraction also issued an appeal to the "American Party" asking it to "do more to help the Chinese Revolution than merely passing resolutions." That is, the party "should contribute financial aid, at least as much as it does to Germany." In concrete terms, the CPUSA CC should "recommend to the membership that it be assessed for the Chinese party the same amount as it is for the German party, money to be transferred to C.C. of

Chinese Party for their use; that money be collected in same manner as it is now for the Germans." This was a bold demand indeed, a testament not only to the strength of the bonds connecting Chinese immigrant Communists in America to revolutionaries in China but also to the activists' awareness of the significance of the revolutionary struggle in China to the cause of the "Proletarian World Revolution"[123] and the well-being of Chinese workers in America.

NOTES

An earlier and longer version of this essay appeared as chapter 8 in *Japanese and Chinese Immigrant Activists: Organizing in American and International Communist Movements, 1919–1933* (New Brunswick, NJ: Rutgers University Press, 2007).

1. "Minutes of DEC Meeting Held Wednesday, May 9, 1928," f. 515, op. 1, d. 1435,1. 85, Communist Party of the United States Papers, Russian State Archive of Social and Political History (RGASPI), Moscow, Russian Federation (hereafter cited as CPUSA); Him Mark Lai, "To Bring Forth a New China, to Build a Better America: The Chinese Marxist Left in America to the 1960s," *Chinese America: History and Perspectives 1992* (1992): 13; Theodore Draper, *The Roots of American Communism* (New York: Viking Press, 1957), 390. On the collapse of the KMT-CCP United Front, see Conrad Brandt, Benjamin Schwartz, and John K. Fairbanks, *A Documentary History of Chinese Communism* (London: George Allen & Unwin, 1952), 89–93; Xenia Joukoff Eudin and Robert C. North, *Soviet Russia and the East, 1920–1927: A Documentary Survey* (Stanford, CA: Stanford University Press, 1957), 301–6; Alexander Pantsov, *The Bolsheviks and the Chinese Revolution, 1919–1927* (Honolulu: University of Hawaii Press, 2000), 127–60; S. A. Smith, *A Road Is Made: Communism in Shanghai, 1920–1927* (Honolulu: University of Hawaii Press, 2000), 190–208.

2. Lai, "To Bring Forth a New China," 3–82; Lai, "A Historical Survey of the Chinese Left in America," in *Counterpoint: Perspectives on Asian America*, ed. Emma Gee (Los Angeles: Asian American Studies Center, University of California, Los Angeles, 1976), 63–80.

3. J. Loeb to Central Committee, C. P., April 10, 1933, "Matter Relating to: NEW MASS ORGANIZATION Pertaining to CHINA," translation into English, f. 515, op. 1, d. 3181,11. 6–8, CPUSA; "GOVERNING PRINCIPLES FOR THE PROGRAM," [April 10, 1933], translation into English, f. 515, op. 1, d. 3181,1. 17, CPUSA; Philip J. Jaffe, "Introduction," to *China Today*, Series 1, Numbers 1–8 (1934) (New York: Greenwood Reprint Corporation, 1968), [2 pages] no page number.

4. Nathan Glazer, *The Social Basis of American Communism* (New York: Harcourt, Brace & World, 1961), 47–48; Theodore Draper, *American Communism and Soviet Russia: The Formative Period* (New York: Viking Press, 1960), 191. The process of Bolshevization of foreign Communist parties actually proceeded slowly over a period of several years. It was initiated at the Second Comintern Congress in 1920 and then formally proclaimed at the Fifth Comintern Congress in 1924. Edward H. Carr, *Twilight of the Comintern, 1930–1935* (New York: Pantheon Books, 1982), 5. The American Communist Party itself formally initiated the process of Bolshevization of the Party at the Fourth Convention of the Workers (Communist) Party of America, held in August 1925. "Call for National Convention–Workers (Communist) Party of America," July 28, 1925, f. 515, op. 1, d. 482,11. 71–74, CPUSA.

5. For examples of the struggle over the Bolshevization process among foreign-language groups, see David John Ahola, *Finnish-Americans and International Communism: A Study of Finnish-American Communism from Bolshevization to the Demise of the Third*

International (Washington, DC: University Press of America, 1981); Paul Buhle, "Jews and American Communism: The Cultural Question," *Radical History Review* 23 (Spring 1980): 9–33; Douglas Monroy, "Anarquismo y Comunismo: Mexican Radicalism and the Communist Party in Los Angeles During the 1930s," *Labor History* 24, no. 1 (Winter 1983): 34–59; and Maria Woroby, "The Ukrainian Immigrant Left in the United States, 1880–1950," in *The Immigrant Left in the United States*, eds. Paul Buhle and Dan Georgakas (Albany: State University of New York Press, 1996), 185–206. On the struggles over the Americanization process, see Gary Gerstle, *Working-Class Americanism: The Politics of Labor in a Textile City* (New York: Cambridge University Press, 1989); George J. Sanchez, " 'Go after the Women': Americanization and the Mexican Immigrant Women, 1915–1929," in *Unequal Sisters: A Multi-Cultural Reader in U.S. Women's History*, eds. Ellen Carol DuBois and Vicki L. Ruiz, (New York: Routledge, 1990), 250–63; James R. Barrett, "Americanization from the Bottom Up: Immigration and the Remaking of the Working Class in the United States, 1880–1930," *Journal of American History* 79, no. 3 (December 1992): 996–1020.

6. For a succinct description of the structure of the American Communist Party following the reorganization of 1925, see Draper, *American Communism and Soviet Russia*, 160–61. See also "General Structure of the Party—Chart No. 1," *Party Organizer* 4, no. 4 (May 1931): 6–7; and J. Peters, *The Communist Party: A Manual on Organization* (New York: Workers Library Publishers, 1935).

7. Glazer, *The Social Basis of American Communism*, 50–51.

8. Minutes of "Meeting of the District Executive Committee, held Wednesday, April 13, 1927," f. 515, op. 1, d. 1169,1. 6, CPUSA; "MINUTES OF ANTI-IMPERIALIST COMMITTEE—June 11, 1927," f. 515, op. 1, d. 1169,1. 20, CPUSA; Tontien to Comrade Gomez, November 26, 1927, f. 515, op. 1, d. 1111,11. 12–14, CPUSA; "Minutes of DEC Meeting held Wednesday, May 9, 1928," f. 515, op. 1, d. 1435,1. 85, CPUSA; Benjamin Fee, "Report on the Work of the Chinese Fraction," Third Session of District 13 Convention, Workers (Communist) Party of America, January 27, 1929, f. 515, op. 1, d. 1791,11. 45–49, CPUSA; "Thesis and Report of the Buro Adopted at the Second National Conference of the Chinese Fraction of the Workers' (Communist) Party of America, February 19–21, 1929," translation into English, f. 515, op. 1, d. 1814,1. 24, CPUSA; and Tontien to Comrade, December 11, 1927, translation into English, f. 515, op. 1, d. 1111,1. 18, CPUSA.

9. For aliases of Chinese Party members in San Francisco in December 1927, see Huang Shih to Comrade Gomez, December 13, 1927, f. 515, op. 1, d. 1111,1. 22, CPUSA.

10. Yang Zuntao and Zhao Luqian, "Shi Huang," in vol. 45 of *Zhonggong dangshi renwu zhuan* [Personages in the party history of the CCP], ed. Hu Hua et al., trans. Jin Yaliang (Xi'an: Shaanxi renmin chubanshe, 1990), 164.

11. The May Thirtieth Massacre occurred on May 30, 1925, when British police fired on a demonstration of Chinese students, killing ten and wounding fifty. The demonstration was held to protest the killing of one Chinese worker and the wounding of others who had gone out on strike at a Japanese-owned cotton mill in Shanghai. Jean Chesneaux, *Le mouvement ouvrier Chinois de 1919 a 1927* (Paris: Mouton & Co., 1962), 372–73.

12. Lai, "To Bring Forth a New China," 8–9; Yang and Zhao, "Shi Huang," 160; Yao Xiaoping, trans. Jin Yaliang, "A Red Revolutionist Seldom Known to Others—Xu Yongying, Founder of China Bureau, U.S.C.P. and Director of English Translation of The Selected Works of Mao Zedong," *Zheng Tan Feng Yun*, 8–10.

13. Yang and Zhao, "Shi Huang," 164.

14. "Thesis and Report of the Buro," 1. 5, 20; and minutes of Political Committee Meeting, held November 2, 1927, f. 515, op. 1, d. 984,1. 67, CPUSA.

15. This "Chinese comrade" may well have been Benjamin Fee, for he had already begun to play a prominent role among Chinese activists, especially in relation to the party leadership, and as a member of the YCL he would have been especially qualified to speak about their activities. FBI report, FBINY 100–98894, 6/1/53, 1, Subject: Benjamin Junt Fee, FBIHQ 100–369886 (in author's possession) (hereafter cited as Fee FBI file); Gil Green, to Party Org. Dept., September 28, 1931, f. 515, op. 1, d. 2326,1. 9, CPUSA.

16. "Minutes of DEC Meeting Held Wednesday, May 9, 1928," 11. 85–86.

17. There is some question about exactly when ACWP was founded and *Xianfeng Zhoukan* was first issued. Writing in 1982, Zhang Bao stated, "The Alliance was first established . . . in 1927." However, the Chinese Bureau's Special Resolution on publication of the paper's successor *Xianfeng Bao* in April 1930 stated, "The Alliance was organised [*sic*] by the Party in January 1928 and the Vanguard was published at the same time." Other sources indicate that the latter first appeared in April of that year and that some time in 1930 during the period following the transfer of the ACWP headquarters to New York, *Xianfeng Zhoukan* was published in Philadelphia. Zhang Bao, trans. Yu Chunmei, "Er-Sanshi Niandai zai Meiguo de Zhongguo Gongchandang ren [Chinese Communists in the United States during the twenties and thirties]," *Guoji gongyunshi yanjiu ziliao* [Historical research materials on the international communist movement], vol. 7 (Beijing: 1982), 154; "THE IMPORTANCE OF THE 'CHINESE VANGUARD WEEKLY' AND OUR TASKS (Special Resolution of the Chinese Buro, C.C., CPUSA)," April 5, 1930, f. 515, op. 1, d. 2159,1. 38; Lai, "To Bring Forth a New China," 34; and Gor Yun Leong, *Chinatown Inside Out* (New York: Barrows Mussey, 1936), 154.

18. Notably, in Philadelphia a branch was led by former KMT leader and "former member of the city government of Canton," P. T. Lau. Minutes of Political Committee DEC, District 3 meeting, held May 27, 1927, f. 515, op. 1, d. 1139,1. 45, CPUSA; "U.S.—'Hands Off': Chinese Here Deplore Excitement over Death of American," *Philadelphia Daily News*, March 28, 1927, 2; and M. James to the Central Committee, CPUSA, May 14, 1932, f. 515, op. 1, d. 2756,1. 3, CPUSA. For the appeal to Japanese comrades, see leaflet entitled "Workers and Farmers of China, Japan, and America!" [May 1928], f. 515, op. 1, d. 1438,1. 36, CPUSA; and "Minutes of Polcom Meeting held Saturday, May 19th, 1928," f. 515, op. 1, d. 1435,1. 95, CPUSA.

19. Yang and Zhao, "Shi Huang," 160–61; and Lai, "To Bring Forth a New China," 8–10.

20. In his study of the relationship between left-wing Chinese students and Chinese hand laundry workers in New York in the 1930s and 1940s, Renqiu Yu points out that just as the activists held an elite status as university students, upon joining the KMT in America they also became members of "the elite within the KMT." Renqiu Yu, "To Merge with the Mass: Left-Wing Chinese Students and Chinese Hand Laundry Workers in New York City in the 1930s," in *Asian Americans: Comparative and Global Perspectives*, eds. Shirley Hune, Hyung-chan Kim, Stephen S. Fugita, and Amy Ling (Pullman: Washington State University Press, 1991), 50. See also Renqiu Yu, *To Save China, to Save Ourselves: The Chinese Hand Laundry Alliance of New York* (Philadelphia: Temple University Press, 1992), 58.

21. Letter to Comrade Gomez, December 29, 1927, translation into English, f. 515, op. 1, d. 1111,1. 26, CPUSA.

22. FBI Investigative Summary Report, FBINY 100–98894, 12/14/51, 4, Fee FBI file; Certificate of Identity of Benjamin J. Fee, in file of Benjamin J. Fee, File No. 12017–49602, Chinese Arrival Files, San Francisco, Records of the U.S. Immigration and Naturalization Service, Record Group 85, National Archives, Pacific Branch, San Bruno, CA; M. James to Secretariat, CPUSA, July 5, 1932, CPUSA; and Lai, "To Bring Forth a New China," 10.

23. Letter to Gomez, December 29, 1927; "Thesis and Report of the Buro," 1. 25.

24. Tontien to Gomez, November 26, 1927, 11. 12–13.

25. "Thesis and Report of the Buro," 11. 20–21, 28, 30.

26. Tontien to Gomez, November 26, 1927, 1. 12.

27. Minutes of Anti-Imperialist Committee meeting, held December 27, 1927, f. 515, op. 1, d. 1110,1. 22, CPUSA.

28. E. Levin to Comrade Lovestone, April 26, 1927, f. 515, op. 1, d. 1043,1. 59, CPUSA.

29. Acting General Secretary to E. Levin, May 9, 1927, f. 515, op. 1, d. 1043,1. 77, CPUSA.

30. "Thesis and Report of the Buro," 1. 19.

31. Tontien to Comrade, December 11, 1927, 1. 18.

32. Huang Shih to Comrade Gomez, December 9, 1927, translation into English, f. 515, op. 1, d. 1111,11. 16–17, CPUSA.

33. As recounted by Shi Huang in mid-December 1927, the paper "was first published in Seattle by S. C. Hueng (Editor) and C. T. Hsieh (manager)" and then later "adopted by the Left wing organization as its official organ and . . . removed to San Francisco with Tontien and Suarez as editor and manager respectively." Financing came from "free contribution by the left wingers [*sic*] in America." Tontien to Comrade, December 11, 1927, 11. 19–20.

34. Regarding the relationship between the two bodies, the Anti-Imperialist Committee ruled at a meeting in late October 1927, "That the structure of the Anti-Imperialist Department be as follows: CEC sub-committee (the present committee), District Anti-Imperialist Committees (sub-committees of the DECs), City Anti-Imperialist Committees (except in residence city of DEC), and special committees (such as the sub-committee in California working in connection with the National Committee of the Kuo Min Tang of China in America, etc.); no anti-imperialist committees to be elected in sections, sub-sections or nuclei." "Minutes of Anti-Imperialist Committee," held on October 31, 1927, d. 515, op. 1, d. 1110,1. 9, CPUSA.

35. "Minutes of Anti-Imperialist Committee Meeting," December 27, 1927, 1. 22.

36. "Questionary," issued by the Language Department C.C. and completed by the Chinese Bureau by May 15, 1929, f. 515, op. 1, d. 1684,11. 21–23, CPUSA. At a meeting of the Anti-Imperialist Committee, held in late December 1927, Gomez refers to "the Provisional Committee for an American Section of the I.L.A.I." Minutes of meeting, December 27, 1927, 1. 22. See also "Proposal for Building American Section of the International League against Imperialism—Submitted by M. Gomez," ca. late 1927, f. 515, op. 1, d. 1110,11. 18–20, CPUSA.

37. "Summary of Recent Activities in the All-America Anti-Imperialist League," ca. January 1929, f. 542, op. 1, d. 35,11. 13–14, CPUSA; "Call for a National Convention of the All-America Anti-Imperialist League (United States Section), to be held in New York City, April 20–21, 1929," f. 515, op. 1, d. 1840,11. 12–15, CPUSA; "Memorandum Concerning Anti-Imperialist League," [1929], Series 2–13, Earl Browder Papers (hereafter cited as EBP), 52 linear feet, Special Collections Research Center, Syracuse University Library (a duplicate set is available in 36 reels of microfilm at the McKeldon Library, University of Maryland); "ANTI-IMPERIALIST TOUR," *Labor Unity*, August 24, 1929, 3; Scott Nearing and William Simon to Fellow Member, August 27, 1929, Series 2–13, EBP; P. Smith to all Language Buro Secretaries, August 19, 1929, f. 515, op. 1, d. 1682,1. 29, CPUSA; and "Communist Party of U.S.A.—District #13, Minutes Secretariat Meeting, October 13, 1929," f. 515, op. 1, d. 1795,1. 45, CPUSA.

38. Soon after the National Conference held in February 1929, the headquarters of the Chinese Buro was transferred from San Francisco to New York City and plans were initiated to relocate the offices of ACWP, although by the time of the fifth meeting of the Buro, held on March 25, 1929, the transfer was not yet "complete," and it was decided that "Com.

Tontien [Shi] should be still responsible for the Agi-prop [*sic*] department and take care of the 'Vanguard,' the official organ of the Alliance." Minutes of the "Fifth Meeting of the Chinese Buro," held on March 25, 1929, translation into English, f. 515, op. 1, d. 1814,1. 33, CPUSA.

39. "Members of the General Council," ca. August 1929, Series 2–13, EBP; and Zhang, "Chinese Communists in the United States," 150–51. Lai writes that toward the end of 1927, left-wing students "gained control of the national student organization," and two former "Chaotai members, Mei Ruao (Mei Ju-ao) and Hu Dunyuan (Thomas T. Y. Hsu), now CPUSA members, held posts as two of the next three chief editors of the Alliance's publication." Lai, "To Bring Forth a New China," 15.

40. Fee, "Report," 11. 46, 48.

41. "Call for a National Convention of the All-America Anti-Imperialist League (United States Section)," 1. 14.

42. The "Far Eastern Anti-Imperialism Conference" was held on May 30, 1929, in New York. Apparently, the Chinese Buro along with "the Japanese comrades" had organized what was described by the secretary of the Chinese Buro as a "mass meeting" on China. Handwritten minutes of the ninth meeting of the Chinese Buro, held on May 15 [1929], original in Chinese (translation by Zhenlin Rang), f. 515, op. 1, d. 1814,1. 37, CPUSA; and Toddy, Chinese Buro, C.P.U.S.A., to Acting Executive Secretary, C.P.U.S.A. May 31, 1929, f. 515, op. 1, d. 1656,1. 71, CPUSA.

43. L. Gibarti, International Representative, A.A.A.I.L., to Secretariat of the C.P.U.S.A., June 7, 1929, f. 515, op. 1, d. 1658,11. 17–18, CPUSA.

44. "District Committee #13, Meeting Tuesday, May 14 [1929], Minutes #4," f. 515, op. 1, d. 1793,1. 20, CPUSA; "District Committee #13, Meeting Tuesday, May 21st [1929], Minutes #5," f. 515, op. 1, d. 1793,1. 23, CPUSA; and E. Gardos to L. Gibarti, May 23, 1929, f. 515, op. 1, d. 1799,1. 24, CPUSA.

45. Regarding the mobilization of Mexicans, Gardos himself admitted in another letter to Gibarti, "unfortunately we have very few connections here in San Francisco; and the Los Angeles comrades, where there are over 200,000 Mexicans living, somehow didn't secure so far any endorsement." Organizer, District #13 to L. Gibarti, June 14, 1929, f. 515, op. 1, d. 1799,1. 30, CPUSA.

46. The Comintern theorized that the period from 1928 to 1934, known as the Third Period, was the last stage in a three-phase development of capitalism during the post-World War I period. The Third Period would be marked by increasingly sharp contradictions in capitalism that would in turn bring about a revolutionary upsurge among workers and the growing strength of Communist parties around the world. Accordingly, the Sixth Comintern Congress, held in 1928, adopted an ultra-left antisocial democratic platform, including the policy of "class against class," that is, the tactic of noncooperation with all reformists and direct confrontation between labor and capital. See Kevin McDermott and Jeremy Agnew, *The Comintern: A History of International Communism from Lenin to Stalin* (New York: St. Martin's Press, 1997).

47. Gardos to Gibarti, May 23, 1929, 11. 24–25.

48. "Minutes of the Western Regional Conference of the All-America Anti-Imperialist League, U. S. Section, Held Sunday, June 30, 1929," f. 515, op. 1, d. 1840,11. 16–18, CPUSA.

49. "Bulletin for League Workers. Building the All-America Anti-Imperialist League," [1929], f. 515, op. 1, d. 1840,11. 38–39, CPUSA.

50. Lai, "To Bring Forth a New China," 17; Lai, "A Historical Survey," 66; and "Thesis and Report of the Buro," 1. 21.

51. There is some confusion about when Fee changed his membership from the YCL to the party. According to a certificate issued by the secretariat of the CPUSA, before Fee

departed from the United States in September 1930 to attend the Lenin School in Moscow, he was a member "in good standing of the Communist Party, U.S.A." However, correspondence between Gil Green of the YCL National Office and W. Weiner of the Organization Department CC indicates that not only was Fee "a very active League member before he left" but further that he was ordered "to remain a Y.C.L. member" following his return in September 1931. Certificate issued by the Secretariat [CPUSA], September 19, 1930, f. 515, op. 1, d. 2266, CPUSA; Green, to Party Org. Dept., September 28, 1931; and Org. Dept. CC to Gil Green, Youth Dept., October 1, 1931, f. 515, op. 1, d. 2326,1. 8, CPUSA.

52. Fee, "Report," 1. 46; Green to Party Org. Dept., September 28, 1931.

53. Report by Minnie Carson, Young Workers League Representative, Third Session of District 13 Convention, Workers (Communist) Party of America, January 27, 1929, f. 515, op. 1, d. 1791,1. 49, CPUSA. In this regard, Renqiu Yu calls attention to the "left's dogmatic application of the CPUSA's theories to overseas Chinese," and to the "quandary" in which the Chinese leftists were placed by "following the theoretical guidance of the CPUSA," as "there were few Chinese industrial workers in the United States." Yu, *To Save China, to Save Ourselves*, 60.

54. Report by Minnie Carson, 11. 49–50, CPUSA.

55. "Thesis and Report of the Buro," 11. 10, 21.

56. Ibid., 11. 20–21.

57. Ibid., 1. 21.

58. Before the strike, the workers were members of the Shih-Fook Tong (Tong for the "Good of the Workers"). The day after the workers began their strike, they decided to change the name of the Tong to "Chinese Laundry Workers Union." "Report to the District Plenum, District #13, On the Chinese Laundry Workers Strike," February 10, 1929, f. 515, op. 1, d. 1791,1. 95, CPUSA.

59. The strikers' other demands were as follows: "1—One day off in seven. 2—Quitting time Saturday 5 PM. Recognition of the Union. Pay for lost time. . . . Recognize as a holiday the Strike Day." "On the Chinese Laundry Workers Strike," 1. 97.

60. Here, Manus added the jarring parenthetical comment "(This committee is in the form of a shop delegation and is formed in a crude manner)," which simply did not make sense unless he was referring to the fact that the committee numbered a somewhat unwieldy sixty-five. Ibid., 11. 95–96.

61. "On the Chinese Laundry Workers Strike," 11. 95, 98; minutes of meeting of Chinese Fraction, S. F. Branch, held on February 5, 1929, f. 515, op. 1, d. 1814,11. 1–2, CPUSA; minutes of meeting titled "Chinese Strike of Laundry Men" [February 1929], f. 515, op. 1, d. 1793, 1. 85, CPUSA; and Lai, "To Bring Forth a New China," 17. I have been unable to identify "Billy." Whereas my sources identify Billy as a representative of the Kung Yu Club and Wood as a representative of the ACWP, Lai identifies Dea as the former.

62. I have been unable to find any further mention of such meetings in the archival records.

63. "On the Chinese Laundry Workers Strike," 1. 96; minutes of meeting of Chinese Fraction, February 5, 1929, 1. 1; "Chinese Strike of Laundry Men"; and minutes of "Enlarged District Executive Committee Meeting," February 10, 1929, f. 515, op. 1, d. 1793,1. 1, CPUSA.

64. "Our Chinese Neighbors," *The Seamen's Journal* 43, no. 3 (March 1, 1929): 73; and minutes of meeting of Chinese Fraction, February 5, 1929, 1. 1.

65. For instance, the report noted, "The C.E.C. of our Party did not give adequate political guidence [*sic*] and financial assistance [to] the Fraction." "Thesis and Report of the Buro," 11. 25, 26.

66. In his January report, Fee gave details on the CED's failure to provide financial assistance. For instance, regarding the sending of delegates to the National Conference: "The CEC promised to give $250 for the comrades to make the trip across the US, three were to go." In the end, they received only $100. Fee, "Report," 11. 25, 26.

67. "Thesis and Report of the Buro," 1. 26; and remarks by Emanuel Levin, Third Session of District #13 Convention, January 27, 1929, f. 515, op. 1, d. 1791,1. 59, CPUSA.

68. The criticism was not directed solely at the Chinese Bureau but rather was part of a broader directive to all language bureaus to "immediately reorganize" and thereby move toward "speedier liquidation of all remnants of federationalism." In this regard, the Language Department's instructions noted, "Not only have we in our Party had the wrong habit of local language membership meetings, we have even had National conferences of certain language groups with delegates from these local 'fractions'!" P. Smith to all District Organizers and Language Bureaus of the Central Committee, July 19, 1929, with "Instructions for Our Work in Non-Party Language Organizations," f. 515, op. 1, d. 1682,1. 20, CPUSA.

69. "Minutes of Twelfth Meeting of the Chinese Buro," held on July 11, 1929, f. 515, op. 1, d. 1680,1. 14, CPUSA.

70. Yang and Zhao, "Shi Huang," 168; "Minutes of the Seventh Meeting of the Chinese Bureau" held on April 5, 1929 original in Chinese, trans. Zhenlin Rang, f. 515, op. 1, d. 1814,1. 35, CPUSA; and "Minutes of Twelfth Meeting of the Chinese Buro."

71. "Minutes of meeting of the Language Department," held on October 22, 1929, f. 515, op. 1, d. 1680,1. 15, CPUSA.

72. Toddy to Comrade Smith, October 25, 1929, f. 515, op. 1, d. 1683,11. 45–46, CPUSA. In line with the move to reevaluate the ACWP, the Buro also decided "to openly declare the dissolution of the SUN Yat Sen Society [Students' Society for the Advancement of Sun Yat-senism in America], and point the reactioary [*sic*] character of the Sun Yat Seninsm [*sic*]."

73. Handwritten minutes of the tenth meeting of the Chinese Buro, held on June 2 [1929], original in Chinese, trans. Zhenlin Rang, f. 515, op. 1, d. 1814,1. 39, CPUSA.

74. Toddy to Smith, October 25, 1929,1. 46.

75. "Party Recruiting Drive: Instruction of the Chinese Buro, Language Depar't, CC, CPUSA," prepared by Toddy, ca. December 14, 1929, translation into English, f. 515, op. 1, d. 1682,1. 51, CPUSA.

76. Ibid., 11. 52–54.

77. Toddy to Acting Executive Secretary, CPUSA, May 31, 1929, f.515, op. 1, d. 1656,1. 71, CPUSA.

78. "Minutes of the seventh meeting of the Chinese Buro," 1. 35.

79. Zhang, "Chinese Communists in the United States," 161; questionnaire issued by the Central Committee, CPUSA, and completed by Henry Hahn, Chinese Buro, C.C., November 23, 1932, f. 515, op. 1, d. 2747,11. 89, 91, CPUSA; M. James to Comrade Browder, August 25, 1932, f. 515, op. 1, d. 2706,1. 23, CPUSA; and Toddy to Acting Executive Secretary, CPUSA, May 31, 1929, 1. 71.

80. Xiaoping, "A Red Revolutionist Seldom Known to Others," 12–13.

81. Lai, "A Historical Survey," 12. See also "Chinese Rout Reds but It's in Mott St.," *New York Times*, July 29, 1929, 1.

82. Some time in the first months of 1930, the *Chinese Students Monthly* was "stopped." "Questionary," 1. 23.

83. "Party Recruiting Drive," 1. 53; and "Questionary," 11. 21–23.

84. In fact, nine days after the appearance of the first issue of *Xianfeng Bao*, Li sent a brief note to Comrade Campbell declaring that the "great problem before us is financial"

and "immediate practical help from the Party and the Eastern Department is very urgent." In spite of such pleas for assistance, the financial situation deteriorated further to the point where *Xianfeng Bao* was "suspended for three months in the summer of 1930 due to lack of finance." T. H. Li to Com. Campbell, April 12, 1930, f. 515, op. 1, d. 1961,1. 15, CPUSA; and M. James to CC, 1. 3.

85. "THE IMPORTANCE OF THE 'CHINESE VANGUARD WEEKLY,' " 11. 1, 38–39; Secretary, Chinese Buro, to M. Alpi, Language Department, April 11, 1930, f. 515, op. 1, d. 2021,1. 74, CPUSA; and Leong, *Chinatown Inside Out*, 150.

86. Lai, "A Historical Survey," 67.

87. See endnote 46.

88. "THE IMPORTANCE OF THE 'CHINESE VANGUARD WEEKLY,' " 1. 2.

89. Ibid. The Chinese Bureau purchased "three sets of Chinese types" ordered "from China" through a "contribution" of $900 from Bishop William Montgomery Brown, D. D. Brown had promised Lovestone at an "election campaign meeting in Harlem" in 1928 that he would "do whatever is deemed necessary by him as representative of the Party, in respect to the finance of obtaining the types" in return for their use in printing a Chinese-language edition of his "booklet, Communism and Christianism." Yung Ying Hsu to Bishop Wm. Montgomery Brown, May 25, 1929, f. 515, op. 1, d. 1658,1. 96, CPUSA; Bishop William Montgomery Brown, D.D., to Mr. Robert Minor, May 27, 1929, f.515, op. 1, d. 1658,1. 97, CPUSA; "THE IMPORTANCE OF THE 'CHINESE VANGUARD WEEKLY,' " 1. 39; and Zhang, "Chinese Communists in the United States," 156.

90. "THE IMPORTANCE OF THE 'CHINESE VANGUARD WEEKLY,' " 1. 2, 38; Secretary, Language Department, CC, to Secretariat, CPUSA, May 6, 1930, f. 515, op. 1, d. 2017,1. 4, CPUSA. There existed both an Eastern Department of the Comintern (dissolved and transformed in 1926 into the East Regional Secretariat) and an Eastern Department (also known as Eastern Bureau) of the Profintern. The former answered to the Central Executive Committee of the Comintern and was divided into Near, Middle, and Far Eastern Sections, whereas the latter was responsible for directing trade union–related work among workers in the so-called Far East. However, well after 1926, the Chinese immigrant Communists continued to refer to the Eastern Department of the Comintern. Peter Huber, "The Central Apparatus of the Comintern: New Statistical Evidence," in *Politics and Society under the Bolsheviks: Selected Papers from the Fifth World Congress of Central and East European Studies, Warsaw, 1995*, eds. Kevin McDermott and John Morrison (New York: St. Martin's Press, 1999), 266, 276–77; Adibekov, Shakhnazarova, and Shirinya, *Organizatsionaia struktura kominterna, 1919–1943* (Moscow: Rosspen, 1997), 114–15, 155–56; and Edward Hallett Carr, *A History of Soviet Russia: Socialism in One Country, 1924–1926*, vol. 3, part II (New York: Macmillan Press, 1964), 607–8, 898, 904, 909, 940.

91. "THE IMPORTANCE OF THE 'CHINESE VANGUARD WEEKLY,' " 1. 1; "Minutes and Report of the Joint Meeting of the Agi-Prop [*sic*] and Language Dep'ts and the Chinese Buro," held on November 4, [1930], f. 515, op. 1, d. 2003,1.5, CPUSA.

92. L. Kovess, "Report on the Influence of the Party trough [*sic*] Language fractions and Language papers," May 19, 1930, f. 515, op. 1, d. 2016,1. 9, CPUSA; "Shortcomings of Party Fractions in Language Work," *Party Organizer* 3, no. 4 (June–July 1930): 10; and "THE IMPORTANCE OF THE 'CHINESE VANGUARD WEEKLY,' " 1. 39.

93. Lai, "To Bring Forth a New China," 18; Lai, "A Historical Survey," 67; questionnaire that was probably prepared by the Language Department, CC, CPUSA, and completed by the Chinese Buro, ca. after July 1933, f. 515, op. 1, d. 3181,11. 14–15, CPUSA; and M. James to Comrades, Secretariat, CPUSA, July 5, 1932, f. 515, op. 1, d. 2756,1. 7, CPUSA.

94. M. James to CC, May 14, 1932, 1. 2.

95. *Resonance* was first published in 1927. On the basis of his interview with Benjamin Fee, Him Mark Lai writes that the newly reissued *Resonance* was intended "to serve the same function for the Chinese Marxist Left in the West that Chinese Vanguard did for the Left in the East." However, in mid-May 1932, the Chinese Bureau described it thus: "A monthly published by the Resonance Ass'n in S.F. essentially for the Chinese youth." Lai, "To Bring Forth a New China," 35; and M. James to CC, May 14, 1932, 1. 3.

96. Questionnaire [February 1931], 11. 51–53; M. James to CC, May 14, 1932, 11. 2–4; "Thesis and Report of the Buro," 11. 17–18. The Chinese Bureau also oversaw publication of the mimeographed *The Seamen Monthly* in New York and *The Chinese Unemployed* in San Francisco. However, the former was still fledgling, and the latter no longer was issued regularly.

97. Questionnaire, ca. after July 1933, 11. 14–15.

98. "Minutes of District Language Bureau, District #13, January 7, 1930," f. 515, op. 1, d. 2135, 1. 30, CPUSA.

99. Questionnaire [February 1931], 11. 49–50; and questionnaire, November 23, 1932, 1. 89.

100. Beatrice Siskind to Earl Browder, December 20, 1930, f. 515, op. 1, d. 1966,1. 153, CPUSA; J. Mo to Comrade Browder, ca. late 1930, translation into English, f. 515, op. 1, d. 1961,1. 92, CPUSA; M. James to George Maurer, C.P. Fraction, I.L.D. National Office, May 11, 1931, f. 515, op. 1, d. 2351,1. 105, CPUSA; John Lewey to Hon. Mr. Doak, Sec'y Dept. of Labor, Washington, DC, May 12, 1931, f. 515, op. 1, d. 2531,1. 106, CPUSA; "Deportation of Aliens," under "CURRENT LEGAL NOTES," *The Seamen's Journal* 45, no. 8 (August 1, 1931): 243; and Zhang, "Chinese Communists in the United States," 159.

101. M. James to Comrade Goodman [1931], f. 515, op. 1, d. 2531,1. 107, CPUSA; M. James to Comrade Brown, Language Department, June 30, 1931, f. 515, op. 1, d. 2336,1. 86, CPUSA; M. James to Comrades, July 5, 1932; "Wei Wins Fight in Deportation Plot; To Go To U.S.S.R.," *Western Worker*, May 1, 1932, 1; and handwritten notes about "MING HUA WEI, USC student," box 14, folder 3, Karl Yoneda Papers, Collection 1592, Special Collections, University Research Library, University of California, Los Angeles.

102. Anglo-American Secretariat, ECCI, to Central Committee, Communist Party, Soviet Union, September 21, 1932, f. 495, op. 72, d. 289,1. 16, Comintern; and Zhang, "Chinese Communists in the United States," 159.

103. H. Hahn to Comrade Browder, September 1, 1932, f. 515, op. 1, d. 2756,1. 9, CPUSA.

104. Hahn to Browder, September 1, 1932; minutes of "Meeting of Chinese Buro, Language Dept. CC" [ca. August 15, 1932], f. 515, op. 1, d. 2756,1. 20, CPUSA.

105. The spelling of "Hwin" is unclear.

106. Chow En Len, Wong Hwin, and Lee Chen to Comrade Han [*sic*], July 10 [1931], translation into English, f. 515, op. 1, d. 1841,11. 117–19, CPUSA.

107. Ibid.

108. In some instances, when dealing with allegations of Trotskyism or other so-called deviations from the correct ideological line, the bureau expelled or forbade interaction with the parties under criticism. See minutes of the "Fifth Meeting of the Chinese Buro," held on March 25, 1929, translation into English, f. 515, op. 1, d. 1814,1. 33, CPUSA; and "Statement of the Chinese Bureau, C.C., C.P.U.S.A. On T. H. Tsiang and His Book, 'Red China,'" [1931], translation into English, f. 515, op. 1, d. 1814,1. 46, CPUSA.

109. Chinese National Bureau to Comrades [mid-July 1931], translation into English, f. 515, op. 1, d. 1051,11. 48–50, CPUSA; and "The decision of the Chinese Bureau on the problem" [July 1931], translation into English, f. 515, op. 1, d. 1814,1. 47, CPUSA.

110. Minutes of "Meeting of a group of comrades to form the organization for support of the Chinese Revolution," held January 18 [1933], translation into English, f. 515, op. 1, d. 3181,1. 12, CPUSA; and "Outline for Program of 'Friends of Chinese People,'" attached to above minutes, translation into English, f. 515, op. 1, d. 3181,1. 13, CPUSA.

111. Xiaoping, "A Red Revolutionist Seldom Known to Others," 15. For a fuller discussion of Xu Yongying's criticisms, see Yu, "To Merge with the Mass," 50.

112. Jaffe, "Introduction."

113. "Campaign for the Defence [*sic*] of the Chinese Revolution" [ca. early 1933], translation into English, f. 515, op. 1, d. 3123,11. 231–33, CPUSA.

114. Ibid., 1. 233.

115. "MINUTES OF MEETING CHINESE BURO, C.C.," held on January 20, 1933, translation into English, f. 515, op. 1, d. 3181,1. 1, CPUSA.

116. Ibid.

117. J. Loeb to Central Committee, April 10, 1933, 11. 6–8; "GOVERNING PRINCIPLES FOR THE PROGRAM."

118. J. Loeb to Central Committee, April 10, 1933, 1. 7.

119. Questionnaire, ca. after July 1933, f. 515, op. 1, d. 3181,11. 14–15; J. Loeb to Central Committee, April 10, 1933, 1. 7. In the "opinion" of the author of these responses, "the lack of collective leadership of the Buro" was hurting "work as a whole."

120. "1500 AT CHINESE CONSULATE PROTEST HUANG PING ARREST; ANTI-WAR MEETINGS ON COAST FIGHT MUNITION SHIPMENTS," *Western Worker*, January 30, 1933, 1; "2500 AT JAPANESE, GERMAN CONSULATES OF S.F. PROTEST FASCIST TERROR AND WAR PREPARATIONS AGAINST THE SOVIET UNION," *Western Worker*, February 20, 1933, 1; and "WORKERS PROTEST MATSUOKA WELCOMES BY DEMONSTRATIONS," *Western Worker*, April 10, 1933, 1.

121. Zhang, "Chinese Communists in the United States," 157–58; "GOVERNING PRINCIPLES FOR THE PROGRAM"; "Statement on the expenses of the $200.00 received from the C.C.," by J. James [1932], translation into English, f. 515, op. 1, d. 2756,1. 17, CPUSA.

122. Zhang, "Chinese Communists in the United States," 158; "MINUTES OF MEETING CHINESE BURO, C.C.," 1. 2.

123. Untitled statement, unsigned, included in a file of documents from the Chinese Buro, C.C. in New York [1933], translation into English, f. 515, op. 1, d. 3181,1. 16, CPUSA.

3

Filling the Rice Bowls of China: Staging Humanitarian Relief during the Sino-Japanese War

Karen J. Leong and Judy Tzu-Chun Wu

Two striking visual images of China captured the U.S. public's attention in 1937. In January, Metro-Goldwyn-Mayer released its much-anticipated epic film, *The Good Earth*, which was based on Pearl S. Buck's 1931 bestselling novel. The film portrayed a Chinese peasant family nobly suffering economic dislocation and political upheaval. Like the book, the movie was widely successful and received critical acclaim; the characterizations of the hard-working and selfless Chinese female protagonist, O-lan, and her driven husband, Wang Lung, became icons of China's resilient spirit. Ten months later, in its October 4 issue, *Life* magazine published a photograph taken after the Japanese bombed Shanghai. The picture of a crying baby sitting amidst the rubble seemed to capture the destruction and lost innocence created by war. Named one of the top ten photographs of 1937, this image would symbolize China's suffering in its war of resistance against Japan. The popularity of both the film and the photograph primed American audiences to see and respond to the anguish of the Chinese people; in the context of the Sino-Japanese War, these visual narratives laid the foundation for a national campaign to generate humanitarian aid for China.

However, the partnership of Chinese Americans and "Old China Hands"—white American missionaries and businessmen formerly stationed in China—who sought to mobilize support among mainstream Americans faced many challenges. The United States had a long history of suspicion of, disdain for, and downright hostility toward people of Chinese ancestry.[1] National and state laws prevented Chinese from immigrating to the United States, obtaining citizenship through naturalization, and marrying white individuals.

In addition, discriminatory social and economic practices resulted in residential and occupational segregation. Although Japan's full-scale invasion of China in 1937 captured the attention of the American public, could the average American be convinced to give money not just for entertainment but also to support humanitarian aid for a country and people that still seemed so foreign?

The solution adopted by China relief organizations offers an opportunity to reevaluate the existing scholarship on the impact of the international conflicts of the 1930s and 1940s on the status of Chinese Americans. Most historians argue that the Sino-Japanese War and eventually World War II fundamentally transformed the position of Chinese Americans from perpetual aliens to worthy citizens. The wartime alliance between the United States and China and, more broadly speaking, the growing sense of sympathy between American and Chinese people led to the repeal of all the Chinese exclusion acts in 1943 and also sparked the greater social, economic, and political integration of Chinese Americans into mainstream society. Historians further point out that Americans of Chinese ancestry, both men and women, played a major role in facilitating this transformation in their status.[2] Chinese Americans initiated relief campaigns for China before America's entry into World War II. They also participated wholeheartedly in the war effort and defense industries following Pearl Harbor. In other words, Chinese Americans demonstrated their worthiness for American citizenship through their civic engagement. They moved out of their racially segregated neighborhoods, and women in particular found opportunities to expand their roles outside of the private realms of family and home.[3]

This chapter suggests a less celebratory and more problematic interpretation of how the Sino-Japanese War shaped representations of Chinese people and facilitated opportunities for racial and gender advancement. The most successful and visible efforts to raise relief funds resulted from interracial and unequal partnerships between Chinese and white Americans. "Old China Hands" like author Pearl S. Buck and publisher Henry R. Luce had ready access to mass media and political lobbying networks. However, they required visible Chinese and Chinese American participation to legitimize and humanize their narratives of a nation in need of uplift. Together, Chinese and white Americans appealed to existing romanticized and Orientalist narratives of China already scripted in the American popular imagination. In other words, in order to "sell" China as an object of compassion, these organizers fostered exotic fantasies about Chinese culture and people to promote humanitarian forms of consumerism and tourism. Women's labors and particularly their bodies played a central role in these efforts to elicit sympathy, curiosity, and financial aid from an American audience. The China relief campaigns of the late 1930s and early 1940s reveal the contradictory processes by which Chinese Americans achieved acceptance in the American nation: People of Chinese ancestry enjoyed greater opportunities to expand their influence and visibility in the public sphere but in so doing they had to fulfill continuing expectations that they perform versions of Chinese culture and identity produced and consumed by white Americans.

Uniting China Relief

American efforts to raise funds for China dramatically increased after the "Rape of Nanjing," wherein Japanese troops invaded and captured China's capital in December 1937. Because of the large foreign presence in Nanjing, reports of the atrocities committed by Japanese soldiers against Chinese civilians circulated internationally as missionaries and businessmen fled China under the protection of their governments. In July 1938, *Reader's Digest* published an eyewitness account about the Japanese army's horrific massacre of Chinese civilians. When readers responded with disbelief, assuming that this was merely propaganda, *Reader's Digest* conducted its own investigation and published a more complete and graphic account of what had happened.[4] The violence of these attacks, widely reported in mainstream media in the United States, ignited an interracial movement to raise humanitarian aid for China.

"Old China Hands" led the effort to demand a greater response to China's war with Japan from the U.S. government and mainstream Americans. These retired white American missionaries and businessmen initiated the formation of a number of organizations and committees to raise aid for China. By 1938, the list of China relief groups included the American Bureau for Medical Aid to China (ABMAC), the China Emergency Relief Committee, the China Aid Council, the Church Committee for China Famine Relief, the American Committee for Chinese Industrial Cooperatives (Indusco, Inc.), the Associated Boards for Christian Colleges in China, and the American Committee for Chinese War Orphans. All of these organizations featured prominent civilians, such as John D. Rockefeller II, Pearl S. Buck, and Henry R. Luce, as supporters. Their lobbying efforts bore fruit when in 1938 the United States began providing China with limited "commodity credits" to purchase supplies domestically. This program continued until early 1941, when President Roosevelt created the Lend-Lease Program.[5]

These China relief efforts not only depended on the goodwill and organizing efforts of white Americans; they also relied on the presence and testimonials of Chinese nationals. For example, the American Committee for Chinese War Orphans was formed after eight white women who were "deeply sympathetic to the Chinese people and their cause" attended a New York meeting where a Chinese diplomat's wife related accounts of children who lost their parents to the war.[6] Because of the impact that prominent Chinese nationals could have on the hearts and minds of Americans, relief organizations frequently featured one or more of the Soong sisters (especially Madame Chiang Kai-shek), novelist Lin Yutang, or China's ambassador to Great Britain, Wellington Koo.

Chinese Americans also played an important role in launching and promoting relief aid for China. As early as 1931, when Japan attacked Manchuria, people of Chinese heritage in the United States had initiated campaigns to protest Japanese aggression and to attract American support for their ancestral country. By 1937, when the political situation became even more urgent, the Chinese War Relief Association (CWRA) "was established to coordinate the fund-raising efforts of some three hundred communities throughout the United States, Mexico, and Central and South America."[7]

The nature of cooperation and coordination between white and Chinese American relief efforts varied greatly depending on the regional context. One of the most successful forms of interethnic fundraising resulted from the Rice Bowl campaigns, elaborate community festivals (alternately called parties or carnivals) that featured parades, cultural performances, carnival concession stands, and fashion shows. Initiated in 1938 by ABMAC, these campaigns—later called "Bowl of Rice" campaigns nationally—were highly visible and effective tools to raise public awareness. Nearly every state boasted local organizing committees that sponsored these events. In San Francisco, home to the largest population of Chinese in the United States, the cosponsors included Paul C. Smith, editor of the *San Francisco Chronicle* and western director of ABMAC; B. S. Fong, the president of the Chinese Six Companies and chairman of the CWRA; and Margaret Chung, a Chinese American physician with connections to mainstream politicians and movie celebrities.[8] Through the large Chinese American population and the contacts of the organizers, San Francisco alone raised $235,000, nearly half of the total Rice Bowl funds.

Interestingly, more modest efforts outside of metropolitan areas with established Chinatowns also relied on interracial forms of cooperation. In the border town of Nogales, Arizona, Frank Y. Wong, the proprietor of Nanking Grocery and secretary of the local Chinese War Relief Association chapter, organized a two-day "Bowl of Rice Carnival." He predominantly recruited white civic leaders, including the mayor and judge, to be speakers, and he exhibited Chinese films. He relied on the support of Tucson's Chinese American community, which was much smaller than San Francisco's but had a history dating back to the nineteenth century. Wong also drew on the assistance of a prominent Chinese national. He secured Madame Kuo, the wife of China's minister of foreign affairs—who spent winters in Arizona—as the featured speaker. Wong's efforts raised over $500 in a primarily working-class town of Mexican Americans. In Silver City, New Mexico, Mrs. Patience Glennon organized a speech and dinner at the local Elks clubhouse; however, it was Chinese American residents of Silver City who prepared and served chop suey as their contribution to the event. The combined efforts attracted attendees from neighboring cities and raised close to $600. Although the amounts donated may have been relatively small, these efforts brought awareness about China to areas that did not have many Chinese American residents, including South Carolina, Virginia, Tennessee, rural Pennsylvania, Oklahoma, and Michigan.[9]

Despite the reach of the Rice Bowl campaign, its success was qualified. British and Greek war relief efforts far outpaced China relief fundraising—in 1940, all China relief organizations raised a little over $1 million compared with over $10 million and $5 million raised by British and Greek organizations, respectively.[10] Part of the problem was the smaller numbers of Chinese Americans in the United States and continuing perceptions that Chinese had less in common with Americans than European peoples and cultures did. In his study of Chicago, historian James C. Schneider found that ethnic identification played a major role in Chicagoans' affiliation with relief organizations.[11] Thus, organizations devoted to raising funds for China faced greater challenges because Chinese American communities—although presumably willing to contribute more than other Americans—were relatively small due to racist immigration restrictions.[12] Furthermore, as numerous scholars including Harold Isaacs, Michael Hunt, and T. Christopher Jespersen have demonstrated, Americans in the 1930s were reluctant to support China emotionally and financially due to perceptions of racial and cultural differences.[13]

As a result of the relatively meager amounts raised by the China relief campaigns, prominent supporters persuaded President Franklin D. Roosevelt to ask the American Red Cross to add China to its fundraising efforts. A belated attempt by Roosevelt and the American Red Cross in 1941 to raise $5 million specifically for China was an embarrassing failure that raised less than $200,000. The Red Cross debacle alerted China relief organizers to the urgency of educating the American public about events in Asia and why the United States should care. In addition, many sympathizers recognized that competition among groups for public funds was increasingly counterproductive, confusing the public and resulting in multiple fundraising and publicity efforts.

In response, Henry Luce, the influential publisher of *Time* and *Life* magazines, proposed a solution: incorporate key agencies into one umbrella organization that would coordinate efforts to raise American awareness about and funds for China. As an "Old China Hand" and son of missionaries to China, Luce was a logical choice to unite the different China relief agencies.[14] Under his leadership, eight major China relief organizations in 1940 incorporated as United China Relief (UCR).[15] The organization relied on the already existing community infrastructures of churches and mission boards, civic clubs, and women's clubs to disseminate information and to raise funds. UCR also incorporated the existing structure of the ABMAC Rice Bowl campaign, which had raised the most funds of all the American China relief organizations.[16]

As in previous relief efforts, UCR sought to establish interracial partnerships. The organization wrote press releases in Chinese for the Chinese-language press. A Chinese American receptionist greeted visitors to UCR headquarters in New York City. However, most of the employees of Chinese ancestry occupied the top floor of the UCR offices and were thus isolated from the other staff members as well as the central workings of the organization.[17] The interethnic cooperation espoused by UCR did not necessarily reflect an equal partnership.

Furthermore, the ways in which UCR and other China relief organizations sought to educate Americans about China raised questions about the power dynamics of cultural and knowledge production. Seeking to build on successful relief efforts and to launch an even more aggressive campaign for humanitarian aid, these friends of China sought increasingly innovative ways to "sell" China to a reluctant mainstream American audience.

Cultivating Compassionate Consumerism

To both educate the American public about the plight of China and to raise humanitarian funds for the besieged nation, UCR organizers faced two sets of obstacles. To overcome the long-held disdain and indifference of mainstream Americans toward Chinese people, humanitarian relief workers had to demonstrate the desperate needs of the Chinese people as well as their worthiness of American assistance; UCR had to find the right balance between presenting China as a victim that required external aid and China as a potential ally that was willing and able to fight for its own survival. In addition, China's sympathizers faced the difficult task of soliciting funds just as American spending showed significant increases in the purchase of luxury goods and significant decreases in charitable giving.[18] China relief organizations developed a solution to these challenges by capitalizing on Orientalist fantasies of China and promoting American consumption as relatively painless ways to offer humanitarian assistance.

UCR, with Henry Luce's contacts and its headquarters in New York City, was uniquely positioned to shape American perceptions of China. The organization appealed to some of the top publicists on Wall Street to develop campaigns for raising funds for China; they, in turn, applied the latest innovations in marketing and advertising to shape positive public opinion about China.[19] A memo for the UCR directors in May 1941 reported the activities of thirty-one staff members, which included developing publicity packets for local committee chairs, distributing twenty-five 16 mm films to those communities organizing screenings and lectures as fundraisers, providing educational information kits to editorial writers throughout the nation, and working with manufacturers for Fifth Avenue shops to develop China-related clothing and items. One subcommittee dealt with the comics industry and negotiated with "Terry and the Pirates," "Superman," and others to "introduce Chinese scenes and personalities."[20] A bulletin sent out to UCR chapters during the first year boasted, "our publicity department is doing a grand and increasingly effective job of educating America on China. If the European war does not engulf us, America will yet wake up about China and be ready to do a typical American job for China."[21]

UCR's media contacts enabled the organization to saturate the American market with emblems and representations of China. However, the organization faced the difficulty of deciding what message it was seeking to communicate to its audience. On the one hand, UCR sought to promote an image of "new China" to appeal to middle-class and mainstream Americans. "New China" distinguished itself with its Christian values, democratic principles, and openness to American ideals, culture, and technology. In other words, the portrayal of China's desire for American tutelage emphasized its worthiness for American aid. Chinese Americans also lauded this image of China as it reflected positively on them as well. Long viewed as undeserving of American citizenship, people of Chinese ancestry in the United States visibly demonstrated their civic capability by appearing in fundraising parades as boy scouts and nurses, male and female versions of civic heroes.

Although these depictions of new China held positive appeal, UCR and other China relief workers discovered that portrayals of victimization generated greater sympathy and hence humanitarian aid from mainstream Americans. According to Harold Isaacs, one of the images that resonated most with Americans was the picture of the baby crying amidst the devastation of Shanghai. China relief publicists named the baby Ping Mei (P'ing Mei in some publications) and created a story about the loss of his parents. The intent of this strategy was explicit: "Perhaps this picture of hurt little Ping Mei screaming his pain and defiance in the ruins of war will do more than a thousand words to bring China's message home to others." China's supporters were asked to solicit donations from friends and acquaintances with postcards featuring a photo of the famous baby.[22] This image was also used in the "Cheer China" program distributed during a UCR benefit at Radio Music City Hall during China Week. Coty, a New York–based cosmetics company, paid for a half-page photo of the baby with the caption "P'ing Mei is Hungry and Afraid" to announce its support for "the cause of a valiant people."[23] The image of the helpless baby, although it did little to educate Americans about Chinese resistance against Japan, nevertheless appealed powerfully to the

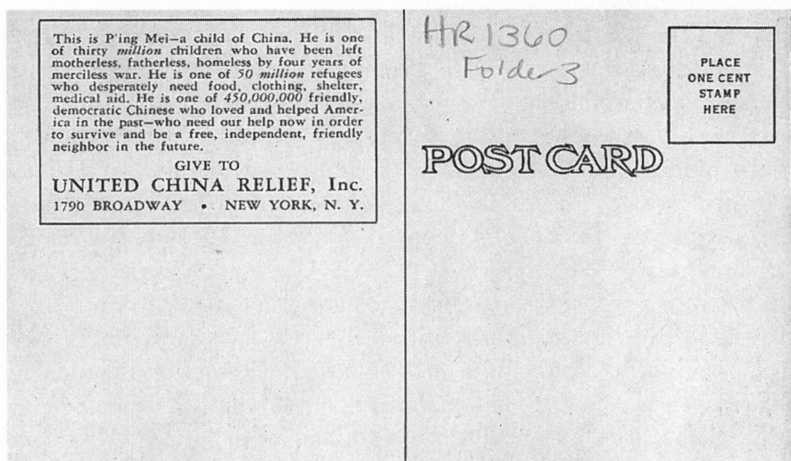
This is P'ing Mei—a child of China. He is one of thirty *million* children who have been left motherless, fatherless, homeless by four years of merciless war. He is one of *50 million* refugees who desperately need food, clothing, shelter, medical aid. He is one of *450,000,000* friendly, democratic Chinese who loved and helped America in the past—who need our help now in order to survive and be a free, independent, friendly neighbor in the future.

GIVE TO

UNITED CHINA RELIEF, Inc.

1790 BROADWAY • NEW YORK, N. Y.

HR 1360
Folder 3

PLACE ONE CENT STAMP HERE

POST CARD

The photographic image on the face of a 1943 United China Relief postcard depicted a lone child crying in a pile of rubble. The message on its reverse, shown here, tugs at the heartstrings by emphasizing why "friendly, democratic Chinese who loved and helped America in the past" deserved support as they struggled to survive as a "free, independent, friendly neighbor in the future." *(Courtesy of the Yale Divinity School Library, Special Collections, HR 1360.)*

emotions and evoked the atrocities committed against Chinese women and children.

As did the ubiquitous image of the Chinese orphan, the signature event for the China Relief campaign, the "Bowl of Rice" Festivals, also conveyed a message of victimization. According to a UCR staff memo, even the title "Bowl of Rice," was selected to emphasize the unique sufferings of China: "[It] is a particularly happy phrase because of its connotations. To the American mind, it suggests at once food for the hungry. It suggests the same thing to the Chinese because the bowl of rice is not only a basic food, but also a symbol of livelihood, as 'bread and butter' is to us."[24] The rice bowl connoted difference; Chinese ate rice and were identified with eating rice. The bowl also signified a beggar's bowl. The deceptive simplicity of the phrase was part of the complexity of effectively advertising China's needs and the monetary functions of the China relief agencies. "Editors," the memo stated, "respond best to simple, uncomplicated appeals and fresh material and give maximum cooperation to short drives."[25]

Chinese and Chinese American responses to the infantilization and victimization of China were mixed. UCR sought to assuage concerns that China would be perceived as helpless by altering its initial slogan from "China Needs Our Help" to "China Shall Have Our Help." However, both Chinese national representatives and Chinese Americans also contributed to the propagation of this image of victimization. During the San Francisco Rice Bowl events, Chinatown residents performed the sufferings of China for their predominantly white American audiences in order to attract their sympathy and political support. One section of the elaborate festival parade recreated the realities of war: "A grim replica of wounded Chinese refugees was carried out by one section [of the paraders]. Children and parents were covered with red bandages. A father trotted by with two babies slung in baskets at the end of the bamboo pole . . . [depicting] the fate of millions of children and peasants in a land torn by war and flood."[26] The Rice Bowl Party also featured Chinese beggars who wandered in the midst of spectators, soliciting donations from the crowd: "Throughout the district, Chinese mendicants and sword dancers begged for coins in the colorful custom of the homeland and all proceeds went to China's empty rice bowls. High priests wandered hand in hand with members of the hastily-organized Beggars Guild to beg for starving China."[27] These performances as refugees and beggars predominantly served to dramatize the helplessness and sufferings of the Chinese. The greater the victimization of the Chinese, the greater was the need for American assistance. As one *San Francisco Chronicle* article explained, the Rice Bowl Party "became a festival where happy people here in San Francisco rained down a shower of silver so that people who no longer ask for happiness might have bread and rice, the barest needs to keep life and hope in their bodies."[28]

In order to stage the scenes of wartime China, the organizers of the Rice Bowl parades reinforced the perception of Chinese Americans as representatives of China. Many Chinese in the United States embraced the opportunity to present their ancestral land in a positive light. However, they also were pushed toward this task by whites who viewed them as non-American while seeking to capitalize on the commercial and political appeal of China. For example, publicists of the Rice Bowl Festival emphasized the "otherness," the alienness, of Chinatown to attract spectators. One journalist explained that "San Francisco, always friendly to those strange yellow people who came from across wide seas to make their homes here, celebrated the New Year with the yellow people who have made themselves part of the city, closer than neighbors, members of the family."[29] Although Chinese Americans are here described as part of the San Francisco family, they also are referred to as "strange yellow people . . . from across wide seas." In order to stage the symbolic unity of China and the United States, Chinese Americans played the role of non-Americans. This point is underscored by the dress requirements for all Chinese Americans. Regardless of their status as performers or spectators, they were instructed to appear in Chinese costume, or what was frequently described as "native" dress.[30]

The desire to accentuate the Chineseness of Chinatown represented a joint effort of both the neighborhood's and city's chambers of commerce. The ethnic community's merchant leaders devised an "11-point program" in the late 1930s to develop the Oriental atmosphere of Chinatown, seeking to "erase the tendencies toward modernization and Occidentalization that had been manifested in certain sections" of the area.[31] San Francisco's economic planners readily agreed with the program, warning that "if Chinatown were to lose any of its quaint charm through modernization, San Francisco would lose proportionately some of the individuality that has characterized this city for many years."[32] The Orientalization of Chinatown and its people did not result from the "natural" retention of culture. Rather, the cultural image of the community was consciously constructed by both Chinese American and mainstream commercial interests. The result, in the words of Anthony Lee, was a "Sinocized theme park."[33]

Such a setting assisted efforts to promote both humanitarian aid and consumption. Rice Bowl Parade organizers balanced the grim portrayals of Chinese suffering, necessary for soliciting aid, with promises of festivities. As one newspaper article explained, "All San Francisco Chinatown and its thousands of friends join tonight in a common cause—the seeming anomaly of making merry while men die of flood, famine and war in the Far East. But they will make merry for the aid of, and not at the expense of, the untold hundreds of thousands of mothers and children who lie within the reach of disaster's fatal fingers."[34] The large-scale Rice Bowl activities deliberately sought to appeal to public consumerism, promising participants spectacular decorations and entertainment. During the festival, one reporter explained, "Stores were open, their proprietors dressed in gowns and red-buttoned mandarin caps, their windows brilliantly lighted. Colorful neon signs of the quarter blazed in soft reds and blues. Buildings were outlined in lights."[35] In addition to the ornamentation of existing structures and businesses, party organizers also staged spectacles such as parades, fashion shows, theater performances, and dragon and lion dancing for the viewing pleasure of tourists.

By attending the festival, visitors could sample cuisine in Chinatown restaurants, one of the key sectors of the community's tourist economy. Publicity for the Rice Bowl Festival featured such menu items as "sliced steamed duckling, smothered with mushrooms, chicken almond chop suey, barbecued duck and Westlake duck; fat prawns served in lichee sauce, birdnest soup, fried rice a la mandarin, flower of egg and mushroom broth, preserves, almond cakes, sesame seed cookies, and rare teas."[36] The consumption of such elaborate feasts by white American visitors demonstrated Sino-American friendship both internationally and domestically. As John Tchen persuasively argues, the symbolism of food figures prominently in anti-immigration rhetoric against Chinese people.[37] Charges that the Chinese enjoyed eating rats, dogs, and even other people supported perceptions of their racial inferiority and subhuman nature. For example, the American Federation of Labor evoked the cultural connotations of food to argue for the undesirability of Asian immigration. In 1902, Samuel Gompers coauthored a tract calling for Asian exclusion, entitled "Meat versus Rice: American Manhood against Asiatic Coolieism—Which Shall Survive?"[38] Although rice once symbolized the degeneracy of the Chinese people, mainstream Americans during the 1930s and 1940s contributed money to ensure that the Chinese be supplied their staple food.[39]

As the organizers themselves noted, promises of frivolity and abundance contrasted starkly with the humanitarian goal of assisting the suffering and starving masses of China. They reconciled the themes of excess and need by defining consumerism and tourism as political acts. One account of a New York Bowl of Rice Party reassured its predominantly white readers, "Chinatown natives look on happily as sympathetic guests celebrate to aid their stricken countrymen across the sea."[40] Giving aid for China's relief effort became more appealing when the experience was novel and fun. In turn, UCR cloaked its goal of promoting consumption in the noble rhetoric of international aid. For example, each participant of the San Francisco Rice Bowl Festivals was expected to purchase a fifty-cent "Humanity badge," a visible representation of the individual's support for sending aid to China.[41] The badge transformed a commercial act, the payment of a cover charge to a party or nightclub, into a political statement. In the context of the Rice Bowl Festivals, other tourist activities also gained political significance. Money spent in Chinatown restaurants and stores became political donations as "merchants . . . pledged to give a percentage of receipts during the evening."[42] In fact, humanitarianism even justified price inflation, for "all stores, bars, theaters and fraternal associations will be open . . . [and] where charges are made the Chinese Six Companies will levy a special assessment to swell the Rice Bowl fund."[43] By defining commercialism and tourism as forms of political support, organizers reconciled their goal of assisting war-torn China through the staging of community carnivals.

To attract more donors to visit Chinatown as a tourist site, organizers also evoked older images of the community as mysterious, exotic, and vice-ridden. In doing so, promoters implied that participants would gain access to an authentic Chinatown. They advertised the parties as opportunities "to see into the most closely guarded quarters of Chinatown,"[44] reminded spectators about the lore of "hatchet men [fighting] one of the greatest inter-tong battles in the history of [Chinatown]," and promised views of "silk clad Chinese girls crowd[ing] the balconies."[45] Although Chinatown merchants had led campaigns to drive organized crime and prostitution underground, they, along with white commercial and publishing interests, also evoked vice to titillate curious spectators. In his study of cultural representations of the community, Lee notes that this practice, "which staged the old world as a commodity available to all," continued after World War II as well.[46]

The exotification of Chinatown and the commodification of humanitarian aid were not unique to San Francisco. The Los Angeles Chinese American community cooperated with the Hollywood film industry to stage spectacles of China in order to promote compassionate forms of consumerism. As films like *The Good Earth* demonstrated the box office appeal of movies set in China, Chinese Americans were regularly called on to recreate China for Hollywood films by filling in as extras and by supplying "Oriental" props.[47] They likewise performed supporting roles for the movie industry during fundraising events. The Chinese Consolidated Benevolent Association of Los Angeles—in collaboration initially with ABMAC in 1938 and then with UCR chapters in 1941—presented the Moon Festival, a street festival replete with entertainment to raise awareness of and funds for China. The 1941 festival attracted thousands of attendees with the appearance of 110 movie stars in nightly parades over the three-day event that spanned Old Chinatown, China City, and New Chinatown.[48] Chinese Americans also contributed to the spectacle by performing in parades, costumes, traditional dancing, and musical performances throughout the three Chinatowns in Los Angeles.[49] Even the ethnic setting of the Moon Festival reflected the influence of the Hollywood movie industry. New Chinatown, the third Chinese-themed commercial area, was constructed based on the Orientalized sets of *The Good Earth*.[50] The movie rendition of China that inspired the creation of an American Chinatown reveals the circularity of Hollywood forms of Orientalism. The Los Angeles Chinese American community sought to take advantage of the fascination with Chinese people and culture promoted by the movie industry to attract patronage of its ethnic economy and humanitarian aid for China. However, the "China" that tourists experienced was a Hollywood creation brought to life by Chinese Americans. Influencing one another, moviemakers and ethnic entrepreneurs projected similar fantasies of the Orient but insisted on marketing their creations as authentic versions of China.

While Chinese American urban communities in California exploited American fascination with Chinatowns and Chinese as a way to raise funds, UCR efforts in New York capitalized on the city's centrality to industry, advertising, and news media to make China a trend in itself, a fashion that could occupy Americans' minds and adorn their bodies. By April 1942, UCR had enlisted to its efforts "two dozen of the top-flight sales executives of most of the big business corporations in America" and reported of this team, "They have been doing a grand job during the last two or three months selling China to the American people instead of their usual products of automobiles, tires, electrical supplies, and other commercial products."[51] Chinese Americans were recruited to legitimize these efforts, but because Chinatowns in the Northeast tended to be smaller than on the West Coast, UCR campaigns just as often relied on high-class European American socialites and businessmen to model the appropriate combination of commercialism and compassion.[52] For example, one New York Bowl of Rice Party featured Mrs. Theodore Roosevelt Jr. eating rice with chopsticks to demonstrate her "sympathy with a destitute Chinese civilian."[53] To capture the interest of the upper classes, UCR scheduled relief events, such as concerts, balls, fashion shows, and teas at Carnegie Hall, the Hotel Waldorf-Astoria, Radio City Music Hall, the Metropolitan Museum of Art, and the Hotel Pierre.

The different strategies employed to raise funds reveal the intersections between specific Chinese American communities' histories and social location and the political economy of different regions in the United States. Organizers in San Francisco and Los Angeles strategically located their fundraising efforts within the economic and cultural borders of Chinatowns, with Chinese Americans welcoming outsiders into a clearly separate Orientalized space. Within these geographic and cultural borders, visitors—already assuming Chinatown to be a distinct cultural space—could traverse these clear boundaries as spectators to experience the exotic. On a national level, however, rendering China accessible to the American public required organizers to breach these perceived borders between Chinese Americans and the whole of the American public, through broad, universal symbols.

Gendering Internationalism

Regardless of specific regions' histories of interactions with Chinese Americans, the visual narratives of orphans and Chinese women served as tropes that could foster compassion for China and consumer desire for things Chinese among a national audience. Ideologies of gender had consistently permeated American narratives of China.[54] Whereas images of Chinese women as morally suspect had justified white American attempts to exclude and contain Chinese immigrant communities through the turn of the twentieth century, images of Chinese and Chinese American femininity during the late 1930s and early 1940s facilitated interracial cooperation and collaboration. To represent China's need for aid from the United States and Chinese American communities' appeal for tourists, two types of performances of Chinese womanhood emerged. While Chinese mothers and destitute children portrayed the helplessness and sufferings of China, the exotic beauty of young women attracted both male and female consumers.

The political demands for international and interracial unity during the Sino-Japanese War and World War II required that Chinese and Chinese American men also be recharacterized. Representing the vigor and strength of China, images of Chinese male soldiers surfaced in the American media. These portrayals of heroic masculinity conveyed the message that China was worthy of American admiration. They also contrasted sharply with the dominant depictions of Chinese men in the United States as emasculated and deviant economic competitors of white laborers. However, an overemphasis on the achievements of Chinese soldiers as a basis for a humanitarian campaign sent a problematic political message, namely that a U.S.-China military alliance was desirable when the American government and people had not yet made such an official commitment. Consequently, alternative models of Chinese manhood, specifically Chinese dignitaries and Chinese American merchants, emerged to serve as positive male representatives of China. However, relief organizers quickly discovered that the most effective figures for stirring compassion for China were orphaned children and suffering mothers.

Especially prior to the official entry of the United States into World War II, humanitarian campaigns sought to emphasize the victimization of China by Japan. Chinese women and children perfectly embodied a nonthreatening and accessible image of China and the Orient. One of the most remarked upon spectacles of San Francisco Rice Bowl festivals centered on the parade of a large Chinese flag held aloft by "hundreds of Chinese mothers" to collect donations for China.[55] The focus on the Chinese ancestry and maternal identity of the women was crucial to the overall appeal for economic assistance. The flag bearers, who figuratively took center stage at the festival, wore "*cheong sam*, China's national dress," to signify their Chineseness.[56] Although some might have been born or lived in the United States for a significant number of years, Chinese American women assumed the responsibility and the privilege of physically representing their ancestral homeland. Furthermore, their reputed maternal identity emphasized a nation in need of paternal support from the United States. The women symbolically and literally gathered money from the predominantly white American spectators to put rice in the bowls of starving children. In this international economic exchange, the fathers of China were absent. As one newspaper article noted, Chinatown was devoted to gathering "wealth for the starving and the homeless, for the maimed and the sick, for the fatherless thousands of Mother China."[57] The absence of a national paternal figure in the festival allowed the United States to imagine itself as the benevolent surrogate father who could provide economic support and eventually military protection for his female partner.[58]

This is not to say that white men were the most active in defending and supporting China. They certainly had a greater role in U.S. military and diplomatic circles and even in the leadership of mainstream relief organizations. However, white women, with their tradition of international maternalism, also participated enthusiastically and especially in humanitarian campaigns to assist the women and children of war-torn China.[59] The lists of China relief organizations and donors featured a substantial number of non-Chinese female benefactors. In addition, white women's groups sought Chinese female spokespersons to educate them about the needs of China. The DeWitt Clinton

Discussion Club contacted the UCR's Department of Speakers and Entertainment to request that a Chinese woman review Pearl Buck's *Dragon Seed* at one of their meetings.[60] Quarterly "Radio Reports" from 1943 reveal an attempt to raise women's knowledge of and interest in China through guest appearances on women's radio shows: Mrs. Lin Yutang appeared on "Frankly Feminine," Madame Chiang Kai-shek's favorite hymn was played on "Hymns of All Churches," Liu Liang-mo spoke on Mary Margaret McBride's "Home Front Forum," and the "Tribute to China" program at Carnegie Hall with Pearl Buck was broadcast over WHN.[61] Nevertheless, the gender symbolism of international and interracial relations tended to spotlight Chinese women as representatives of their ancestral land and white men as the leaders of the United States, overshadowing the contributions of both white women and men of Chinese ancestry.

Although Chinese women were featured as mothers of a helpless nation at the Rice Bowl festivals, they also appeared as seductive figures who could entice viewers to patronize Chinatown establishments and encourage consumption of Chinese luxuries. In contrast to the dignified portrayals of Chinese mothers, the coverage of the festivals emphasized the exotic beauty of young Chinese women. For example, one of the highlights of the festivals was the ethnic fashion show, which "featured scores of Chinese American women modeling elaborate clothing from the Tang dynasty to modern times."[62] One organizer recalled that the event was "very popular in those days. . . . Ticket lines were so crowded that the lines formed around the block. . . . After each show, we had to let the audience out the back door. As soon as we let one group out, new people were pushing in already."[63] As in the parade of flag-bearing mothers, "native" costumes were essential to the appeal of the show. Especially for younger women who were more likely to be American-born and acculturated, the clothing emphasized their connections with an ancestral land and clearly marked them as Chinese. Furthermore, the exotic silk costumes reinforced perceptions of the wearers as possessing a sensuous beauty. The coverage of the fashion show suggested that "Occidental mannequins could well take a lesson in poise, graciousness and gracefulness from their Oriental sisters. . . . Undulating across the stage came flower-like girls with glossy black hair."[64]

Newspaper accounts of other Rice Bowl festival events offered similar descriptions of physically alluring young Chinese women. For example, one parade observer declared, "the feature of that parade was, of course, beauty. It is well known that all Chinese girls are beautiful, but when they come by the hundreds, by the thousands, under colored lanterns and in their costumes of silk that robbed a million-million flowers for their colors—the effect was overpowering. It has all the quality of a strange dream of beauty which comes from a sleep induced by a magic draught."[65] The writer's description makes subtle allusions to the similarities between the seductive appeal of Chinese female beauty and the magical, dreamlike effects of opium, a drug popularly associated with the Chinese. These passages reveal how Orientalist perceptions of Chinese culture encouraged organizers and promoters to emphasize the physical appearance and sexual allure of Chinese American women to enhance the commercial and political appeal of the festival.

Rice Bowl Festival organizers used women of Chinese ancestry to attract both male and female audiences. White men might imagine themselves surrounded by the enticements of "Oriental" beauties, as depicted in one publicity photograph that featured San Francisco Mayor Angelo Rossi next to three performers from a Chinatown nightclub.[66] In fact, the humanitarian goals of the Rice Bowl festivals provided legitimation for men interested in gazing on the physical allurements of Chinese women. In addition, white women also were invited to view and admire the beauty and attire of Chinese women. Fashion shows traditionally target female audiences and seek to encourage consumption by arousing their desire for possession. The stagings of Chinese femininity communicated the message that racialized women or at least their ethnic costumes were worthy of emulation.[67] The fact that the articles on fashion tended to be written by female journalists underscored the homosocial and perhaps even homoerotic nature of the event.

China Relief publicists recognized the importance of appealing to American women as well as men for their campaign to be successful, and so encouraged the simultaneous marketing of China and femininity. Wes Bailey, a publicist on loan from *Life*, suggested that the Philadelphia UCR chapter hire a woman to assist with promotion efforts. She should be "gracious enough to sit across a tea table on the Main Line and talk intelligently about China, and who, at the same time, would have energy and ability enough to persuade the top-flight department stores that they should have China displays, fashion shows, et al., and who could contact all the women's clubs."[68] American women had been an increasingly important factor in the consumer market for decades; even if the products had changed, the audience profile remained much the same.

Conclusion

Both Chinese American and white relief organizers were responding to a similar set of cultural, economic, and political conditions. During the 1930s and 1940s, opportunities for interracial, international, and cross-gender cooperation emerged due to the nature of the worldwide conflicts. Individuals of Chinese ancestry and women became valued members of America's national and international family not only because they demonstrated civic agency, but also because they could affirm hierarchical assumptions regarding race, culture, and gender. Rice Bowl organizers and participants strategically staged performances to fulfill Orientalist fantasies in order to gain humanitarian aid for China. But these images did little to provide mainstream Americans with a more realistic view of China and the Chinese. Because appeals were shaped as much by marketing concerns as they were by the goal of raising awareness, they often perpetuated and relied on long-standing stereotypes. Even after the United States and China became allies in 1941 and after Chinese immigrants gained the right of naturalization, the shift from stranger to friend relied on further gendering Americans' already exoticized images of China. Emphasizing the role of Chinese women allowed UCR publicists to celebrate China's modernity and progress, while also containing any threat to the United States.[69] Underlying the idea that Americans could express their compassion through consumption was the continued assumption that the United States' future relationship with China would be one based not in equality but in economics and utility. The fact that Chinese Americans participated in these commercialized humanitarian efforts demonstrates both the limited possibility for political transformation during the international conflicts of the 1930s and 1940s and the continued economic profitability of performing Orientalism for a mainstream American audience.

NOTES

1. For overviews of Asian American history, see Ronald Takaki, *Strangers from a Different Shore: A History of Asian Americans* (Boston: Little, Brown, 1989); and Sucheng Chan, *Asian Americans: An Interpretive History* (Boston: Twayne Publishers, 1991).

2. See Yong Chen, *Chinese San Francisco, 1850–1943: A Trans-Pacific Community* (Stanford, CA: Stanford University Press, 2000); Gloria Heyung Chun, *Of Orphans and Warriors: Inventing Chinese American Culture and Identity* (New Brunswick, NJ: Rutgers University Press, 2000); Takaki, *Strangers from a Different Shore*; K. Scott Wong, "War Comes to Chinatown: Social Transformation and the Chinese of California," in *The Way We Were*, ed. Roger W. Lotchin (Urbana: University of Illinois Press, 2000), 164–86.

3. Judy Yung, *Unbound Feet: A Social History of Chinese Women in San Francisco* (Berkeley and Los Angeles: University of California Press, 1995).

4. Charles R. Shepherd, "All Too True," condensed version of his article in *Chung Mei Chronicle*, October 1938, as reprinted in *Chinese Digest*, November 1938, 5, 19.

5. Michael Schaller, *The U.S. Crusade in China, 1938–1945* (New York: Columbia University Press, 1979). See especially chapters 3 and 4.

6. "Children of China, a Fifth Year Report." (New York: China Aid Council, n.d.), 3.

7. Yung, *Unbound Feet*, 227.

8. For information about the Rice Bowl Parades, see Yung, *Unbound Feet*, 239–40; and Judy Tzu-Chun Wu, *Doctor Mom Chung of the Fair-Haired Bastards: The Life of a Wartime Celebrity* (Berkeley and Los Angeles: University of California Press, 2005), 133.

9. "Outstanding Chairmen (and Workers) Bowl of Rice Committees," May 19, 1941, "Bowl of Rice Parties," American Bureau for Medical Aid to China (ABMAC) Archive, Rare Book and Manuscript Library, Columbia University, New York; Memorandum,

ABMAC to Mr. B. A. Garside, February 10, 1941, 4, "Bowl of Rice Parties," ABMAC Archive; Memorandum, Mr. Hedrick to Dr. McConaughey, October 18, 1943, 3–5, box 22, folder 3, United Service to China (USC) Archives, Seeley Mudd Library, Princeton, NJ.

10. Untitled list of war relief organizations and funds raised, 1941, box 10, folder 2, USC Archives.

11. James C. Schneider, *Should America Go to War?: The Debate over Foreign Policy in Chicago, 1939–1941* (Chapel Hill: University of North Carolina Press, 1989), 74–78. Schneider notes, however, that "great care" was taken to "prevent the [Committee to Defend America by Aiding the Allies from becoming publicly identified with East European groups, especially the Jews" (76).

12. The 1940 U.S. census recorded 75,000 persons of Chinese origin residing in the United States.

13. Harold Isaacs, *Scratches on Our Minds: American Images of China and India* (New York: John Day Co., 1958); Michael Hunt, *Ideology and Foreign Policy* (New Haven, CT: Yale University Press, 1987); and T. Christopher Jespersen, *American Images of China, 1931–1949* (Stanford, CA: Stanford University Press, 1996).

14. Henry Luce also produced the *March of Time* dramas and newsreels and wielded his considerable influence in shaping Americans' perceptions of China. Patricia Neils, *China Images in the Life and Times of Henry Luce* (Savage, MD: Rowman & Littlefield, 1990); and Jespersen, *American Images of China.*

15. B. A. Garside, "Items for Consultation with Madame Chiang Kai-shek," April 28, 1943, box 22, folder 7, USC Archives. UCR's board of directors subsequently defined three goals: to raise funds for relief in China, to demonstrate American support and friendship for China, and to educate Americans about the importance of China in the past and future.

16. Under ABMAC, Bowl of Rice events had been staged by sixty-one local committees; of these, two-thirds continued as UCR committees.

17. The tensions between the Chinese Americans and the white Americans on staff are discussed in executive correspondence found in box 3, folder 5, and box 4, folder 10, USC Archives. In a summary of UCR activities during 1942, Wes Bailey noted of the Chinese American staff, "they taught all of us who worked with them something of the Chinese point of view, and with their help and consultation we have avoided many errors of judgment in all departments." Wes Bailey, "Report on Feb. 15–May 1 Activities," n.d., folder 7, box 22, USC Archives.

18. Arthur Rugh to B. A. Garside, "Occasional Bulletin No. 11," June 4, 1941, box 17, folder 10, USC Archives. According to this memo, between 1932 and 1937, Americans increased spending on theater by 41 percent, autos by 188 percent, radio by 220 percent, jewelry by 24 percent, and beer by 600 percent. Donations to churches, benevolent societies, and community chests declined by at least 20 percent.

19. The success of UCR, however, ultimately may have raised concerns on the part of the federal government about generating funds for all of its allies. In 1943, the Roosevelt administration proposed a more centralized fundraising effort, the National War Fund, which would eliminate competition among U.S. allies' relief organizations.

20. O. P. Swift, "Informal Report to Chairman Jas. Blaine Prepared by Otis Peabody Swift for Directors Meeting, Monday, May 12, 1941," May 8, 1941, box 5, folder 3, USC Archives.

21. Arthur Rugh, "Occasional Bulletin No. 17," July 10, 1941, p. 1, USC Archives.

22. It apparently accomplished its purpose, for Harold Isaacs declared it "one of the most successful 'propaganda' pieces of all time." See Harold R. Isaacs, *Scratches on Our Minds,* 168, fn. 84. Also see Robert Fyne, *The Hollywood Propaganda of World War II* (Metuchen, NJ: Scarecrow Press, 1994), 38.

23. "Cheer China" Program, Radio City Music Hall (New York: United China Relief, Inc., 1941), 31, box 84, folder 3, USC Archives.

24. "The Bowl of Rice Party: A brief history and recommendations for its future," n.d., 1, "Bowl of Rice Bulletins," box 4, ABMAC Archive.

25. Ibid.

26. " 'China, China, My Chinatown,' Chant Paraders" and photo caption in *San Francisco Chronicle*, June 18, 1938, A.

27. Ibid.

28. Willis O'Brien, "S.F. and a New Year Start Filling the Rice Bowls of China," *San Francisco Chronicle*, February 10, 1940, 1.

29. Ibid.

30. "Chinatown's Rice Bowl Celebration: Humanity Legion Buttons Yield $1,000 at Bay Meadows," *San Francisco Chronicle*, April 28, 1941, 15.

31. "Two Chambers of Commerce Pledge Support of Chinatown Beautification Program," *Chinese Digest* (April 1938), 14.

32. Ibid.

33. Anthony W. Lee, *Picturing Chinatown: Art and Orientalism in San Francisco* (Berkeley and Los Angeles: University of California Press, 2001), 251.

34. "Chinatown Holds Open House Tonight," *San Francisco Chronicle*, June 17, 1938, 1.

35. "300,000 Throng Chinatown for Rice Bowl Fete," *San Francisco Chronicle*, June 18, 1938, 1.

36. "Chinatown Holds Open House Tonight," 5.

37. John Kuo Wei Tchen, *New York before Chinatown: Orientalism and the Shaping of American Culture, 1776–1882* (Baltimore: John Hopkins University Press, 1999).

38. Samuel Gompers and Herman Gutstadt argued that Asian abilities to survive on rice allowed them to work for less pay than American men who required higher wages in order to sustain their diet of meat. Samuel Gompers and Herman Gutstadt, "Meat versus Rice: American Manhood against Asiatic Coolieism—Which Shall Survive?" originally published by the American Federation of Labor and printed as U.S. Senate Document 137 (1902), reprinted by the Asiatic Exclusion League (San Francisco: 1908).

39. The Chin and Lee Company in New York City shipped materials for dinners for up to one hundred people anywhere in the United States. Mrs. James E. Hughes, form letter, February 27, 1942, 3, box 19, folder 4, USC Archive.

40. Bill Utley (photographer), "Bowl of Rice Party, 1939," Photograph File, box 94, ABMAC Archive.

41. Individuals in Chinatown without humanity badges were required to stand before a kangaroo court and were fined appropriately. The collected fines became contributions to the Rice Bowl Funds. Stanley Bailey, "Before the Magistrate—Fun, Frolic and Funds," *San Francisco Chronicle*, February 10, 1940.

42. "300,000 Throng Chinatown for Rice Bowl Fete," A.

43. "Twelve Tongs to Participate," *San Francisco Chronicle*, June 17, 1938.

44. "Chinatown's Bowl of Rice Invites Everybody Tonight," *San Francisco Chronicle*, June 17, 1938, 18.

45. "300,000 Throng Chinatown for Rice Bowl Fete," 1.

46. Lee, *Picturing Chinatown*, 251–52.

47. Lisa See, *On Gold Mountain: The One Hundred-Year Odyssey of My Chinese-American Family* (New York: Vintage Books, 1995), 213. In the ABMAC Bulletin for the Bowl of Rice Parties, organizing committees were informed, "In a large city, where there are Chinese residents, Chinese entertainers . . . will be glad to cooperate to make the Festival a

success. In other places, gifted Americans may substitute for them." ABMAC Bulletin, no. 24, 1941, "Bowl of Rice Bulletins," box 4, ABMAC Archive.

48. Lyman Thompson to Henry Luce, August 15, 1941, folder 1, box 18, USC Archives. Thompson states that an estimated 250,000 people participated in raising between $75,000 and $125,000.

49. Ibid. As with San Francisco's Rice Bowl Parties, Chinese restaurants were expected to operate food concession stands with the profits going to the fundraising effort as well. The UCR Hollywood committee noted that had the streets been less crowded, they would have certainly raised more money through the food stands.

50. See *On Gold Mountain*, 221–22. For a history of the three Chinatowns in Los Angeles, see Suellen Chan and Munson Kwok, "The Golden Years of Los Angeles Chinatown," reprinted from *The Los Angeles Chinatown 50th Year Guidebook, June 1988,* http://oldchinatownla.com/history.html (accessed August 16, 2005).

51. B. A. Garside to Peter Rhodes, April 9, 1942, box 23, folder 29, USC Archives.

52. The regional differences in Chinatowns are suggested by K. Scott Wong, " 'The Eagle Seeks a Helpless Quarry': Chinatown, the Police, and the Press. The 1903 Boston Chinatown Raid Revisited," *Amerasia Journal* 22, no. 3 (1996): 81–103; and Mary Ting-yi Lui, *The Chinatown Trunk Mystery: Murder, Miscegenation, and Other Dangerous Encounters in Turn-of-the-Century New York City* (Princeton, NJ: Princeton University Press, 2005).

53. Utley, "Bowl of Rice Party, 1939."

54. See, for example, Gina Marchetti, *Romance and the "Yellow Peril": Race, Sex, and Discursive Strategies in Hollywood Fiction* (Berkeley and Los Angeles: University of California Press, 1993); and Karen J. Leong, *The China Mystique: Pearl S. Buck, Anna May Wong, Mayling Soong, and the Transformation of American Orientalism* (Berkeley and Los Angeles: University of California Press, 2005).

55. Abe Mellinkoff, "The Parade: Thousands Marched Last Night So Millions Might Live," *San Francisco Chronicle*, February 10, 1940.

56. Yung, *Unbound Feet*, 240.

57. "Chinatown Holds Open House Tonight: Thousands Will Join Rice Bowl Fete to Aid Far East's Disaster Refugees," *San Francisco Chronicle*, June 17, 1938, 1.

58. The Chinese American community recognized the value of female leadership in war relief work. Judy Yung notes that the male-dominated CWRA viewed fundraising as a "female task." Whereas the CWRA could tax businesses in Chinatown, women used their networks to solicit "door-to-door." The male leaders and members of the community may have viewed the act of requesting aid, similar to the act of begging, to be more suited for women. Yung, *Unbound Feet*, 230, 232.

59. Patricia R. Hill, *The World Their Household: The American Woman's Foreign Mission Movement and Cultural Transformation, 1870–1920* (Ann Arbor: University of Michigan Press, 1985); and Jane Hunter, *The Gospel of Gentility: American Women Missionaries in Turn-of-the-Century China* (New Haven, CT: Yale University Press, 1984).

60. Lorraine Talbott, "Speakers and Entertainment Department," March 24, 1942, box 80, folder 1, USC Archives.

61. "Radio Reports, 1943–44," box 58, folder 1, Publicity, USC Archives.

62. Yung, *Unbound Feet*, 237.

63. Ibid.

64. Ninon, "Beautiful, Svelte and Poised, They Walk," *San Francisco Chronicle*, February 10, 1940.

65. Willis O'Brien, "S.F. and a New China Start Filling the Rice Bowls of China," *San Francisco Chronicle*, February 10, 1940, 9.

66. "Rice Bowl: Rossi Buys First Button for Chinatown Party," *San Francisco Chronicle*, April 26, 1941, 11.

67. For a study of white women's investment in Orientalism, see Mari Yoshihara, *Embracing the East: White Women and American Orientalism* (New York: Oxford University Press, 2003).

68. Wes Bailey to Mr. Fletcher, April 10, 1942, box 22, folder 7, USC Archives.

69. Jespersen, *American Images of China*, 45–58.

4

From Pariah to Paragon: Shifting Images of Chinese Americans during World War II

K. Scott Wong

When the United States entered World War II in late 1941 and became allies with China in the shared fight against Japanese aggression, the first sizable American-born generation of Chinese Americans was reaching adulthood.[1] Their parents and grandparents had suffered the indignities of the Chinese exclusion acts, which had greatly curtailed the number of Chinese allowed into the country, denied them the right of naturalization, and shaped the composition of the Chinese immigrant population, giving preference to males, merchants, students, and others seen as more desirable than common laborers. The racial and cultural stereotypes of the Chinese in America centered on their supposed inability to embrace American political and social values; they were seen as "perpetual foreigners," forever on the margins of American society. When this American-born generation came of age, however, they were determined to claim a place in the broader American political, social, and cultural landscape. In this pursuit, Chinese Americans sought to take control of their public portrayals, which in turn reflected how they saw themselves as Americans.

This chapter examines three interrelated trends in the late 1930s and early 1940s that would greatly improve the image of Chinese Americans and would allow them to move from the status of social pariahs to paragons—what would later be called the "model minority": the distinguishing and distancing of the Chinese from the Japanese, Madame Chiang Kai-shek's tour of the United States, and the congressional repeal of the Chinese exclusion acts. These developments were played out in the public sphere through political and cultural activities, congressional hearings, and the print media—both the mainstream press and English-language Chinese American newspapers.

The Chinese American Press

The rise of the Chinese American periodical press was one of the most important developments in the shaping of second-generation Chinese Americans' identity formation. Although there were Chinese-language newspapers available, most American-born Chinese did not read or write Chinese well enough to read them; thus, English-language publications were vital. As Dorothy Eng of Oakland, California, remarked, "Our generation couldn't read or write Chinese, we spoke English among ourselves, as it was faster thinking in English. By the time you could figure the Chinese, the person had left." Mary Wong of Philadelphia echoed this position: "Our parents spoke Chinese and we would usually answer them in Chinese, or the parents of our friends. But among ourselves, my brothers and sisters, and friends, we only spoke English to each other."[2]

Founded in San Francisco in 1935 by Thomas Chinn and Chingwah Lee, the *Chinese Digest* was the first newspaper published in English specifically for American-born Chinese. It tried to bridge the gap between the second generation's ties to the culture of their parents and Chinatown and their own attempts to enter the American mainstream. In its inaugural issue, an editorial titled "Why the Digest?" clearly stated the mission of the paper: "The *Chinese Digest* is not just a hobby or a business—it is all that with a full-sized battle thrown in. We are fighting on five fronts."[3] The first front was "Killing a Celestial":

> There are no people in America more misunderstood than the Chinese. From the time of 'Sand-lot Kearny' [*sic*] to the present, the Chinese is pictured as a sleepy Celestial enveloped in the mists of opium fumes or a halo of Oriental philosophy, but never as a human being. The pulp magazines and Hollywood have served to keep this illusion alive. The 'Chinese Digest' is fighting this Celestial bogey and substitutes a normal being who drives automobiles, shops for the latest gadgets, and speaks good English.[4]

The second front was "The Truth Is Our Battle Cry," meaning that the paper wanted to report accounts of Japanese aggression in Asia that were more accurate than those appearing in most American newspapers. The third, "Bridging the Pacific," referred to the desire to cultivate an appreciation for and understanding of Chinese history and culture among Chinese Americans who might feel estranged from their ethnic heritage. The fourth, "Inter-Trench Communication," was a call for better ties among the Chinese American communities in America, as the editors recognized that the "Chinese in Boston or Portland have natural ties and common interests. Adverse legislation in one is adverse to all."[5] The final front was "The War on Neglect," a call for more economic opportunities for Chinese Americans. This initial editorial showed the editors' conscious effort to articulate the concerns of their generation and to educate, unify, and mobilize the community.

Soon after the *Chinese Digest* folded in 1940, William Hoy and Charles Leong, Chinatown journalists, began another Chinese American publication, the *California Chinese Press* (the title would later be shortened to the *Chinese Press*). According to Karl Lo and Him Mark Lai, the circulation of the *Chinese Digest* never reached a thousand, but the *Chinese Press* enjoyed a national readership.[6] In the opening editorial, Hoy made it clear that this paper would be geared toward second-generation concerns. He wrote, "Over sixty per cent of the 30,000 Chinese [in California] are those of the second or younger generation, the generation that speaks, reads and writes predominantly in the English language. The language of the California Chinese today is the language of their fellow Americans, and therefore their voice should also be in English."[7] The following paragraphs clearly set this newspaper apart from its predecessors:

> The California Chinese today are predominantly Americans, either through the privilege of birth or by derivative citizenship. As Americans of Chinese descent their future is the future of America, and their social and political ideals are those of American democracy. As they become rapidly Americanized there is an urgent need for a newspaper to act as a voice for this large group. The California Chinese Press hopes to become this voice.
>
> The California Chinese also look across the Pacific Ocean, seeking opportunities to help China in her present plight and to plan for the reconstruction of a greater China to come. The American people have always been the staunchest helpers of China. And the California Chinese, bound by the ties of race to the people of that Republic across the Pacific, can do no less than to bend their every effort in helping China emerge victorious from her present war with Japan, and later aid her in the gigantic task of reconstruction.[8]

Although the *Chinese Digest* was geared toward the second generation as well, there was still a tension between its desire to honor Chinese traditions and its determination to adopt American cultural mores. The group of second-generation Chinese Americans represented by the *Chinese Press*, however, felt wedded to America. Without rejecting China or Chinese culture, the editors fully embraced the United States as the land where their futures would unfold. Even though they referred to themselves as "California Chinese," they also called themselves "Americans," thereby forcefully claiming a place and role in American society. China was now "that Republic across the Pacific" rather than the "motherland." Although Chinese immigrants and their offspring had long desired to claim America as their rightful home, the weight of social, cultural, and legislative pressures constrained them from doing so. By the late 1930s and early 1940s, however, they were asserting their identification with American society and culture with strong conviction, and much of this would be articulated through the Chinese American press.

"How to Tell Your Friends from the Japs"

Once allied with China in the war, many Americans thought it necessary to distinguish Chinese from Japanese—a distinction that became important in how the two groups of Asian Americans would be perceived and treated by the American public. Two of the best-known examples came from Henry R. Luce's *Time* and *Life* magazines. On December 22, 1941, *Time* ran a three-quarter-page illustrated article in the "Home Affairs" section entitled "How to Tell Your Friends from the Japs." Photographs of two Chinese and Japanese men ran across the top and bottom of the article, with the text in between. The text is replete with cultural and physical stereotypes of Chinese and Japanese, but the author also warns that the guidelines offered are not always reliable: "There is no infallible way of telling them apart, because the same racial strains are mixed in both. Even an anthropologist with calipers and plenty of time to measure heads, noses, shoulders, hips, is sometimes stumped." Nevertheless, the article listed nine general differences between the two, ranging from height (the Chinese being taller than the Japanese), to weight (the Japanese are seldom fat, whereas in China being fat is a sign of prosperity), body hair (the Chinese seldom grow an impressive mustache), eyes (Japanese eyes are set closer together), and social demeanor (the Japanese are hesitant, nervous in conversation, and laugh loudly at the wrong time). Nothing, of course, was significant about these so-called differences, and none of them could hold up from one individual to the next, but the idea that there were important differences between the Chinese and the Japanese, and that one might be able to tell the two apart because of these traits, helped set the tone by which the Chinese became "friends" and the Japanese became "Japs."[9]

The *Life* version, which appeared on the same day, "How to Tell Japs from the Chinese," took a similar tack of explicating subtle physical differences between the Chinese and Japanese, couching them in pseudoscientific theories of race and racial origins: "To physical anthropologists, devoted debunkers of race myths, the difference between Chinese and Japs is measurable in millimeters. Both are related to the Eskimo and North American Indian. . . . Physical anthropology, in consequence, finds Japs and Chinese as closely related as Germans and English. It can, however, set apart the special types of each national group." Unlike the *Time* article, which featured four small pictures of Chinese and Japanese men for comparison, the *Life* article provided readers with a large portrait of a pleasant-looking Chinese government official and a menacing picture of Japanese General Tojo. Both portraits were inscribed with lines drawn to facial features and comparisons made in hand-written labels, such as "scant beard," "parchment yellow complexion," "never has rosy cheeks," and "more frequent epicanthic fold" for the Chinese and a "heavy beard," "earthy yellow complexion," "sometimes rosy cheeks," and "less frequent epicanthic fold" for the Japanese. Another set of pictures on the following page compared the height and leg length of "tall Chinese brothers" and "short Japanese admirals." The caption under the Chinese brothers stated, "Most Chinese in America come from southern and coastal cities, Canton and Shanghai. They are shorter than Northern Chinese, but retain the slight proportions of the young men shown here. When middle-aged and fat, they look more like Japs." In contrast, "aristocratic Japs . . . are proud to approximate the patrician lines of the Northern Chinese."[10] Despite the pictures and text, the articles were not really useful for distinguishing between Chinese and Japanese Americans. Nonetheless, the message was clear that the Chinese were friendly whereas the Japanese were ruthlessly militaristic; all of the pictures of the Japanese showed them in military uniforms.

If it was important for Americans on the home front to be able to distinguish between Chinese and Japanese Americans, it was vital that service personnel in Asia be able to tell the difference between Chinese and Japanese soldiers. To help meet this need, the Army issued *A Pocket Guide to China* to American military personnel stationed there. In addition to explaining Chinese cultural customs and habits and suggesting how Americans should behave in China, it offered a section entitled "How to Spot a Jap," written and drawn by cartoonist Milton Caniff and featuring characters from Caniff's best-known work, the comic strip "Terry and the Pirates." The title frame of this strip showed an officer asking Terry and his friend Ryan to show "the men a few points of difference between the Japs and our Oriental allies." As in the articles in *Time* and *Life*, these differences were constructed around physical traits supposedly common to the two nationalities. According to this guide, the skin color of the Chinese and Japanese is slightly different (the Chinese having a "dull bronze" skin tone and the Japanese, a "lemon yellow"); the Chinese have evenly set teeth, whereas the Japanese have buck teeth; when walking, the Chinese stride, whereas the Japanese shuffle (conversely, the *Time* article maintained that the Japanese walked "stiffly erect," whereas the Chinese shuffled); the Chinese and "other Asiatics have fairly normal feet," but the Japanese had a wide space between their first and second toes because of the wooden sandals they wore before being "issued Army shoes"; and finally, the Japanese had less ease with the English language, sucking in on any "s" sound and unable to pronounce the letter "l." Terry even advised the reader to "try 'lalafalooza' on them! That's a panic!" To sum up, the strip emphasized that "spotting a Jap" depended on three things: appearance, feet, and pronunciation; and that, in general, a Japanese individual was "short, squat, [with a] fairly heavy beard, with lemon-yellow skin and slanted eyes."[11] Although the Chinese are not described in as much detail, the general judgment is that they are much like Americans and should be treated with kindness and respect, whereas the Japanese—or, as they were more commonly called, "Japs"—could not be trusted nor did they deserve to be treated with respect or humanity.

Once the United States entered the war, many Chinese Americans took immediate steps to express their support for the American war effort and to separate themselves from the Japanese and Japanese Americans. Within days after the attack on Pearl Harbor, the Chinese consulate in San Francisco, with the assistance of various Chinese American community organizations, issued identification cards to Chinese immigrants and Chinese Americans in order to verify their ethnicity. Soon, buttons were available, for ten cents each, which declared "I'm Chinese," or simply "China"; other buttons depicted American and Chinese flags crossed in unity. The editors of the *Chinese Press* urged its readers to carry some sort of identification in order to distinguish themselves from Japanese: "For your own protection, the authorities MUST distinguish you from the Japanese, a people at war and an enemy of China and the United States."[12] Despite the use of such buttons, Chinese Americans found themselves frequently mistaken for Japanese Americans. Newspapers published many reports on such incidents. "Identification cards, buttons, and car stickers are displayed and wore [*sic*] by the thousands, but still the practice of Chinese being mistaken for Japanese goes merrily on. Minor incidents, such as Chinese being refused service in department stores and restaurants, etc. are still making the rounds. Here is this week's 'So sorry—thought you were a Jap' news stories."[13] Chinese Americans were urged to be patient and understanding if mistaken for a Japanese American. The editors of the *Chinese News*, a semimonthly founded by Thomas Chinn after the *Chinese Digest* ceased publication in 1940, wrote,

> The average American cannot tell the difference between Chinese and Japanese. With this thought in mind, we wish to caution every Chinese to bear with patience if the salesgirl does not wait on you; show that you're Chinese in some way, but do not do so arrogantly. In all cases, remember that most people cannot tell the difference between flags, so even the display of a flag is best augmented with the word "Chinese" in connection with it. The duty of every Chinese in America is to participate in the defense of this country.[14]

In conjunction with distancing themselves from Japanese Americans, there was little mention of the incarceration of Japanese Americans except when it might benefit Chinese Americans.[15] When Japanese Americans were taken from their homes and placed in concentration camps in the spring of 1942, there was a severe shortage of farm laborers on the West Coast, especially in California. The United States Employment Service issued a call for a thousand Chinese Americans to fill the ranks of the depleted farm workers. The *Chinese Press* urged Chinese Americans to respond to this call, mentioning that "Food is just as important as machine-guns to help win the war. . . . This is an opportunity for all Chinese with farm experience to develop a business as well as perform a patriotic duty. All types of produce and berry farms, vacated by the Japanese are available."[16] Thus, some Chinese Americans saw the internment as an opportunity to make gains in the name of patriotism.

The *Chinese Press* also participated in spreading the belief that Japanese Americans may have been guilty of fifth column activities to aid Japan. When writing about Chinese Americans taking over stores and business spaces left vacant by Japanese Americans, H. K. Wong reported that a "Japanese-owned hotel" on the corner of California and Grant Avenue in San Francisco had been leased by Albert and Nellie Lee and would reopen as a residence hotel for girls and businesswomen. When workers arrived to begin remodeling, "they found chairs and tables all set up for (could be fifth columnist) conferees. . . . The whole works were torn down in record time."[17] The fifth column message, however, had been made even more explicitly in an earlier article, which reported that Dr. Gordon S. Watkins, professor of economics and Dean of the College of Letters and Science at the University of California, Los Angeles, lectured to an alumni group and stated that "Pearl Harbor's fall was mainly caused by fifth column work by American-born Japs."[18] Watkins placed the blame on those Japanese Americans who had gone to Japan, claiming that some had become "officers for the mikado" and that "a number of them were fliers."[19] He concluded that Japanese parents and teachers from Japan prevented the *Nisei* from assimilating into American life. Japanese schools and Buddhist priests saw "to it that the boys and girls do not lose the virtues of their ancestors."[20] The editors of the *Chinese Press*, although acutely aware of the generational conflicts within the Chinese American community, were apparently not willing to acknowledge that similar tensions existed in the Japanese American community and that, like themselves, their Japanese American counterparts were overwhelmingly loyal to the United States and the American war effort.

The internment of Japanese Americans also provided Chinese Americans with the unlikely opportunity to make temporary gains in the motion picture industry. The war created a demand for films about the conflict, and stories set in the Pacific theater or China were popular. A piece in the *Chinese Press* describing the call for Chinese American actors began, "If your cheekbones are high and prominent, if your eyes will slant with the aid of a little adhesive tape, Hollywood's harried casting directors may be looking for you. And if you're really an Oriental, you haven't a Chinaman's chance of ducking a movie job unless you can run faster than the sprinting scouts of half a dozen studios where China is in just about every other title on the production lists."[21] Before the war, about a thousand Chinese Americans worked occasionally in the movie industry, but the war effort drew them into the military, defense industries, and other jobs that offered steady employment, and there was such a shortage of Asian actors at this point that the Screen Actors' Guild waived its membership requirements for hiring. The article emphasized, "The Japs are gone to internment camps. So many Chinese are playing Jap roles that there are practically no Chinese left for Chinese roles. Koreans are scarce. Malayans are scarce [and] Filipinos are so busy they have to stop and think which side they are really on."[22] An executive for Metro-Goldwyn-Mayer, speaking of the need for Chinese American actors for Pearl S. Buck's *Dragon Seed*, remarked, "I'll venture to say that every Chinese man, woman, and child west of Denver can get work in that picture. The only ones we definitely don't want are those in the army or defense plants."[23] On the one hand, Chinese Americans took this opportunity to make a statement about their loyalties and concerns about playing roles to portray the enemy. Filipinos, however, were said to relish the roles because "they all get killed at the end."[24] On the other hand, Mei Lee Foo, a San Francisco-born Chinese opera and concert singer, agreed to play a Japanese geisha girl because "the geisha girl is symbolic to many people of the moral decadence of Japan."[25] Thus, Chinese Americans could express their antipathy toward the Japanese while making economic gains for themselves.

In addition to the performing arts, Chinese Americans engaged in other forms of cultural production in the public sphere that boosted their status as loyal Americans. On May 16, 1943, the Department of the Treasury's War Savings Staff hosted an "I Am an American" Day at the Civic Auditorium in San Francisco. Representing Chinatown, May Jeannette Wong joined groups of Armenian, Austrian, Czechoslovakian, Danish, Dutch, Filipino, Finnish, French, German, Greek, Hungarian, Italian, Norwegian, Polish, Portuguese, Romanian, Spanish, Swedish, and Yugoslavian Americans to celebrate the climax of American Citizenship Week. Each of the twenty-two participating groups sponsored a booth, some of which sold "art objects and native trinkets," while others sold coffee and refreshments. All the proceeds would be used to buy war bonds. An evening show featured each nationality performing "folk dancing, singing, and a variety of other features that [would] illustrate the cultural contribution of each group to the development and upbuilding of America."[26] All new citizens were honored during a ceremony in the afternoon. The newspaper account of the event is striking in its praise of those participating: "They are the people who came to America to enjoy the freedoms guaranteed under our American form of government—the freedom of speech and of press, the freedom of worship, and the freedoms of petition and assembly. They show by

The Chinese American chapter of the American Women's Volunteer Service, 1942. *(From the Martha Taam collection. Courtesy of Judy Yung.)*

their participation that they appreciate what America has given them and want to give all they can to preserve the American way of life."[27] Although German and Italian immigrants were among those honored as loyal Americans, Japanese Americans were not. And although Chinese Americans were invited to participate, there was no mention of the fact that Chinese immigrants were still barred from citizenship at this point.

This pageant was consistent with other expressions of ethnic patriotism during the war. Eleanor Roosevelt and Frances Cooke MacGregor published a volume of photojournalism in which the "American Chinese" were the first ethnic group covered. The text praised their patriotism while acknowledging that "Under our laws, some of our older Chinese people have never been able to become American citizens . . . [but] we have today many young Chinese, also born here, serving in our armed forces. They are serving equally the nation from which their parents or grandparents came, since China and the United States are now Allies."[28] As in the pageant held in San Francisco, Italian and German Americans were celebrated as part of the American mosaic. There is no mention of Italy as part of the Axis powers, and the German immigrant featured is described as a loyal American "though he may grieve for the second war which has now come between the country of his origin and the country of his birth."[29] Not surprisingly, Japanese Americans do not appear in the book.

The two themes, that the Chinese are similar to Americans and that they are loyal patriotic Americans in the war effort, are echoed in the film series *Why We Fight*, directed by Frank Capra at the behest of the War Department. In the sixth installment, *The Battle for China*, China is praised for being the world's oldest country, a civilization of "art, learning, and peace," one that has never "waged a war of conquest." Furthermore, the war had brought the oldest and the youngest nations together to fight "side by side in a struggle that is as old as China itself; the struggle of freedom against slavery, civilization against barbarism, and good against evil."[30] The final film of the series, *War Comes to America*, stresses that "we the people, all the people" were involved in the war and that the war was being fought in defense of all Americans, including the "English, Scotch, Dutch, Italians, French, Swiss, Danes, Norwegians, Poles, Welsh, Negroes, Spaniards, Mexicans, Greeks, Portuguese, Germans, Hungarians, Russians, Irish, Slavs, and Chinese."[31] Chinese Americans were pleased to participate in these events and to be included in similar publications, for these venues allowed them to parade their ethnic heritage while demonstrating their loyalty to America. Thus, many Chinese Americans consciously claimed their place in American society during the war, often at the expense of Japanese Americans. Most Japanese Americans, powerless behind the barbed wire of concentration camps, had little recourse to counter this trend. One wonders how different the Chinese American response to Japanese Americans would have been had Japanese Americans not been interned.

As Chinese Americans separated themselves from Japanese Americans, and other Americans distinguished between friendly Asian allies and hostile Asian enemies, the general perception of Chinese Americans improved. In an article published in the *San Francisco Chronicle* and later reprinted in the *Chinese News*, a reporter wrote about Chinatown's readiness to aid the war effort. The end of the article is most revealing of the changing attitudes toward Chinese Americans. The reporter writes, "Next time you're eating or drinking in the district, don't let the fancy neon lights, the Cantonese talk, or the Oriental architecture fool you. These people are American through and through. The fact that their parents may have come from the old country and that their children have a tougher Americanization job on their hands than most of us makes them all the better Americans."[32] In 1942, Earl Warren, running for governor of California, issued a statement in observation of China's "Independence Day" (October 10) declaring, "Like all native born Californians, I have cherished during my entire life a warm and cordial feeling for the Chinese people. Under your great leader, Generalissimo Chiang Kai-Shek you have long been in the forefront of the battle for freedom. My sincere congratulations to you on this anniversary of Chinese independence, and with it my prayer that the Jap invaders will be driven from Chinese soil before the beginning of the New Year."[33] Wartime relations between the United States and China had created a new interpretation of both American history and Sino-American relations in which the hostilities between the two countries and the mistreatment of Chinese immigrants and Chinese Americans were conveniently forgotten.

Madame Chiang Kai-Shek's Tour of the United States

If there was one Chinese who changed the image of the Chinese and Chinese Americans in the American public's imagination, it was Madame Chiang Kai-Shek, the wife of the leader of wartime Nationalist China. Chiang's well-publicized and well-orchestrated tour of the United States officially began in the nation's capital on February 17, 1943. A guest of the Roosevelts, she stayed in the White House and was photographed often chatting with Eleanor Roosevelt on the White House lawn and meeting various politicians and military figures. On February 18, she made history by becoming the first private citizen and only the second woman to address both houses of Congress. *Time*'s account mentioned her poise, clothes, figure, and presence, characteristics that would be commented on throughout her visit:

> The Senators watched in curious silence as Madame Chiang walked down the aisle of the Senate Chamber. They saw a still face with dark eyes. They saw a slim, straight figure in a black Chinese gown, with a tiny splash of jade, there a black sequin's unstated sparkle. Madame Chiang stepped to the rostrum, listened as Vice President Wallace introduced her, shot a smile at the Senators, and then, after apologizing for not having a set speech, knocked their silvery blocks off extemporaneously.[34]

Chiang's speech was eloquent, witty, flattering of the United States, and forceful in presenting China's case. At one point, she stressed the commonalities between the two countries, giving it a personal bent, "I came to your country as a little girl. I knew your people. I have lived with them. I spent the formative years of my life among your people. I speak your language, not only the language of your hearts, but also your tongue. So coming here today, I feel that I am also coming home."[35] When her speech ended, the chamber erupted in generous applause. As *Time* put it, "The U.S. Senate is not in the habit of rising to its feet to applaud. For Madame Chiang it rose and thundered."[36]

Chiang's tour took her from Washington, DC, to New York City, her alma mater Wellesley College, and across the country by rail to San Francisco and Los Angeles. In both New York and San Francisco, she often delivered speeches to both white audiences, to whom she stressed China's plight, and to Chinese

American audiences, whom she exhorted to support China's efforts while being loyal Americans. After a stay in San Francisco, Madame Chiang traveled south to Los Angeles, where she appeared at the Hollywood Bowl on the afternoon of April 4, 1943. Produced by David O. Selznick, "China: A Symphonic Narrative" was an elaborate spectacle in front of 30,000 people with music provided by the Los Angeles Symphony Orchestra, a narration read by Walter Huston, and five hundred Chinese Americans acting out scenes of China's history and its role in the war. As the performance ended, Madame Chiang rose to give a speech that recounted China's struggle against the Japanese and also touched on the close relationship between China and the United States. Hailed as a great success, this was viewed as a proper ending to her impassioned tour.

Throughout Madame Chiang's time in the United States, the response from the American public was overwhelming. She received hundreds of cards and letters a day. One sent by Mrs. Cathleen Quinn of East Orange, New Jersey, included a money order for three dollars and a note reading, "It is from my three daughters and it is for the little guy on the railroad tracks somewhere in China."[37] As Carl Sandburg wrote, "What she wants, she wants for the Family of Man over the entire earth."[38] Referred to affectionately as the "Missimo" (to match her husband Generalissimo Chiang Kai-shek's abbreviated title of "Gissimo") and more formally as "Madame" or "the First Lady of China," she was embraced by Americans with a level of respect and kindness that contrasted starkly with how most Chinese immigrants and Chinese Americans had been received throughout American history. She represented not the heathen Chinese slave girl of the past but the modern Christian woman of China's future. Historian Karen Leong claims that Chiang was "the ultimate symbol of a modern and Americanized China"; historian T. Christopher Jespersen views her from a different angle, stating, "As a women who fitted squarely within domestic ideas about gender roles, Mme. Chiang could be viewed as the foreign equivalent of an American woman."[39] In her, Americans could embrace China's cause because Madame Chiang made China more familiar to them. She was American-educated, Christian, attractive, fluent in English, and an outstanding orator. For many Chinese Americans, she was all these things and more. She represented a modern and respected China: a heroine they could believe in, one who made them proud of their cultural roots, and one to whom all of America's press and celebrities eagerly paid homage.

Some scholars have criticized Madame Chiang for not confronting the issues of racial discrimination faced by the Chinese in America or the continued enforcement of the Chinese exclusion acts.[40] Although it is true that Madame Chiang said little in public about them, she apparently played her hand in mid-May of 1943, when she invited several key congressmen to dinner, days before the House Committee on Immigration and Naturalization was to begin hearings on the various bills before them. She is said to have stressed how much the repeal of the Chinese exclusion acts would boost Chinese morale and thus contribute to the war effort.[41] Throughout the congressional hearings and debates over the scope of repeal, those supporting repeal repeatedly invoked Madame Chiang.

The Repeal of the Chinese Exclusion Acts

The push for repeal came primarily from the Citizens Committee to Repeal Chinese Exclusion, a group of well-connected white Americans who had ties to China. In early 1943, Richard J. Walsh, editor of *Asia* and the second husband of Pearl S. Buck, published an article by Charles Nelson Spinks calling for the repeal of the Chinese Exclusion Act, declaring, "As our allies, the Chinese deserve racial equality now. As fellow human beings, they have been entitled to it ever since the United States first came into contact with their country."[42]

The article received considerable attention, and support for repeal grew. The Citizens Committee to Repeal Chinese Exclusion began meeting in New York to map out their strategy while Madame Chiang was touring the United States. Seizing on her presence in the country, Martin Kennedy (D-NY) introduced HR 1882, which called for repeal of the exclusion acts and made the Chinese eligible for naturalization.[43] Once this bill was introduced, other versions and amendments would follow in steady succession. Some supporters wanted to repeal all the laws that excluded Asians from immigrating and naturalization, whereas others advocated putting the Chinese on the quota system established by the 1924 Immigration Act. Some wanted to include a provision to allow Chinese men to bring their wives into the country as nonquota immigrants. In the end, it would be the bill sponsored by Warren Magnuson (D-WA), HR 3070, that emerged as the version that carried the most support. It called for the repeal of the Chinese exclusion statutes, establishing an annual quota based on the system outlined in the 1924 Immigration Act and allowing Chinese immigrants to apply for citizenship. This bill passed the House on October 21 and the Senate on November 26; President Roosevelt signed it into law on December 17, 1943.

As Congress debated repeal, much of the rhetoric employed on both sides was reminiscent of the debates over "the Chinese Question" in the late nineteenth and early twentieth centuries. Those opposed to repeal came from four main constituencies: labor, veterans' groups, "patriotic" societies, and some West Coast interests. Among those who supported some form of repeal were commercial interests, religious groups, "China Hands," and Chinese Americans and Chinese nationals. The debate over repeal focused on a number of overlapping and interrelated issues: countering anti-American propaganda employed by the Japanese; raising Chinese morale vis-à-vis their war effort; addressing the meaning of racial equality; and navigating the fear that repeal would allow a mass influx of Asian immigrants into the country, which would threaten the postwar economy and create racial tensions.

The issue of Japanese propaganda was at the forefront of much of the congressional discussion. Pearl Buck testified that "the Japanese have not failed to taunt them [i.e., the Chinese] with the friendliness of our words and the unfriendliness of our deeds. The Chinese have heard this propaganda and while they have not heeded it much, it has nevertheless been true. As a war measure, it would simply be the wisest thing we could do to make it impossible for Japan to use this sort of propaganda any more, by making it untrue."[44] The argument to establish an annual quota for the Chinese was a controversial issue for many. Although some believed that a quota would signify that the Chinese were seen as equals to other immigrants, others did not want to tamper with the nation's immigration laws during wartime, and yet others saw it as the beginning of a deluge of Asian immigrants and refugees. Supporters pointed out that "Hitler could come in under a quota, Mussolini could come in under a quota, but Madame Chiang Kai-shek, or the finest type of Chinese people, cannot because we say they are ineligible to come here."[45] Opponents, such as the national committees of the American Federation of Labor, the American Legion, and the Veterans of Foreign Wars, feared that a rise in Asian immigration would threaten the job prospects of returning veterans after the war, and that by allowing the Chinese to immigrate, other Asians would then seek the same privileges as "there would be no tenable argument after this war to deny admission to the Japanese, Hindus, Malays, and all other people of the brown and yellow races."[46]

Underlying the arguments for and against repeal was the American attitude toward race and citizenship and how Chinese and Chinese Americans figured into that discourse. Those who supported repeal often denounced the racial discrimination that was practiced through exclusion, although it was usually in relation to the war effort, Japanese propaganda, and the international reputation of American policy, and not necessarily to the moral questions of racism and social justice. The rhetoric among those opposed to the repeal may have included issues of economics and wartime conditions, but racial antipathy toward the Chinese was evident, as was their general opposition to racial equality and integration. Many of those opposed to repeal often asked witnesses whether they supported equality for all racial groups in all social situations, implying that their position on exclusion was linked to their stand on segregation. One of repeal's most ardent supporters, Walter Judd (R-MN), appealed to his colleagues in Congress to pass the bill on the grounds of fair and equal treatment. He remarked, "The Chinese are good enough to die by the millions in a war against Axis tyranny—but a Chinese who is not born in the United States is not good enough, so the law implies, to become an American citizen by naturalization. A man of German descent may so be naturalized, and so may an Italian. But a Chinese alien is not so fortunate. He is beyond the pale." He then pointed out that many Americans knew that the Chinese were not inferior as American laws had deemed them to be, for "in the United States we have come to admire the Chinese for his industry, his intelligence, his patriotism, and his good faith, and we have come to see, in the person of Mme. Chiang Kai-shek, the symbol of a truly great people."[47] Pearl Buck concurred on the quality of the Chinese as citizens, using language that would reappear in the 1960s as Chinese Americans were hailed as the "model minority." She declared, "the Chinese we have here are among our best citizens—they do not go on relief; their crime record is very low; they are honest and industrious and friendly."[48]

Organized labor and its affiliates saw repeal as a threat to the postwar job opportunities of returning veterans, whereas others were against changing immigration policies during a time of war. Some opponents simply continued the racialized attacks on the Chinese and the perceived inability of the Chinese to become Americans. William Green, president of the American Federation of Labor, was quoted as saying, "People from other countries are absorbed in a few years and you can't tell where they came from. A Chinaman is a Chinaman. Haven't you noticed that?"[49] Echoing his predecessors from the West Coast in the late nineteenth century, Compton White (D-ID) declared, "I do not think we can take the Chinese with their habits and mentalities in this year and time into our great American melting pot and in 10 years or a hundred years bring them up to our standards of civilization. It is impossible. We may be placed in the same position as the sentimentalists were in the South after the Civil War who wanted to do something grand for civilization. You have got a long, tough job to bring them up, and you still have race riots and other racial problems confronting you." Not content to stop with an obvious white supremacist tirade, White asked his colleagues, "How many of you Members know anything of the devious ways of the 'wily Chinese?' " He went on to discuss their slavelike labor conditions, their penchant for gambling and opium smoking, and their filthy standards of living. Yet he finished by stating, "I have no animosity against the Chinese. We children loved the Chinese cooks and laundrymen who lavished Chinese 'goodies' on us on Chinese New Year's—and even remembered our own Christmas. Let us help the Chinese—but help them in their own country!"[50]

One of the most striking aspects of the repeal movement is the absence of a strong Chinese immigrant or Chinese American presence in the public campaign. According to Fred Riggs, the Citizens Committee to Repeal Chinese Exclusion decided early on to limit its membership to "American citizens not of Asiatic origin so as to give the impression that the demand was completely indigenous, and not fostered by the Chinese or anyone with a personal 'axe to grind.' "[51] This approach was a continuation of a patronizing and paternalistic attitude that many so-called well-meaning white Americans maintained toward Chinese Americans. Fearing that opponents would brand the movement as one of special interests, the Citizens Committee's decision to limit membership to "Americans" served to disenfranchise Chinese Americans of their legal status as "Americans" and made one writer feel as if "we were just outside observers."[52] Nevertheless, Chinese Americans were not silent on the issue. They wrote letters to political figures, and they let it be known that the repeal of the exclusion laws was indeed something important to them. Taking a very accommodating, yet direct line, Theodora Chan Wang, representing the Chinese Women's Association of New York City, took advantage of Madame Chiang's visit to the United States and wrote Eleanor Roosevelt to express support for the establishment of an immigration quota for the Chinese. She stressed the issue of equality with other nations, although never mentioning them by name, by voicing her hopes that "a quota may be established—however limited it might be—whereby members of the Chinese race would be accorded the privileges enjoyed by our companions in ideology and arms." Wang addressed the concern that repeal might lead to an influx of unwanted labor. She emphasized that the establishment of a quota would simply send a message to the Chinese that the United States was sincere in its proclamations of equality; otherwise, the Chinese would continue to be "savagely assailed by the irrefutable claims of [the] Japanese that those who would accept us as their brothers-in-arms yet regard us as strangers within their gates. . . . They see only the cold facts before them."[53]

As the national campaign for repeal picked up, the Chinese American press ran more articles and advertisements in support of these efforts. When the San Francisco Chamber of Commerce voted to support repeal and to establish a quota for the Chinese, it was front page news. The *Chinese Press* also urged its readers to send letters to their representatives in Congress urging them to support the movement for repeal.[54] And when the City Board of Supervisors of San Francisco voted to support repeal, the paper commented that "sixty years ago [the city] was the chief center of violent 'The Chinese must go' discriminatory measures, this week repaid its debt to justice" with this vote. To add to the significance of their appeal, this article ran beneath a large photograph of Mr. Chow Fong accepting Silver Star and Purple Heart medals on behalf of his son Lt. Albert P. Fong, who had fallen in combat.[55]

In addition to articles of this kind, there were advertisements that proclaimed support for the Chinese American community. One taken out by the International Longshoremen's and Warehousemen's Union, CIO, was especially poignant. It read, "Here is where we Stand. . . . From 1935 on we refused to pass the picket lines of the Chinese People as they protested the sending of scrap iron to Japanese militarist murderers. We stand now for repeal of the Chinese exclusion laws, and for full equality of the Chinese people with all of us. We are united with the Chinese People and with them we will fight for the right of all to use the maximum energy against the common enemy on an equal basis."[56] The appearance of such appeals in the Chinese American press indicates that Chinese Americans were indeed concerned with repeal and issues of equity, and they appreciated the support they received from the broader community.

When the details of repeal were worked out, there were three main advances for Chinese immigrants and Chinese Americans: Sixty-one years of excluding aspiring Chinese immigrants on the basis of race and class ended, an annual quota based on the Immigration Act of 1924 was established, and Chinese immigrants were allowed to apply for naturalization. However, it was a limited victory. Chinese wives of American citizens were still not allowed to enter as nonquota immigrants; the annual quota was set at a mere 105; and naturalization was open only to those who could prove they had entered the country legally, pass an English-proficiency test, and demonstrate a knowledge of American history and the Constitution. These hurdles would prove insurmountable for many Chinese immigrants.[57] The annual quota of 105 was most revealing of persistent racial antagonism toward the Chinese. Although the quota was on a par with some other nations according to the Immigration Act of 1924, it was assigned to the Chinese as a "race," rather than on the basis of their nativity. Seventy-five percent of the entrants were to come from China and the remaining immigrants from elsewhere. Moreover, the language used also shaped who was to be considered "Chinese." The definition of "Chinese" was broad yet specific. It defined Chinese persons and persons of Chinese descent as "persons who are of as much as one-half Chinese blood and are not as much as one-half blood of a race ineligible to citizenship."[58] Therefore, those Chinese who were of mixed heritage with a parent who was of another Asian origin could not enter. Despite its limitations, the repeal of the Chinese exclusion laws in 1943 would eventually prove to be the "entering wedge" that its opponents feared. It paved the way for legislation that would eventually allow Filipinos, South Asians, Koreans, and Japanese to immigrate freely, culminating in the Immigration Act of 1965, which did away with racial and geographic restrictions to immigration.[59]

Conclusion

If the Chinese were social pariahs during much of their prewar presence in the United States, the war years saw Chinese Americans become the paragons of American assimilation and patriotism. As they embraced "the internal experience of citizenship" and developed a better sense of themselves as Americans, others also came to view them in a more positive light. Both the American mainstream and Chinese American periodical press played a role in the early

1940s in shaping how white Americans and Chinese Americans would see the Chinese American community. By becoming the "good Asian in the good war," they continued to be portrayed, and they portrayed themselves, in an increasingly normative light, gaining a degree of social acceptance previously denied them. These positive images, however, would shift in the postwar era as China turned to Communism and Japan became an important ally of the United States. Sociologist Rose Hum Lee perspicaciously foresaw this possibility when she wrote in 1944, "As violently as the Chinese were once attacked, they are now glorified and mounted on a pedestal. It is impossible to predict how lasting this change will be. . . . Largely grounded on the sandy loam of sentimentality, one is left conjecturing what the tone of the literature toward the Chinese will be in 1954."[60] Although Lee could not have predicted the course of events from the founding of the People's Republic of China, the Korean War, the Vietnam War, or the more recent incarceration of Wen Ho Lee, she was well aware that American images of Asians and Asian Americans would be dependent on American relations with the nations of Asia.

NOTES

1. This chapter is drawn from K. Scott Wong, *Americans First: Chinese Americans and the Second World War* (Cambridge, MA: Harvard University Press, 2005). The native-born Chinese American population of the United States in 1900 was 5,621. By 1930 it was 17,320, and by 1940 it had reached 22,880. *Sixteenth Census of the United States: 1940, Population, vol. 2: Characteristics of the Population* (Washington, DC: U.S. Government Printing Office, 1943), 516.

2. Interviews with Dorothy Eng, June 9, 1995, and Mary Wong, August 20, 2002. A different perspective on this is offered by Him Mark Lai, "Retention of the Chinese Heritage: Chinese Schools in America before World War II," *Chinese America: History and Perspectives* (2000): 10–31; and "Retention of the Chinese Heritage, Part II: Chinese Schools in America, World War II to the Present," *Chinese America: History and Perspectives* (2001): 1–30.

3. *Chinese Digest*, November 15, 1935, 8.

4. Ibid. It is difficult to determine how the term *celestial* came to be associated with the Chinese. One possibility is that the term for the Chinese imperial court, "Tian chao," translates as "Heavenly Court," which gave rise to the Western term *celestial* for Chinese.

5. Ibid.

6. See Karl Lo and H. M. Lai, *Chinese Newspapers Published in North America, 1854–1975* (Washington, DC: Center for Chinese Research Materials, 1977), 14; and Marjorie Lee, "Hu-Jee: The Forgotten Second Generation of Chinese America, 1930–1950" (M.A. thesis, University of California, Los Angeles, 1984), 57. Him Mark Lai estimates that the circulation of the *Chinese Digest* probably never exceeded five hundred, whereas the *Chinese Press*, published "during a period of relative prosperity," may have had a circulation of 1,000–1,500. Correspondence with Him Mark Lai, April 16, 1999.

7. *California Chinese Press*, November 22, 1940, 1.

8. Ibid.

9. *Time*, December 22, 1941, 33.

10. *Life*, December 22, 1941, 81–82.

11. United States Army, *A Pocket Guide to China* (Washington, DC: War and Navy Departments, n.d.), 65–75.

12. *Chinese Press*, December 19, 1941, 1.

13. *Chinese Press*, January 9, 1942, 1.

14. *Chinese News*, December 15, 1941, 6. After the *Chinese Digest* ceased publication in 1940, Thomas Chinn began publishing the *Chinese News*. This latter periodical was published semimonthly until early 1942, when Chinn entered government service in support of the war effort.

15. When I asked Thomas Chinn about the lack of coverage of Japanese American internment in his papers, he simply stated, "My papers were for and about Chinese Americans," implying that there was little need to address Japanese American concerns. Interview with Thomas Chinn, June 6, 1995.

16. *Chinese Press*, May 1, 1942, 1.

17. *Chinese Press*, May 1, 1942, 6.

18. *Chinese Press*, January 30, 1942, 1.

19. Ibid.

20. Ibid.

21. *Chinese Press*, May 14, 1943, 5.

22. Ibid.

23. Ibid. This statement is rather ironic because the film starred Katherine Hepburn, rather than an Asian actor, in the lead female role.

24. Ibid.

25. *Chinese Press*, August 13, 1943, 1.

26. *Chinese Press*, May 14, 1943, 1.

27. Ibid.

28. Eleanor Roosevelt and Frances Cook MacGregor, *This Is America* (New York: G. P. Putnam's Sons, 1942), no page number.

29. Ibid.

30. "The Battle for China," directed by Frank Capra, 1944.

31. "War Comes to America," directed by Frank Capra, 1945.

32. Bill Simons, "Chinatown Ready for Any Emergency for She Knows Aggressor," *Chinese News*, January 15, 1942, 3. Originally published in the *San Francisco Chronicle*, January 14, 1942.

33. *Chinese Press*, October 16, 1942, 7.

34. *Time*, March 1, 1943, 23.

35. Harry J. Thomas, *The First Lady of China: The Historic Wartime Visit of Mme. Chiang Kai-shek to the United States in 1943* (New York: International Business Machines, 1943).

36. *Time*, March 1, 1943, 23.

37. Quoted in Barbara W. Tuchman, *Stilwell and the American Experience in China, 1911–1945* (New York: Macmillan, 1970), 349.

38. Quoted in Tuchman, *Stilwell and the American Experience in China*, 350.

39. Karen Janis Leong, *The China Mystique: Pearl S. Buck, Anna May Wong, Mayling Soong, and the Transformation of American Orientalism* (Berkeley and Los Angeles: University of California Press, 2005), 144; and T. Christopher Jespersen, *American Images of China, 1931–1949* (Stanford, CA: Stanford University Press, 1996), 88.

40. See especially Lorraine Dong, "Song Meiling in America 1943," *The Repeal and Its Legacy: Proceedings of the Conference on the 50th Anniversary of the Repeal of the Exclusion Acts* (San Francisco: Chinese Historical Society of America, 1994), 39–46.

41. Fred W. Riggs, *Pressures on Congress: A Study of the Repeal of Chinese Exclusion* (New York: King's Crown Press, 1950), 116.

42. Charles Nelson Spinks, "Repeal Chinese Exclusion!" *Asia* (February 1942): 94.

43. The bill's number, 1882, matched the date of the passage of the first exclusion bill to prohibit the immigration of Chinese laborers for ten years.

44. U.S. Congress, House of Representatives, *Hearings before the Committee on Immigration and Naturalization*, 78th Cong., 1943, 68 (hereafter cited as *Hearings*).

45. *Congressional Record* 89, U.S. House, 78th Cong. (June 16, 1943): 5966.

46. *Congressional Record* 89, U.S. Senate, 78th Cong. (November 26, 1943): 10014.

47. *Congressional Record*, 89, Appendix, 78th Cong. (June 11, 1943): A2928.

48. *Hearings*, 69–70. Buck's comments are very similar to those found in the seminal "Model Minority" article in the 1966 *U.S. News and World Report* article, which remarked, "At a time when it is being proposed that hundreds of billions be spent to uplift Negroes and other minorities, the nation's 300,000 Chinese-Americans are moving ahead on their own—with no help from anyone else. . . . Visit 'Chinatown USA' and you will find an important racial minority pulling itself up from hardship and discrimination to become a model of self-respect and achievement in today's America." "Success Story of One Minority Group in U.S.," *U.S. News and World Report*, December 26, 1966, 73.

49. Quoted in Riggs, *Pressures on Congress*, 67.

50. *Congressional Record* 89, U.S. Senate, 78th Cong. (October 21, 1943): 8626–27.

51. Riggs, *Pressures on Congress*, 113. See also Renqiu Yu, *To Save China, to Save Ourselves: The Chinese Hand Laundry Alliance of New York* (Philadelphia: Temple University Press, 1992), 130–37.

52. L. Ling-chi Wang, "Politics of the Repeal of the Chinese Exclusion Laws," in *The Repeal and Its Legacy: Proceedings of the Conference on the 50th Anniversary of the Repeal of the Exclusion Acts* (San Francisco: Chinese Historical Society of America, 1994), 66.

53. *Hearings*, 6.

54. *Chinese Press*, June 11, 1943, 1.

55. *Chinese Press*, September 10, 1943, 1.

56. *Chinese Press*, July 9, 1943, 3.

57. Wang, "Politics of the Repeal," 80.

58. Roger Daniels, *Asian America: Chinese and Japanese in the United States since 1850* (Seattle: University of Washington Press, 1988), 198.

59. For a study that examines the racial ideologies embedded in the repeal of the various exclusion laws, see Neil Gotonda, "Towards Repeal of Asian Exclusion: The Magnuson Act of 1943, the Act of July 2, 1946, the Presidential Proclamation of July 4, 1946, the Act of August 9, 1946, and the Act of August 1, 1950," in *Asian Americans and Congress: A Documentary History*, ed. Hyung-chan Kim (Westport, CT: Greenwood Press, 1996), 309–37.

60. Rose Hum Lee, quoted in Harold R. Isaacs, *Scratches on Our Minds: American Views of China and India* (Armonk, NY: M. E. Sharpe, 1980; originally published in 1958), 120.

5

From Chop Suey to Mandarin Cuisine: Fine Dining and the Refashioning of Chinese Ethnicity during the Cold War Era

Madeline Y. Hsu

> *At Johnny Kan's restaurant in Chinatown, Mayor H. Roe Bartle of Kansas ordered chop suey, to the annoyance of Kan. "Chop suey," he pointed out, "is an imitation of Chinese food, we wouldn't insult our customers by serving it."*[1]
>
> —Herb Caen

With the 1953 founding of his eponymous Grant Avenue restaurant in the heart of San Francisco's Chinatown, Johnny Kan (1906–1972) established new standards for elegance and authenticity in Chinese dining. Unlike the dingy chop suey joints of pre–World War II years with their bastardized dishes and rude waiters, Kan's Restaurant featured white tablecloths and Chinese art on the walls, trained waiters who offered gracious service, a convivial and informed host, and the "centuries old" cuisine of China's emperors prepared in modern stainless steel kitchens displayed to the world from behind plate glass windows.[2] Drawing on decades of experience as an entrepreneur, Kan began redefining Chinese ethnicity to appeal successfully to a broadening and increasingly affluent swathe of American consumers. The decades-long success of Kan's Restaurant, and the market transitions it helped to engender, reflects the shift from racialization to ethnicization of Chinese Americans during the cold war years. Together with the even more upscale Mandarin, founded in 1961 by the elegant former foreign-service wife Madame Cecilia Chiang (b. 1919), Kan's Restaurant popularized Chinese-style fine dining in San Francisco. The success of these two restaurants demonstrates the continuing salience of ethnicity in Chinese American lives even as cold war ideologies proclaimed their increasing acceptance into the American mainstream. In the face of such contradictions, these two highly acculturated and ambitious entrepreneurs refashioned representations of Chinese cuisine and ethnicity to enhance the desirability, and thus the consumption and profitability, of Chinese foods and restaurants for a general American public.

The Chinese started gaining greater acceptance in the United States only in the late 1930s, after decades of open hostility that produced America's earliest race-based immigration restrictions and a raft of other forms of institutionalized discrimination. According to Karen Leong and Colleen Lye, changing American foreign policy goals in Asia, and the developing alliance with China's Nationalist Party, the Kuomintang (KMT), stimulated ideological shifts that accelerated with the anti-Japanese partnership of World War II and extended through the cold war era.[3] In what Lye refers to as "processes of naturalization," the Chinese evolved from the unassimilable aliens of the Chinese exclusion era (1882–1943) to the model minorities of the late twentieth century.[4] Even as they morphed from the yellow peril to model American citizens, however, race and ethnicity remained essential components of Chinese American experiences. The upgrading of Chinese restaurants and Chinese cuisine reveals how the content of Chinese ethnicity shifted and gained desirability during the cold war years. Rather than attempting to blend into the mainstream by erasing their racial and ethnic distinctiveness, Chinese American entrepreneurs such as Kan and Chiang became increasingly skilled at selectively marketing versions of Chineseness so that the ethnic restaurant industry could become an extremely profitable niche rather than a dead-end career path imposed by discrimination. By the time America's cold war with China ended in 1972 with a flurried exchange of ping-pong players and pandas, Kan and Chiang were among those who helped to engineer some of the domestic shifts in racial ideology that made this new friendship more feasible.

During the 1950s and 1960s, the salience of Chinese ethnicity did not diminish despite the civil rights movement and the anticipated fruition of an American melting pot protected from significant immigration flows by the most severe legal restrictions in the nation's history.[5] In *Cold War Orientalism*, Christina Klein argues that

> In the 1930s and 1940s the racial formation of people of color within the U.S. began to change, as racialization gave way to ethnicization. With ethnicization, the socially and culturally defined category of ethnicity replaced the biological category of race as the preferred way to explain differences among populations. During World War II, official and unofficial propagandists celebrated America as a racially, religiously, and culturally diverse nation, and in the process they transformed the ethnic immigrant from a marginal figure into the prototypical American.[6]

America was supposed to integrate under such conditions. In reality, it was difficult to eradicate the connection between racial differences and inequality despite the ideological implications of Supreme Court decisions such as the 1954 case *Brown v. Board of Education.*

For Chinese Americans particularly, this new agenda of racial inclusiveness paralleled the war on Communism. Klein juxtaposes the global imaginary ideology of containment against the global imaginary ideology of integration. She notes that the former "imagined the cold war as a crusade against communism. . . . Much of the energy it generated, however, was directed inward and aimed at ferreting out enemies and subversives within the nation itself."[7] The latter, however, "represented the cold war as an opportunity to forge intellectual and emotional bonds with the people of Asia and Africa. Only by creating such bonds . . . could the economic, political, and military integration of the 'free world' be achieved and sustained. When it did turn inward, the global imaginary of integration generated an inclusive rather than a policing energy."[8] As minorities whose ethnicity could now serve to bolster American democracy, Chinese Americans gained social and cultural acceptance even as they faced the considerable risk of racialization as enemy agents working on behalf of Communist China. This confluence of opportunity and danger shaped the choices made by Chinese American entrepreneurs who developed strategies for marketing their ethnicity in ways that affirmed America's democratic and capitalistic ideals.

The examples of Kan's Restaurant and the Mandarin illustrate that domestically palatable representations of Chinese American-ness could also generate tremendous profits. These consumer-oriented approaches toward packaging Chinese American ethnicity were rooted in ideological and generational shifts dating back to the 1930s.

An Enterprising Generation

Johnny Kan was one of a new breed of American-born Chinese, a generation that came of age during the 1930s and 1940s and were determined to transcend the economic and social constraints imposed by racism. They sought alternatives to the economic ghetto that had confined so many of their immigrant parents and grandparents in the service industries of laundries, Chinatown stores, domestic service, and cheap chop suey restaurants. Highly acculturated Chinese Americans such as Charlie Low and Jade Snow Wong managed to acquire wealth and fame by packaging "Chinese" culture in ways that appealed to mainstream consumers. As American conceptions of democracy became inclusive of its minority components, Chinese Americans learned to turn their ethnicity into profits.

Charlie Low established the Chinese American nightclub Forbidden City in 1939 with a small fortune inherited from his mother. He had dreamed of creating a Chinese American version of the nightclubs then dominating the nightlife of big cities like New York. Low was ambitious: The Forbidden City featured a floorshow, a restaurant seating more than three hundred diners, a kitchen equipped to prepare both American and Chinese menus, a reception area ornamented with arches and temple awnings, a separate bar that could hold ranks of patrons four to five deep, and a long hallway displaying photos of himself shaking hands with celebrity visitors.

As suggested by its name, the Forbidden City catered willingly to the Orientalist fantasies of mainly white audiences. The all-"Chinese" revue included singers, dancers, magicians, comedians, and strippers wearing embroidered silk robes and using fans and gongs.[9] These entertainers performed as the "Chinese Frank Sinatra" or the "Chinese Fred Astaire and Ginger Rogers." Although they confounded audience expectations when they spoke, sang, and joked in perfect English and displayed a sense of rhythm when they danced, they also reinforced stereotypes of the Chinese as exotic and foreign. Low's show pandered to the basest of Euro-American curiosity in the form of the Chinese American bubble girl, stripper Noel Toy. Although local Chinatown residents spurned the nightclub, Low and his performers profited handsomely for almost a decade from the thousands of Euro-Americans who flocked to enjoy the illicit pleasures of the Forbidden City.[10]

The writer and ceramicist Jade Snow Wong chose a far less scandalous approach in her representations of Chinese American life. Wong is most famous for her autobiography, *Fifth Chinese Daughter*, which remains in print to this day. It offered the archetypical tale of an unappreciated Chinese daughter who defied tradition to find a balance between her Chinese and American selves. Wong overcame her parents' lack of support by working her way through college. After receiving her B.A. and working briefly as a secretary in a shipyard, Wong forged a lucrative career path in marketing her Chinese American-ness for non-Chinese, first as a writer and a ceramicist, then as a travel agent specializing in trips to Asia.

As a potter, Wong selectively promoted desirable aspects of Chinese culture by producing an elite art form for American consumers. In this phase of her career, Wong continued to emphasize her uniquely Chinese American melding of tradition and defiance by choosing a very public storefront near Clay Street in San Francisco as her studio. In full view of Chinatown tourists, she practiced this renowned Chinese craft to make her living as an artist, a rare career choice for Chinese Americans at that time. As a travel agent and tour guide, Wong specialized in leading Euro-American groups on trips to visit America's Asian allies—Taiwan, South Vietnam, and Cambodia. Although *Fifth Chinese Daughter* has been heavily criticized for its one-dimensional portrayals of Chinese American patriarchy, it helped to domesticate and familiarize Chinese American lives for mainstream readers. Authors such as Maxine

Hong Kingston and Amy Tan acknowledge their debt to Wong in developing broader audiences for Chinese American writers.[11]

Low's and Wong's achievements occurred during the early stages of major ideological and institutional shifts in American attitudes regarding racial and ethnic minorities. In the wake of World War II, the federal government banned racial discrimination in the defense industries, electoral rights, the military, housing covenants, and public schools.[12] These legal and social shifts permitted the percentage of Chinese in the professional and technical occupations to increase from 2.8 percent to 26.5 percent between 1940 and 1960.[13] During these same years, Chinese Americans also began leaving Chinatown, a phenomenon reflected in the quadrupling of Bay area Chinese living in the suburbs.[14]

Even as they gained unprecedented access to the comforts of middle class life, however, many Chinese Americans understood that their greatest prospects for wealth rested not in the hope of integrating into the American melting pot but in enhancing the desirability of their ethnic heritage through the tourist and food service industries. The careers of George Hall and John C. Young of Wing Nien Foods suggest how this generation of Chinese Americans negotiated these contradictions.

Both Hall and Young were well educated and received their engineering degrees during the 1930s. During the 1940s, they knew that they could finally get jobs that reflected their educational attainments but that as Chinese Americans they would not advance in them.[15] Nor would they get rich. Instead of security and respectability, they chose the creativity and potential profits of entrepreneurship and founded Wing Nien Foods to become the first domestic manufacturers of soy sauce. Although soy sauce did not make them wealthy, Hall and Young profitably invested in Kan's Restaurant.

As dedicated businessmen developing ethnic products for domestic consumption, Hall and Young fitted well into the capitalist and integrationist agendas promoted by cold war America. Unlike many other Chinese Americans, they were never suspects in the FBI's war on Communism and did not face the surveillance and threatened loss of citizenship and deportation experienced by thousands of immigrant Chinese.[16] Hall and Young were representative of Chinatown's emerging generation of entrepreneurs, who secured their place in America by embracing the kinds of economic and racial opportunities available during the cold war to forge new ways for Chinese Americans to succeed as ethnic Americans.

Hall's and Young's generation of entrepreneurs boosted Chinese American businesses through the Chinese Chamber of Commerce, a new type of organization that developed the Chinese New Year's Parade and beauty pageant to attract tourists to Chinatown. In their campaigns to broaden mainstream consumption of Chinese American goods, Chinese American entrepreneurs focused their energies on promoting ethnically flavored festivals, young women, districts, and food.

Restaurants and the Continuing Salience of Chinese Ethnicity

The cold war successes of entrepreneurs like Charlie Low, Jade Snow Wong, George Hall, and John C. Young demonstrate that being Chinese could be lucrative business, if marketed in the right way. As analyzed by Klein, domesticated Chineseness served to vindicate American claims of democracy. "Although they are not exclusively foreign, their partial foreignness makes them worth assimilating into American society, because it legitimates the nation's claim to be a 'nation of nations.'"[17] Closer examination of the founding and marketing of Kan's Restaurant and the Mandarin highlights the usefulness of ethnic identity in Chinese American business efforts during the cold war era. For American-born and elite émigrés alike, Chinese restaurants remained reliable and sometimes tremendously lucrative ways of making a living as they produced increasingly desirable representations of Chinese ethnicity for non-Chinese consumption.

The Chinese have been making money by feeding the non-Chinese since they first arrived in search of gold. At Chinese-run eating establishments, hordes of rough-and-tumble miners could choose from both Chinese and American selections washed down with coffee and hot tea.[18] Despite rumors of rats and dogs in the larder, Chinese restaurants continued to attract patrons through the late nineteenth and early twentieth centuries. In these early decades, Chinese dining was associated with dingy quarters and poor service offset by tasty food, low prices, and delivery services.

Chop suey became the much maligned but most recognizable symbol of Chinese adaptations to American tastes. The term chop suey derives from the Chinese phrase *zasui* (*zapsui* in Cantonese), which refers to a miscellany of chicken livers, gizzards, fungi, bamboo shoots, pig tripe, and bean sprouts in a brown sauce. Chinese cooks later adapted these ingredients for American tastes by replacing internal organs with the more familiar chicken, pork, or shrimp.[19] To explain the pervasiveness of chop suey, Renqiu Yu argues that Chinese American businessmen capitalized on the publicity accompanying Chinese minister Li Hongzhang's 1896 visit to popularize the dish as the Mandarin official's favorite.[20] Although Yu convincingly demonstrates that this tale is apocryphal and that Li never encountered chop suey during his trip, Chinese restaurants and chop suey became staples in the American dining experience.[21]

Sociologist Ivan Light argues that the growing popularity of Chinese restaurants was part of the rise of the Chinatown tourist industry as a whole. Beginning in the 1890s, Chinatown merchant leaders attempted to attract more customers by simultaneously sanitizing and exoticizing their communities. They embarked on a decades-long struggle to quell the secret societies whose public violence and criminal activities fed the image of Chinatowns as dangerous places.[22] They lighted and swept the streets and ornamented buildings to produce an Oriental quarters that was enticingly foreign but safe and clean. The rebuilding of San Francisco's Chinatown after the 1906 earthquake, with pagoda roofs, bedragoned lamp posts, and temple-cum-telephone exchange, exemplifies this shift toward wooing the curiosity and tastes of non-Chinese. Such strategies were successful as observed by George Hsiong of New York in 1939: "Approximately eight thousand to ten thousand people come to Chinatown every weekend for the purpose of getting Chinese food."[23]

The rising popularity of Chinese restaurants promoted growth in the Chinatown tourist industry. Between 1903 and 1923, the Los Angeles city directory listings of Chinese restaurants rose from only five to twenty-eight despite the fact that the local Chinese population fell during those same years. According to the 1870 U.S. census of population, nationally only 164 Chinese worked as restaurant keepers or employees. By 1920, these numbers had increased to 11,438.[24] Although restaurants employed fewer Chinese than laundries did, the former industry generated more growth by channeling business toward "grocery stores, butcher shops, and fish markets from which the restaurants procured samples." In Chinatown, "import outlets, bric-a-brac and curio stores also prospered . . . in response to the increased traffic of white tourists."[25]

In pre–World War II America, chop suey restaurants provided steady incomes for thousands of Chinese denied employment in other occupations. Newspaperman Leong Gor Yun observed that "generally a Chinese restaurant with good management and a decent chef can easily be successful, thanks to American fondness for chop suey and chow mein."[26] However, restaurants also served as bitter reminders that even American-born, college-educated Chinese had few other options. "Before World War II, native-born Chinese youths who wanted to stay in this country had little choice. They were confined to restaurant work."[27] Those with more ambition, however, began to contemplate the potential of restaurants to become something more than a dead-end means of making a living.[28] To make Chinese restaurants more profitable and prestigious, ambitious entrepreneurs and self-taught experts in Chinese cuisine, such as Johnny Kan and Cecilia Chiang, had to liberate Chinese food and the reputation of Chinese restaurants from the disreputable shadow of greasy chop suey joints and grimy Chinatown ghettos.

From Chop Suey to Fine Dining

As suggested by the anecdote that begins this article, Johnny Kan was on a mission to combat the bastardization of Chinese cuisine and culture represented by chop suey. Legendary San Francisco raconteur Herb Caen recalled in his eulogy for Kan: "To tourists (and natives) who would innocently order chop suey, Johnny would purr, 'I'm sorry, we serve only Chinese food here.'" Caen credited Johnny Kan with being the first to educate non-Chinese about "the wondrous subtleties and intricacies of true Oriental cuisine" at a time when "Chinatown . . . was still a mysterious world to most whites" characterized by small restaurants, tables with bare marble tops, and rude waiters that served the working-class foods of chop suey and "beetle juice."[29]

Kan was a fervent advocate of Chinese cuisine among non-Chinese. His friend and tour book author, Jack Sheldon, celebrated Kan as something akin to a prophet of Chinese fine dining:

> There is one man who surely deserves the credit for making San Franciscans as well as visitors to our city anxious to dine in Chinatown. He was Chinatown's Mr. Ambassador to the world. Not only did he bring Chinese restaurants out of the alleys and proudly onto Grant Avenue and either side of it, but he never turned down an opportunity to spread the word extolling the delights of Cantonese cookery. He traveled, he wrote, he spoke, he greeted, he welcomed. And through it all, he kept his own restaurant highly distinguished among Chinatown's most famed. He, Johnny Kan, gave this awakening to us.[30]

The man who accomplished such transformations in the minds and palates of white Americans was unusual both for his level of acculturation and for the scope of his vision and ambition of what could be accomplished in America by an entrepreneur who was enthusiastically Chinese. When interviewed by Victor and Brett de Bary Nee in 1963, he seemed strikingly different from the beaten-down working-class "bachelors" who also worked in San Francisco's Chinatown: "We are surprised at how tall he is when he walks into the room. In a dark formal suit, Johnny seats us and orders drinks for everyone. Although we know he is fifty-seven years old, in dress, manner, and speech he is completely different from the old men with whom we have spent the last few weeks learning about the history of Chinatown."[31] Kan stood tall, not only as an American, but also as a self-confident visionary who sought ways to profit by improving mainstream impressions of Chinese people and their food.

From his first job as a clerk in a peanut-roasting firm, Kan sought to improve and expand business by attracting non-Chinese customers. Over his employers' objections, Kan advertised in the mainstream magazine *Variety*. A buyer from Barnum and Bailey's Circus noticed the exceptionally good prices and proceeded to buy their entire stock, thereby paving the way for a lucrative new business relationship.[32] As manager of the Fong Fong soda fountain and bakery, Kan initiated another innovation in 1935 by manufacturing and serving Chinese-flavored ice creams, such as lichee, kumquat, and ginger. Fong Fong became the popular gathering place for Chinatown's youthful elites.[33]

By the late 1930s, Kan had developed his vision for instilling elegance into the experience of Chinese dining to attract non-Chinese customers, as he recounted to the Nees:

> I realized that the reason there were no first-class restaurants in Chinatown was because no one ever bothered to study, and to teach their employees, how to run a really fine place. And nobody had tried to educate Caucasians to an appreciation of Chinese food. There were over fifty restaurants in Chinatown—papa-mama, medium-sized, juke and soup joints, tenderloin joints, and others—where waiters just slammed the dishes on the table and cared less about the customer or what he wanted to eat. So we decided to launch the first efficiently operated and most elaborate Chinese restaurant since the collapse of the old Mandarin. Our concept was to have a Ming or Tang dynasty theme for décor, a fine crew of master chefs, and a well-organized dining room crew headed by a courteous maître d' host, hostesses, and so on. And we topped it off with a glass-enclosed kitchen. This would serve many purposes. The customers could actually see Chinese food being prepared, and it would encourage everybody to keep the kitchen clean.[34]

High-class Chinese restaurants had flourished during the 1920s in the Chinatowns of New York and San Francisco but had closed during the Great Depression. Kan sought to emulate their scale and refinement but packaged his restaurant to attract more non-Chinese diners.

It would take Kan more than a decade to realize this dream because he lacked capital.[35] Only after serving in World War II and managing other restaurants would Kan gain the financial backing of Hall and Young to establish Kan's Restaurant in 1953.

With a flurry of flyers and personal letters, Kan publicized the opening of his restaurant and distinguished it from its lesser competitors by proclaiming the authenticity of its dishes, their links to China's imperial past, and his strong commitment to service. At Kan's Restaurant, "patience, careful thought, and finest ingredients together offer you a new adventure in time-honored recipes of Old China." Even the most discriminating of Euro-American consumers could enjoy "all that is genuine and worthwhile in Chinese cooking," knowing that they could view through large plate glass windows the modern metal kitchen presided over by five Chinese cooks tending their woks while wearing chef's whites and hats.[36] They could experience a foreign adventure that was safe, clean, and exotic all at the same time.

Kan's Restaurant introduced many innovations to the Chinese restaurant industry. It offered early "exotic" dishes, such as crab à la Kan, bird's nest soup, Peking duck, and asparagus beef.[37] Kan's Restaurant was also the first to feature the much-imitated round lazy susan and steaming perfumed towels after meals.[38] The combination of elegant foods, setting, and service brought many accolades, and Kan's Restaurant made frequent appearances on national lists of the ten best places to eat in San Francisco and received an impressive fourteen consecutive *Holiday* magazine awards for excellence in hospitality.[39] Such fame attracted celebrity diners, and Johnny Kan hobnobbed with the likes of Danny Kaye, Cary Grant, Joan Sutherland, Nancy Kwan, Lily Valentine, Dong Kingman, Joe DiMaggio, and Marilyn Monroe.[40] As depicted in an advertising postcard from 1959, Kan's was the place to go for a "Luxurious Adventure in Chinese Food." Chinese and Western diners, although apparently never sitting at the same table, enjoyed "the charm, the elegance of Kan's, most colorful of Chinese restaurants. Here, hospitality is a way of life . . . reflecting a tradition . . . serving extraordinary native Chinese dishes of unsurpassed quality."[41]

Kan took seriously the goal of educating Americanized Chinese and non-Chinese alike to understand and respect the rich culture and long history of Chinese people and their food. Kan's Restaurant featured the Gum Shan (meaning Golden Hills) Room, a private dining salon decorated with "watercolors depicting the history of the Chinese in the United States."[42] The restaurant's famously thick menu described the rich and extensive history of Chinese food and culture. In the cookbook that he published in 1963, Kan claimed the slogan of "tell the truth" when stressing the imperial roots of Chinese cuisine and criticizing the inauthentic offerings of chop suey joints. "Chinese cooking, with a recorded history of 47 centuries, is one of the world's oldest and is the essence of the highest art of cuisine. To misrepresent it constitutes an unforgivable sin." In contrast, Kan's Restaurant offered real Chinese food from "within the heart of San Francisco's Chinatown—the recognized mecca for the best Cantonese food in the world, outside of Hong Kong—[which] authenticates further the recipes selected from an unfathomable range of the best in Chinese food offerings."[43] To eat at Kan's was to consume authentic Chinese cuisine that reflected the best of Chinese culture.

Kan's educational campaign also had its practical agenda. Even as he complained about the "comparatively small number of Americans [who] actually know what real Chinese cuisine is," he also described the "average of 35 million dollars per year [that] is spent on America's supermarkets for frozen and canned American-packed Oriental products."[44] Unfortunately from Kan's perspective, much of this market in canned chop suey and chow mein was dominated by the likes of the Chun-King brand, which had been founded in 1947 by the Italian American entrepreneur Jeno Paulucci.[45] If Kan could teach Euro-Americans to appreciate real Chinese food, more of these dollars might flow into Chinese American hands.

Actor Danny Kaye learning to cook Chinese food in the kitchen of Kan's Restaurant, San Francisco, 1969. Johnny Kan is standing to the back and center with an unknown man and cook at the left. Kaye later ordered a stainless steel Chinese-restaurant kitchen for his own home from the Frank Yick Company. *(Photographer unknown. Courtesy of Connie Young Yu.)*

Kan became rich as he paved the way for other Chinese restaurants to attract a higher class of clientele. Some other notable successes include the Empress of China and the Imperial Palace. Unfortunately, Kan passed away in December 1972, just as the Chinese restaurant industry was on the cusp of its greatest popularity in the aftermath of President Richard Nixon's visit to China.[46] Herb Caen acknowledged the improvements that Kan had spearheaded in American appreciation of Chinese food: "After Johnny, Chinatown cooking was never the same. Chop suey has all but disappeared and you seldom hear anyone calling for beetle juice. In his wake came restaurateurs who tried to emulate him, and patrons who know the infinite variety that stretches beyond chow mein. . . . In Canton and Peking, they should be aware that there lived in San Francisco a man who raised their cuisine to the highest level."[47] The rise in respectability of Chinese cuisine made it possible for other restaurateurs to flourish and gain even greater celebrity and wealth.[48]

Mandarin Cuisine

Cecilia Chiang founded her restaurant, the Mandarin, after Kan's Restaurant had been in operation almost a decade. The door had been opened for Chiang to introduce yet more innovations to the business, for by the early 1960s, China and Chinese people had become more interesting to many Americans. Travel to Asia had increased, and growing affluence in the post–World War II decades encouraged consumers to actively seek out cosmopolitan tastes and experiences. Although an immigrant, Chiang was born of a wealthy family and enjoyed the advantage of being part of the privileged KMT-connected émigré elite. As such, she occupied an even more strategic position from which to channel elegance and good taste into the experience of dining Chinese.

Chiang's personal background offered not only tantalizing glimpses into the privileged lives of China's wealthiest classes but also a Horatio Algeresque tale of a striving and self-made immigrant entrepreneur. Chiang grew up in China in the courtyards of her affluent family's mansion surrounded by a dozen siblings and even more servants. She famously claimed that until coming to the United States, she had never had to cook for herself.[49] The Japanese invasion ended these happy times, and under the threat of occupation, Chiang and her fifth sister decided to escape to KMT-controlled territories in western China. The two young women traveled 2,500 miles by train and on foot to reach the Chinese wartime capital of Chongqing. Six months after they had set out, they arrived covered with dust and fleas and still disguised as peasants. Chiang survived the Sino-Japanese War and married the diplomat husband with whom she would flee the Communist takeover in 1949. They moved with his career to Tokyo, where Chiang started the first of her successful restaurant ventures.

Without training in cooking or running a business but nostalgic for the foods of her childhood, she opened a restaurant called the Forbidden City.[50] It soon attracted the wealthier members of both the Chinese and American expatriate communities, although the local Japanese could not afford the high prices. At the Forbidden City, Chiang became practiced at recalling the foods of her childhood and at hiring talented kitchen staff to translate her memories into consistently reproducible restaurant cuisine.

Chiang possessed considerable entrepreneurial experience when she came to the United States in 1958, although her original intent in coming to the country was to comfort a recently widowed sister.[51] After deciding to remain, however, she agreed to help a group of friends open a restaurant and even invested $10,000 as a deposit for the site on Polk Street that they had selected.[52] Chiang later recalled: "Afterward they backed out, leaving me committed, as I had already put up the money. It was about a year after I had arrived in the States and there was still much that was new and unfamiliar to me."[53] Chiang forged on alone, in part because she was reluctant to lose her money but also because she looked down upon the poor fare offered in Chinatown. "Egg drop soup everywhere . . . soup that tasted like the water that's left after you wash your wok. If people can make money with chop suey and egg foo yong, then I can do better with the real dishes from my homeland." On her own, Chiang applied for a business license only to learn from the city clerk that seven businesses had folded at that location during the past six years.[54] Despite this inauspicious beginning, Chiang persevered. "I named the restaurant the Mandarin, and selected dishes for the menu from northern China, Peking, Hunan and Szechwan: real Chinese food, with a conspicuous absence of chop suey and egg foo young."[55]

The Mandarin opened in 1961 but struggled initially. Its location outside Chinatown and the novelty of its offerings confounded expectations of where and what Chinese food should be: "In those days of the early sixties, the restaurants in San Francisco served Cantonese food exclusively, and the unfamiliarity of the hot and spicy cuisines of the northern provinces of China puzzled our first guests. Many of them were even defeated by the pronunciation of Szechwan."[56] Chiang recalls of that time: "I had to do everything: welcome guests, wash dishes, shop for provisions and rack my brains for what I had eaten in China and what I had learned from my mother. I worked sixteen hours a day, and became thin from my incessant activities."[57] After a year and a half of losses, Chiang's efforts began paying off. She hired skilled and reliable staff. "I had found a couple from northern China to cook, and was luckily joined by Mr. Linsan Chien, the former Chinese consul in San Francisco. He had elected to stay on in the States at the conclusion of his term of office, and consented to become my manager."[58] More important, perhaps, she gained the support of established restaurateurs such as Alexis Merab and Johnny Kan who in turn brought the local writers Herb Caen and Marion Conrad. A rave review by Caen piqued the curiosity of local San Franciscans, and the very next day, a hundred telephone callers demanded reservations.[59]

Within a few years, business had become so successful that Chiang expanded her operation. She chose another site outside Chinatown that offered the advantages of spectacular harbor views and enough space for a truly grand presentation of Chinese culture and cuisine. In 1968, the Mandarin grew from sixty-five seats to three hundred in a well-financed and architecturally planned setting that incorporated "the brick walls and long wooden rafters" of the original Ghirardelli chocolate factory and ornamented them with a "virtual gallery of oriental arts and crafts," including a painting by Chang Dai-chen and "forbidden stitch" embroideries reputed to have once hung in "the palace in Peking." The centerpiece was a Mongolian open barbeque, "adapted from the outdoor firepits in China."[60] This transformation garnered Chiang her first *Holiday* award in 1969.

Throughout the 1970s and 1980s, the Mandarin remained one of the premier Chinese restaurants in San Francisco. As a pioneer in offering Mandarin cuisine, it spawned many imitations. "As the fame of my restaurant grew, northern dishes started to appear on the menus of many Chinese restaurants in San Francisco for the first time, and a number of cooks who had originally worked in my kitchen branched out to start their own establishments, where they featured dishes prepared in the northern style."[61] The continuing popularity of such dishes as pot stickers, sizzling rice soup, and Chinese chicken salad first began with the Mandarin's innovations. Chiang continued to expand her business by opening branches in other locations and by 1986 presided over a four-restaurant chain that employed some three hundred people.[62]

Chiang's success was due in part to timing and in part to her personal appeal as a purveyor of Chinese culture and food. By the 1960s, the Chinese faced less hostility because America's cold war friendship with the KMT had enhanced the appeal of Chinese people and things. Chinese Americans also gained status as their middle-class ranks grew with the ascendance of the American-born generations and with the arrival of a new class of better educated, KMT-affiliated, and often affluent Chinese immigrants.

During the 1970s, growing interests in the conjunction of food and tourism contributed to the rising stardom of restaurateurs, chefs, and food writers. In a way that Johnny Kan could not, Cecilia Chiang became a public celebrity through friendships with influential restaurant critics as she embodied for them an appealing representation of China.

Chiang became famous not only as an authority on Chinese food but also as a symbol of the long-gone splendor and luxury of China's imperial past. In her 1998 memoir, *Tender at the Bone*, former *New York Times* food critic and *Gourmet* magazine editor Ruth Reichl recalled the first time she met Chiang: "Cecilia Chiang stood in the doorway of The Mandarin restaurant, dressed entirely in green silk. She had shiny black hair pulled into a severe chignon that emphasized the small oval of her skull. Her smooth, beautiful face was a mask offering no clue to her age. When she waved her manicured hands, gold and diamonds flashed in the sun."[63] Chiang herself described her privileged childhood in the courtyards of her family's mansion as a "way of life [that] no longer exists. The last ten years have completed its destruction: yet . . . my family background and the path of my life have given me unusual opportunities of knowing both the manner of living of the Mandarin classes and of the Chinese people at large in the first half of this century."[64] Non-Chinese food writers were fascinated by the hints of extraordinary wealth and luxury that Chiang suggested. Cookbook author Marion Cunningham introduced Chiang to Reichl with the comment, "Did you know that Cecilia walked out of China with gold sewn into the hem of her dress?"[65]

Chiang's persona also included the satisfying narrative arc of the successful immigrant businesswoman. Chiang's flight from the Japanese invasion and the many obstacles she overcame as a northern Chinese, an immigrant, and a woman in the United States became well-known components of her story.[66] Long after she had become successful and hobnobbed with the cream of America's restaurant elite, Chiang recalled with pride her early experiences scrubbing the floors of her restaurant late at night. She emphasized the independence that she had gained in coming to America and building her own business: "I feel sorry for the women I grew up with who did not have a chance to discover that they could take care of themselves."[67] She explicitly preferred American modernity to the leisurely life of affluence of the now vanished Chinese society in which she had grown up. "Admittedly, it was a very different kind of home from those I had known in China. . . . In seeing first-hand the push-button efficiency and economy of the American way of living, I realized there would be no room in the United States for the formal, diffuse layout of a Chinese house as I had known it."[68] By coming to America, however, Chiang had realized more of herself through hard work and as a self-made success.

Chiang claimed ultimate authority in her knowledge of Chinese food and described herself as "knowing how": "I have confidence. . . . I love people, I love food, and about Chinese food, I think I know better than all the people I know."[69] Non-Chinese, however, viewed Chiang not only as an incomparable expert on Chinese cuisine but also one who provided access into the heart of what it meant to be Chinese. As recalled by Chinese food specialist Barbara Tropp, "Cecilia became an institution. You felt, as you entered her restaurants, that you were in the weave of Chinese culture."[70]

Chiang's achievements resonated with the ideological agendas of cold war America. As a successful entrepreneur, she was a model capitalist. And by embracing the kinds of opportunities available to her as an immigrant Chinese woman, and in turn helping Americans to understand and consume Chinese cuisine, she affirmed that America was truly a multiracial, diverse democracy. Chiang grew rich because she was a member of an exemplary ethnic minority.[71]

Concluding Remarks

Johnny Kan and Cecilia Chiang helped to engineer a shift in consciousness whereby American people learned to value authentic and well-prepared Chinese cuisine rooted in China's rich imperial past. After decades of the disreputable but cheap and tasty satisfactions of chop suey, Americans came to associate Chinese dining with elegantly appointed settings and refined tastes in food. Some Americans even grew to believe that Chinese food in America was better than that available in Asia. In 1965, *Holiday*'s food critic, Silas Spitzer, observed that "My firm opinion is that for every first-rate Chinese restaurant in

Hong Kong there are at least ten in New York or San Francisco as good or better. . . . My feeling is that the poetic and imaginative Chinese cuisine today available is today at its best in the United States."[72] In this critic's opinion, Americans no longer had to leave home to consume the best of Chinese cuisine.

The successes of Kan and Chiang suggest how marketable ethnicity can be in the lives of racial minorities and how the values attached to ethnic cultures may change. Rather than seeking to erase their Chineseness, Kan and Chiang strategically promoted aspects of Chinese culture and cuisine to attract more mainstream consumers to their restaurants. Their triumph was not that they disappeared into the American melting pot so celebrated by Robert Park and his Chinese American disciple, Rose Hum Lee, but that they domesticated "authentic" versions of Chineseness so appealingly for American consumption.

Throughout the cold war and up to the present, Chinese restaurants remain a reliable form of employment, even for Chinese Americans with more prestigious options. The sociologist Betty Lee Sung observed in 1967 that "surprisingly, many young men and women who hold good positions in commercial and professional capacities elsewhere go back to restaurants on week ends to supplement their income. . . . Offhand, I can name an architect, a vice-president of a finance company, a welder in an aircraft factory, a medical student, and a dental student who work regularly over the week ends as waiters or headwaiters in various Chinese restaurants."[73]

Chinese restaurants increased dramatically in both numbers and popularity during the early 1970s. Nixon received much of the credit for starting the trend. "When we opened," said Susan Sih, co-owner of Chicago's Dragon Inn, "I couldn't give away a Peking Duck. And then President Nixon went to China. He's been the greatest salesman for Peking Duck.'" In 1972, the Chinese-American Restaurant Association estimated that one restaurant had opened each week during the previous year and that there were twelve hundred Chinese restaurants in New York and Long Island and another five to six hundred in New Jersey and Connecticut.[74]

The Hall family of Wing Nien Foods suggests the continuing appeal of entrepreneurship and the economic potential of ethnic food services for Chinese Americans. Wing Nien Foods is now in its third generation of family management. George Hall's son and grandson, David and Gregory Hall, earned their college degrees and pursued white-collar employment in pharmaceuticals and engineering before returning to run the family business because it offered greater opportunities for creativity, independence, and profit.[75]

Many Chinese Americans continue to run Chinese restaurants because they generally provide reliable incomes in return for relatively low start-up costs. Although the Chinese American community has grown in numbers, socioeconomic status, and educational attainments since the 1940s, running a restaurant remains for many the most preferable means of making a living in the United States. Most of these family-run establishments seek to do little more than satisfy their customers with the now standard favorites of General Tso's chicken and broccoli beef, but at least they rarely serve chop suey.

The theorist Rey Chow has critiqued the implications of power and inequality bound up in the production of Chinese food for non-Chinese. She notes that "food transaction in this instance points up the need to rethink Orientalism not simply as an externally imposed system of ideological mystification and manipulation . . . but also as an elusive process of self-realization, a process that can be vital even when it is, as is often the case, demeaning."[76] Chow highlights the tension between necessity and ethnic misrepresentation in this most typical of ethnic enterprises. How many Chinese American entrepreneurs can afford to choose authenticity over the economic rationality of giving their customers what they want and expect to eat?

Neither Johnny Kan nor Cecilia Chiang shirked at occasionally serving "Chinese" dishes, such as crab rangoon and Chinese chicken salad, that suited the tastes of their non-Chinese customers. In calling her first restaurant Forbidden City and the second the Mandarin, Chiang clearly understood the importance of evoking the exotic to attract more customers. The very concept of Mandarin cuisine that she made so famous was an amalgamation of many different foodways, as Chiang explained in her cookbook. "And let me say, as a last introductory comment, that there is no such thing as 'Mandarin' cuisine. The cuisine of the Mandarin classes was a combination of the cuisine of the capital, augmented by the specialties of every province: the finest produce, from the limitless resources of the whole of China, prepared by chefs whose skill had been handed down from time immemorial."[77] While acknowledging that she had creatively repackaged Chinese food for non-Chinese consumers, Chiang managed to remind Americans of the fascinating traditions associated with China's emperors, its varied and vast empire, ancient history, and richly diverse cultural heritage. Even as Kan and Chiang knowingly skirted the slippery boundaries of authenticity in some of their offerings, both insisted that their restaurants convey pride and skill in the cuisine and culture served to their customers. By instilling class and prestige into the associations Americans had with the consumption of Chinese food, Kan and Chiang greatly enriched the content of Chinese ethnicity to help transform Chinese food from being merely a cheap and sometimes suspect convenience into an experience in culture that could at times attain the level of culinary art.

NOTES

1. Herb Caen, *Only in San Francisco* (Garden City, NY: Doubleday, 1960), 266.

2. See Johnny Kan, "A 'Thank You' Message from Johnny Kan" (Letter dated September 10, 1953); and Johnny Kan with Charles L. Leong, *Eight Immortal Flavors* (Berkeley, CA: Howell-North Books, 1963), 15–16.

3. Karen J. Leong, *The China Mystique: Pearl S. Buck, Anna May Wong, Mayling Soong, and the Transformation of American Orientalism* (Berkeley and Los Angeles: University of California Press, 2005); and Colleen Lye, *America's Asia: Racial Form and American Literature, 1893–1945* (Princeton, NJ: Princeton University Press, 2005).

4. The Chinese are the only group to have been specified by race for exclusion from the United States. First passed in 1882, the Chinese exclusion laws prohibited the Chinese from gaining citizenship by naturalization and restricted entry to four tightly defined "exempted classes": diplomats; merchants and their families; students, teachers, and religious ministers; and tourists and persons in transit. In addition, returning laborers with the requisite documentation could also enter.

5. Between 1924 and 1965, immigration was controlled by a highly discriminatory system of quotas based on national origins. Designed to preserve the pre-1890 ethnic and racial composition of the United States, the quotas were based on census data and gave Western and Northern European nations large numbers of immigration slots compared with the rest of the world. Asian nations, if they received an allotment at all, received annual quotas of 200 or less during this era.

6. Cristina Klein, *Cold War Orientalism: Asia in the Middlebrow Imagination, 1945–1961* (Berkeley and Los Angeles: University of California Press, 2003), 224.

7. Klein, *Cold War Orientalism*, 23.

8. Ibid.

9. Although not all the performers were ethnically Chinese, with some being Japanese, Filipino, or multiracial, they adopted Chinese names. For example, the Portuguese-Spanish-Filipino-Chinese American Caruso Lagrimas became Tony Wing.

10. The Forbidden City's performers were born and raised primarily outside of San Francisco's Chinatown.

11. See Jade Snow Wong, *Fifth Chinese Daughter* (New York: Harper, 1950), 241; and Klein, *Cold War Orientalism*, 242–43.

12. Klein, *Cold War Orientalism*, 225.

13. Henry Shih-shan Tsai, *The Chinese Experience in America* (Bloomington: Indiana University Press, 1986), 195.

14. S. Y. Yuan, *Chinese-American Population* (Hong Kong: UEA Press, 1988), 61–62.

15. Young worked for Standard Oil during the 1940s and was told openly that he would never receive a promotion. Author's interview with Connie Young Yu, December 31, 2003.

16. In response to the Chinese exclusion laws, the Chinese began claiming fraudulent names and family relationships in order to enter the United States. After 1950, the Immigration and Naturalization Service (INS) and the FBI feared that Chinese Communist spies could use this well-organized system to enter the United States. Between 1956 and 1965, the INS implemented the Chinese Confession Program to induce Chinese Americans to cooperate in revealing false names and identities. In exchange for confessing their fraudulent status, Chinese Americans could regain their real names and receive American citizenship. Less than 10 percent of the Chinese American population of the time trusted the INS enough to participate in this program. Of those who confessed, only 11,336 did so willingly. Another 19,124 were implicated in the confessions of others. Most of these Chinese Americans benefited from the confession program, but the INS used evidence of fraudulent entry to deport left-wing activists and strip other leftists of their U.S. citizenship. See Mae M. Ngai, *Impossible Subjects: Illegal Aliens and the Making of Modern America* (Princeton, NJ: Princeton University Press, 2004), 218–23.

17. Klein, *Cold War Orientalism*, 240–41.

18. Philip C. Choy, "The Chinese Food Experience in San Francisco," in *WOKing through Time: The Chinese Food Experience in San Francisco* (San Francisco: Chinese Historical Society of America, 2003), 26.

19. Renqiu Yu, "Chop Suey: From Chinese Food to Chinese American Food," *Chinese America: History and Perspectives* (1987): 89.

20. Yu, "Chop Suey," 95–96.

21. Ivan Light, "From Vice District to Tourist Attraction: The Moral Career of American Chinatowns, 1880–1940," *Amerasia* 43, no. 3 (1974): 384–85.

22. Light, "From Vice District to Tourist Attraction," 376–77.

23. Cited in Light, "From Vice District to Tourist Attraction," 394.

24. Ibid., 385.

25. Ibid., 384–85.

26. Gor Yun Leong, *Chinatown Inside Out* (New York: B. Mussey, 1936), 168.

27. Betty Lee Sung, *Mountain of Gold* (New York: Macmillan, 1967), 208.

28. Sung, *Mountain of Gold*, 207.

29. Herb Caen, "Babble by the Bay," *San Francisco Chronicle*, December 11, 1972. "Beetle juice" was a derogatory term for soy sauce.

30. Jack Sheldon was also a restaurant critic who authored the *Private Guide to Restaurants*. He described Kan as "the man many called the Honorary Mayor of Chinatown." I thank the author Connie Young Yu for generously sharing her collection of documents regarding Johnny Kan and Wing Nien Foods.

31. Victor and Brett de Bary Nee, *Longtime Californ': A Documentary Study of an American Chinatown* (New York: Pantheon, 1973), 110.

32. Ibid., 113.

33. Ibid., 114.

34. Ibid., 115.

35. See Ken Wong, "A Death in the Family" in *The Oriental Express* (December 20, 1972); and Caen, "Babble by the Bay."

36. See *San Francisco Bulletin*, advertisement, February 2, 1960. Kan also helped to promote awareness of Chinese cooking as performance. His kitchen featured the leaping flames, flashing cleavers, and dramatic tossing associated with stir-frying in woks. This show went on the road in 1972, so to speak, when Johnny Kan helped to organize an exhibition of Chinese chefs and their woks at the Sixth Western National Restaurant Convention for an audience of 750 industry insiders. Charles Petit, "Master Chefs at Work on the Wok," *San Francisco Chronicle*, August 28, 1972.

37. Caen, "Babble by the Bay."

38. Engineer George Hall developed the round lazy susan as well as the process for perfuming the hot towels.

39. Wong, "A Death in the Family."

40. See Caen, "Babble by the Bay," *San Francisco Chronicle*, September 12, 1953; and Wong, "A Death in the Family." Caen reported his sighting of the baseball star and his luminous wife in the following way: "On the off-chance that you're still interested in what Joe Di Maggio and Mmonroe are up to, we can tell you that they were at Johnny Kan's last Sat. night, seated at the bar. After they left, all the men at the bar lined up and sat, one after the other, in the seat she'd vacated. (Mr. Freud must have a whole chapter on this.)"

41. *San Francisco News*, advertisement, February 12, 1959.

42. Doris Muscatine, *A Cook's Tour of San Francisco: The Best Restaurants and Their Recipes* (New York: Charles Scribner's Sons, 1963), 103. The paintings were commissioned from Jake Lee, a Chinese American artist who devoted a year to historical research for the

job. According to Muscatine, "His paintings show the first immigrants disembarking in 1849, Chinese miners in the gold fields, lantern-making in San Francisco, railroad workers laboring on the first transcontinental track, and the once-famous China Camp Shrimp fishery. They also depict some less well-known aspects of Chinese-American cultural history: Chinese shoemakers in Massachusetts in the 1870s, vineyard workers in Sonoma county, San Francisco cigar-making, a 1862 view of the Chinese Opera House, and the champion Chinese firehose team of Deadwood, South Dakota, 1888" (103).

43. Kan and Leong, *Eight Immortal Flavors*, 12.

44. Ibid.

45. Donna Gabaccia, *We Are What We Eat: Ethnic Food and the Making of Americans* (Cambridge, MA: Harvard University Press, 1998), 167–68.

46. J.A.G. Roberts, *China to Chinatown: Chinese Food in the West* (London: Reaktion Books, 2002), 166–67.

47. Herb Caen, *One Man's San Francisco* (Garden City, NY: Doubleday, 1976), 111.

48. Kan's Restaurant is still located on Grant Avenue but operates under different management. Since Kan's death, its reputation has declined considerably.

49. Cecilia Chiang with Allan Carr, *The Mandarin Way* (San Francisco: California Living Books, 1980), 263.

50. This Forbidden City is different from Charlie Low's nightclub.

51. The oft-told tale of Chiang's life story has been published with slightly different details. Sometimes her year of arrival is listed as 1961, and the number of siblings she had is given as twelve or thirteen in varying reports.

52. Emerald Yeh, "Cecilia Sun Yun Chiang," http://www.asianpacificfund.org/awards/bio_chiang.shtml (accessed June 15, 2005).

53. Chiang, *The Mandarin Way*, 265.

54. Yeh, "Cecilia Sun Yun Chiang."

55. Chiang, *The Mandarin Way*, 266.

56. Susan Edmiston, "The Year of the Woman Immigrant: Self-Selected for Success," *Working Woman* (July 1986): 56.

57. Chiang, *The Mandarin Way*, 266.

58. Ibid., 267.

59. Yeh, "Cecilia Sun Yun Chiang."

60. Doris Muscatine, *A Cook's Tour of San Francisco*, rev. ed. (New York: Charles Scribner's Sons, 1969), 147.

61. Chiang, *The Mandarin Way*, 267.

62. Edmiston, "The Year of the Woman Immigrant," 56.

63. Ruth Reichl, *Tender at the Bone: Growing up at Table* (New York: Random House, 1998), 277.

64. Chiang, *The Mandarin Way*, vii.

65. Reichl, *Tender at the Bone*, 278–79. Another anecdote conveys Chiang's fascinating persona. Cunningham, Chiang, and California cuisine guru Alice Waters had visited China together. Throughout their three-week trip, the two Euro-American women obsessed about what Chiang carried in her twelve suitcases. Baffled by their interest in her luggage, Chiang offhandedly explained that their contents included cloth to have clothes tailor-made in Hong Kong and the then-scarce ingredients of shark's fin and hair vegetable for her restaurants.

66. Edmiston, "The Year of the Woman Immigrant," 56.

67. Reichl, *Tender at the Bone*, 280.

68. Chiang, *The Mandarin Way*, 259.

69. Edmiston, "The Year of the Woman Immigrant," 56.

70. Peggy Knickerbocker, "Empress of San Francisco," *Saveur* (May/June 2000), http://saveur.com/article.jsp;jsessionid=3927F5D27A54324E851A755FA2AA5?ID=15171&typeID=100 (accessed June 15, 2005).

71. Chiang retired in 1991 but continues to consult for new restaurants. The Mandarin remains in Ghirardelli Square but has recently changed ownership. Chiang's son Phillip was one of the founding partners of the Chinese restaurant chain P. F. Chang's.

72. Silas Spitzer, "Dining in the Far East," *Holiday* 38, no. 6 (1965): 107.

73. Sung, *Mountain of Gold*, 208. Sung also described the importance of the restaurant business even for the relatively privileged groups of refugees and graduate students immigrating to the United States during the 1950s and 1960s: "Another group of Chinese revised their attitude toward the restaurant business too. These are the intellectual and political refugees who once held high office in China. . . . At first, these émigrés disassociated themselves from the 'overseas Chinese,' whom they looked down upon as laundrymen and restaurateurs. When they began to look around for means of earning a livelihood or investing their capital, they found that restaurants can yield a good living and handsome returns" (209).

74. Ralph Blumenthal, "The Chinese Restaurant Boom," *San Francisco Chronicle*, September 6, 1972.

75. Author's interview with Connie Young Yu, December 31, 2003.

76. Rey Chow, "Have You Eaten?: Inspired by an Exhibit," *Amerasia* 31, no. 1 (2005): 20–21.

77. Chiang, *The Mandarin Way*, xi.

A village watchtower in Heshan District, Guangdong Province, China. *(Photograph by Andrea Louie, 1992. Used with permission.)*

6

Searching for Roots in Contemporary China and Chinese America

Andrea Louie

Like many Asian Americans, I grew up in two seemingly different worlds. In elementary school I was the little pudgy Chinese boy with slanted eyes and bad English. At home I was the youngest of three sons with a strong craving for McDonalds and television. And with bad Cantonese. . . . Not until I moved to the [San Francisco] Bay Area of Northern California did I realize that I did not have to choose between my "two cultures" and that a strong desire for both rice and McDonalds is quite acceptable, and indeed common. I realized that it is acceptable to have limited skills in Chinese, and acceptable to have limited skills in English. I realized that names like "Jook Sing" and "Banana" are insults only if I take offense at them. I realized how to be proud of being a Chinese American. And I also realized that I knew nothing about my Chinese heritage. . . . All along China has been a mythical and legendary place, touched upon briefly and distantly in high school history [courses]. Yet history is not merely a subject that students study in a classroom. Rather, history is "Roots." History can be a personal exploration of one's heritage. To the children of immigrant families, we especially must make an attempt to understand what the Something is when we call ourselves Something-American. This is the beginning of my attempt.

Roots Narratives

The above vignette is typical of the narratives produced by participants in the "In Search of Roots Program" that is jointly sponsored by the Chinese Culture Center and the Chinese Historical Society of America in San Francisco and the Overseas Chinese Affairs Office in the People's Republic of China

(PRC). The major focus of the program is a two-week journey to China, where the participants visit their ancestral villages in the Pearl River Delta of Guangdong Province. This journey is preceded by detailed lessons taught by Him Mark Lai, a noted Chinese American historian, in bimonthly meetings. The lessons begin with a history of the emigrant region, followed by an analysis of Chinese immigration to the United States and the subsequent experiences of Chinese Americans. The program's founders guide the participants as they research and write their family histories and narratives of identity exploration that trace family roots to the emigrant villages in China.

These narratives are written about a year after the participants join the program and approximately six months after they travel to China. Thus, they show a retrospective coherence that most likely did not exist during the evolutionary process through which the writers came to a more "complete" understanding of what it means to be Chinese American. After portraying their initial fear or ignorance of China and their uncertain status both as Chinese and as Americans, the authors discuss how they can now negotiate changing relationships to people and places in both China and the United States by taking advantage of their mobility to draw on various resources. They create identities that reference multiple sources, near and far, past and present. However, the stories are almost too neat: They do not reflect clearly the process of negotiation that characterizes identity production. That is to say, although the process itself is uneven and messy, participants in hindsight portray it as a progressive route toward self-discovery. Such identity narratives are characteristic of the identity politics of U.S. multiculturalism, in which identity is viewed as something "out there" waiting to be discovered. Such an assumption implies that Chinese Americans cannot form a complete identity without going to China and that the identities they discover there are somehow final. Although the identity narratives illustrate how Chinese Americans can move beyond the limitations imposed on them by U.S. society to craft identities attached to, but not derived solely from, China, they also show how these productions involve identity politics on multiple levels. American-born Chinese Americans in the Roots program find themselves caught within a politics of U.S. multiculturalism that excludes them from cultural citizenship in the United States while associating them, willingly or not, with their ancestral homeland. Their relationship to China and their understandings of Chinese culture within the context of the United States are therefore complex and often ambivalent. China is simultaneously an unknown entity filtered through an Orientalist lens and a place to which they are involuntarily and inextricably attached.

However, by constructing alternative genealogies and family narratives that are localized in Chinese American experiences, participants in the Roots program can begin to negotiate viable identities within these constraints. They discover that it is possible to carve out a "place" for American-born Chinese

Americans such as themselves within a politics of cultural citizenship that focuses on mobility: The "places" that they create simultaneously draw on historical connections to ancestral villages in China, contemporary relations with friends and relatives in the United States and in China, and transnational flows of popular culture originating in Asia. The mobility of Chinese Americans, however, is ironically facilitated by the very nation-states that are trying to shape their identities in restrictive ways. Thus, the PRC's sponsorship of their roots-searching activities and the mobility that U.S. citizenship affords them jointly create the road map for their mobility.

At first glance, it may appear that in going to China, Chinese Americans are recovering their ancestral roots in the traditional romanticized sense. Most become more conscious and proud of their Chinese heritage; some even get involved in the Chinese American community or later travel to China to study or do business. This process of re-ethnicization, in which Chinese Americans selectively adopt parts of their Chinese heritage and consciously incorporate them into their lives, is a flexible one that involves more than adopting the "traditional" practices of earlier generations. So, although some exercises, such as tracing genealogies, preparing traditional foods, or learning to speak Chinese, may appear to replicate the cultural assets of older generations, the meanings assigned to these practices may differ greatly between the generations. Recognizing these differences is essential, as one of the controlling processes[1] that disempowers American-born generations within the politics of U.S. multiculturalism is its emphasis on traditional cultural knowledge as a marker of cultural authenticity and legitimization. U.S. multiculturalism, in its reliance on symbolic representations of diversity, oversimplifies and essentializes the diversity of racial/ethnic groups in the United States. Distinctions of class, gender, and intraracial/ethnic diversity are often glossed over in the superficial representations that lump people into broad, undifferentiated categories, such as "Asian," "Chicano/Latino," "African American," or "Native American." When cultural authenticity is measured in these terms, American-born Chinese Americans who know little about China are left with little to display. They also may not be able to identify with these representations and may even feel inadequate in comparison to recognized culture bearers.

In a more specific sense, categories that encompass a range of identifications may also be insufficient to express the diversity among people of Chinese ancestry. As Aihwa Ong notes in her analysis of cultural citizenship, it may be premature to suggest that there is a shared panethnic Asian American identity. The Cambodian refugees and upper-class Hong Kong immigrants she studied, both of whom fall under the category "Asian Americans," have been inserted into U.S. racial politics at opposite ends of the black–white spectrum. Cambodians and Chinese from Hong Kong share little in terms of class status and cultural practices. Similarly, the experiences of participants in the Roots program tell us that even pan-Chinese or pan-Chinese American forms of identification may not adequately represent the identities of those subsumed under these concepts. Although Roots participants gain knowledge about China and Chinese culture during their visits, they often find these forms of Chinese identity inappropriate for describing their own experiences. Instead, the identities expressed in Roots narratives are often formed in relation to or sometimes in contrast to other ways of being Chinese. Therefore, the generic forms of Chinese arts and "high culture" presented to Chinese Americans who visit China actually make them feel less Chinese. Roots participants also continually make distinctions between themselves—American-born Cantonese Americans from peasant origins—and newer, often wealthier immigrants from Hong Kong and Taiwan. Thus, they selectively negotiate among the available categorizations. Ultimately, their identification as persons of Cantonese descent from specific villages or a particular region, for example, may coexist with other identities, such as Asian American, Chinese American, or just plain American. Moreover, these categories may intertwine with class and gender identities, specific family histories, broader Chinese American history, or the fact that their families had emigrated to Southeast Asia or Latin America before coming to the United States. One participant in the Roots program sums up the process of identity exploration in this way:

> I think that for me I'm looking at it more as a Chinese American now, not necessarily as an ABC, or as a Chinese, but as a Chinese American. I'm very comfortable sort of knowing my personal family history, knowing [about the] exclusion laws, knowing factual things, teaching, and researching on that. . . . And that's my community, that's the stuff that I do, and definitely [the Roots Program] is important, Asian American Studies, my friends, family. All those things are definitely Chinese American. And I'm still trying to figure out exactly what does that mean. I don't want to make it that, well we pull some Chinese stuff, we pull some American stuff. It's a lot more complex, and I don't even know how to approach it, it's a much bigger thing and I think that's why . . . even though it's hard to describe what it is, I'm growing comfortable in saying I know what Chinese American culture is, but don't ask me to define it.[2]

Chinese Americans and China: Redefining the Relationship

Although American-born Chinese Americans may identify with China as an exotic tourist site, geopolitical entity, historical region, or place of origin, most have had little first-hand contact with China or mainland Chinese people.

Most of them have not been to China and do not speak Chinese fluently, if at all. Prior to their involvement in the Roots program, many had little knowledge about China or their family histories. During the Chinese exclusion era (1882–1943) and for some years after it ended, many Chinese families avoided talking about their history for fear that their "paper son" status might unwittingly be disclosed by children who do not understand the need for secrecy. In addition, after a Communist government came to power in China in 1949 and before the resumption of diplomatic relations between the PRC and the United States in 1979, a majority of Chinese Americans seldom acknowledged any connections with the PRC because the U.S.-supported government in Taiwan dominated Chinatown politics. Even for the children of post-1965 immigrants, China remains at least a generation away.

For Chinese Americans, family histories frame images of "Chinese culture" and of China as an ancestral home. At the same time, it is difficult to distinguish between what is particular to one's own family and friends and what is generally true of Chinese and Chinese American culture and society. Because they live in a society where there are multiple and conflicting images about China and Chinese culture, it can be difficult for Chinese Americans to contextualize their own families' experiences and practices within Chinese and Chinese American cultures. Family experiences and home culture must be resolved with what they learn outside the home about China and other Chinese from the mass media, school textbooks, and popular culture.

For American-born generations, "Chinese culture," often learned outside the home, takes form and meaning as something consciously learned and explored. One twenty-two-year-old second-generation Chinese American said he grew up thinking he should know how to do kung fu (*gongfu*) because he was Chinese. Growing up in the Midwest, the only images he saw of the Chinese people were on television; he thinks these media images taught him how to be Chinese. For some Chinese Americans, these conceptions of their (lack of) Chineseness shape their images and attitudes toward China as a reservoir of an essentialized Chinese culture and source of family secrets that can be tapped to fill in the holes of their own incomplete and perhaps quirky understandings of their Chineseness.

Chinese Americans and the Asia-Pacific Region

The relationship between Chinese Americans and China emerges from historical processes that go far beyond the particularities of stories about ancestors who had emigrated. These broader developments shape how Chinese Americans conceive of their Chineseness. As Arif Dirlik argues, the idea that the Asian continent and the Pacific Ocean form a region is a product not only of geography but also of Eurocentric thinking and capitalist processes.[3] That is,

"Asia-Pacific" is a sociohistorical construction. It has defined the relationships between Chinese Americans and China, and between Chinese Americans and the United States. Thus, ideas of cultural difference in U.S. definitions of relations between "East" and "West" have shaped Asian American history and identities. From the beginning, the conflictual relationship between Asians and the United States has taken form around issues of labor and capital. However, the debates have always been framed in terms of cultural differences rather than political or economic tensions. The exclusion of Chinese immigrants was justified not because Chinese workers posed a threat to white labor but because irreconcilable differences supposedly existed between Eastern and Western cultures.[4] Although the Chinese were integral to building the economy of the American West, they remained exotic and dangerous outsiders who needed to be controlled.

The difficulty faced by Asian Americans, then, is how to comfortably claim either Asian or American roots. As Dirlik observes, "to the extent that trans-Pacific ties of Asian Americans have been recognized within the dominant culture . . . this recognition has served primarily to deny their 'Americanness' and their history." In light of the recent attention paid to the Asia-Pacific region, new emphasis is being placed on those connections.[5] However, for the Chinese Americans on whom my research focused, this emphasis puts them in a double bind. Lacking strong connections to Asia, they are nevertheless viewed through the prism of cultural difference. Whereas black Americans are seen as lacking a cultural heritage, Chinese Americans are viewed as having too much culture.[6] But the "Asian" and "American" parts of Asian Americans represent two irreconcilable parts of a single identity within U.S. multiculturalism, neither of which can be recognized as whole. The idea that the Asian and American parts of Asian America cannot be integrated into a cohesive singular identity makes it very difficult to conceive of cultural changes that blend Asian and American elements.

When China Is Brought Closer

Ideas of relative Chineseness become even more salient as diasporic or historically transnational relationships between immigrant populations and their homelands are redefined under globalization, which is reshaping the boundaries of historical diasporas and multiplying the channels through which identities can be negotiated.[7] In many ways, increased access to China has opened up new possibilities for the formation of identities within the context of a still-racist U.S. society that continues to construct Chineseness in restrictive ways.

Increasing contacts between the United States and China through trade, migration, and popular culture constantly remind Chinese Americans of their "motherland." The prominent presence of the Pacific Rim in the mass media makes representations of Chinese culture available on a daily basis, be they attached to discussions of economics, international relations, illegal immigration, or campaign finance scandals. Through these transnational flows of commodities, popular culture, and the mass media, Chinese Americans are sometimes unwillingly reattached to their homeland. The mass media portray transnational Chinese business and social networks as a diaspora driven by Confucian values and a culturally ingrained entrepreneurial spirit—a powerful force to be reckoned with. China is discussed in the news, and it is found on product labels, in popular culture, and in many other dimensions of American life. Andrew Lam, a Pacific News Service commentator originally from Vietnam, satirizes the ease and extent to which Asian Americans are tied to Asia in the American imagination. He marvels at the power and influence that he and his Asian American friends surely must now have to influence U.S. politics. All they have to do, he quips, is to make "a few well-placed campaign contributions" to ruin the careers of politicians. After all, his "transpacific web of connections is extensive." He has an uncle in Saigon, cousins confined in refugee camps in Hong Kong at the time he wrote the essay, and the ability to make a "wicked Thai soup."[8]

As one participant in the Roots program remarked, images of China, though changing, still strongly affect his ideas of what it means to be Chinese in America:

> I think the idea of China always having an effect on your perception of Chineseness, I would tend to agree with that, because no matter what I think, . . . the media plays a role in what I absorb and what I don't, whether I agree with it or not, it affects the way I think. Whatever is going on in China or . . . what Congress says about China, or what movies are out about China, it always has this effect. . . . Basically it seems to me like it's opening up a little more, and China is becoming more like any normal country. Whereas twenty years ago I thought it was this dark, Evil Empire II kind of thing.

This cognitive and emotional distance from China, combined with the pressure to know and identify with it, results in a complex and confusing relationship between Chinese Americans and their ancestral land, a relationship mediated by the discourses of multiculturalism and race in the United States. Whereas Hong Kong transnational migrants deftly use multiculturalism to their advantage,[9] Chinese Americans are in many ways controlled by American multiculturalism without realizing the extent of its impact. This fact both opens up new alternatives and raises new complications for rooting (and routing) identities. Although meant to be empowering, the identity politics of U.S.

multiculturalism provides a distorted lens through which Chinese Americans view their "Chineseness," their "Americanness," and their relationship to both China and America.

Roots in the Context of U.S. Identity Politics

The structure and focus of the Roots program arose out of Chinese American community-based politics originating in 1960s activism that claimed that American-rooted identities developed through a reinvolvement in community issues in Chinatown, Japantown, and Manilatown on the part of second-generation Asian American college students.[10] A corollary of these activities was involvement in Third World movements overseas. One group of Chinese Americans visited China in the 1970s to participate in Chairman Mao's Great Proletarian Cultural Revolution, which in their eyes paralleled the revolutionary struggles of Third World peoples of color in the United States. Many individuals combined their revolutionary goals in China with roots-searching experiences in interesting ways through a political lens that differed from modern multicultural identity politics.[11] An important element of 1960s and 1970s Asian American politics was the development of a pan-Asian American identity that focused less on roots and origins and more on the shared struggles of Asians as minorities in the United States. "Yellow Power" did little, however, to remove essentialized notions of ancestral roots in Asia as the basis for Asian American cultural and political legitimacy. The cultural politics of diversity, moreover, had the unintended effect of perpetuating racialized categories, referencing Native Americans, Chicanos/Latinos, African Americans, and Asian Americans as the only legitimate and recognized minority groups. Such racial dynamics work against more nuanced understandings of racialization. The linking of "Asian" and "American" did not remove the ambiguity of how racialized "minority" groups fit into U.S. society. The "Asian" part of Asian American was produced through a broader set of discourses stemming from the history of U.S. involvement in Asia and its hegemonic definition of Asia as a region.[12] Asian Americans were and are seen as perpetual foreigners who maintain deeply ingrained ties to Asia. These perceived ties have taken on new meanings in recent years as the transnational potential of connections between Asian Americans and Asia has received increasing attention. Asian Americans, especially those born in the United States, who usually have fewer connections with Asia, are placed in awkward positions when they are cast in these popular and political discourses as bridge builders across the Pacific. Although renewed pride in Asian cultural roots cultivated through these connections can be viewed as a basis for Asian American political empowerment, Evelyn Hu-DeHart has asked, "Can Asian Americans . . . claim . . . 'ethnic nationalism' without jeopardizing their cultural and political citizenship in the

United States?"[13] In a similar vein, Dirlik notes that Asian American "groups have acquired a new significance in light of global economic developments, and the localized identities that they acquired in their settlements abroad have been overwhelmed in reassertions of cultural nationalism that stress their 'essential' unity across global spaces."[14] These racialized and essentialized forms of cultural nationalism are dangerous because they emphasize cultural origins over the complex national contexts that shape the varied meanings of what it means to be Chinese in particular times and places.

The Problem with Assimilation

Chinese American culture is defined within U.S. multicultural politics as a form of inherent and immutable difference from U.S. mainstream culture, whatever that might be. Chinese immigrants have been portrayed as unassimilable and incapable of being democratic or civilized.[15] They have thus been marginalized and excluded from mainstream American society and its political, economic, and cultural realms. An emphasis on such inherent differences is used to criticize Chinese Americans as "less American," while at the same time forcing them to adhere to China and Chinese culture, about which they know little. The hybrid blend that Chinese American culture has become is not recognized by mainstream U.S. society or by Chinese Americans themselves as legitimately "Chinese." Therefore, Chinese Americans are forced to form a relationship with China or to claim a wholly "American" identity, something that is difficult, if not impossible, to do in a racialized society.

Conceptions of cultural change and adaptation to U.S. culture must be understood within the larger context of the social science, folk, and official models used to describe minority experiences in the United States, each of which is based on implicit assumptions that one's true identity is "out there," waiting to be found through a process of self-reflection. Within the consciousness-raising identity politics of U.S. multiculturalism, assumptions about cultural change, preservation, and authenticity constrain identity exploration and expression.[16]

Assimilation models do not deal adequately with processes of cultural change and issues of race. Nonetheless, they provide a framework for folk understandings of cultural change. Theories of race relations with regard to U.S. minorities have been shaped by the legacy of Robert Park's race relations cycle, which described a continual four-stage drive toward assimilation.[17] Although it has become evident that racial minorities do not melt into a uniform blend, the assimilation paradigm remains influential despite newer discourses of multiculturalism that have arisen to replace it due in large part to its inability to deal effectively with race, which is now relegated to the realm of biology, subsumed under class, or hidden by ethnicity.[18]

Both folk and academic discourses on Asian American adaptation to U.S. culture have been subsumed under the framework of assimilation, within which the differential abilities of immigrant versus American-born generations to adapt to American ways is seen as the main source of intergenerational conflict. Lisa Lowe argues that this vertical generational model of understanding both the conflicts and the diversity within Asian American communities and families should be replaced by a horizontal model that acknowledges the heterogeneity of the Asian American community, a first step toward strategic political action. One particular difficulty with a generational model, Lowe observes, is the relationship that it constructs between authenticity and assimilation, and consequently of positing China as a place of origin. The further one is removed from China, the more assimilated to U.S. culture one will be, and therefore, the less authentically Chinese.[19]

The idea that one can be more or less authentically Chinese places Chinese Americans in an ambivalent relationship with people whom they view as being "more Chinese" (those who speak the language or have immigrated more recently). On the one hand, the assimilation model prescribes that Chinese Americans must identify strongly with their U.S. roots; on the other hand, racial politics codes them as perpetual foreigners. Chinese Americans are told that although their "home" is in the United States, their "roots," and therefore the missing pieces of their identity, are somewhere in China. Furthermore, U.S. multiculturalism conceives of some societies, such as the United States, as being composed of multiple cultures, and of other nations as having a single culture. As David Segal and Richard Handler put it,

> Culture, in this view, is not itself "multi"; rather, multiplicity and diversity arise from the aggregation of cultures. Cultures, in short, are figured as elemental. From this perspective, it is not that diversity is intrinsic to social formations, nor simply that the U.S. is diverse, but more specifically, that the U.S. consists of some unspecified number of cultural elements.[20]

In addition, because there is a tendency in Western thinking to view "culture as a thing: a natural object or entity made up of objects and entities ('traits')," culture is often objectified and commodified within movements for cultural preservation.[21]

In the Chinese American case, culture is not only objectified but also broken down into discrete practices, customs, and traditions, such as using chopsticks, eating certain foods, and celebrating certain holidays. These elements carry symbolic weight as features and traits that can be used to measure the authenticity of a culture. Chineseness thus becomes a measurable and commodified form of cultural capital.[22] Some people have "more" Chinese culture, whereas others (having lost it or never having learned it) have "less." This sets up a situation whereby some are said to lack culture while others have too much of it. Chinese American culture, compared with "authentic" Chinese culture, is considered impure, diluted, and devolved. Meanwhile, Chinese tradition or culture is rendered static—something that has been left over or "preserved." Thus, in folk cultural terms, Chinese Americans critically describe one another as "not very Chinese" or "too Chinesey." Some are accused of being *jook sing* (hollow bamboo); others are viewed as "bananas" (yellow on the outside, white on the inside). The term "ABC" (American-born Chinese) also carries a negative connotation, implying assimilation to the dominant American culture and loss of Chinese culture.

Popular ideas about Chinese culture often comprise essentialized and static representations of "Chinese tradition" perceived through an Orientalized filter. The American public at large view these traditions, customs, food, language, and history as rooted in a Chinese past—a past about which many American-born Chinese Americans know very little. In U.S. multiculturalism, specific "racial" backgrounds are associated with packages of cultural traits, ranging from an admirable work ethic to superstitious beliefs. As "Chinese people," Chinese Americans are expected by the larger society to know the Chinese language as well as cultural practices despite the fact that many families have lived in the United States for generations and view Chinese culture with ambivalence and as something mysterious, foreign, or irrelevant to their daily lives. The specificities of family history are disassociated from these more visible identity markers.[23]

In mainstream American constructions of Chineseness, the emphasis on knowledge of such identity markers makes many Chinese Americans feel inadequately and inauthentically Chinese. Yet, they are inescapably trapped because American racialization marks them as inherently and immutably Chinese. Folk models conceive of culture as natural, possessed, and innate; they assert that "pure" cultures can be neither created nor invented. People "have" or "possess" culture, "just like animals have fur." It is acquired slowly through a lifetime of personal development. Rapid cultural change results in acculturation—in other words, a loss of the culture of origin.[24] For Chinese Americans, these naturalized conceptions imply that consciously learned culture is less authentic or even inauthentic. A fourth-generation Chinese American woman shared the following experience in a discussion session with fellow American-born Chinese:

> I was having a conversation with a friend of mine who was born in Hong Kong. He was saying that . . . he was kind of disgusted how ABC I was. I think he used the wrong word. He was kind of joking to me . . . and was saying that I have no culture. And I was saying that I can't help

> the way I was born, I'm fourth or fifth generation, and whatever culture that I have is going to be learned culture, and then he said, and I think that this is controversial, he said that you can't learn culture, it's something that you're born with.

The idea expressed by this woman's Hong Kong friend that culture cannot be learned but is "something that you're born with" is consistent with folk ideas about culture change. Such thinking leaves no room for processes of re-ethnicization. Many Chinese Americans consciously research and adopt practices, material culture, and beliefs that signify "Chineseness" or "Chinese Americanness." Or they mark certain values, traits, and customs as their family's ethnic core. Re-ethnicization often involves learning Chinese history and culture, studying Chinese American and Asian American history, becoming active in Asian American or Chinese American "community" issues, going to China, learning to speak Chinese, consciously associating with other Chinese Americans or Asian Americans, and watching Chinese or Hong Kong movies. But in claiming Chinese culture, Chinese Americans must negotiate a politically charged atmosphere in which both the sources of the culture and the contents of its parts are contested by other people of Chinese ancestry and by members of the broader U.S. society. In this sense, re-ethnicization takes place within a context that both cooperates with and resists state-sponsored identities.

Chinese American Identity Narratives

Although family histories are the routes through which Chinese Americans explore their identities, not all versions of history and the means for exploring them are relevant. Histories are versions of the "past" created in the present within a context of power relations. The past carries heavy symbolic weight, and the creation of narratives of the past is necessary for the legitimization of interests, ranging from personal to national, in the present.[25] But the question of the past is problematic in the Chinese American case because the symbolism remains largely embedded in the traditions, customs, food, language, and histories of a Chinese past, a past that many view with ambivalence or as irrelevant and foreign. At the same time, this history is hard to escape because traditions, like cultures, are viewed as bounded entities that embody a group's cultural heritage,[26] expressed largely through ritual exercises of solidarity that incorporate powerful symbols.[27] Symbols, whether of unity, protest, authority, or equality, are the language in which cultural battles are fought. The power of symbols lies in their ability to remain stable in form, yet be flexible in content. They can be co-opted and reinterpreted, empowered and disempowered, through the manipulation of social actors. Kertzer argues that because of the existence of this symbolic diversity, symbols can play a role in fueling and legitimizing alternative viewpoints. In the case of Chinese Americans, the symbols are bound within a Chinese culture that in the context of U.S. multiculturalism represents a grouping of elements that merge unproblematically as Chinese American culture.

Chinese American identity narratives demonstrate this merging and the processes through which the meanings of Chineseness and Chinese Americanness as heritage, racial category, and political identity are negotiated. They translate family history and heritage into a contemporary social and political framework created and made meaningful to Chinese Americans or Asian Americans. These identities are embedded in social experiences. For many people, coming to an understanding of their Chinese American identities involves developing an awareness of class and ethnic differences between themselves as descendants of Cantonese immigrants who came to the United States before World War II and Chinese from other parts of the world who emigrated under different circumstances in more recent times. This "Cantonese consciousness" signals an identification with the history, language, and food of the Pearl River Delta; with American Chinatowns; and with other Chinese Americans as these elements intersect with their own family experiences.

Class, Language Competency, and Regional Identities

Participants in the Roots program often mention China as something unknown or only partially understood. The political activities of Chinese Americans, Asian Americans, or women of color also play a significant role in how they express their identities to varying degrees. What their narratives most strongly bring out are the processes of sorting out what is particular to one's own and one's family's experiences and those of a larger Chinese American community and one's place in it. For all of the individuals I interviewed, their experiences in the Roots program were a major factor impelling these processes.[28] They conceptualize China and Chinese culture in ways that are influenced by their class and positions within U.S. society. Most were born and raised in the United States, grew up primarily in middle-class areas outside of Chinatown, and identify strongly with the Cantonese dialect and its various subdialects (even if they do not speak any fluently, if at all). These factors defined their relationship to other Chinese groups in the San Francisco Bay Area, such as newer immigrants from Taiwan, as well as Chinese who reside in Chinatowns.

Susan, a third-generation participant who grew up in a Bay Area suburb, said that until she arrived on her university campus (at the time of the interview she was a senior biology major), she did not have any consciousness about being of Cantonese descent. "I used to think that if you're Chinese, you're Chinese." Growing up, she did have Asian and Chinese classmates, "but it didn't seem like they were as culturally aware" as the ones at the university. "We never talked about 'our Chinese pasts' as people here do. Here [at the university] it seems like it's more on people's minds." She indicated a belief that her growing awareness of her Cantonese identity came from the heightened distinctions made among students of Chinese descent at her university and reinforced by her participation in the Roots program and visit to her ancestral village. She related a story about how, upon her arrival at the university, others asked her "what kind of Chinese" she was. She recalled knowing that she was not Taiwanese, but could not remember whether she was Cantonese or Mandarin, and had to ask her mother. She used to wonder why people seem to make such big distinctions between people of various regional origins. But now she thinks that these differences are significant because they reflect how she was brought up in relation to Chinese from other backgrounds: "My grandparents' past, when I read them in the archives,[29] [differed from] other people's parents. . . . I don't think [the latter] had to go through as much interrogation and they weren't here when there weren't that many Chinese. . . . I think it affects how they were brought up and how I was brought up, so I think that's where I make the most distinctions, how we were raised."

A few anecdotes Susan told are indicative of issues faced by third-generation Chinese Americans and their understandings of their communities and the stereotypes of themselves. These involve a feeling of incompleteness, of not knowing about how one's own experiences fit in with those of other Chinese Americans, and not having the ability to differentiate "what is Chinese" and "what is American." When her elementary school teacher gave her class an assignment to create a family tree, Susan filled in the names of members of her nuclear family, as well as those of her maternal grandparents, who had English names. She knew her maternal grandmother's name because the family visited her often, but she did not know the names of her paternal grandfather or any of her great grandparents.

> So I was like, my teacher will never know, and I knew they were from China so that they would have Chinese names, so I kept that [last] name and then I went to look at Chang, or whatever in the phone book, and so I just chose some. I never thought much of it. I didn't care that I didn't know my great grandparents' names, though I knew that other people probably did. . . . It was mainly because I didn't want to turn it in blank because the teacher would probably ask me about it and I didn't want people to think, "she doesn't know." I didn't want it to be blank. . . . It just looks bad if it's blank.

In elementary school, Susan thought that all Chinese Americans were like herself—they spoke English at home to their parents, and their parents spoke half English and half Chinese to them. But then she realized that some of her friends spoke half Chinese and half English to their parents, and in high school she concluded that half of the Chinese Americans were like her, and the other half were like her parents. "I always thought that if they were Chinese American, they were like me, but if they were Chinese from China, they would be more in touch with their Chinese background, like speaking to their parents in Chinese."

Susan recalls seeing public service announcements on KPIX, the local Public Broadcasting System station, that portrayed people from various "ethnic" backgrounds claiming "I'm proud to be . . . [Chinese, Jewish, etc.]." One spot showed a Chinese American girl walking through the streets of Chinatown, proclaiming, "I'm proud to be Chinese American."

> And I was thinking, how could she be Chinese American if she was in Chinatown, because I always related Chinatown to Chinese from China, and I always thought that Chinese Americans were more like me. I never really thought that they were really different from anyone else, but from those public service clips, it made it look so different . . . like she was Chinese from China. I didn't really relate to them because it didn't seem like she had the same experiences that I did.

Susan says she does not remember when she figured out that she is Chinese. In junior high school, one classmate said to her, "I bet you eat Chinese hamburgers." She recalls just brushing off his comment, not knowing exactly how to respond because she did not know whether there really was such a thing as Chinese hamburgers.[30]

Many of the Roots participants grew up with negative or ambivalent ideas of China. Few remember learning much about China in school; even fewer knew anything about Chinese American issues. In the images they were exposed to, China was either romanticized as an ancient and proud civilization or vilified as dark, evil, and Communist in the Orientalist discourses disseminated by the American media and educational systems. In essence, rather than representing a place that is familiar and comfortable to Chinese Americans, China is depicted as a foreign and unknown location to which they have, somehow, an ancestral connection.

Thus, it is not surprising that Roots participants are influenced by essentialized ideas about Chinese culture as portrayed in the American media and through interactions with first-generation immigrants who (are thought to) have a better command of the language and the customs. Most of the Chinese Americans I interviewed felt that they are not authentic Chinese. Even those who had a fluent command of spoken Cantonese felt inadequate in terms of their ability to write Chinese or to use a vocabulary more complex than a child's stock of household words. At the same time, some entered public school not speaking English; this was the first time they had to recognize themselves as Chinese. Before entering school, they never had a label for the kind of "Chinese" they were or the type of Chinese they spoke.

Carl, a graduate of San Francisco State University and active in the Chinese Historical Society of America, is fourth generation on one side of the family, and fifth generation on the other. He and his cousin created an extensive family tree based on immigration files at the National Archives branch at San Bruno, a project that continued long after this assignment for the Roots program had been turned in. I asked him to what degree he was conscious of being of Chinese descent as he was growing up. He observed that at the school he attended in the Richmond district of San Francisco, there was a "distinct difference between those who have just arrived here and those who have been here for a few generations." He thinks this distinction is correlated with the ability to speak Chinese.

Carl went to the same Chinese school that his father had attended as a child. But he lacked the Chinese language background at home that many of his classmates had. "To me it was kind of awkward. I wasn't afraid and I didn't want to rebel, or block myself from being Chinese or anything, but [in] the Chinese school I went to, now that I think of it, I should have gone to a CSL (Chinese as a Second Language) program. . . . I was brought up with English and didn't know Chinese." He remembers going to friends' houses and being spoken to in Chinese by his friends' parents. He often felt embarrassed because he could comprehend only the gist of what they said as he did not know that much Chinese. He thinks his friends' parents found that odd.

"I'm willing to admit, the Roots program and the Taiwan Study Tour [nicknamed the Love Boat][31] made me realize I [should] accept my identity the way I am. I'm not one or the other. I'm not Chinese or Chinese American. I'm an American of Chinese descent."

In certain contexts, not only generation but also "Cantoneseness" become a social marker closely tied to class distinctions. Roots participants viewed their Cantonese background and their families' history of emigration from Guangdong Province as one of struggle, a challenge met with a strong work ethic that paved the way for the success of later generations. Although most of their families had risen to solid middle-class status, many still identified with the struggles of their immigrant ancestors. Thus, for many Roots participants, their rural Cantonese background reflects a class identity that distinguishes them from the more prosperous immigrants from Hong Kong and Taiwan whom they encounter at their universities.

One participant recalls that he did not identify with the Chinese culture he learned about in a college course in Chinese history because he could not see any connections to his own family background. "When I took history of China, which I just barely passed, I didn't find any connection to the history of Beijing or to the empires. It didn't mean anything. I could have studied the history of any other country and it would have been the same."

Kim is a graduate of Harvard's Kennedy School of Government, specializing in housing and urban development. As a child, she and her family occasionally went shopping and visited her grandmother in Chinatown. But to her, Chinatown seemed "sort of crowded and dirty. . . . It was always a place to do errands rather than a destination." Growing up, she was "always that shy Chinese girl." She recalls how at school recent immigrants and American-born Chinese formed two separate groups that did not associate with each other. She does not recall having what she terms a "Cantonese consciousness" until she participated in the Roots program. Like Susan, she became aware of class and cultural differences among different types of Chinese when she arrived at Stanford University. Her view of the Chinese American experience that she read about in class or heard about from her family differed from those of her classmates, many of whose parents emigrated from Taiwan after 1965.

> I think when we would read all these books, like *Longtime Californ'*, *Angel Island*,[32] I would identify with them. I would think, "Oh my grandfather went through that." My grandfather picked fruit when he came over, and just from seeing Chinatown I knew that there were garment workers, they were poor, . . . but then a lot of the Taiwanese had a really different experience. They were well educated . . . no sense of connection to . . . Chinatown . . . sort of the class difference that began to emerge.

While a student, Kim fought to add classes in Cantonese to her university's curriculum, but both administrators and students asked why she wanted to learn Cantonese, a peasant language.

> I . . . feel like language is a key element of culture, especially for me . . . well, my case is a little bit different since I was adopted, I mean I was like a day old, so for all intents and purposes my parents are my parents, and they're Cantonese, but biologically I'm half Cantonese and half Italian, so I don't look completely Chinese, so for me language is a way of connecting with that culture that is very important, it's one thing that really separates the generations . . . you know it separates sort of your identity.

After I last interviewed her, Kim went to Hong Kong to study Cantonese for a year.

Henry's family roots extend through Latin America. His mother is of Chinese descent, born and raised in Peru, and his father's family is Chinese from Hawaii. He remembers that as a youth he went with his mother to shop in both the Mission district (the Chicano/Latino section of San Francisco) and in Chinatown. He speaks Spanish at home with his grandparents. It was not until he entered school that he was forced to distinguish between the Peruvian and Chinese parts of his family's background when other children asked about his ethnic origins.

I asked him what his impressions of China were while he was growing up. Henry says that he didn't think about China that much. He recalls seeing pictures of Chinese kids in Chinese school textbooks. The stories of China he heard at school conjured up images of a countryside with isolated farms. China is ancient, with a history thousands of years old. Images of Peru are more vivid to him. Peru and Hawaii are the "old countries" for his family. Although his grandfather listens to Chinese opera at home, he thinks that in the Richmond district where he grew up, "being Chinese" wasn't stressed, despite the fact that there was a large concentration of Chinese Americans there. He had trouble relating to Chinese Americans in Chinatown, who seemed "more Chinesey," having grown up in the Chinatown environment.

Henry became involved in Asian American Studies while attending the University of California, Berkeley. He studied for a year at the Chinese University of Hong Kong and returned fluent in spoken and written Cantonese. He identifies strongly as a Chinese American of Cantonese descent from Zhongshan District with a Peruvian background. When I asked him which aspect of himself he considers to be Chinese, he mentioned language, a group-oriented attitude, his custom of celebrating Chinese holidays, his tendency toward eating certain foods and deferring to authority, and his physical characteristics.

Another example of the complex forms of identity created through secondary migration is Laura's family. Laura was born in Burma, which her family left when she was a young child. Burma figures prominently in her interest in her ancestral roots. She knows that she spoke Burmese and some Toisanese (a subdialect of Cantonese) at one time, but now sees those languages as having been taken away from her in the process of getting an English-language education that marginalizes multicultural literature. When I first met Laura in 1992, she was a recent graduate of Lowell High School, waiting to enter a private women's college in the Bay Area. When I interviewed her in 1995, she was packing for a semester of study abroad in Thailand, after which she hoped to cross the border into Burma to contact relatives there. In recent years, she has become actively involved in Asian American feminist politics, which strongly influences her views. I asked her how she identified herself before participating in the Roots program and becoming involved in politics in college. Although she attended Lowell High School, where Asian American students are a majority, upon reflection she thinks that at the time she did not have the resources available to "inspire me to become more active." The first Asian American literature she read was in a college course. The only Asian high school teacher she had was her Mandarin teacher. It was "almost a complete turnaround for me having teachers of color [in college]. I always felt that in English class I had to take myself out of myself and try to relate to the author, and when I write it seemed I had to take on this academic voice, something that wasn't real to me. When I took an Asian American literature course it brought the two together, my love of writing, and my cultural history and family issues."

Laura had not heard the term "people of color" until she began filling out college applications. Her first year in college was the first time that she really learned about the Asian American movement. Despite her activist and political leanings, she sees her family background as consistent with her values. She thinks that her family has given her a "real grounding of my culture. . . . There isn't just one way of doing a movement, marching down the street with a sign, it's more than that, it's your daily acts of preserving your culture, and I think I owe a lot to my parents for passing down the history and preserving traditions, teaching me where I'm from."

Gender and Ethnicity

Participants in the Roots program desire to adopt flexibly Chinese customs and practices that are meaningful and familiar to them, while at the same time modifying these practices in a Chinese American context. In this way, rather than feeling that irrelevant traditions are being imposed on them as a measure of their Chineseness, they are taking ownership of them in new ways. Many of the women I interviewed see the gendered practices associated with traditional Chinese culture, such as the exclusion of female names from written genealogies, as practices that they can change in their own reworkings of Chinese culture in an American context. They find customs, such as generational naming and not washing one's hair on New Year's Day, to be practices that no longer apply to modern U.S. society. They often do not know the original meanings and functions of these traditions, which make the latter seem even more irrelevant. They think generational naming is part of a patriarchal system, as only males receive these formal names. Also, descent is traced through the male line. Many young women strongly object to the gender-biased nature of these traditions, but they still express a desire to perpetuate certain customs, stressing that understanding them is an important part of remembering one's Chinese American history: "To me the [generational] name doesn't mean as much, but it could also be because I'm a woman, so most likely, I won't have my own anyway. But I also think the most important thing is that we remember our history, so I think that if we just remember that and remember how the [paper] name got changed, then I think that it's sufficient for me."[33] In de-emphasizing the importance of generational naming, but reinforcing the importance of genealogy as an avenue for reclaiming family history, these women are recasting genealogical writing in a new light. Thus, tracing genealogies are important both as a way to symbolize the linkages between China and the United States, past and present, and as a way to reclaim the family's rightful identity that had been forcibly altered to skirt unfair immigration laws. At the same time, they change not only the function but also the form of the genealogies: Many trace both sides of the family and include both men and women.[34]

Conclusion

The content of Chinese American culture consists of far more than traditions deemed "Chinese" on the basis of their association with traditional Chinese customs. As Chinese Americans construct their own versions of culture, they employ a selection of symbols from China's past that acknowledges, yet falls outside of, the ritual constraints of traditional Chinese culture. They emphasize things that seem a unique part of the Chinese American experience, such as the history of Chinese immigrant railroad workers and the common experiences of racial oppression they share with other minority groups. But their Chinese heritage makes them different from other "Americans," so Chinese Americans have to decide how much of this past they wish to claim. Regardless of the degree to which they are adamant about claiming the "American" part of their identity, they continue to face judgment, by both Chinese and non-Chinese, as "Chinese."

Thinking of "culture" as fine arts and elite traditions increases the feeling of cultural "lack" among Chinese Americans and devalues their everyday practices and family traditions. Indeed, their rewriting of genealogies in many ways represents their spurning of "high culture." Their efforts to alter genealogical forms thus can be read not only as a rejection of "high culture" but also as a celebration of new Chinese American cultural forms. Being Chinese American ultimately has a subjective meaning, created variously through experiences with valorizing families, investigating family histories, learning about the history and current situation of Asians in America, visiting ancestral villages, and engaging in political activism. The meaning of each of these experiences is left to the individual to fashion. The Roots program was instrumental both as a way for participants to learn about Chinese and Chinese American history, family history, and ancestral places in China and as a means for them to recontextualize their personal experiences within a larger context by understanding the meanings behind many customs and traditions, of which they saw only disjointed pieces at home. For many, the Roots experience involved relearning, or learning for the first time, aspects of "Chinese culture."

Although the Roots program did not focus explicitly on issues of power, its format allowed the participants to rework various hegemonic constructions of Chineseness and Chinese Americanness, of which participants were aware to differing degrees. Rather than dwell on the state of in-betweenness that many say they feel, the program provides a basis on which identities can be supported independently of the dichotomized categories they are caught between.

What the Roots program does most effectively is to help participants begin to reach an understanding of themselves in relation to China and its traditions by researching their family histories, visiting their ancestral villages, and getting involved in a peer group whose members are concerned with similar issues. These experiences are instrumental to the reworking of the bounded categories assumed within U.S. multiculturalism and offer a way for participants to counter the hegemony of the cultural authenticity of China in the Chinese American past by building their own cultural capital, writing their own histories, and creating their own family rituals based on their experiences in the United States. The hybridity of Asian American identities[35] must be recognized as authentic and complete; they result from ongoing cultural construction and acknowledge the validity and richness of heterogeneity.

NOTES

This chapter is a shorter, revised version of Chapter 3 in Andrea Louie, *Chineseness across Borders: Renegotiating Chinese Identities in China and the United States* (Durham, NC: Duke University Press, 2004).

1. Laura Nader, "Controlling Processes: Tracing the Dynamic Components of Power," *Current Anthropology* 38, no. 5 (1997): 711–37.
2. J. O. in a roundtable discussion, 1996.
3. Arif Dirlik, "The Asia-Pacific Idea in Asian-American Perspective," in *What Is in a Rim? Critical Perspectives on the Pacific Region Idea*, ed. Arif Dirlik (Lanham, MD: Rowman and Littlefield, 1998), 283–308.
4. Dirlik, "The Asia-Pacific Idea," 296–97.
5. Dirlik, "The Asia-Pacific Idea," 294, 184.
6. Paulla Ebron and Anna Tsing, "From Allegories of Identity to Sites of Dialogue," *Diaspora* 4, no. 2 (1995): 125–51.
7. Madeline Y. Hsu, *Dreaming of Gold, Dreaming of Home: Transnationalism and Migration between the United States and South China, 1882–1943* (Stanford, CA: Stanford University Press, 2000); Nina Glick Schiller, "Transmigrants and Nation-States: Something Old and Something New in U.S. Immigrant Experience," in *Handbook of International Migration: The American Experience*, eds. Charles Hirschman, Josh DeWing, and Phillip Kasinitz (New York: Russell Sage Foundation, 1999), 94–119; Schiller, "Who Are These Guys? A Transnational Perspective on National Identities," in *Identities on the Move: Transnational Processes in North America and the Caribbean Basin*, ed. Liliana Goldin (Austin: University of Texas Press, 1999), 15–44.
8. Andrew Lam, "An Asian American Argues It's Better to Be Feared Than to Be Invisible," Pacific News Service, http://pacificnewsservice.org/jinn/stories/3.06/970314-invisible .html.

9. Katharyne Mitchell, "In Whose Interest? Transnational Capital and the Production of Multiculturalism in Canada," in *Global/Local: Cultural Production and the Transnational Imaginary*, eds. Bob Wilson and Wimal Dissanayake (Durham, NC: Duke University Press, 1999), 219–51.

10. Community, in this sense, was envisioned as a discrete geographic location, rather than as a population dispersed throughout the city and suburbs.

11. Andrea Louie, "When You Are Related to the 'Other': (Re)locating the Chinese Homeland in Asian American Politics through Cultural Tourism," *positions: east asia cultural critique* 11, no. 3 (2003): 735–63.

12. See Dirlik, "The Asia-Pacific Idea."

13. Evelyn Hu-DeHart, "Introduction: Asian American Formations in the Age of Globalization," in *Across the Pacific: Asian Americans and Globalization*, ed. Evelyn Hu-DeHart (New York: Asia Society; and Philadelphia: Temple University Press, 1999), 3.

14. Arif Dirlik, "Asians on the Rim: Transnational Capital and Local Community in the Making of Contemporary Asian America," in *Across the Pacific*, ed. Hu-DeHart, 40.

15. Philip Choy, Lorraine Dong, and Marlon Hom, eds., *The Coming Man: Nineteenth-Century American Perceptions of the Chinese* (Hong Kong: Joint Publishing, 1994; repr. Seattle: The University of Washington Press, 1995).

16. Liz Bondi, "Locating Identity Politics," in *Place and the Politics of Identity*, eds. Michael Keith and Steve Pile (London: Routledge, 1993), 84–101.

17. Michael Omi and Howard Winant, *Racial Formation in the United States: From the 1960s to the 1990s*, 2nd ed. (New York and London: Routledge, 1994).

18. Omi and Winant, *Racial Formation*; and Kamala Visweswaran, "Race and the Culture of Anthropology," *American Anthropologist* 100 (1998): 70–83.

19. Lisa Lowe, "Heterogeneity, Hybridity, Multiplicity: Marking Asian American Difference," *Diaspora* 1, no. 1 (1991): 24–44.

20. David A. Segal and Richard Handler, "U.S. Multiculturalism and the Concept of Culture," *Identities* 1, no. 4 (1995): 391–407.

21. Richard Handler, *Nationalism and the Politics of Culture in Quebec* (Madison: University of Wisconsin Press, 1988).

22. Pierre Bourdieu, *Distinction: A Social Critique of the Judgment of Taste*, trans. Richard Nice (Cambridge, MA: Harvard University Press, 1984).

23. A cartoon strip, *Angry Little Asian Girl* (ALAG), makes fun of these assumptions. The girl walks into a classroom and the teacher says, "Oh my, you speak English so well, where did you learn to speak so well?" The ALAG says, "I was born here, you stupid dipshit, don't you know anything about immigration? Read some history, you stupid ignoramus."

24. Jean Jackson, "Culture, Genuine and Spurious: The Politics of Indianness in the Vaupes, Colombia," *American Ethnologist* 22, no. 1 (1995): 3–27.

25. David Kertzer, *Ritual, Politics, and Power* (New Haven, CT: Yale University Press, 1988).

26. Segal and Handler, "U.S. Multiculturalism."

27. Kertzer, *Ritual, Politics, and Power*.

28. One participant commented, "I think that Roots was the first feeling of the cultural and political feeling of being a part of the Asian American community. That was the first experience I had that gave me a sense of that community outside my family."

29. This refers to the National Archives branch in San Bruno, California, which houses the Immigration and Naturalization Service records from the Angel Island Immigration Station.

30. After a Roots meeting, a small group went out to dinner at a family style restaurant. One of the dishes ordered was *yuk beng* (*zhuroubing*), consisting of steamed minced

pork mixed with eggs. Susan looked with surprise at the dish, recognizing it as something her mother cooks at home, something that she always had thought was a type of American meatloaf.

31. The "Love Boat" is a program for overseas Chinese youth run by the Taiwan government.

32. Victor G. Nee and Brett de Bary Nee, *Longtime Californ': A Documentary Study of an American Chinatown* (New York: Pantheon, 1972; 1986); and Him Mark Lai, Genny Lim, and Judy Yung, *Island: Poetry and History of Chinese Immigrants on Angel Island, 1910–1940* (San Francisco: Hoc Doi, Chinese Culture Foundation of San Francisco, 1980; repr., Seattle: University of Washington Press, 1991).

33. "Paper sons" were young men in China who evaded the Chinese exclusion laws by buying documents from Chinese immigrants residing in the United States. These residents, after visits to China, would report to immigration officials upon their return to the United States that their wives had given birth to sons, thereby creating "slots" that could be used later either by their own sons or by "paper sons" to gain admission into the United States. The paper sons had to memorize minute details of the family histories of their "paper fathers" in order to convince interrogators that they were the real sons of the immigrants.

34. As Susan Brownell and Jeffrey Wasserstrom observe in *Chinese Femininities/Chinese Masculinities: A Reader* (Berkeley and Los Angeles: University of California Press, 2002), 1–42, genealogical forms are also changing in the People's Republic of China.

35. Lowe, "Heterogeneity, Hybridity, Multiplicity."

The Changle American Association in New York City. Note that the sign on the building spells Chang Le as two separate words. However, in scholarly writings, all the transliterated characters in a Chinese place name are linked together and spelled as one word. *(Photograph © Xiaojian Zhao, 2007. Used with permission.)*

7

The "Spirit of Changle": Constructing a Chinese Regional Identity in New York

Xiaojian Zhao

Most of the signs for the Chinese American associations in New York's Chinatown are permanently carved on stone walls or tiled on huge buildings with Chinese architectural touches to signify their long history and prominence in their community. The eye-catching awning of the Changle American Association (CAA) on Chatham Square, at the tip of East Broadway, in contrast, points to the organization's youth—it was established in 1998—and suggests that the office space is leased. Located on the second floor of 2 East Broadway, the headquarters of the CAA is a busy place. Men and women go in and out of the small office and the adjourning meeting room, speaking loudly in the Fuzhou dialect. The door of the office is also open to visitors: The association takes public relations seriously. More than anything else, the leaders of the organization want their people to be known to the world. This chapter examines how recent Chinese immigrants from the Changle (pronounced *Chang-le*) region of Fujian province negotiate power within the Chinese American community. In their struggle against discriminatory stereotypes, the leaders of the CAA attempt to create a distinctive image for immigrants from their native place.

Immigrants from the Changle region are no strangers in the minds of the American public. Beginning in the 1990s, they have been the subject of a number of headline stories: They were targets of the U.S. government's crackdown on human trafficking from China. While the mass media and the general public focused on the tragedies that often accompanied this type of smuggling, the immigrants were working hard to create a new image for themselves. As the fastest-growing Chinese American regional group, the Changle immigrants exemplify the new dynamics and power relations in post-1965 Chinese America.

Changle and the Image of the Changle Immigrants

Located along the Min River in Fujian Province on the southeastern coast of China across the strait from the island of Taiwan, Changle is the homeland of a majority of the new Chinese immigrants in New York. With a population of a little over 672,000 in 2001, the county (which acquired cityhood in 1994) is not as big as most of its neighbors, largely because a significant portion of its natives have emigrated. A 2001 census compiled by the Fuzhou municipal government, which has administrative jurisdiction over Changle, revealed that about 400,000 Changle natives and their descendents were living outside China, in such places as Hong Kong, Taiwan, Macao, the United States, and Europe.[1]

Nineteenth-century Chinese immigrants in the United States came primarily from the coastal districts of the southeastern province of Guangdong, where the Chinese have had frequent contacts with outsiders since the first Opium War (1839–1841). Some natives of Fujian emigrated to California during the Gold Rush that began in 1849, but before 1965 the vast majority of the Chinese population in the United States was Cantonese. During the last two decades of the twentieth century, however, Fujian replaced Guangdong as a major base for U.S.-bound emigration. A majority of the new Fujian immigrants have come from the region around Fuzhou, the provincial capital, about 80 percent of them from Changle, one of the ten cities or counties under the administrative jurisdiction of Fuzhou. Because all the people from Fuzhou share the same dialect, the Changle people [*Changle ren*] often address themselves or are referred to as Fuzhou people [*Fuzhou ren*] even though the relatively few immigrants from the Fuzhou metropolis do not like to be associated with immigrants from rural areas like Changle, nicknamed the Village of Smugglers [*toudu zhi xiang*].

Because of its location, Changle has had a long history of maritime activities and overseas migration since the Song Dynasty. Some of its natives settled in Taiwan, Hong Kong, Southeast Asia, Britain, and Holland. Not until after 1980, however, did their numbers in the United States begin to grow. This wave of immigration was stimulated by the normalization of U.S.–China relations and economic reforms in China that began in the late 1970s. Inspired by those Chinese Americans who built big brick houses for their families and donated money to the village schools, going to America instead of going to college became the dream of young people, but at that time the number of Changle natives in the United States was very small, which meant that the 1965 Immigration Act—and in particular, its family unification provision—could not be utilized by Changle ren who wished to emigrate to the United States. Those eager to leave had to seek alternative means to do so.

In the 1980s, groups of Changle natives began to leave their home villages through arrangements made by individuals the Chinese call snakeheads [*shetou*]. At first some were able to travel to the United States with falsified or fake documents. When obtaining these papers became difficult, many individuals and families tried to go to the United States by crossing the open sea without the required passports and visas. The media coverage of intercepted boatloads of people from Fujian, alive or dead, captured the fascination of the world.

Their story, as told in the American mass media, began with the *Golden Venture*. In the summer of 1993, this run-down freighter registered in Honduras ran aground on the Rockaway peninsula in Queens Borough, New York. The smugglers had promised to send small boats to pick up the passengers, but in the midst of a bloody battle among members of the Fuqingbang, a Fuzhou natives' gang that was responsible for the task, no one showed up.[2] The 286 Chinese on board were reportedly forced to jump off the ship and swim to shore; ten drowned. It was soon revealed that most aboard were from Changle, which gained the region undesired international fame. The *Golden Venture*, as Peter Kwong points out, has "defined the discourse" of contemporary Chinese immigration. In the months and years that followed, the cruel exploitation of illegal immigrants would make headlines in many nations and became the topic of several U.S. government reports and scholarly works. In December 1998, thirty-five people were charged in an immigrant-smuggling operation that investigators said made $170 million in two years by bringing 3,600 Chinese across the Canadian border through the St. Regis Mohawk Indian reservation into the United States. The Chinese were said to be from three Fujian counties, including Changle. In 1999 and 2000, U.S. and Canadian authorities intercepted several boatloads of undocumented immigrants. On June 18, 2000, another tragedy captured international attention: A customs officer working at the English port of Dover discovered in a truck, under a cargo of tomatoes, sixty Chinese, fifty-eight of whom had already suffocated. Twenty-three of the dead were later identified as emigrants from Changle.[3] Such sensational stories made Fuzhou immigrants in general and Changle immigrants in particular a synonym for smuggled Chinese. An Internet search on Changle immigrants in September 2004 resulted in 175 entries; almost all of them concerned smuggling activities.

It cost in U.S. currency about $20,000 per person in the late 1980s and $30,000 in the early 1990s to be smuggled into the United States. By 2004, the price had risen to $80,000, a 300 percent increase over twenty years. As the per capita income for urban residents in Fujian province was only about U.S. $1,400 (11,175 yuan) in 2004, very few individual families could afford to pay such an exorbitant amount.[4] As with the early Chinese immigrants, families and relatives in the villages pooled money from various sources and some took out high-interest loans. Once a deposit of half of the fee was paid, the snakeheads would provide the prospective emigrants with fake documents to travel to Hong Kong. From there, they would go to other countries before entering the United States. The remaining payment would be due once these people arrived in the United States.[5]

According to U.S. media reports, the majority of Fuzhou immigrants were lured to the United States by snakeheads who minimized the dangers of the smuggling process. Some of the snakeheads, however, were highly respected members of the community because they provided opportunities otherwise not available in their villages. When Cuiping Zheng, known as Pingjie (Sister Ping), was on trial in New York in 2005, many immigrants from Fujian expressed their sympathy and concerns for her. According to the *Chinese Daily News*, the majority of the villagers in Changle thought that Zheng was a *da hao ren* (great person) who helped her fellow villagers search for opportunities overseas.[6] Although economic reforms in the 1980s and 1990s brought significant improvements to the villages, the income of the peasants was far lower than those in China's big cities. If U.S. dollars were converted to Chinese yuan, the amount of money a dishwasher in a Chinatown restaurant could make would be very large by village standards.[7]

In the early 1990s, the Chinese government lifted its special exit permit policy, making it relatively easier for people to leave the country. Young and middle-aged men left in large numbers; those who stayed were seen as people with no promising future [*mei chu xi*]. A twenty-six-year-old restaurant worker in New York City explained why he decided to leave in 1998:

> At that time everyone thought America was the place to get rich. My situation was not bad at home; I had an iron rice-bowl—a job paid by the city government. But my prospects were not so good. My uncle, my cousin, and my sister's husband were all in New York. My uncle built a very nice house in the village, and my grandfather's grave was the one everybody admired. My mother never said that I had to leave, but she kept on telling me so and so had left and so and so had found a job in the United States. For my own future and the future of my family, I decided that going to America would be the best thing to do.[8]

If the emigrants were not completely ignorant about the risks involved, they were not overly concerned. For some, the ordeal was a test of will and ambition. One of them said,

> I was young and physically strong. The question was whether I was brave enough to make the crossing. So many of my villagers had done that; why couldn't I? Once I had announced that I wanted to go, everyone started to save money for me. Of course people whispered about the tragedies. A classmate of mine died, and we were all saddened. But

> I did not want that to stop me; I did not let that shatter my dreams. When I was about to leave, no one in my family talked about those things; everyone wished the best for me.[9]

Some scholars estimate that between 1986 and 1996, over 100,000 Chinese entered the United States illegally.[10] People in New York's Chinatown believe that out of a total of 200,000 Changle immigrants in the United States, 80 percent were either smuggled or trafficked into the country. That number may be exaggerated; most of those who got caught, however, were indeed from Changle. The number of people who disappeared en route is unknown.

The new arrivals started working in the United States in restaurants, garment shops, or construction companies. Many of them used family networks to find jobs, working mostly for business owners who spoke the Fuzhou dialect. Qingming Chen, a takeout restaurant owner who came to New York in 1997 at age twenty-five, was picked up by "big brother Lin," a distant cousin on his mother's side, when he first arrived. Two days later, Chen started working at a Manhattan restaurant owned by a friend of Lin's: "I made $40 that day and was very excited about it! I called my family and they were all very happy. Most people would have to work for at least two weeks to get $40 in Changle."[11]

If the new immigrants found that money was easy to make, they also learned that it was hard to save if they wanted a comfortable place to live. In the village visitors could stay at their relatives' houses, but in America the newcomers were on their own even if they had relatives. "It is better this way, I guess," said a man in his late thirties, now a homeowner himself, "but it was hard for me to understand at the beginning when my relative said he had found a place for me. I had just started to work and had borrowed a lot of money. Why couldn't he let me sleep on the couch? All I needed was a place to sleep!" Eventually he took a job in Georgia. "I did not want to leave New York," he said, "but that restaurant owner provided shelter."[12]

Another man, a new business owner, described the four years he lived in an apartment shared by many laborers as the most difficult part of his life: "I didn't mind hard work. If I stayed healthy and there was work, I was thankful. But those long nights were hard. I watched videotapes on my bed and chatted with my roommates, also on my bed—that's the only space that I had. To beat homesickness I played cards with friends, sometimes all night. And I drank a lot."[13]

The new immigrants were subjected to social prejudice. "I would not rent any of my apartments to those *Fuzhou lao* [guys from Fuzhou], even if they pay cash in advance," said one woman from Hong Kong. "I would not let them stay in my apartment either—they are too loud," said another, who is also from Hong Kong. "Besides, they borrowed too much money to get here. How can they pay off debt by working in Chinatown? Some of them became ill, mentally ill [pointing at her own head]. I don't want to see this kind of people in my place." Some landlords or business owners do not want to deal with Fuzhou people, saying simply that they do not want to be bothered by the gangs.[14]

The Changle Entrepreneurship Style

About 80 percent of the Changle immigrants live in the New York area, where Chinatown encompasses more than twenty blocks on Manhattan's Lower East Side. The new immigrants have brought new life to Chinatown. East Broadway and Eldridge Street, once quiet, are now filled with shops, restaurants, vendors, and employment services. Instead of Cantonese or Mandarin, the Fuzhou dialect is now the official language of the neighborhood. As Jane Lii, who reported for the *New York Times*, pointed out, the "new blood" of the Fujianese in Chinatown began to play an increasingly important role in the community in the mid-1990s, posing a real challenge to the old Cantonese population and the more affluent immigrants from Taiwan.[15]

In early 2004, Wai-Yin Tsang, a reporter for the Chinese-language newspaper *Chinese Daily News*, interviewed twenty prominent businessmen from Changle in New York. Her three-part special report, *Changle ren zai meiguo* [Changle people in the United States], appeared in the paper's weekly magazine, *Shijie zhoukan*, from late September through early October, and provides the first in-depth coverage of the experiences of a young immigrant group. According to Tsang, the early arrivals made their living by relying on "three knives"—one for chopping meat and vegetables, a second for sewing clothing, and a third for mixing cement. By early 2004, however, the Changle immigrants dominated the small takeout restaurant business in the New York area, had opened some of the largest buffet restaurants in the United States, and had entered a variety of economic activities. Relying on connections from home, they have also built an extensive business network utilizing market, labor, and financial resources among themselves.[16]

The typical Changle immigrant begins working in the United States at a Chinese restaurant. Once the person has paid off his or her debt and saved some money, he or she tries to go into business, usually borrowing money from friends and using family members as labor. If the person succeeds, he or she expands the business a few years later or moves to a better location. Beyond the New York area, restaurants operated by Changle immigrants may now be found in Washington, DC, Baltimore, Boston, Cleveland, Houston, Denver, and various cities in California, as well as in Toronto and Vancouver. One immigrant interviewed by the author recalled his early experiences:

> I was an all-purpose restaurant worker [*dazhade*] for two years before I started out on my own. Don't laugh at me—I had never cooked a

> grain of rice before coming to the United States. At home my mother would not allow her only son to work in the kitchen! But everyone I knew here made money in the restaurant business, and I figured that's what I would have to do. I had a partner and we bought a place together. I was the chef—can you imagine? I don't think any of the customers who came during the first week ever returned [laugh]! But I got help from friends and some of them taught me how to cook.[17]

To cut down the cost and avoid competition, Changle immigrants open businesses in run-down neighborhoods or other less desirable locations. Quandi Chen, who served as the first president of the Changle American Association, started a takeout place in Harlem in 1987. "In those days gunshots were heard just about every day," he recalled. "I made a living under gunfire." One day, Chen's restaurant was hit by eight bullets, and one of them went through the supposedly bulletproof glass window and lodged deep in the stove. "I was a little scared by that incident," Chen admitted.[18]

A fellow Changle immigrant had a similar experience:

> When that restaurant was up for sale, a friend told me that the location was bad: there were gangs in the neighborhood. At that time I just saw the good deal. I was in my early thirties and what would people think they could get from me? I did not have the money to be choosy anyway. One day someone broke into my car. A little later the window of the storefront was smashed. After that, I decided to move.[19]

To expand business, many of these takeout restaurants provide delivery service despite the risk. In areas where few places offered delivery, the residents welcome affordable food brought to their homes. Owners of these establishments do not have to compete with bigger and fancier restaurants for customers. However, the delivery people, who carry only a small amount of cash, are often the victims of robberies or even homicides. From December 1998 to early 2004, six Chinese restaurant workers were killed while delivering food. On October 15, 2002, thirty-six-year-old Jianchun Lin was shot in Brooklyn while bicycling to deliver food for the Happy House Restaurant. At the time he was killed, Lin was still $10,000 in debt and his ten-year-old son was left behind in Changle. In the late evening of February 13, 2004, eighteen-year-old Huang Chen, whose parents owned the Ming Garden restaurant in Queens, fell prey to a group of teenagers looking for cash to buy athletic shoes. The young Chen, who had left Changle as a ten-year-old, had just graduated from high school. Although he offered the attackers the $49 he carried as well as the dinner they ordered, the young men hit Chen's head repeatedly with a baseball bat before stabbing him to death with a knife. His body, wrapped in a garbage bag, was discovered the next day in a lake in Brookville Park near Kennedy Airport.[20]

To some extent, the success of a Changle immigrant can be measured by the grandeur as well as the number of restaurants he or she owns. The smallest takeout places, where customers order food through a small hole in a bulletproof window, are operated by immigrants who had moved up from being laborers not too long ago. After a few years, the owner might open another establishment or move to a more desirable area. The highest standards have been set by such giant restaurants as Jingfeng in Manhattan and the luxury eateries operated by the East Buffet Restaurant Corporation. Jingfeng can seat 1,500 patrons, and the East Buffet restaurants in New York, Long Island, and Connecticut can each serve 800 to 2,200 customers at a time. With 120 employees on its payroll, Jingfeng operates like a medium-sized company. It is the place of choice for formal community gatherings and banquets in New York's Chinatown.[21]

Zhonggao Zheng, a major shareholder of Jingfeng, served as the director of a business board that runs several other eateries and a real estate company. He is active in community affairs in both the United States and China and is no doubt one of the most respected community leaders in New York's Chinatown. Zheng's personal achievement has a symbolic value among the immigrants as they pursue the American dream. In February 1995, when a group of labor union activists picketed Jingfeng, local establishments backed the restaurant. At the "Thousand Plate Dinner Party in Support of Jingfeng," attended by notables of New York's major Chinese American organizations, Lin Song, the head of the labor union that had organized the picket line, was labeled a "devil" who wanted to destroy the community's economic prosperity. Although union organizers had raised legitimate concerns, Jingfeng did provide its employees with working conditions and benefits that many smaller eateries could not match.[22]

Their concentration in the restaurant business has allowed the Changle immigrants to develop other types of businesses as well. One of the three owners of the East Buffet Restaurant Corporation, Tianming Zheng, came to New York in 1982 after living in Hong Kong for a few years. He opened Flushing's first Chinese restaurant, Ming Yuan, and later sold it for a good profit. Over the next decade, he purchased one restaurant after another. Each time he would remodel the place thoroughly, open the business, and then sell it and move on. At a certain point in his business expansion, Zheng decided to display restaurant menus by projecting colorful slides of the dishes in lighted frames. He deposited $2,000 on an order of twenty slides. When the advertising company failed to deliver the product on time, he went to its office and waited until the job was completed. There Zheng learned that the advertising business was less labor intensive than the restaurant trade, so he soon opened the New

Generation Advertising Company in Chinatown. As a large portion of the approximately 50,000 Chinese restaurants in the United States at the time were operated by Changle immigrants, and many of them wanted similar slides, he never had to worry about getting customers. Within a decade, the company had accumulated $2 million in assets, and its workspace had expanded from 700 square feet to 5,800 square feet.[23]

Chuanshu Wang, another prominent member of the CAA, moved up by remodeling restaurants as well. Arriving in New York in 1990 by "jumping the airplane" [*tiaoji*], Wang took three years to pay off his debt to the snakeheads before starting out on his own. His first business was to remodel a takeout restaurant in upstate New York, near the Canadian border. At that time, he had no office space, no car, no cell phone, and he could not speak English. As he soon found out, shopping for building materials was very time consuming and difficult because most suppliers did not carry what was needed for Chinese restaurants, and preassembled or ready-to-use materials were even harder to find. Wang eventually started a business to serve Chinese restaurants only. Making one stop at his 100,000-square-foot company, Yongxin, one can find all the construction tools, building materials, dining sets, kitchen cabinets, and other materials needed to put together a Chinese restaurant. Over the years, Wang's business received orders from all over the United States, Canada, and even Changle. By 2004, it had its own iron and woodwork shops to make customized furniture and restaurant signs; the company also carried lights and lamps as well as other decorative accessories.[24]

Centered in the restaurant business, the Changle immigrants have built a network of entrepreneurship that utilizes their own resources and markets. They make business deals among themselves. In the words of one of the leaders of the CAA, the idea is to "let no fertile soil be washed into the land of others" [*feishui bu ru wairen tian*]. Business owners provide services to one another; a market base supported by the large Changle immigrant population assures their success. Dohua Chen, the owner of the 999 Florist in Flushing, New York, started in New York by selling soft dofu drinks (*dohua*) from a cart on the street. Over eight years, especially on cold winter afternoons, Chen recalled, many people from his native place purchased drinks so that he could go home earlier. Some even brought him hot coffee to keep him warm.[25]

The trust built on ties to their place of origin plays an important role in the economic activities of the Changle immigrant community. It is not easy for newcomers to secure bank loans; however, lending money to each other is common among relatives and fellow villagers. Some companies even let their customers purchase goods on credit. Such practices certainly make it more convenient for Changle people to do business within their own group even if they might also create problems. Tianming Zheng, for example, eventually gave up his advertising company because too many of his acquaintances made purchases on credit, and it was difficult for him to collect from friends and fellow villagers even when the company was having cash flow problems.[26]

The expanding businesses created a huge job market for new immigrants. The restaurants owned by Fuzhou people provide some 400,000 jobs. "There are lazy Changle immigrants," said one business owner, "but I have never heard about anyone from Changle who could not find a job in New York."[27] Chuanshu Wang feels good about being able to provide jobs for the new immigrants. The more than seventy employees of Yongxin all speak the Fuzhou dialect, and each worker receives a starting wage of $70 a day. Experienced workers are paid up to $100 a day.[28]

By 2000, Changle immigrants had entered a variety of businesses. In addition to restaurants, garment shops, and construction companies, there are real estate agencies, employment services, beauty salons, discount stores, family-run motels, bridal shops, and cell-phone booths. A long-distance bus service operated by Fuzhou immigrants along the East Coast poses a real challenge to the Greyhound monopoly.

The purchasing power of the new immigrants is a big factor in the Chinatown economy. The luxury weddings traditional among the people of Fuzhou, for example, have given rise to a number of lucrative businesses. During Chinatown's wedding season, which runs between late September and Chinese New Year, immigrants speaking the Fuzhou dialect host about 1,500 banquets and generate $20 million in restaurant business. A location for a wedding banquet over the Thanksgiving weekend has to be reserved at least two years in advance. The biggest winners, of course, are the bridal services. In the late 1980s, there were no specialized bridal shops; only a few clothing stores carried wedding dresses. In 1995, the *Chinese Yellow Pages* listed four bridal shops, all operated by Cantonese or Taiwanese entrepreneurs. By 2004, the number of bridal shops had increased to thirty-two, many owned by Fujianese. Moreover, the services of these bridal shops have expanded to meet the demands of those planning elaborate weddings. In addition to formal Western-style suits and both Western- and Chinese-style dresses, a complete package includes hair styling, facial treatments and makeup, manicures, and photographic services. During the wedding season, each establishment might cater to as many as a hundred clients each month. Employees of these shops work around the clock during the Thanksgiving weekend, for each store might have as many as twenty weddings in a single day. Florists, jewelers, and the owners of specialty gift shops all enjoy expanded businesses opportunities at this time of year. Newly arrived performing artists from China are hired to sing or perform magic at these celebrations.[29]

The new immigrants have not only revitalized the economy of New York's Chinatown; they have also pushed up real estate values in other areas of the city. Housing prices that had been declining in the late 1980s picked up quickly in the 1990s. Apartments vacated by Cantonese or Mexican tenants were rented by immigrants from Fuzhou, generating twice as much income for landlords in Chinatown and in Flushing, Queens. In the late 1990s and early 2000s, about 80 percent of the luxury housing development units in Queens were purchased by Fuzhou immigrants.

The Changle Social Network

Historically, immigrants from Guangdong Province dominated the Chinese American community in New York. As late as mid-2004, the ability to speak Cantonese was still a prerequisite for leadership positions in community organizations; most organizations used the dialect at public events. Because the Fuzhou dialect is quite different from Cantonese, immigrants from the region were underrepresented in leadership positions within the community despite the fact that after 1980 they emerged as the majority group in New York's Chinatown. Moreover, new immigrants from Fuzhou, especially Changle and its neighboring county Lianjiang, were looked down upon by other Chinese Americans: Even natives from other parts of Fujian Province did not want to be identified with them.

Instead of working through the existing hierarchy of the community power structure, the new immigrants organized among themselves. With support from the old Fuzhou Countrymen's Association, the expansion of Fuzhou business entrepreneurship led to the formation of the Fuzhou-America Chamber of Commerce and Industry; meanwhile, immigrants from Changle and other regions formed numerous smaller groups based on family or village ties. In 1998, a group of businessmen pulled together these small and informal alliances and officially established the Changle American Association. In just a few years, the association has emerged as a powerful force in Chinatown, posing a direct challenge to the existing community establishment.

To a large extent, it was the desire to combat social prejudice, to change their "twisted image," that brought the Changle immigrants together. They did not want to be seen as lawless people. As more and more gained legal status and financial stability, they demanded social recognition and political rights. The association's publications stated that its members had suffered more than any other immigrant group from China because they had been subject to social prejudice within the ethnic community itself. Such prejudice not only had a psychological impact on the new immigrants and imposed hardships on their social life, but it also made it difficult for them to find work and shelter. Human smuggling, the CAA pointed out, was not an invention of the Changle people: It has been well documented that many early immigrants also had various tactics to circumvent the laws of the United States. Urging the Chinese American community to reassess the quality of this regional group, the association emphasized the cultural heritage of Changle and the accomplishment of its people.[30]

The campaign to create a positive image brought the new immigrants together, for Changle natives are a proud people. Despite the fact that they are looked down upon by other Chinese Americans, few Changle immigrants are ashamed of their regional identity. "I am proud of where I came from. Wherever I go, I tell people loudly that I came from Changle," said one business owner. "We are loud. If you see a group of people talking loudly, that's us. That's our Fuzhou people," said another with a big smile. Almost every leader of the CAA can recite memorable anecdotes about his or her place of origin as they remind others that they came from the same region where some of China's most distinguished historical figures were born.[31]

Members of the CAA understand prejudice in class terms. They believe that they are looked down upon mainly because most have had to start at the very bottom of the social ladder, so they emphasize their economic achievements in the United States. Starting low is not something to be ashamed of, they argue. The fact that Changle immigrants have already made inroads toward success ought to be seen as a clear indication that they possess unusual courage, strength, and talent. Individuals who project a positive image, usually successful entrepreneurs, have been selected to lead the group to exemplify their native-place pride. "We have many outstanding people in our community. My duty in the organization is to identify these people and persuade them to come forward to serve the community," said a leader of the association. "We need these people to provide leadership. We need to show others that these are our people, not the smugglers or gang members."[32]

Almost every president, vice president, director, or board member of the CAA has been an entrepreneur. Being financially stable allows these people time for public service. Zhonggao Zheng, the owner of a number of restaurants, including Jingfeng, and the Fuxing Real Estate Company, has gained social recognition from his career in the restaurant business. A member of the Fujianese Association's board of directors in 1973, he served as the association's president from 1981 to 1985. In 1988, he represented New York's Chinese Americans at George H. W. Bush's inauguration. In 1993, he received the Distinguished Asian American Award from the mayor of New York. Zheng has also been recognized for his charity work and praised for his generosity in raising funds for his native place. When the CAA was established, it created a special position just for Zheng: As permanent chief advisor, he was ranked above the president.[33]

Although it is not an official requirement, holders of prominent positions in the CAA have all been recognized for their monetary contributions. Names of donors at major fundraising events are posted in the association's office and printed in its publications. Those who hold the highest positions have usually donated the largest sums. "I gave money at every annual meeting and fundraising event. We [the leaders] all did," said one leader of the CAA proudly. In his opinion, those who have succeeded have an obligation to the community: "I am lucky to have gotten to where I am. The more capable you are, the more you should give [*neng zhe duo lao*]."[34]

To reach its members effectively, the CAA utilizes family and kin networks based on place of origin. Quandi Chen, the association's first president, worked for years to form village- or town-based alliances among fellow Changle immigrants. Leaders of twenty-six such alliances have served as president, vice president, or on the board of directors. Because these people are at the center of their own alliances and have probably played an important role in assisting their fellow immigrants, the CAA has been able to build a substantial network through them. "The only way to make our association strong is to organize from the bottom," said Chen. "My goal is to form more village groups. I want immigrants from every village [*cun* and *xiang*] or town [*zhen*] to have an alliance of their own so that every Changle immigrant can be mobilized."[35]

This effective network building has enabled the CAA to become a major factor in New York's Chinatown. At the celebration of the fiftieth anniversary of the People's Republic of China (PRC), in the parade celebrating the handover of Hong Kong to China, and at other major events, the largest crowds have followed the banner of the CAA. Although most of its members are laborers who have to work long hours, the association can send thousands of people into the street at any given time, something that even the Chinese Consolidated Benevolent Association (CCBA), which had long claimed to be the spokesperson of the community, can no longer do.

Regardless of its extraordinary energy and strength, the CAA is by no means a part of the community establishment. Its newness and its pro-PRC stance make the association look like an oppositional force to the CCBA. Maintaining its independence, however, has been important to the leaders of the CAA, and they have their own take on community power relations. Shuimei Shi, who served as the president of the association from 2000 to 2004, feels very comfortable with the position of his association:

> It is our duty to show the world who we are and what we can accomplish, and it is up to them [the establishment] to decide what to do with us. I am not concerned whether they are going to accept us or take us seriously. Our association is still young. On the other hand, the growth of our association does not depend on the recognition of others. The question is what they can do without us. How many people can they gather without the participation of our Changle immigrants? We don't need them; they need us![36]

The Changle Spirit

In the campaign against social prejudice, the CAA attempts to publicize a new image for its own people. It urges its members to keep up what they call the Changle spirit. According to the official publications of the association, the Changle spirit reflects three distinctive characteristics of its people. First, they are very loyal to each other, value the sentiments of their native place [*xiang-qing*], and have a strong commitment to group solidarity. "In my village," said one community leader, "if one person were in trouble, support would arrive from everywhere" [*yiren you nan, sifang zhiyuan*]. "People often ask how Changle ren overcome seemingly insurmountable difficulties to come to America. My answer is very simple: we help each other along the way." The Changle immigrants see themselves as being different from the Cantonese, who arrived in the second half of the nineteenth and early twentieth centuries: "Money to the Cantonese people is like a wife to a man; he would not lend money to anybody, even to his own brothers. If we Changle people were like that, none of us would have made it to America."[37]

Strong native-place sentiment is manifested as mutual support among the immigrants in the United States. One leader of the CAA who came to New York in 1983 as a teenager made this point, referring to the people in his group as members of his extended family, calling them "big brother Shi," "big brother Chen," or "big sister" so and so. He declared: "Every elder villager here is a big brother of mine, and I have many big sisters too. Once I left the village, I depend on these members of my extended family for help. When I bought my first takeout place, I did not know how to run it. But this big brother [pointing at an elder person in the room] came to help. He basically held my hand and showed me how to run the place. I would not starve in New York with all these big brothers and big sisters around."[38]

The fact that most business owners have hired workers from their home villages is seen as another distinct characteristic of the Changle people. "It is easy to work with those who can speak the Fuzhou dialect," said one employer, "but that's not the only reason that I prefer them over others. A newcomer from Changle understands his situation, he appreciates the opportunity to work, and he tries to work twice as hard." Being able to provide jobs for fellow villagers who needed work has given the greatest satisfaction to many business owners, for it is presented as a service to their own community: "I gave jobs to more than forty people who started at the bottom of society. Nothing makes me happier than watching them paying off their debts and then getting settled," said one CAA leader. Shuimei Shi, who jumped ship in 1971, especially values native-place sentiment: "I knew absolutely nobody in New York when I arrived. On my first day here, I wandered the streets thinking, 'Where am I going to sleep tonight?'" In Chinatown, Shi asked whether there was anyone from Fujian, and someone pointed him to a barbershop. He was very relieved when he finally heard the Fuzhou dialect. "Nowadays we have so many native-place people [*tongxiang*] in New York. We should not let the newcomers suffer the way I once did."[39]

Forging group unity is the main concern of the CAA. According to its leaders, the Changle people understand the importance of group solidarity: they want to "twist" themselves into "one rope." In community gatherings, the immigrants are urged to see each other as equals, which helps ease tensions between employers and their employees. Newcomers toil long hours in small restaurants, often juggling two or more jobs, but they rarely complain about their bosses in public. Most new arrivals from Changle do not have the legal status or the language skills necessary for better jobs. It is necessary for a new immigrant to work hard for a living. At the same time, "helping" a relative or fellow villager can also give a laborer a sense of satisfaction. A forty-year-old business owner did not see fairness as an issue when working his first job in a restaurant:

> When I first got here I did the job of two people. The boss was my second cousin. He had borrowed a lot of money and could not afford to hire another hand. When I finished work in the evenings, he and his wife still had more work to do and her health was not good. It was not easy for them. How could I complain? They were nice enough to give me that job, and they were the only family I had in New York. They would say now that I helped them in those years. Well, I am glad that I did.[40]

The close-knit network also functions to set rules for work ethics as well as labor relations. One woman who has become a business owner spelled out how the unwritten rules work:

> Laziness is not accepted here. Some newcomers had easy lives in China and they do not understand the concept of working hard. They will have to change because no one in America will spoil them the way their parents did at home. If they can't figure that out and refuse to work hard, they will lose their jobs. Business owners, on the other hand, are not completely free to do what they want. There is a common understanding about the minimum sum a person should be paid. Some restaurant owners take advantage of those who have no work permits and pay these people as little as possible. Things like that do happen. But usually people don't treat fellow villagers like that; they do not want to gain bad reputations. It is true that the newcomers do not always have the resources to seek help, but their friends or whoever

introduced them to their jobs understand what is fair and what is not. Word spreads quickly if one treats his fellow villagers poorly.[41]

Another business owner who had more than twenty people on his payroll in mid-2004 said he rarely advertises available jobs in the newspapers:

> People would contact me when they need jobs for their relatives. A friend would call to say that his nephew was looking for a job, something like that. If it was a close friend I would have to give him face [*gei mianzi*] and offer the nephew a job right away even if I was not looking for extra help. Once my mother in China called and asked me to hire so and so. What could I do? I couldn't turn away people from my own village. I sometimes had to find work for them to do.[42]

Mutual obligations within the group, as stressed by community leaders, make the organization of laborers along class lines difficult, if not impossible. When union workers picketed Jingfeng restaurant in a dispute over how tips should be divided, no employees of the restaurant, almost all of them from the same region, talked to reporters. The workers even organized their own counterdemonstration to show their support for their bosses—in this case, their native-place fellow immigrants.[43]

The second element of the Changle spirit, as articulated by leaders of the CAA, is the immigrants' ability to endure hardships and their willingness to take risks. If most other immigrants started with little to nothing in the United States, they argue that the Changle immigrants started from a negative point, as most of them were heavily in debt when they first arrived. Members of the community, however, are encouraged to develop a rather philosophical attitude about such disadvantages: "Only the ones who have tasted the most bitterness could command others" [*chi de ku zhong ku, fang wei ren shang ren*]. Or, quoting another popular Chinese expression, they often say, "The sweetest taste comes after bitterness" [*ku jin tian lai*]. Following such logic, enduring hardship is just a way to anticipate success. The Changle immigrants have certainly endured more hardship than most. In order to pay off debts and support their families, it has been common for the newcomers to work sixty to seventy hours a week. Although life in the United States is much harder than they had imagined, they are proud of the fact that very few have returned home without having earned a good amount of money. It takes at least three to four years of hard labor to pay off a typical debt, but very few have reneged. The trust they have in one another, one leader of the CAA said, made it easier for families to borrow money to finance trips to the United States.[44] Asked by a reporter from the *Chinese Daily News* what he thought about the criminal charges against Cuiping Zheng, the snakehead who allegedly hired gang members to collect debts, one Mr. Zheng (no relationship to Cuiping Zheng) said, "Everyone knows smuggling is a business—you pay to go to America. If you refuse to pay what you have agreed to pay after your arrival, of course you would be in trouble."[45]

Although the snakeheads did not inform their clients about the risks involved, few immigrants see themselves as victims. "We come from a fishing community," one of them said. "You don't give up fishing because of the storms." The immigrants are fully aware of the tragedies, but they do not think the relatively small number of deaths resulting from human smuggling is statistically significant compared with the tens of thousands who have successfully made the journey. Bravery and courage, argue the CAA leaders, are the keys to the success of their people. "Our people are not afraid of taking risks," one of them said. "We go to the mountains knowing full well there are tigers [*mingzhi shan you hu, pian xiang hu shan xing*]. That's why we could quickly establish ourselves in the United States. Very few others would dare to open restaurants in neighborhoods controlled by street gangs. Without doing that, however, many of us would not be able to have businesses at all." Although a few Changle immigrants have been shot or killed while delivering food and many more have been robbed, the practice of starting businesses in high crime areas did not stop. Since the death of Huang Chen in February 2004, however, leaders of CAA have been cautious not to advocate taking excessive risks, and they suggested that takeout restaurants give up delivery service.[46]

The third element of the Changle spirit, according to the CAA, is their people's flexibility. It is a tradition for the people of Changle to leave their overpopulated home villages in search of new opportunities. Adjusting to life in a strange land, however, has not been easy. The immigrants came from all walks of life: They were peasants, fisherman, factory or construction workers, teachers, government officials, and business operators. Once in the United States, however, all of them have had to start at the very bottom of society. They have had to work as menial laborers and to accept very low wages. Being flexible, to the Changle immigrants, means being able to move up and down the socioeconomic ladder [*neng shang neng xia*] regardless of one's previous social status. Ronghua Chen, a prodigy who started publishing poems in China when he was twelve, personifies such flexibility. After an airplane trip and a sea voyage, he crossed mountains and rivers on foot, passing through more than ten countries before being instructed to swim ashore near New York six months later. In Chinatown, Chen started by laboring in restaurants and delivering food by bicycle. Once he was arrested by the police while distributing flyers on the street. In a television interview, a tearful Chen said, "Not a single day I did not regret. I often worked for more than ten hours a day. Even though I couldn't go to bed until one o'clock in the morning, I had to rely on sleeping pills to get two or three hours of sleep each night. I worked the lowest job in the restaurant; anyone could boss me around and anyone could bully me."[47]

But Chen did not return to China. Being a Changle native, his responsibility to his family is more important than his own pride. He learned to be humble and flexible, and that allowed him to find ways to survive and use his talents. In time, he worked as the manager of a big restaurant before entering into a partnership with a florist and opening his own restaurant. After his wife joined him, Chen picked up his pen again; he first served as the secretary of the Fujianese Association and later became the secretary of the CAA. He also found opportunities to lecture on Chinese calligraphy at American University in Washington, DC. In 1997, during the historic handover of Hong Kong to China, Chen's poem "Greetings, My Homeland!" appeared in several major newspapers and magazines in China. "I became famous overnight," said a joyful Chen.[48]

From the viewpoint of CAA leaders, being flexible has allowed the Changle immigrants to grasp new opportunities, and they have been willing to start with the very smallest business available. By mid-2004, about 70 percent of the Changle immigrants were involved in the food businesses, ranging from street carts stocked with drinks and steamed pastries, to mom-and-pop takeout places serving fast and affordable food, to large restaurants geared for formal dining and social gatherings. Their restaurants are not limited to Fuzhou cooking. Large eateries such as those operated by the East Buffet Restaurant Corporation hire chefs specializing in traditional Chinese regional dishes as well as Japanese, Korean, Thai, and Western cuisines. Business owners operate according to market demand, and their entrepreneurship has expanded at a remarkable speed.

Their insistence on solidarity, willingness to endure hardships, and flexibility has enabled the CAA to utilize group resources and help members to adjust to new lives. In mid-2005, a third of the 200,000 Changle immigrants still had not attained legal status; many are still toiling in restaurants and garment shops and on construction sites. It has been the spirit of Changle, spread through stories of those who have succeeded, that has kept their American dreams alive, and it is this spirit that the CAA wants its members to carry forward.

Combating Prejudice: The Yidong Marketplace Incident

Although a significantly large number of Changle immigrants own businesses, most of their establishments are small. Manhattan's East Broadway is bursting with small vendors and shops ran by Changle immigrants. Most single-unit shop spaces are divided for multiple-business operations. To make ends meet, these businesses rely on the labor of family members and stay open for very long hours.

In the summer of 2004, the shareholders of the Yidong Shopping Mall on East Broadway, who held a fifty-year lease from the city government, announced a rent increase that would double or triple the amounts that its tenants had paid earlier. In addition, each new lease would be subject to a deposit of six months' rent plus another two months in advance. This drastic increase would no doubt have imposed grave hardships on the small vendors who have little capital. In response, the vendors of the shopping mall, many of them members of the CAA, organized the Yidong Mall Small Vendors Alliance in late July and staged a three-day demonstration in front of the Emperor's Seafood and Hui Shi Jia restaurants, which are owned by the major shareholders of the mall, Yanming Chen and his wife, Liuzhen Huang. The landlords, however, did not take the vendors seriously. Given the high demand for business space in Chinatown, they believed that finding new tenants would not be difficult. In a heated exchange with the tenants, Huang called Fuzhou immigrants "trash" and threatened to "clean them out," and her son was seen videotaping the demonstrators during their first street rally on July 28.[49]

Agitated, about one hundred vendors scheduled another three-day demonstration to start on August 7. Before the rally and picketing took place, however, the local police, invited by the vendors' alliance to come to the event, were informed that the demonstration had been cancelled. Similar rumors also reached the vendors. As a result, some of them went home after work. Only about one hundred demonstrators showed up that evening as scheduled. The picket line attracted many onlookers, and some sympathizers donated large amounts to support the demonstrators, who soon noticed that their actions were again being videotaped. They suspected that the man holding the camera had been hired by the Yidong landlords. When confronted, the Spanish-speaking cameraman began to shout at the demonstrators and was soon taken away by the police.[50]

To win support from the community, the protestors situated their struggle within the broad context of the city's economic difficulties. Arguing that the terrorist attack of September 11, 2001, had slowed down Chinatown's economy, they urged the city government to support small businesses as a means of speeding up recovery. Drastic rent increases, they reasoned, would force many small vendors out of business, which would further slow down Chinatown's commercial activities. They wanted the government to interfere because the property belonged to the city. A flyer written in both English and Chinese was distributed on the streets, asserting that "the shareholders of the Yidong Mall want to destroy our community harmony and prevent the reconstruction of Chinatown's economy." "What Chen and Huang tried to do," the flyer continued, "was no different from the terrorists. If the rent increase cannot be stopped, Chinatown's economy will be destroyed."[51]

The Chinese text of the flyer spelled out the demonstrators' cause in clear class terms. Calling Chen and Huang "vampires" who would grow bigger by "sucking the blood of Fuzhou immigrants," the alliance stated:

> Chen Yanming and Huang Liuzhen use their wealth to oppress small vendors, sabotage community solidarity, and prevent the economic growth of Chinatown. To double or triple our rent is to completely ignore the sluggishness of the economy and the hardships of small businesses; it is to bring our livelihood to an impasse. . . . Compared with the rich and arrogant shareholders we are small and vulnerable. For the dignity of us Fuzhou fellow immigrants, for our right to survive, for a stable and healthy development of the Chinatown community, and for harmony, unity, and peace, we are going to fight for our cause to the end.[52]

Moreover, the protestors also defined their struggle as one against social prejudice within the Chinese American community. "We are not trash! Say 'No' to Discrimination!" one of their signs read. The protestors viewed Huang's attitude toward the Fuzhou immigrants as a reflection of the prejudice of more established Chinese Americans against the new immigrants, which is deeply rooted in the class structure of the new Chinese American community. Huang certainly did not want to be identified as a hater of the Fuzhou immigrants. Denying that she had ever used the word "trash" to describe the Fuzhou people, she now claimed that her ancestors were also from Fujian Province. Nevertheless, she and her husband would not let the small vendors have their way. They hired lawyers and forced individual vendors to sign new leases. To further intimidate those who had participated in the demonstration, they reported unauthorized sales of telephone cards in the mall to the local police. In late August and September, police raided Chinatown and searched the merchandises of more than one hundred small vendors. Thousands of dollars' worth of telephone cards were confiscated.[53]

A combination of class oppression and social prejudice finally generated overwhelming community support for the protesters. The picketing of the two restaurants was a huge success, and the idea of a vendors' alliance, originally organized to protest the rent increase by the Yidong shareholders, now appealed to merchants throughout the East Broadway commercial district. In October, the leaders of the first small vendors' alliance announced the establishment of the East Broadway Vendors' Alliance and took legal action against the local police for the attack on the small business owners. The Consulate of the People's Republic of China in New York immediately announced its support of the group as almost all its members were immigrants from the Chinese mainland.[54]

The struggle between the small business operators and the landlords who controlled the commercial space at Yidong is part of a larger struggle between new immigrant groups and the community establishment. Although they controlled fewer resources, the CAA pointed out that the new immigrants had become an indispensable force in the community's economy. The newcomers might have a lower standard of living, they said, but compared with the American-born Chinese, they are more likely to spend their money in Chinatown. As one of the leaders of the CAA noted, "Many large business owners still believe that they can run Chinatown the way they want because they control community resources. What they ought to understand is that their numbers are few. Without us as business operators and consumers, Chinatown would have to be shut down."[55]

Back to Changle

The media coverage of human trafficking painted a darker picture of the country that Chinese immigrants have left. To the American public, the circumstances these Chinese left behind must be extremely harsh in both political and economic terms. Nevertheless, as some scholars have pointed out, relatively few post-1965 immigrants left China for political reasons. Neither was absolute poverty a consideration for the natives of Changle. Stimulated by economic reforms in China since the late 1970s, Fujian has been especially successful in attracting foreign investments, which allowed the province to establish thousands of new business enterprises and significantly increase its volume of foreign trade. The living standard of Fujian natives is now higher than in other areas of China. For the peasants in Changle, however, opportunities to earn money are still fewer compared with those in China's large cities, let alone those in developed countries in the West.[56]

To a large extent, a negative image of China generated sympathy toward the new immigrants, which has led to more generous U.S. policies. Many Changle immigrants have tried to attain their legal status by claiming political asylum, arguing that they are victims of China's one-child policy. Thousands of successful petitioners have obtained legal residency in the United States, which not only allows them to work but also to qualify their family members for legal entry. Few individuals with legal status are interested in challenging China's government policies; neither do they want to be identified as political dissidents. Having legal status makes life in the United States easier: Claiming asylum is just a practical path to take.

During the last two decades of the twentieth century, some established community organizations shifted from a strong anti-Communist stance to one that accepted both China and Taiwan. The Changle American Association has always been known as a pro-PRC group. The constitution of the CAA states that the central goals of the association are to advance the spirit of patriotism, to promote friendship between the United States and China, and to push for a united China. Patriotism in this case implies loyalty to both the United States and China. Not only do the immigrants value their ties with China; they also understand that social prejudice against them in the Chinese American community has much to do with China's status within the international community. Shuimei Shi, the former president of the association, was a seaman in Hong Kong and had traveled around the world before coming to the United States in 1977. "In those days, Chinese people were discriminated against because China was backward," he said. "Not until 1979, when China formally established diplomatic relations with the United States, did the situation begin to improve." The immigrants could have blamed China for their low social status in the United States, but more often than not, that has not been the case. One leader of the CAA explained his sentiments toward China in a vivid way: "America is my boss; China is my mother. I would not disown my mother because she is poor."[57] The CAA displays flags of both the United States and the PRC in its office, and it has offered strong support to the PRC consulate in New York. On August 15, 2004, when Shi completed his term as president of the association, he delivered a formal speech entitled "My Heart Is Still Chinese."

Although CAA does not have any formal political connections with the PRC, its members have cheered every Chinese achievement as though it were one of their own. In the parade celebrating Hong Kong's return to China on June 30, 1997, the CAA and many other new immigrant groups from Fujian, such as Fuqing and Lianjiang, sent huge floats and banners bearing the names of their native places. As one young immigrant put it, "We were looked down upon by old-timers as well as immigrants from Taiwan and Hong Kong mainly because China delayed its economic reform for three decades. But the Chinese people are now standing up." In other words, the development of China's economy can change the power structure within the Chinese American community.[58]

For that reason, the immigrants want China to be stronger and stronger, and they want to do whatever they can to speed up that process. Support for China's economic reform is the most recognized activity of the CAA. Earlier immigrants built big houses for their families and elaborate graves to honor their ancestors, and their donations went to the construction of pavilions and the refurbishing of schools and temples. Beginning in the late 1990s, money earned overseas has been invested in building apartments, factories, and hotels and in many other economic enterprises as well.

The remittances the immigrants have sent to Changle have helped increase commercial activities in their native place. Although some scholars in the West are concerned about the importance of preserving rural economies, those who left Changle do not share such concerns. They have no intention of maintaining the rural traditions built by their ancestors; they want their fellow villagers to grasp every economic opportunity available. If an earth-shaking change [*tian fan di fu*] were needed to bring prosperity immediately and improve people's standard of living, the immigrants would definitely like to see that happen.

At the beginning of the twenty-first century, Changle is moving in the right direction, in their view. Old fishing and rice-farming villages have been moving away from self-sufficient agriculturally based economies, and old dusty, sleepy towns are being taken over by bustling areas featuring broad streets, high-rise apartments, elaborate gated single-family residences, fancy hotels, and new stylish stores. In addition to developing highly commercialized agricultural products, each of the eighteen towns under the jurisdiction of Changle City has built its own business infrastructure. The town of Wuhang, for example, operates twelve hotels, and its two industrial centers occupy about forty-one acres of land (250 *mu*). The 139 factories in Hangcheng produce a wide range of merchandise, including machinery, plastics, electronics, textiles, crafts, foodstuff, bottled drinks, and construction materials. Although most towns or villages have developed their own grassroots industries utilizing local resources, it is the nontraditional industrial establishments that have made the immigrants most proud. "No iron ore has ever been found in Changle, but our people built a four-billion yuan steel plant; the soil is not suited for growing cotton, but we developed a one billon yuan textile industry. We can do anything we want," said one of the leaders of the CAA. Even an international airport has been built in Changle, allowing travelers to fly directly to or from Hong Kong and countries in Southeast Asia.

To business-minded entrepreneurs from Changle, China is an enormous market with great economic potential that has provided many opportunities for investment, and the government of the PRC offers various incentives to attract money from overseas, but money is not the only return available. One businessman put it this way: "I could have stayed here to make more money. I could expand my business here. But I do not want to have another restaurant in New York. If you have the money you can do so many things in China. It is very exciting to do something new in my hometown. Besides, our native place [*jiaxiang*] needs money and appreciates the investment. It's hard for me to describe this, but doing business there makes me feel great."[59]

Attracting investment from overseas has been an important part of the Chinese government's agenda. During his visit to New York in May 1999, the mayor of Changle, Baochu Lin, met with about three hundred immigrants at the Jingfeng Restaurant. He presented the immigrants with a detailed plan for the city's economic development and laid out opportunities for them. In late September of the same year, the CAA sent a delegation of more than sixty people to Beijing to celebrate the fiftieth anniversary of the PRC. When the delegation arrived in Changle, it was warmly welcomed by the heads of the city. The once-ordinary peasants and workers who had sneaked out of the country illegally and given up their Chinese citizenship not too long ago were now guests of honor at banquets hosted by local and provincial government officials. "My goal," said Chuangshu Wang of the CAA, "is to pull the capital of our immigrants together and invest it in large projects. In our native place we can rely on people we know to do business."[60]

The immigrants have made an impact on their native place: Changle has become one of the fastest-growing regions in Fujian Province despite the fact that a large portion of its working population is abroad. The improved economy means that more people can afford the $80,000 smuggling fee currently being charged to come to the United States. Family members and relatives already in the United States can help find jobs for prospective immigrants. The rapid growth of the local economy, however, has also offered more options at home, while a significantly improved living standard has made staying more desirable. More jobs have become available in both local businesses and the larger steel and textile factories, and some Changle natives have found business opportunities in Shanghai and Beijing. Relatively few young people in Changle are left working in the rice paddies; most of them today are wage earners or business operators who frequent restaurants, coffee shops, and karaoke bars. Migrants from Sichuan Province are now hired to cultivate the farmland; they also perform domestic chores for well-to-do families. Some young Changle ren, products of China's single-child policy, own motorcycles and automobiles: When the first shipment of sixty Mercedes Benzes was delivered to Changle, it sold out the first day.[61]

On September 9, 2003, a reporter from the *New York Times* revealed that the attractions of America that had lured thousands of Chinese from their home villages were no longer strong because at present not as many Changle people were desperate enough to seek the opportunity to come to America. "I won't say that young people do not want to come to America anymore, but they would only if they could board a flight to New York. They would not [want to go] unless the trip is safe," said Chuangdi Chen. The villagers now have a more realistic picture of the United States. From those who have returned home, they have learned that America is no paradise. Zheng, a college graduate who returned home to Changle after seven years in the United States, told a news reporter that he never laughed or smiled while he was there. "It was the same routine every day," he said. "Get up. Work for sixteen hours. Go to bed. Get up again. I was a fool. A machine." In his hometown, Zheng's job generates a modest income even by local standards, but his life is less stressful and he enjoys hanging out with friends and spending time with his wife and son. Moreover, going to America is no longer the only way to pursue a good life. "Our home village [*jiaxiang*] is moving forward at a fast pace," said a CAA official proudly. "Many people can see there are more opportunities at home, and the situation will only get better every day."[62]

If the Changle immigrants view their low status in the United States as a reflection of the failure of China's socialist economy after 1949, the emergence of China as a new world economic power at the beginning of the twenty-first century gives them courage and inspiration. To some extent, the immigrants see the improvement of China's status in the global economy as a primary reason for a reorientation of power relations in the Chinese American community.

NOTES

I thank Wai-Yin Tsang and members of the Changle American Association for making this study possible.

1. Changle American Association, *Changle American Association, Inc.* (New York: Changle American Association, 2001), 37.

2. Testimonies of Lianqi Guo, the head of Fuqingbang, during the Cheng Cuiping trial, *China Daily News*, May 9, 2005, B10.

3. David Chen, "Exodus Slows from Fujian Province to U.S.," *New York Times*, September 7, 2003, 1; James K. Chin, "Reducing Irregular Migration from China," *International Migration* 41, no. 3 (2003): 49; John Pomfret, "Smuggled Chinese Enrich Homeland, Gang Villagers Work, Chase Dreams in U.S.," *Washington Post*, January 24, 1999, A19. There are many more such reports. According to the *New York Times* and the *Los Angeles Times*, 203 people were caught as container stowaways in Pacific Coast ports in 1999. Canadian and American authorities detained an additional 136 people on eight ships in the period between December 25, 1999, and January 14, 2000. On January 6, 2000, ten Chinese teenaged women about to cross the U.S. border were detained by Canadian authorities. U.S. border patrol officials further found a boatload of fifteen immigrants, along with three corpses, in Seattle on January 9, 2000. In December 1999, authorities found thirty immigrants in Long Beach, Los Angeles County, and arrested three men waiting near the ship. On January 5, 2000, another fourteen were detained in Seattle, while Canada intercepted one ship and caught twenty-five would-be immigrants. There were also reports of Chinese illegal immigrants caught in Guam and along the coasts of Australia and New Zealand. See also Ko-Lin Chin, *Smuggled Chinese: Clandestine Immigration to the United States* (Philadelphia: Temple University Press, 1999); Zai Liang, "Demography of Illicit Emigration from China: A Sending Country's Perspective," *Sociological Forum* 16, no. 4 (2001): 677–701; and David Kyle and Rey Koslowski, eds., *Global Human Smuggling: Comparative Perspectives* (Baltimore, MD: Johns Hopkins University Press, 2001).

4. According to one report, the average income of urban employees in Fujian Province was 974 yuan. See "Introduction to China's Provinces, Municipalities, and Autonomous Regions," http: //www.china.org.cn/English/features/ProvinceView/164868.htm (accessed September 30, 2007).

5. Xinjing yi re san (Arai Hifumi), "*She zhi dao: Fuzhou–Xianggang-Niuyue*" [The snake road: Fuzhou-Hong Kong–New York], part I, "Ershi wan ren hengyue taipingyang" [The Pacific crossing of 200,000 people], *Jiushi niandai*, July 1995, 34–40.

6. *Chinese Daily News*, May 7, 2005, A3; Zheng was convicted in June 2005.

7. In Ko-Lin Chin's study, 86 percent of the three hundred people surveyed cited money as among the principal reasons for choosing to be smuggled into the United

States. He noted that the average monthly income in China was around $100 compared with an average monthly income of $1,359 in the United States. See Chin, *Smuggled Chinese*, 14.

8. Interview by the author, August 8, 2004.

9. Interview by the author, August 8, 2004.

10. Chin, *Smuggled Chinese,* 6.

11. Interview by the author, August 10, 2004.

12. Interview by the author, August 8, 2004.

13. Interview by the author, August 12, 2004.

14. Group interview by the author, August 13, 2004.

15. Jane Lii, "The New Blood in Chinatown: On the Eve of Hong Kong Takeover, A Revolution Takes Hold in Lower Manhattan," *New York Times,* June 22, 1997.

16. Wai-Yin Tsang, "*Changle ren zai meiguo*" [Changle people in America], *Shijie zhoukan* [*China Daily News Weekly Magazine*], September 21, 2003–October 5, 2003.

17. Interview by the author, August 12, 2004.

18. Interview by the author, August 12, 2004. See also Wai-Yin Tsang, "*Changle ren zai meiguo*," part I, "*Shijie pa meiguo, meiguo pa Changle*" [The world is afraid of the United States; the United States is afraid of Changle], *Shijie zhoukan*, September 21, 2004, 17.

19. Interview by the author, August 12, 2004.

20. Wai-Yin Tsang, "*Zhong can waimailang, beige he shi liao*?" [When will the sad song of the delivery boys of Chinese food end?], *Shijie zhoukan*, March 7, 2004, 24–26. Chen's killer was convicted in March 2005, *Chinese Daily News*, March 17, 2005, B10.

21. *Changle American Association, Inc.*, 55–56.

22. Xinjing, "*She zhi dao*," part III, "*Niuyue tangrenjie qitan*" [Strange tales from New York's Chinatown], *Jiushi niandai*, September 1995, 90–91.

23. Tsang, "*Changle ren zai meiguo*," part III, "*Chenggong Changle ren: xiao zhong you lei*" [The successful Changle people: tears amid smiles), *Shijie zhoukan*, October 5, 2003, 29.

24. Ibid., 34; interview by the author, August 12, 2004.

25. Tsang, "*Changle ren zai meiguo*," part III, 34.

26. Ibid., 29.

27. Interview by the author, August 12, 2004.

28. Interview by the author, August 12, 2004.

29. *Chinese Business Directories* (titles vary), New York and East Coast edition, 1990, 1995, 1997, and 2004.

30. *Changle American Association, Inc.*, 52–53.

31. Interviews by the author, August 12, 2004.

32. Ibid.

33. *Changle American Association, Inc.*, 56.

34. Interview by the author, August 12, 2004.

35. Ibid.

36. Ibid.

37. Ibid.

38. Ibid.

39. Ibid.; Tsang, "*Changle ren zai meiguo*," part I, 17.

40. Interview by the author, August 13, 2004.

41. Interview by the author, August 10, 2004.

42. Interview by the author, August 12, 2004.

43. Xinjing, "*She zhi dao*," part III, 90–91.

44. Interview by the author, August 12, 2004.

45. *Chinese Daily News*, May 17, 2005, A3.

46. Interview by the author, August 12, 2004; Wai-Yin Tsang, "*Fangfan beiju zai fasheng, zi bao shouze lao ji zai xin*" [Preventing tragedy from happening again: keep in mind rules of self-protection], *Shijie zhoukan*, March 7, 2004, 28–29.

47. Tsang, "*Changle ren zai meiguo*," part III, 31.

48. Ibid.

49. "*Yidong shanghu shiwei huodong xian zhao quxiao*" [The Yidong vendors demonstration almost got canceled], *Ming bao* [Ming Newspaper], August 8, 2004.

50. Ibid.

51. "*Shi ke ren, shu be ke ren*" ["If this can be tolerated, what cannot?"], undated flyer distributed in New York's Chinatown on October 8, 2004.

52. Ibid.

53. *Fazhi wan bao* [Legal Evening News], October 10, 2004.

54. *Ming bao* [Ming Newspaper], October 15, 2004, A14.

55. Interview by the author, October 9, 2004.

56. Chen, "Exodus Slows from Fujian Province to U.S.," 1.

57. Interview by the author, August 12, 2004. See also, Tsang, " "*Changle ren zai meiguo*," Part III, 31.

58. Interview by the author, August 12, 2004.

59. Ibid.

60. *Changle American Association, Inc.*, 60.

61. Interview by the author, August 12, 2004.

62. Chen, "Exodus Slows from Fujian Province to U.S.," 1; interview by the author, August 12, 2004.

Contributors

Sucheng Chan is Professor Emerita of Asian American Studies and Global Studies at the University of California, Santa Barbara. She received her Ph.D. in political science from the University of California, Berkeley. The recipient of numerous awards for her scholarship, teaching, and public service, her latest books are *Survivors: Cambodian Refugees in the United States* (2004), *In Defense of Asian American Studies: The Politics of Teaching and Program Building* (2005), *Chinese American Transnationalism: The Flow of People, Resources, and Ideas between China and America during the Exclusion Era* (ed., 2005), and *The Vietnamese American 1.5 Generation: Stories of War, Revolution, Flight, and New Beginnings* (2006).

Josephine Fowler received her Ph.D. in American Studies from the University of Minnesota. Her book, *Japanese and Chinese Immigrant Activists: Organizing in American and International Communist Movements, 1919–1933*, was published posthumously in 2007. She had also published an article in *International Labor and Working-Class History* before she passed away in 2006.

Madeline Y. Hsu is Associate Professor of History and director of the Center for Asian American Studies at the University of Texas at Austin. She received her Ph.D. in history from Yale University. Her book, *Dreaming of Gold, Dreaming of Home: Transnationalism and Migration between the United States and South China, 1882–1943* (2000), won the Association for Asian American Studies' 2002 Outstanding Book in History Award. Her articles have appeared in the *Journal of Asian Studies*, *Amerasia Journal*, *China Review*, *International Review of Social History*, and as chapters in various books.

Karen J. Leong is Associate Professor of Women's and Gender Studies and director of the Asian Pacific American Studies Program at Arizona State University, Tempe. She received her Ph.D. in history from the University of California, Berkeley. A cowinner of the 2001 Lerner-Scott Prize from the Organization of American Historians for the best dissertation in U.S. women's history, she is the author of *The China Mystique: Pearl S. Buck, Anna May Wong, Mayling Soong, and the Transformation of American Orientalism* (2005). Her articles have appeared in the *Journal of American Ethnic History* and *Quarterly Review of Film and Video.*

Andrea Louie is Associate Professor of Anthropology at Michigan State University. She received her Ph.D. in anthropology from the University of California, Berkeley. Her book, *Chineseness across Borders: Renegotiating Chinese Identities in China and the United States* (2004), won the Association for Asian American Studies' 2006 Outstanding Book in the Social Sciences Award. Her articles have appeared in *American Ethnologist, Identities: Global Studies in Culture and Power*, and *Positions: East Asia Cultures Critique.*

Mae M. Ngai is Professor of History at Columbia University. She received her Ph.D. in history from Columbia University. Her book, *Impossible Subjects: Illegal Aliens and the Making of Modern America* (2004), won the American Historical Association's 2004 Littleton Griswold Award, the Immigration and Ethnic History Society's 2004 Theodore Saloutos Award, the Berkshire Conference of Women Historians' 2004 First Book Prize, the Organization of American Historians' 2005 Frederick Jackson Turner Award, and the Association for Asian American Studies' 2006 Outstanding Book in History Award. Her articles have appeared in the *Journal of American History, Law and History Review, Journal of American Ethnic History*, and *American Quarterly.*

K. Scott Wong is the James Phinney Baxter 3rd Professor of History and Public Affairs at Williams College, where he chairs the American Studies program. He received his Ph.D. in history from the University of Michigan. His book, *Americans First: Chinese Americans and the Second World War* (2005), received an honorable mention in the Association for Asian American Studies' 2007 Outstanding Book in History Award. He also received the Immigration and Ethnic History Society's 1992 Carlton Qualey Prize. He is coeditor of *Claiming America: Constructing Chinese American Identities during the Exclusion Era* (1998) and *Privileging Positions: The Sites of Asian American Studies* (1995). His articles have appeared in *American Quarterly, Amerasia Journal, Journal of American Ethnic History*, and as chapters in various books.

Judy Tzu-Chun Wu is Associate Professor of History at Ohio State University. She received her Ph.D. in history from Stanford University and an honorable mention for the 2000–2001 Audre Lorde Prize. The author of *Doctor Mom Chung of the Fair-Haired Bastards: The Life of a Wartime Celebrity* (2005), her articles have appeared in the *Journal of Women's History*, the *Journal of Social History*, and as chapters in various books.

Xiaojian Zhao is Associate Professor of Asian American Studies at the University of California, Santa Barbara, where she chairs the Asian American Studies Department. She received her Ph.D. in history from the University of California, Berkeley. Her book, *Remaking Chinese America: Immigration, Family, and Community, 1940–1965* (2002), won the Association for Asian American Studies' 2004 Outstanding Book in History Award. Her articles have appeared in *California History* and as chapters in several books.

INDEX